GROUND RULES

12/97

D1230783

GROUND RULES

Baseball & Myth

DEEANNE WESTBROOK

UNIVERSITY OF ILLINOIS PRESS

Urbana & Chicago

Library of Congress
Cataloging-in-Publication Data
Westbrook, Deeanne.
Ground rules : baseball and myth /
Deeanne Westbrook.
p.   cm.
Includes bibliographical references
and index.
ISBN 0-252-02226-2 (alk. paper). —
ISBN 0-252-06529-8 (pbk. : alk. paper)
1. American literature—20th century—
History and criticism. 2. Baseball stories,
American—History and criticism. 3.
Baseball in literature. 4. Myth in
literature. 5. Literature and
anthropology—United States—
History—20th century. I. Title.
PS169.B36W47
1996
810.9´355˙dc20
95-4433
CIP

And in the earth itself they found a green—

The inhabitants of a very varnished green . . .

There was a muddy center before we breathed.

There was a myth before the myth began,

Venerable and articulate and complete.

Wallace Stevens,

"Notes Toward a Supreme Fiction"

In loving memory of my parents,

Cameron and Esther Williams,

and my parents-in-law,

Curtis and Joyce Westbrook

CONTENTS

ACKNOWLEDGMENTS

According to an old joke, "The good news is, there's baseball in heaven; the bad news is, you're pitching Friday." I suppose that this study was born out of my sense that any perfect place would have two things, baseball and books.

My father seemed always to have a baseball game on the radio, the sounds of the game forming the white noise of my childhood's summer weekends and evenings. So it's his fault, really, that the only things I wanted for my tenth birthday were a ball and a bat. Against her better judgment (she feared I'd ruin my knuckles or knock out my teeth), my mother presented me with said items, and I immediately became somebody in the neighborhood. Years later my mother-in-law taught me to watch major league baseball on television, and later still, when my husband enrolled our sons in Little League, I learned how to keep score and how to be comfortable for hours in the bleachers of city parks. So in many ways my family is responsible for this book, and I thank them for their contributions.

More immediate contributions have come from colleagues and students who have brought me a thousand stories, notes, copies of newspaper or magazine articles, reports of games, poems, and books – all presented with a sort of laughter or sense of amazement that they constituted matter for academic work. Three of my prized possessions are an original poem about Fenway Park, a Chicago Cubs cap, and an old *Baseball Magazine* mouse pad, all of which are gifts from colleagues. Carol Fokine, Carol Franks, and Henry Carlile, also colleagues, performed the generous and thankless tasks of reading and commenting on the manuscript as it evolved. Thank you, my friends.

As the book neared completion, thoughtful, pertinent, expert advice came from Jerry Klinkowitz, Eric Gould, and Christian K. Messenger. For their generous contributions of time and knowledge I am deeply grateful. And finally, to Richard Martin, whose fine, dedicated, and humane editorship made this book possible, my heartfelt gratitude.

GROUND RULES

ONLY A HORIZON RINGED ABOUT WITH MYTHS CAN UNIFY A CULTURE. THE FORCES OF IMAGINATION AND APOLLONIAN DREAM ARE SAVED ONLY BY MYTH FROM INDISCRIMINATE RAMBLING. THE IMAGES OF MYTH MUST BE THE DEMONIC GUARDIANS, UBIQUITOUS BUT UNNOTICED, PRESIDING OVER THE GROWTH OF THE CHILD'S MIND AND INTERPRETING TO THE MATURE MAN HIS LIFE AND STRUGGLES. Friedrich Nietzsche, *The Birth of Tragedy* 136–37

[MYTH] ORGANIZES A WORLD WHICH IS WITHOUT CONTRADICTIONS BECAUSE IT IS WITHOUT DEPTH, A WORLD WIDE OPEN AND WALLOWING IN THE EVIDENT, IT ESTABLISHES A BLISSFUL CLARITY: THINGS APPEAR TO MEAN SOMETHING BY THEMSELVES. Roland Barthes, "Myth Today" 132

[BASEBALL] IS PROFOUND ALL BY ITSELF. Stephen Jay Gould, "The Creation Myths of Cooperstown" 26

TO BE A POET IN A DESTITUTE TIME MEANS: TO ATTEND, SINGING, TO THE TRACE OF THE FUGITIVE GODS. Martin Heidegger, *Poetry, Language, Thought* 94

INTRODUCTION

BASEBALL AND MYTH

My subject is baseball and myth, which encompasses the subject of baseball and its texts as constituting a genuine American mythology. I became interested in the topic several years ago when I designed and taught a summer course on baseball and mythology. As a teacher of myth, literature, and criticism, I had become aware that baseball literature has more coherence, more common themes and figures, more "familiar" characters and acts, a greater tendency to approach the mysterious and the sacred, and more echoes of ancient myths than can be accounted for easily, given the secular topic and modern setting. At the time, although I called this set of characteristics mythological, I had not worked through the implications of this claim or the very basic problems of definition. In any case, I found the texts to be interconnected in the manner of traditional mythologies, or canons; reading them provides a sense that the action of each newly encountered text is performed by familiar figures in a well-known landscape with similar results. We expect a Greek hero, for example, to kill a female monster and make a journey to the underworld; we expect a Nordic god or hero to overcome magic or trickery to defeat a giant.

To take a seemingly inconsequential example of what I have in mind, consider the figure of the dwarf. James Thurber ("You Could Look It Up"), Bernard Malamud (*The Natural*), W. P. Kinsella (*The Iowa Baseball Confederacy*), and Philip Roth ("Every Inch a Man," in *The Great American Novel*) all include in key roles the figure of a dwarf who suffers violence within the confines of the field and park: Thurber's dwarf is hurled bodily into center field;[1] Malamud's is purposely struck with a foul ball; Kinsella's is killed by a beanball; and Roth's is blinded by a beanball thrown by another dwarf, a violent, evil-tempered pitcher. Jerome Charyn (*The Seventh Babe*) and John Sayles (*Pride of the Bimbos*) both include dwarfs as central characters, and in neither of these works does the dwarf survive his own narrative. The presence of such a figure is puzzling in itself, but his reappearance from text to text, along with the violence he suffers, suggests more than it says, a meaning hidden in figure. Reinforcing this sense of unspoken significance is a feeling that such characters are archaic and incongruous in a modern setting: as recurring figures they (along with giants) seem to be of other times, other places, carrying with them into the modern texts some ancient meaning.

Another figure whose reappearance fosters our sense of interconnectedness in baseball literature is the absent or abusive mother. We may wonder about the presence (often as trace or mere memory) of the "terrible mother" (the one who abuses or abandons her son, thwarts him, or hinders his progress) in a literature based on a game whose goal is simply to "come home." Complementing the concern with the mother is the recurrent theme of the fostering but failed father, in reaction to whom, on whose behalf, or in whose name the son performs his action – in the process working variations on the Oedipus myth, expressed in terms that Freud never considered yet repeated, insistent, and familiar. Beyond presenting these figures, baseball literature evokes the sense of a universe where time and space may obey the laws of an unknown physics or be measured not in mechanistic terms but in human, psychological ones. There are opportunities in such a world to encounter the sacred, the numinous, the uncanny.

At the outset these and like matters led me to recognize the mythic character of baseball literature and, as a body, its status as a mythology. To make this point, however, I need to discuss the difficult terms *myth, mythology,* and *mythicity,* along with their relationships to literature and critical theory.

MYTH, MYTHOLOGY, AND MYTHICITY: SOME DEFINITIONS

Myth is now so encyclopedic a term that it means everything or nothing. We can find in it whatever we want to say is essential about the way humans try to interpret their place on earth. Myth is a synthesis of values which uniquely manages to mean most things to most men. It is allegory and tautology, reason and unreason, logic and fantasy, waking thought and dream, atavism and the perennial, archetype and metaphor, origin and end.
—*Eric Gould,* Mythical Intentions in Modern Literature 5

The word myth is used in such a bewildering variety of contexts that anyone talking about it has to say first of all what his context is.
—*Northrop Frye,* Myth and Metaphor 3

As the two epigraphs to this section indicate, what I now seek to do is not without risk. I need a definition that not only captures the essential in myth but also reflects the prevailing thought of those who turn their attention to the intersection of myth and literature. To do this I have to make excursions into extraliterary fields that have generated ideas or approaches relevant to the myth-literature question. I begin, therefore, not with a definition but with a demonstration to which I will return from time to time.

Paul Ricoeur has said that it is impossible to speak of metaphor nonmetaphorically, and various theorists bear this out.[2] A similar claim can be made for attempts to define myth (which often reveals itself to be metaphor pushed into motion, time, predication, and narrativity): it is impossible to speak of myth nonmythically. Consequently, before I attempt the impossible, I yield to the necessary and present a myth that captures the sense of current thinking about myth, what it is, what it does, and why. The story is called "The Tower of Babel"; later I will show that its subtitle might well be "The Myth of the Gap":

And the whole earth was of one language and of one speech. And it came to pass as they journeyed from the east, that they found a plain in the land of Shinar; and they dwelt there.

And they said one to another, Go to, let us make brick, and burn them thoroughly. And they had brick for stone, and slime had they for mortar.

And they said, Go to, let us build us a city and a tower, whose top may reach unto heaven; and let us make us a name, lest we be scattered abroad upon the face of the whole earth.

And the Lord came down to see the city and the tower, which the children of men builded.

And the Lord said, Behold, the people is one, and they have all one language; and this they begin to do: and now nothing will be restrained from them, which they have imagined to do.

Go to, let us go down, and there confound their language, that they may not understand one another's speech.

So the Lord scattered them abroad from thence upon the face of all the earth: and they left off to build the city.

Therefore is the name of it called Babel; because the Lord did there confound the language of all the earth: and from thence did the Lord scatter them abroad upon the face of all the earth. (Gen. 11:1–9)

From the outset it is clear that this is a myth about language – the possibilities implicit in its origins (when "the whole earth was of one language and of one speech") and its failures after the divinely spoken confusion. At first perfect language is capable of bridging the gap between earth and heaven, human and divine, time and eternity, known and unknown. The bricks and slime are, figuratively, the stuff of language (words, sentences, phonemes, morphemes, semantemes, and syntax); the tower is discourse-as-bridge. Here, in the prelapsarian phase, to imagine, to speak, and to do are congruent acts. In this language there is no gap between signifier (word) and signified (concept/thing). Possessed of such language, humans are powerful indeed. The Lord seems to have a commitment to the gap, however, perhaps a fear of its closure, and his solution is to confound and confuse the language of humans, opening further fissures between one person and another, between concept and word, and scattering (further dividing) them over "the face of all the earth."

The ruined tower with its rubble of words is an apt metaphor for both the mythic enterprise and, more broadly, the general use of language about language, including the metalinguistic activities of philosophers, social scientists, theologians, and literary critics, many of whom have in recent years – according to their own lights – addressed the nature of language, the subject of myth, and the problem of the gap. All of us involved in such an enterprise are ironically compelled to work with language and within language to analyze and (if possible) repair its failures, to muck around in the rubble, inside the tower. Lévi-Strauss recognized this curious structural fact of myth early in his career. Taking his cue from Franz Boas, Lévi-Strauss saw in the mythic enterprise the work of the *bricoleur,* the artificer who "make[s] do with whatever is available" to construct a new thing, building, as Boas said, "new mythological worlds" from the shattered remains of the old (Lévi-Strauss, "Structural Study of Myth" 50). Mythological thought, as Lévi-Strauss defines it, is "a kind of 'intellectual *bricolage'* " (*The Savage Mind* 17). As I show later, he will make a similar assertion about the mythologist's work, a claim whose implications have crucial significance in modernist anthropology;[3] Gérard Genette will echo the claim on behalf of the literary critic and the critical enterprise.

The story of the tower is thus about language, yet it is also about myth, about human attempts to make sense of the world through words. The dual referent of the tale is not surprising, for the words *language* and *myth* have traveled together from a common origin. Both, as William G. Doty points out, go back to a single Indo-European root, **ma-,* realized in Greek as *mythos,* "word," "speech," and related to "mother" – hence the "mother tongue" (3). So myth is language, but as Barthes insists, "language needs special conditions in order to become myth" ("Myth Today" 93), and Lévi-Strauss says similarly that myth "is both the same thing as language and also something different from it" ("Structural Study of Myth" 52). It is the special conditions and the something different that I am attempting to specify.

Complicating the picture is the word *mythology,* which sometimes means simply "myths" but has traditionally been used ambiguously to mean both "a body of myths" and "the study of myths." The word (which combines *mythos,* "word," and *logos,* "word"), is a reiterative term meaning something like "word words," or as Doty says, "words concerning words" (3) (which is another term for *metalanguage* and which, in turn, is a term frequently applied to critical discourse). In Plato both *mythos* and *logos* could mean "account" or "story," but the two terms were already taking on connotations, at times, of the "false" and the "true," or the narrative and the discursive.[4] By Aristotle's time *mythos* had come to mean "plot" or "story," Greek plots typically dealing with material that we would call mythic but that was religious to the Greeks, tales like those in the Bible or the Koran of gods and humans and significant events in the deep past or at the beginning. Anthropologists tend to make few distinctions between "the mythic" and "the religious" as subjects of myth. Hence from its origins *myth* meant "language" or "speech" and gradually took on the meaning of speech in plot or story form, true or false, often concerning the sacred. This is close to the position of philosopher Lawrence J. Hatab, who begins his analysis of philosophy and myth by acknowledging the difficulties of defining myth and offering instead a "generalization": "A myth is a narrative which discloses a sacred world" (19). As soon as one opens the door to the sacred, however, the question arises whether myth can function in a profane world. Is myth a thing of the past?

Some mythographers, such as Frazer, have viewed myth as a relic, a form produced in one developmental stage of consciousness but later outgrown as science replaced magic and religion as means of confronting nature. In this vein H. J. Rose saw "true" myth as "the result of the working of naïve imagination upon the facts of experience" (12), a claim that implies not only that myth is primitive or unsophisticated but also that there is such a thing as false myth – modern mythic imitations, one assumes, by the no-longer naïve. Seen as primitive or archaic, myth is variously said to be the precursor of science, history, politics, "linguistic awareness" (Kort 118), "discursive conceptual language" (Falck 116), and literature (Frye, *Great Code* 35).

Today, however, many have begun to suspect that myth is not something humans outgrow, like nursery rhymes, or evolve beyond, like an appendix, but something they retain as an enduring, functional strategy that mind pursues to conduct its dialogue with the world. Not all observers see this as cause for celebration, and certainly the value of myth and mythmaking has, over time, risen and fallen on the intellectual market. Although conflicting attitudes continue to exist, at least since the late eighteenth century (with the impact of Herder and the rise of German romantic philosophy), one school of mythographers has assumed myth to be an intellectual impulse of enduring nature and redemptive qualities, a mode of the imagination that may atrophy from disuse but that remains indispensable to the health and vigor of a people, its politics, art, religion, and exchanges with nature.[5] Moreover, although the aura (some would say "odor") of the distant past continues to cling to myth, or its persistently recurring structures, images, and themes, conflicting attitudes about both its value and its status in the modern world persist. There are mytho-phobes who find in modern myth not only the archaic but the irrational, the manipulative, and the muddled. In this view myth is a system used by some for the control of others. Despite his extensive analyses of mod-ern myths, Roland Barthes remained an inveterate mythophobe,[6] seeing myth as a political tool bourgeoisie use to control the thought and behav-ior of the people ("Myth Today" 125–49). Paul de Man, speaking of met-aphor as the coin of myth (he says the former relates to the latter as "knot" to "plot"), expresses a fear not so much of control by others as of powers implicit in figural language itself to confuse and deceive each of us. Lit-erature, he says, "is . . . the place where the possible convergence of rig-or and pleasure is shown to be a delusion. The consequences of this lead to the difficult question whether the entire semantic, semiological, and performative field of language can be said to be covered by tropological models, a question which can only be raised after the proliferating and disruptive power of figural language has been fully recognized" ("Epis-temology of Metaphor" 28).

It is probably not accidental that de Man's fears about language, its knots and plots, are expressed in pervasively figural terms, for his own fields of language sprout their mythic weeds. Surprisingly, among the my-thophobes must be numbered Joseph Campbell, comparative mytholo-gist and one of the premier mythographers of our time, who simultaneous-ly finds a human need for myth but sees danger in the continuing power of outmoded mythic systems. Every functioning mythology is "a control system" (*Inner Reaches* 20), he says, and the question is whether outmod-ed systems impel us toward real destruction in an outgrown, mythically determined world.[7]

But there are mythophiles, too, who emphasize other characteristics of modern myth, especially its ability to express the essential in human life, its ties to fundamental ontological and psychological "truths," its links with reality, and its ability to impose order on the apparent chaos of ex-istence. Although he acknowledges the primitive nature of myth and "the mythic mode of apprehension of reality" as a "universal stage through which the developing human linguistic consciousness passes" (116), Colin Falck claims as well that myth and the mythic are not left in the past but continue to exert their influence in the present: "Myths seem in practice to be quite ineliminable from human perception or vision, and . . . their function in human life appears to be a primal, and an irreplaceable, ex-pressive one" (129). Myths are a universal phenomenon, "not merely as a primitive residue which has not yet been superseded by rationality or true belief, but seemingly as a continuing substratum of the basic structures of experiencing" (129). Lévi-Strauss, taking a different tack, argues that there is nothing primitive about "the savage mind" and that, on the contrary, mythic thought is indistinguishable from modern thought: "The kind of logic which is used by mythical thought is as rigorous as that of modern science, and . . . the difference lies not in the quality of the intellectual process, but in the nature of things to which it is applied"; furthermore, "the same logical processes are put to use in myth as in science, and . . . man has always been thinking equally well" ("Structural Study of Myths" 66). Northrop Frye agrees with Lévi-Strauss on the nonevolutionary nature of human mental processes but reverses the claim. Accepting Shelley's notion that poetry is "primitive" in that it maintains "a fundamental and persisting link with reality," Frye observes that "in mythology the issues are more confused: it apparently takes social scientists much longer than poets or critics to realize that every mind is a primitive mind, whatever the varieties of social conditioning" (*Great Code* 37).

Among these seemingly contradictory attitudes and claims, one thing is clear: whether fragmentary or coherent, dangerous or life enhancing, primitive or modern, evolutionary or constant, myth, the narrative that discloses (and as often as not at the same time veils) a sacred world, abides and exerts its influence, for good or ill, in our world.

The last of the three terms I seek to define, *mythicity,* is a neologism that, despite its apparent meaning – "the nature of the mythic, or the attributes or qualities of the mythic" – not only insists on but more carefully defines the *linguistic* nature of myth implicit from the beginning in the word itself. Eric Gould's analysis of *mythicity* is the most comprehensive, as well as the most congruent with recent developments in criticism. Gould's analysis foregrounds mythicity as a quality of some modern literature, a quality related to the mythic but not identical with it. Gould's ground-breaking work, *Mythical Intentions in Modern Literature,* addresses the myth-literature relationship from the perspective of structural and poststructural theory, emphasizing text or language as antecedent to and foundational of such constructions of traditional myth criticism as the unconscious, the archetype (the repeated structure, motif, figure, or image), and the sacred. Starting from the Lacanian notion that the unconscious is a product of language and linguistic in its own right (31–32), Gould takes his cues from Lévi-Strauss to argue cogently that, contrary to Jungian analysis, the archetype (long a sign of mythicity) is not a mental given but rather a linguistic construct that has begun as a signified (a thing referred to by language) and then changed roles to that of signifier (itself a form of language) (45), becoming in the process endlessly repeatable but, like other signifiers, equivocal, evolving, undergoing transformation, and requiring endless interpretation.[8] Gould's redefined archetype is a concept very similar to Lévi-Strauss's bricolage: both are made of mythic remains, and both are linguistic and therefore necessarily implicated in the eternal linguistic contest between semantic tradition and evolution. In this way Gould identifies what I think is the soundest, most theoretically coherent of approaches to the study of myth and its relationship to, or intersection with, literature. Although Gould's analysis is not primarily of myth per se but, as he says, of modern manifestations of "mythical intentions" in literature, he has nevertheless rewritten myth criticism, placing it midstream in contemporary criticism and pointing the way to an enhanced understanding of mythic texts, ancient and modern.[9] His work thus proves an invaluable guide to my own study of the relationship of myth and baseball literature and of their common linguistic enterprise.

As Gould uses it, *mythicity* reflects the structuralist principle that the word is not the thing; it is born in just this recognition of the primacy of language and the insistence "that mythicity is no less modern than it is ancient, that it is preserved in the gap which has always occasioned it, through our attempts symbolically to represent and give meaning to our place in the world through discourse. Insofar as literature preserves the fullness of that intent, then it preserves mythicity" (12). *Intent,* as used here, does not suggest merely the conscious willing toward a goal but implies both an autonomy of language and a strong unconscious element that, as Gould says, finds that the "genetic mechanism accounting for myth must have something to do with language and its interpretation, especially since *language is in full complicity with human desires,* ranging from ontological yearnings to our very existential need to solve the compromises of the self among other selves" (30; emphasis added). More specifically the essential quality of myth – that is, mythicity – is "its exemplary function of intending-to-interpret, whether its object is social compromise, the supernatural, questions covering the self and its place in the world, or those issues we think of as ultimate, unanswerable and metaphysical" (34).[10]

Although my project here differs from Gould's, I want to claim the quality of mythicity for baseball's texts: this body of texts – baseball literature – has the status of a functional modern mythology. The texts are archetypal (in Gould's sense); they reveal the work of the *bricoleur;* they "make do" with the "shattered remains" of old mythological worlds; and they are characterized by the kind of coherence one finds in traditional mythologies, presumably growing from ethnic shapings of both consciousness and the unconscious, from congruence in time and space, and most significantly, from a metaphor-made reality shared to a greater or lesser degree among the mythmakers and supplied by the game itself, in both its scene and its progress, which is by nature "poetic," that is, evocative of that which is ultimately unrepresentable in language but nevertheless may be felt, thought, feared, and desired. The mythicity of baseball's texts emerges almost of necessity from a mythicity in the game itself – its rituals and roles, its characters, the tropological nature of its space and time, its "plot" (the progress and rules of play), its object (to make the circular journey from home to home), its ground (a solid stage in a shifting cosmos), and its ground rules (the principles of order within this [con]text).

Moreover, mythicity's intention to interpret and thus to fill the semiotic gap between word and thing, language and world (Gould 42), is manifest not only in the realm of myth as narrative but also in adjacent interpretive realms of psychoanalysis, philosophy, anthropology, and literary criticism, all of which are fields bearing on this study. Mythicity is a quality not solely of ancient tales or literature but of "texts," even those purporting to be objective or scientific. As a quality of written or spoken discourse, mythicity (with its interpretative intent and its recognition of the essentially metaphoric ground of texts) is hatched in the nest of poetry. As Gould says, mythic discourse "reveals a heightened sense of reliance on metaphor" (54). It is to be contrasted with representation, traditionally said to characterize the language of science. Whereas representation seeks to "present again" in language that (usually) nonlinguistic "truth" which unequivocally *is,* mythicity evokes the conceivable, the truth merely glimpsed through the veils of language in which it is necessarily swaddled. Mythicity is thus associated, one might argue, with two kinds of recognition, one as old as language and the other sputtering into consciousness over the last two hundred years: the recognition that language is the human vehicle in which truths are shaped and transmitted and the postmodern recognition of the tangled web of what Marc Manganaro calls "representational complexes" and the resulting "disillusionment with adequate representation" (10). As time passes and texts on the subject accumulate, one thing becomes clear: mythic texts are characterized by mythicity, an eternal quality of language. They are poetic, evocative, relying on metaphor to find meaning in, or assign meaning to, the "facts" of existence. Mythicity is most transparent in myth, but it inheres also in modern texts, the literature itself, as well as in those several forms of discourse that function to interpret that literature – resulting in an entanglement of first and second and even third orders of mythicity, a virtual linguistic web in which authors, "poetic" and "scientific," struggle. Such authors work amid the rubble of the ruined tower of language and myth. Their task is most difficult.

I have shown that *myth,* originally "language" or "speech," evolved to mean a plot, account, or story, but retained its birthright, its mythicity, its essentially linguistic nature. That linguistic nature exerts its influence on the behavior of the genre, with all the creative possibilities, equivocations, and surpluses of language, its intent to interpret, to fill the voids of understanding, knowledge, and being with significance or intelligibility. Myth cannot escape its past, its diachronic dimension, and the use of old signifiers and their ancient etymologies; therefore, its gaze is often retrospective, and its subject – to put it broadly – is human interaction with the facts both of nature and of the numinous, or uncanny. That myth endures into our age as an essential fact of human speaking and imagining is generally accepted, at times with regret. Given this situation, we must ask why and how (if at all) myth today differs from both its "primitive" character and function and from nonmythic texts, literary and discursive. We must ask about the grounding of myth in the sacred, the extent to which that basis persists, and whether and how it is transformed. What profitable commerce can transpire betweeen us, inhabitants (we are told) of a decentered, largely secular universe, and the sacred, the numinous, the uncanny? To address these problems, and to say how all these matters bear on the subject of baseball and mythology, we need to return to the ruined tower and the myth of the gap.

Chapter 1, "The Myth of the Gap," presents the theoretical background for the present study of modern myth. The chapter takes its direction from Gould's work and finds its most useful texts among the French structuralists – anthropological, semiological, and psychological. Jacques Lacan is a pivotal theorist here, standing at the crossroads of Freudian and structural interpretations of texts. All such theories rest on the metaphor of the gap, a gap that, despite its claim to discursive truth, is no less mythic than the phenomena it seeks to explain. That we can enlist a myth – and an academic one at that – in the work of understanding myth and its career in our world seems paradoxical until we recognize the power of plots to organize our experience, direct our searches for meaning, and even define the nature of the world we inhabit. In the last section of chapter 1 I discuss the problem of the sacred in modern myth and its fundamentally linguistic nature, adopting in the process Gould's redefinition of archetype and relating this to Lévi-Strauss's notion of bricolage. Chapter 2 applies some of the strategies of structural and psychological theories to a reading of August Wilson's *Fences*. It finds that the protagonist inhabits a space crowded with battered and now ironic mythic archetypes and that he makes sense of his life through metaphors emerging from ancient narratives through the medium of baseball – all of which offer their equivocations and ancient echoes to the myth of Troy Maxson.

In chapter 3 I use the Freudian notion of "key narratives" to examine two recurring plots or archetypal structures – the classic and American monomyths (*mono,* "one," and *myth,* "plot, story") – and their affinity with the game of baseball, its progress, and its ground. I also consider whether the essentially masculine patterns are replicated in baseball narratives by and about women. The concept of the monomyth (both classic and American) and its grounding in the quest structure is a clear example in baseball and its literature of the mythic signified having emerged in modern ritual and text as signifier. Continuing with this subject, in chapter 4 I analyze Mark Harris's *Bang the Drum Slowly,* showing that in its dual protagonists it combines classic and American plots, using baseball's scene and structures to weave two structures into a single text. The link between the structures is language, wherein a comic voice, lexicon, syntax, and structure become the media for the tragic narrative; the mythic task in the work is to bridge the gap between life and death, the comic and the tragic; and the materials of bridge building (the bricolage) are taken from baseball, its figurative ground and ancient archetypes. The resulting narrative performs a delicate balancing act, attempting to overcome the most basic of contradictions through language.

In chapter 5 I explore the (meta)physics of baseball, the dimensions of the game and its literature – space and time as created, represented, and occupied by the game and its texts. Here the mythic dimensions Mircea Eliade describes are transformed into signifiers, which have through history, as Gould says, "endlessly repeat[ed] the so-called archetype[s]" (45) of sacred time and space. Within the precincts of the game and its lore, space takes on the significance of the originary, first place; time, the fluidity and malleability of dream time. Baseball's time, like the mythic time of its archetypes, often leads back into the distant past – to the beginnings, individual or collective. Baseball's space often represents the archetypal scene of origins – garden, home, motherland. I look at works by women, exploring gender issues implicit in the feminization of "ground" and the metaphoric identification of woman and nature. In chapter 6 I explore the narrative labor within baseball's mythic dimensions in W. P. Kinsella's *The Iowa Baseball Confederacy* and William Kennedy's *Ironweed*, two works whose protagonists, both time travelers, are distant kin of Odysseus and Oedipus. Their progress leads them, willingly or not, and for good or ill, back to a primordial garden, home, (en)closure.

In chapter 7 I explore the relationships among myth, religion, and art – what I will call crisis art – as these converge in the literature of baseball. Drawing on insights of Friedrich Nietzsche, William James, and Joseph Campbell, and focusing on the subjects of death, spiritual catastrophe, the uncanny, illumination, and conversion, I demonstrate the fan's typical reaction in forms of art, the mythmaking reaction to limit situations resulting in the creation of gods (Dionysian and Apollonian), texts, sermons, and visual and plastic arts. The chapter contains a reading of illumination and mythmaking in W. P. Kinsella's *Shoeless Joe*. Continuing in this vein, in chapter 8 I examine the masterful presentation of fan psychology and crisis art in Eric Rolfe Greenberg's novel *The Celebrant*.

Chapters 9 and 10 deal, respectively, with Bernard Malamud's *The Natural* and Robert Coover's *The Universal Baseball Association, Inc., J. Henry Waugh, Prop.* Both analyses explore the effects of bricolage, mythic signifiers become signifieds, and the intertextual invasions and invitations, echoes and distortions, between these texts and the mythic past of Western literature.

In chapter 11 I look at a particular theme of baseball's mythology, that of father-and-son atonement, a oneness gained when the father, a "good guy," dies young. Focusing on Mark Harris's *The Southpaw*, David Small's *Almost Famous*, and David James Duncan's *The Brothers K*, I show that baseball often centers the father-son relationship and provides a trope both for the father's blessing of the son and for the son's movement into adulthood. Atonement with the father is, however, costly and hard-won, usually achieved not only through the death of the father but also through a decentering, dislodging, destructive "plot" against the mother – a "whore," "feeb," or "denier of life."

Chapter 12 returns to the subject of the baseball dwarf, analyzing his personal and collective implications. The dwarf embodies both the individual past, the Oedipal child, and the primordial form of the species, a figure who brings along with him associations gained through countless representations in myth, legend, and literature. Special attention is given to the figures of Scarborough in Jerome Charyn's *The Seventh Babe* and of Pogo Burns in John Sayles's *Pride of the Bimbos.*

In chapter 13 I take up the difficult problem of aesthetics in myth criticism, asking, for example, how one tells good myth from bad. In addition to treating other matters, I explore what Christian K. Messenger appropriately objects to as a "complacent" inclusion in baseball's texts of "magic" and "history," and include a discussion of Tidewater's "counterhistory" or "autobiography" in Jay Neugeboren's *Sam's Legacy.*

MYTH IS LANGUAGE: TO BE KNOWN, MYTH HAS TO BE TOLD; IT IS A PART OF HUMAN SPEECH. IN ORDER TO PRESERVE ITS SPECIFICITY WE SHOULD THUS PUT OURSELVES IN A POSITION TO SHOW THAT IT IS BOTH THE SAME THING AS LANGUAGE AND ALSO SOMETHING DIFFERENT FROM IT. . . . THIS IS PRECISELY WHAT IS EXPRESSED IN SAUSSURE'S DISTINCTION BETWEEN *LANGUE* AND *PAROLE*, ONE BEING THE STRUCTURAL SIDE OF LANGUAGE, THE OTHER THE STATISTICAL ASPECT OF IT. Claude Lévi-Strauss, "The Structural Study of Myth" 52

MYTH IN FACT BELONGS TO THE PROVINCE OF A GENERAL SCIENCE, COEXTENSIVE WITH LINGUISTICS, WHICH IS SEMIOLOGY. Roland Barthes, "Myth Today" 95

IF PSYCHO-ANALYSIS IS TO BE CONSTITUTED AS THE SCIENCE OF THE UNCONSCIOUS, ONE MUST SET OUT FROM THE NOTION THAT THE UNCONSCIOUS IS STRUCTURED LIKE A LANGUAGE. Jacques Lacan, *Four Fundamental Concepts of Psycho-Analysis* 203

WHAT BASEBALL PLAYERS SAY AND WHAT BASEBALL WRITERS WRITE IS TRANSLATABLE EVEN IN CONCEPTUAL PLAY, AND IT IS THIS SPECIAL AFFINITY FOR LANGUAGE AS A SYSTEM – BEYOND DIALECT AND IDIOM, MORE TOWARD THE ESSENTIAL NATURE OF COMMUNICATION ITSELF – THAT IS THE FIRST GREAT DISTINGUISHING POINT IN BASEBALL'S FUNDAMENTALLY *WRITABLE* NATURE. Jerry Klinkowitz, *Writing Baseball* 2

THE MYTH OF THE GAP

The epigraphs indicate something more than an intellectual fashion; they reveal the presence of a full-blown, interdisciplinary, cross-cultural mythology that arose in the intellectual movement known as structuralism.[1] According to Fredric Jameson, structuralism understood "in its strictest and most limited sense" is "work based on the metaphor or model of a linguistic system" (ix). The linguistic system itself (Saussurean linguistics) is not part of structuralism; it merely provides the model or metaphor. In fact Jameson dates the rise of structuralism to 1955 and the publication of Lévi-Strauss's *Tristes tropiques*. The first three epigraphs at the opening of this chapter belong to three of the four names most frequently associated with the intellectual movement of structuralism,[2] and the last citation comes from another place, another time; between the first three and the last, numerous reiterations of this central idea have been written and spoken (and structuralism has been transformed into an anxious form of itself, namely, poststructuralism). The idea may be stated thus: *X is structured like a language,* and for X we can substitute any number of abstractions, for example, *narrative,* or more broadly, *literature.* Turbayne, for the purposes of demonstration, went so far as to substitute *the universe* for X.[3] More pertinent to my examination of baseball and myth, in the epigraphs *myth, the unconscious,* and *baseball* are the substituted terms. It follows that among them a structural analogy must obtain, for if A, B, and C are structured like language, then, of necessity, A, B, and C share a structure. As a result the analogy by itself is an invitation to interdisciplinary probing and helps to account for numerous cross-disciplinary applications of the formula.

I do not need to review again the structuralist model; many good analyses are available. My purpose here is to focus on the figural core (or knot) of the Saussurean linguistic model, to analyze its diffusion into, and transformation in, anthropology, psychology, and literary theory, and to relate this metaphor to a theory of modern myth in which I include baseball and its literature. In this enterprise I draw on Jonathan Culler's *Structuralist Poetics,* Eric Gould's *Mythical Intentions in Modern Literature,* Gérard Genette's "Structuralism and Literary Criticism" (in *Figures of Literary Discourse*), and Mark C. Taylor's *Tears.* As I mentioned previously, Eric Gould's book is particularly helpful, integrating in a single study structuralism, myth criticism, and key aspects of poststructural theory. I argue that at the center of the linguistic model as structuring principle, and of those theories based on it or evolving from it, is an indispensable figure, the spatial metaphor of gap. Above this gap, metaphorically situated, are the manifest, the conscious, the known, the empirically observable, the seemingly random facts of existence, the language of the text; beneath are the hidden, the unconscious, the unseen, the mental, and the systematic, the ambiguous, evocative utterance of the unconscious – with a structuring energy that flows into the gap and exerts its influence within the realms of the manifest.

As I have suggested by this chapter title, the academic notion of the gap is itself of the nature of myth, characterized by "mythicity" – Gould's "intention-to-interpret" – and taking its cues from myth and myth's methods.

The academic myth has a figural core, using the spatial metaphor of the gap to explain myth, a genre that likewise uses the same metaphor in an attempt to reconcile contradictions or to transcend the boundaries between known and unknown, seen and unseen, and conscious and unconscious. The gap of myth is a great void of nonmeaning, nonsense, or contradiction in which the mythic purpose operates within the medium of language, attempting to fill that emptiness with meaning, to render experience intelligible, to create narrative bridges across the abyss.

To discover exactly what sort of structure these authors have in mind when they say that X is structured like a language, we need to seek answers in Saussurean linguistics. It is deeply ironic to find that the myth of the gap arises from a radically demythologizing gesture by Saussure. When he declared that the word is not the thing, he denied what Hatab sees as a principle of mythic thought – that the word *is* the thing in a conceptual system where language and world are understood as coextensive, where language does not merely represent but actually presents the thing of which it speaks (Hatab 37), the Tower of Babel, for example. This, the first of the Saussurean gaps, opens up a space between signifier and signified and denies any contact between words and "reality," whether phenomenal, metaphysical, or mental.

Another gap is created by a second Saussurean principle: *parole* (speech) must be distinguished from *langue* (language). This latter principle makes a distinction, as Culler reminds us, roughly equivalent to that which Noam Chomsky makes between performance and competence (Culler 3–31). *Parole* (or performance) is on the side of the empirically observable; *langue* or competence, by contrast, is the largely unconscious, never directly observable system (grammar) internalized in the minds of speakers. The rules of this grammar can be formulated only through a process of deduction and interpretation of empirically observed speech and from speakers' reports of their understanding of utterances.[4] Thus tropological gaps open up – at some times mere fissures, at others yawning abysses – between "deep" and "surface" structures, between *langue* and *parole,* between word and thing, between unheard, unspoken, unconscious linguistic knowledge and talk in the world. Current theory seizes on this space and uses it, making myth, metaphor, archetype, interpretation (of whatever sort), and play things and acts of the gap, a figurative maneuver inspired by the linguistic model but performed outside linguistics, in anthropology, philosophy, theology, and psychology – in all fields bearing on critical theory and the problem of mythicity. Indeed, *gap* and its synonyms (aporia, abyss, lack, cut, absence, and numerous others) bear to current theory (structuralist and poststructuralist) a relationship analogous to that of *imagination* to early nineteenth-century theory. Both gap and imagination are metaphors, and both attempt to name a middle "playground" of language, art, or text. Their difference lies in part in the fact that whereas imagination was seen to have a mediating, reconciling function as "third thing"[5] between reason and sense, self and world, or subject and object, gap insists on separation (a meaning inherent in the trope), irreconcilability, or eternal *différance*. Nevertheless, a clear line of descent extends from the German and English romantics to the structuralists and poststructuralists as concerns this "play space" of the gap.

Friedrich von Schiller in 1795 posited such a play space between the determinisms of reason and sense (or mind and body) in which both sorts of "necessity" are nullified by the "play drive." Schiller associates the play drive with art, whose energies, exerting on the psyche both moral and physical constraints, will "set man free, both physically and morally" (14:424). Such a tripartite structure whose middle ground is the realm of play or art is implicit in precisely those authors whom Derrida cites as forwarding the inquiry that led ultimately to his own "decentering" of Western metaphysics: Nietzsche, in his "critique of the concepts of Being and truth, for which are substituted the concepts of play, interpretation, and sign"; Freud, in his "critique of self-presence, that is, the critique of consciousness"; and Heidegger, in his "destruction of metaphysics, of ontotheology, of the determination of Being as presence" ("Structure, Sign and Play" 85). Despite their questioning of the history of Western metaphysics, these authors, along with Lévi-Strauss and even Derrida himself, face a dilemma, for they "have no language . . . which is foreign to this history [of Western metaphysics]" (85), and so each of Derrida's predecessors has fallen victim to the discourse of structure, with its space between, its center. According to Derrida, the space between reflects the "concept of centered structure," which is "the concept of a play based on a fundamental ground, a play constituted on the basis of a fundamental immobility and a reassuring certitude, which itself is beyond the reach of play" (84).

Derrida's response to what he sees as an implicitly structural metaphysics is to accept the notion that every critic is a *bricoleur* (in Lévi-Strauss's sense, of which I say more later) faced with the necessity "of borrowing . . . concepts from the text of a heritage which is more or less coherent or ruined" ("Structure, Sign and Play" 88) and to adapt, change, or transform those concepts as suits his needs. Derrida, in this role of *bricoleur,* borrows the concept of structure, with its necessity of center, and decenters it, replacing the center with a hole (an abyss) and placing everything within the reach of play. Derrida uses the term *free-play* to describe this unrestrained activity of discourse. Of course, a hole – an absence or an abyss – will in some ways center a structure, a play space, as will play itself in a more compelling manner. James S. Hans, in his analysis of play, walks a line between the ideas of Derrida and Gadamer on the subject of play, accepting Derrida's notion of play as "free from Being" but modifying Derrida's notion of freeplay by showing that play creates its own structures:

> Whereas play is free in the sense that there is no Being in which to ground it, it is also bound in two crucial senses: first, the beginning of play is always necessarily connected to a foreproject, to a series of pre-judgments that are at issue in the activity of play itself, that give an orientation to the play; and second, the result of play is a structure, a framework or order that has been confirmed by the play itself. *It is this structure which is – this structure which is confirmed as true – that will become part of the structure of prejudgments that will affect future play.* Thus play is always bound by the results of its own activity, though those results can always be called into question in future play. (*The Play of the World* 10–11; emphasis added)

Play may be, for Derrida, "The Exciting Game Without Any Rules" (Mark Harris's card game in *Bang the Drum Slowly*), but it is not innocent of prejudgment or purpose and, therefore, of structure. It arranges itself around a center, whether point or hole, presence or absence. This centering gap, then, is play-space, and as I will argue, baseball – the game and its texts – is the artifact par excellence of the gap and in the gap.

MYTHOLOGY, PSYCHOLOGY, BASEBALL, AND THE GAP

A good metaphor seems to be important because it is useful. When we are confronted by a model or metaphor uprooted from one field of reference (in this case linguistics) and transported to another (anthropology, or psychology, or literary criticism), we are dealing with what Ricoeur refers to as the "intersection of spheres of discourse," one established and the other waiting, as it were, to be born. The metaphorical utterance (e.g., Lévi-Strauss's claim that "myths are structured like a language")[6] functions, Ricoeur says, "in two referential fields at once." It is already established in the first field (in this case linguistics), with a system of predicates attached: "This already constituted meaning [Ricoeur explains] is raised from its anchorage in an initial field of reference and cast into the new referential field which it will then work to delineate. But this transfer from one referential field to another supposes that the latter field is already in some way present in a still unarticulated manner, and that it exerts an attraction on the already constituted sense in order to tear it away from its initial haven" (*Rule of Metaphor* 299).

The unarticulated field exerts a sort of physical attraction on the network of predicates in the first field, but two forces contribute to the *epiphora* (the transfer of meaning) from field to field: "Two energies converge here: the gravitational pull exerted by the second referential field on meaning, giving it the force to leave its place of origin; and the dynamism of meaning itself as the inductive principle of sense." In the end, the effect of the metaphorical transfer is to bring "an unknown referential field towards language" (299). That linguistic birthing increases the number of fields of discourse, thus advancing "knowledge" by building one more annex to the house of language known through the metaphor and the narratives constructed thereon.

Ricoeur's analysis, couched in metaphor, helps to explain the way in which the new field of discourse can come into being through the transfer of meanings from one established field of reference to another "ghostly" realm of meaning waiting to be born. The predicates (narratives) applicable in the first field emigrate with the initial *epiphora*. In the process, Ricoeur says, two energies operate, the gravitational pull of the new field and the dynamism of meaning; both are language-driven. I want to include a third, Lacanian sort of energy, a mental or "symbol"-driven force inherent in the unconscious of the metaphor maker and consisting of perceptual, partly preverbal images with their associated affects, fragmentary sound, and all the unconscious refuse of conscious language. The obvious way in which the unarticulated field can be present is in the mind (another metaphor) of the metaphor maker (who, Turbayne says, is a wizard, a creator of new realities, a cross-sorter). Perhaps language, in some ways innate in the human animal (as Chomsky argues), is the source, determinant, and outer limit of all meaning, the metaphor of metaphors. Nevertheless, we sense that there are word magicians among us, those whose peculiar experiences or ways of sorting those experiences conjure the ghostly field of reference in the first place and invent ways to talk about it.[7]

What we can say with some degree of certainty is that when there is a field of discourse waiting to be articulated, whether it is humanly made or linguistically determined, humans will work with the bricks and slime – the rubble – they find at hand. Old predicates will find new work; new meanings will take form and speak. The new field, too, is a gap that must be filled with language. Lévi-Strauss's application of the language metaphor and its gaps to re-create mythography (so as to speak of it as structure) contributes several interesting notions to my inquiry into the status of baseball as myth. As Eric Gould points out, Lévi-Strauss's intellectual bent is interdisciplinary; he is an "anthropological scientist concerned with mythology, the arts, and hermenutics" (89). Lévi-Strauss's anthropological discussions of myth thus tend to lead to application or discussion in the realms of literature, psychology, or philosophy, for he permits himself to wander freely into speculations about what the myths reveal of human logic and epistemology; his famous analysis of the Oedipus myth's in "The Structural Study of Myth" from the outset plunged him and his ideas into cross-disciplinary discussions (he claimed, for example, that a myth consists of all its versions, the Oedipus myth thus including Freud's version of it) – discussions demonstrating analogies among the disciplines that have continued with varying amounts of fervor ever since.

Working with the linguistic metaphor, on the analogy of the phoneme (an abstract, unconscious, unhearable, unspeakable bundle of phonetic features), Lévi-Strauss formulated the notion of the "gross constituent unit" ("Structural Study of Myth" 53), or "mytheme," which is a narrative primitive whose systematic influence is discoverable at the sentence level. Lévi-Strauss suggests that the way to discover the unconscious infrastructure of myth is "by breaking down [a mythic] story into the shortest possible sentences." Just as phonemes (the smallest units of language) are bundles of features, so mythemes are "bundles of . . . relations," and "it is only as bundles that these relations can be put to use and combined so as to produce a meaning" (53). A mytheme is meaningful only within its system; transporting it to another system will change its meaning, because it will exist in a structural relationship with other bundles of relations with which it is contrasted and from which it derives meaning.

To return to the motif I identified in the introduction (that of the baseball dwarf who suffers violence and exclusion), following Lévi-Strauss I propose that the several appearances of this motif are manifestations of some underlying mytheme. Between this unseen, unconscious structural principle and its manifestations is a gap that the mythologist/critic must fill with interpretation. This interpretative act is crucial because associated with the mytheme is the notion that, like a phoneme, a mytheme reveals its meaning not alone but in its binary opposition to some other mytheme.[8] This principle shows the baseball dwarf to be a surface manifestation of an underlying mytheme, a bundle of relations. Does the mytheme also have alternate forms ("allomyths") within its system at the manifest level? Are there analogues to the baseball dwarf that are likewise manifestations of the mytheme, for example, the aging and aged, the young, the ailing, the female, or the inept? Any decision about what the mytheme signifies will depend on prior analyses and intuitions about just what constitutes a manifestation of it and the discovery of its binary opposite within this myth or body of myths. The baseball dwarf presumably must be assigned a meaning different from that of the dwarfs of Nordic myth, or the Munchkins "over the rainbow," or the dwarf who accompanies Una in book 1 of *The Faerie Queene*, although he may be a transformation of those ancient signifiers. Thus, in Lévi-Strauss's scheme, to be understandable a myth must be reduced to a system of mythemes, each of which is meaningful in contrast to another within the system. The myth itself will address the problem of "bridging the gap" ("Structural Study of Myth" 64) between the polar opposites represented by mythemes juxtaposed at the manifest level. Lévi-Strauss claims that the purpose of myth "is to provide a logical model capable of overcoming a contradiction (an impossible achievement if, as it happens, the contradiction is real [e.g., the living and the dead])" (65). Myth thus arises in response to need. There is an absurdity, a mystery, a contradiction – two things or conditions or facts "speaking against" each other, denying each other. Language seeks a logical model (a means through language, or logos) of overcoming the contradiction. Whereas myth attempts to close the gap between such polar opposites, the mythologist attempts to bridge the gap between unconscious and conscious. Hence, for Lévi-Strauss, the mythic and the mythographical enterprises are analogous: to fill a gap with language in pursuit of meaning.

Returning for a moment to my suggestion that some of the figural energy is provided by the metaphor maker, some insight into Lévi-Strauss as metaphor maker and his affinity for this linguistic model may be seen in his account of the making of an anthropologist in *Tristes tropiques*. Here, having spoken about his early interest in geology and of his own ontological speculations, he tells of a personal "quest," of following a particular geologic formation that contained in juxtaposition rocks laid down by ancient seas separated by immense periods of time but now revealed in a "pale blurred line." He says that the object of his quest is "to recapture the *mas-*

ter-meaning, which may be obscure but of which each of the others is a partial or distorted transposition" (emphasis added). When "the miracle occurs" and the quester discovers "on one side and the other of the hidden crack" evidence of the "gap of several tens of thousands of years," then "suddenly space and time become one"; the mythic work has been done: "Thought and emotion move into a new dimension where every drop of sweat, every muscular movement, every gasp of breath becomes symbolic of a past history, the development of which is reproduced in my body, at the same time as my thought embraces its significance. I feel myself to be steeped in *a more dense intelligibility,* within which centuries and distances answer each other and speak at last with one and the same voice" (56–57; emphasis added).

Here is a demonstration of uncommon power, for the mythologist not only creates a myth about myths, using a metaphor from geology and demonstrating the mythic task (momentarily) achieved, but actually lives the myth, occupying mythic time and space and revealing the impact on and value to the human experiencer. The hidden crack, the gap, is closed; time and space, thought and emotion, physical effort and history – all these are reconciled, as master-meaning is made or discovered and thought embraces significance. To find oneself in this "more dense intelligibility" is, one might say, the object of all mythmaking. Eric Gould uses a similar phrase – "ultra-signification" – to describe myth's purpose, "especially to confront the unanswerable" (178). The phrases "master-meaning," "more dense intelligibility," and "ultra-signification" refer beyond the known to the unknown and sometimes beyond the mundane to the sacred, uncanny, or numinous – to some crucial, life-enhancing ontological or metaphysical truth.

At least by 1964 Lévi-Strauss came to see his own analyses as not only figurative (a fact that he acknowledged from the start) but also, in their movement, mythological in their own right. Myths, he explains, are secondary codes based on the primary codes of language. The anthropologist's interpretation is a "tertiary code," "intended to ensure the reciprocal translatability of several myths. This is why it would not be wrong to consider this book [*The Raw and the Cooked*] in itself as a myth; it is, as it were, the myth of mythology" (12).

Lévi-Strauss clearly works as *bricoleur,* making do with what is at hand – a geologic formation, the mythemic raw and cooked, archetypes (in Gould's redefinition) – to create his own structures, his myths of mythology. As mentioned, Derrida follows Lévi-Strauss in seeing his own critique of language as a form of bricolage and himself as necessarily a *bricoleur* ("Structure, Sign and Play" 88), and although he does not go so far as to call his enterprise "mythmaking," he implies as much. Gérard Genette, however, explicitly characterizes as bricolage not only mythmaking in so-called primitive civilizations (and Lévi-Strauss's interpretative work to construct a myth of mythology) but also his own critical enterprise, an intellectual activity of more "developed" cultures (i.e., a nonprimitive mythmaking): "I mean criticism, more particularly literary criticism, which distinguishes itself formally from other kinds of criticism by the fact that it uses the same materials – writing – as the works with which it is concerned; . . . [it] speaks the same language as its object; it is metalanguage" (3–4). That is, he explains, literary criticism, like mythmaking, primitive or anthropological, has a "*secondary* character" to which "Lévi-Strauss's remarks on *bricolage* may find a somewhat unexpected application": " 'Critical thought,' one might say, paraphrasing Lévi-Strauss, 'builds structured sets by means of a structured set, namely the work. But it is not at the structural level that it makes use of it: it builds ideological castles out of the debris of what was once a literary discourse' " (4–5). With both Derrida and Genette, not surprisingly, we find ourselves amid familiar rubble, returned to the ruined tower and its linguistic debris – its bricks and slime, its shards and fragments – to perform the craft of literary criticism.

There is, however, an interesting anomaly in Genette's exposition based on Lévi-Strauss's metaphor. Lévi-Strauss's primary code of language underlies the secondary code of myth (bricolage or metalanguage), which in turn underlies the tertiary code of anthropological interpretation, the "myth of mythology" (more mythmaking, bricolage, a meta-metalanguage). In contrast Genette moves from literature, which is for him a primary code, to the secondary code of mythmaking (a metalanguage or a "metaliterature" [4]). For Genette, the maker of the literary work is not a *bricoleur* but an *engineer* (a term he borrows from Lévi-Strauss), using instruments tooled for the purpose, not those lying at hand, the debris of other structures (4–6). Derrida correctly sees that the "engineer, whom Lévi-Strauss opposes to the *bricoleur,* [and who] should be the one to construct the totality of his language, syntax, and lexicon. . . . , is a myth." Derrida explains: "A subject who supposedly would be the absolute origin of his own discourse and supposedly would construct it 'out of nothing,' 'out of whole cloth,' would be the creator of the verb, the verb itself. The notion of the engineer who supposedly breaks with all forms of *bricolage* is therefore a theological idea; and since Lévi-Strauss tells us elsewhere that *bricolage* is mythopoetic, the odds are that the engineer is a myth produced by the *bricoleur*" ("Structure, Sign and Play" 88). The mythical engineer as the origin of his own discourse, the creator of the verb, speaking an Adamic, a first, or a divine language (the Logos), speaking the speech of the first tower builders, would antedate the *bricoleur,* who is condemned to suffer the effects of his or her own belatedness, to work with the verbal debris of such original speaking. Obviously this positing of a privileged first speaker is another version of the story of Babel, in which there is an unspoken sense that the work of the tower builders, mythical engineers, must somehow be better or more legitimate than that of the *bricoleur.*

Genette's position, which perhaps is based on the impulse to dissociate literature from myth or to elevate the poet-novelist above the critic-mythmaker, fails to account for the crucial observation that, in Derrida's terms, "we have no language . . . which is foreign to this history [of metaphysics]"; Derrida of course includes in that "we" not only the philosopher and critic but the novelist and the poet as well. Genette's position also discounts the pervasively intertextual nature of language in general and literature in particular, its "mythicity" (and the presence therein of "archetypes" as signifieds become signifiers), a subject to which I return later.[9]

Nevertheless, the metaphors of gap, engineer, and *bricoleur* reveal the energies Ricoeur described, the "gravitational pull" of the fields of mythology, anthropological interpretation, and literary criticism desiring to be reborn or reconstituted and the dynamism of language itself – both of these operating in concert with the third force, the creative energy of the metaphor maker. That at least part of the energy of the metaphor (and its transplantation from one field of reference to another) must be ascribed to the metaphor maker is shown with even more vividness in the difficulties and feints of a Lacanian text. Lacan, a post-Freudian psychoanalyst, adopts and adapts the linguistic model to suggest the structure of the mind and the relationship between consciousness and the unconscious: "Linguistics, whose model is the combinatory operation, functioning spontaneously, of itself, in a presubjective way – it is this linguistic structure that gives its status to the unconscious. *It is this structure, in any case, that assures us that there is, beneath the term unconscious, something definable, accessible and objectifiable"* (*Four Fundamental Concepts* [hereinafter *FFC*] 20–21; emphasis added).

A pattern is emerging. There is something hidden, unknown, and unconscious that influences the manifest in all its diversity and apparent inexplicability. If the nature of that unknown could be discovered, it would offer clues to the meaning of the manifest. If we find the right metaphor, if we uproot a network of predicates from the field of linguistics by asserting that myth is structured like language, that literary criticism is structured a myth, or that the unconscious is structured like language, the unknown becomes suddenly knowable through the metaphor. In the linguistic model actual utterances, together with speakers' intuitions about them, provide evidence about the underlying structure, *langue* or competence. Once the initial metaphor is made, narrative takes over. Myths grow mythemes; the unconscious takes on "body." To claim, as does Lacan, that the linguistic model provides assurance that there is, beneath the term *unconscious,* something definable, accessible, and objectifiable is to make a metaphoric leap from "as if" to "is," from pretense to belief, terms I borrow from Turbayne. If I say that the distant mountain is made of ice cream, and that I therefore am assured of food at my journey's end (and I had better take a spoon), I am making a similar claim. I point this out not to deny the efficacy of such claims or to denigrate the metaphoric work but simply, on the one hand, to reveal the presence here of a genuine mythicity and of realities constructed of myths and, on the other, to reiterate my point that it is impossible to talk (about) myth nonmythically.

In adopting the metaphor Lacan is interested not so much in revealing the psychoanalytic equivalents of phonemes, morphemes, or deep syntactic structures as he is in investigating the linguistic gap between *langue* and *parole,* which he identifies with the gap between the unconscious and consciousness. The linguistic model insists that the unconscious aspect of language imposes, through specifiable rules, a structuring force on speech and comprehension of speech. What we know when we know a language (whether we know it or not) is structure. Linguists do not concern themselves with the causal nature of the relationship, but Lacan does notice the problem in the model he has adopted and goes back to Kant to wrestle with it: "In his *An attempt to introduce the concept of negative quantities into philosophy,* we can see how closely Kant comes to understanding the gap that the function of cause has always presented to any conceptual apprehension. In that essay, it is more or less stated that cause is a concept that, in the last resort, is unanalysable – impossible to understand by reason . . . and that there remains essentially in the function of cause a certain *gap,* a term used by Kant in the *Prolegomena*" (*FFC* 21). If the relationship between underlying system and surface manifestations is understood as one of cause and effect, and if it is impossible to understand causality by reason, the linguistic metaphor finds another embodiment in psychoanalytic theory: it is not only the gap between unconscious and conscious but between (unconscious) cause and (conscious) effect.

Explaining Freudian ideas of the unconscious, Lacan freely applies the language of the model: "What the unconscious does is to show us the gap through which neurosis recreates a harmony with a real. . . . In this gap, something happens." This gap, Lacan believes, is the place where Freud finds "something of the order of the non-realized"; the gap is not the unconscious itself but a "hole," "split," or "gap" (*FFC* 22) at the "infernal opening" (29) of the unconscious, the hollow entrance to an underworld. "At first," Lacan says, "the unconscious is manifested to us as something that holds itself in suspense in the area, I would say, of the unborn"; "That repression should discharge something into this area is not surprising. It is the abortionist's relation to limbo" (23). Within the Lacanian prose the metaphor is becoming myth again; its spatial nature provides a stage for events, stretches out like a universe, a world where the shades walk.

For Lacan, the spatial metaphor provided by the linguistic model becomes the center of a myth that seeks its own realization in the language of yet older myths. We hear the mythmaker's art in Lacan's caution to his audience:

> It is always dangerous to disturb anything in that zone of shades [the unconscious "realm" beneath the gap], and perhaps it is part of the analyst's role, if the analyst is performing it properly, to be besieged – I mean *really* – by those in whom he has invoked this world of shades, without always being able to bring them up to the light of day. . . . It is not without effect that, even in a public speech, one directs one's attention at subjects, touching them at what Freud calls the navel . . . which is simply, like the same anatomical navel that represents it, that gap of which I have already spoken. (*FFC* 23)

Lacan has a commitment to the gap. Some analysts since Freud have, he says, occupied themselves with "stitching up this gap"; "Believe me," he adds, "I myself never re-open it without great care." It is a frightening boundary, this gap, and the unconscious that lies beyond is "infernal," a "realm of shades." All Lacan's imagery insists both on the otherworldly, mythic character of the unconscious and on a vertical orientation to the mental universe. He invokes the person of Odysseus in his notion of the proper approach to the opening: "Since Freud himself, the development of the analytic experience has shown nothing but disdain for what appears in the gap. We have not – according to the comparison that Freud uses at a particular turning-point of *The Interpretation of Dreams* – *fed with blood* the shades that have emerged from it" (*FFC* 32). Freud's and then Lacan's allusion is to book 11 of *The Odyssey*, the scene where Odysseus is required to dig a pit and fill it with blood for the shades to drink. Without the blood they cannot become conscious or speak their secrets to him. How does the unconscious speak to consciousness? What is the metaphoric blood? I discuss these questions later.

Is there mythology today? Undoubtedly, yes. Ancient mythical geography has, through language, become internalized (as Wordsworth announced nearly two hundred years ago);[10] its plots, persons, and progress have become "archetypal" – that is, part of our language, the system of signs that constitutes our unconscious minds as well as our world; and we, at the end of the twentieth century, traverse that mythical landscape in text after text, in this or that field of discourse, as well as in our dreams and nightmares. As it was for Wordsworth, the mind is the "haunt" of Saussure, Lévi-Strauss, Derrida, Genette, and Lacan, and as I argue later, it is in such inner reaches and their linguistic terrain – mostly, of course, terra incognita – that we will find room for the numinous, a matter already suggested by Lacan's metaphors: the underworld, the shades, the feeding with blood.

What is the blood that we must feed the shades that emerge from the linguistic realms of desire, of ecstasy and terror, in our underminds, and step into that pit, gap, hole, or slit? Lacan can answer in a word: *language.* The shades are ghostly embodiments of the essence of unconscious language, preverbal sign and (largely rhetorical) language; they make their presence known through language; and at times they become conscious and capable of communication with the light through language. In short, there is language in the gap, and as Eric Gould explains, beneath the gap is fugitive language (the unspeakable words of shades): "For Lacan, quite simply, the unconscious is that discourse which has 'escaped' from the subject, which we produce without knowing why. It is the language which we give birth to, which humanizes us, but which we cannot fully control, and which instead appears to control us" (74). On the linguistic model such fugitive language has its structure, its grammar (as *langue*), and will exert its influence across the gap.

There is a paradox at the center of Lancanian psychology, and it lies in the coexistence of two tenets, one a simile and the other a metaphor: the unconscious is at the same time structured *like* language and *is* a language. If

Robert Burns had said, "my luve's like a red, red rose, and is a rose," the enigma would have complicated his text, too. I call attention to this paradox here because it has gone unnoticed in Lancanian literary analyses. The two principles are treated as one, with predictable confusions and complications. The previously discussed phenomenon of the gap belongs to the simile; the analysis that follows concerns the claim (metaphorical or not) that the unconscious is a language. The distinction between simile and metaphor is crucial, for I make a similar claim concerning baseball: it is structured like language, and it is a language.

The notion that the unconscious is structured like language is intended to reveal the systematic nature of the unconscious and its ability, as system, to exert a structuring effect on conscious discourse; it creates the analogy that the unconscious is to consciousness what *langue* is to *parole*. The tropological claim permits the gap to appear and its profundities and functions to be explored. The second claim, that the unconscious is a language, calls for the construction of a "grammar" of the unconscious, including rules for the functioning of its symbols and narratives, its semantic and syntactic components. The attempt to construct a grammar of the unconscious takes the analyst into fields of discourse whose subject is, broadly, the text (understood in psychoanalysis as the narratives and dreams of the analysand and in literary criticism as drama, story, or poem). This places the unconscious as text side by side with other texts and leads to the further claim that the unconscious reveals itself in texts – the myth, the poem, the literary narrative.

From this relationship it follows that the best preparation for the psychoanalyst is that exemplified by Freud, who according to Lacan enjoyed not only scientific training but also "a profound assimilation of the resources of language (*langue*), and especially of those that are concretely realized in poetic texts," including literature, classics, folklore, and ethnography (*Écrits* 76–77). Lacan cited with approval Freud's list of disciplines supporting an "ideal" psychoanalytic faculty: "Besides psychiatry and sexology, 'the history of civilization, mythology, the psychology of religions, literary history, and literary criticism.'" In addition, Lacan would include "rhetoric, dialectic. . . , grammar, and . . . poetics" (76). Such lists make explicit a further analogy: the reader is to the text what the analyst is to the narratives and dreams of the analysand. This analogy does not extend to metaphoric identity; the analyst is not a literary critic, and the literary critic is not an analyst, although their enterprises are similar.

Psychoanalysis and critical reading both involve interpretation, hermeneutics, stylistics, and most importantly, rhetoric. They can proceed along parallel lines because "readers" in both disciplines share a language with the object of interpretation – the language of the unconscious. The relationship is one in which, in a sense, deep calls to deep, for although each unconscious is absolutely particular (built on the perceptions and experiences of the individual), it nevertheless has a universal character in that it is the "language of desire, that is to say, . . . the *primary language* in which beyond what [the subject] tells us of himself, he is already talking to us unknown to himself, and, in the first place, in the symbols of the symptom"; the language of the symbol "has the universal character of a language (*langue*) that would be understood in all other languages (*langues*), but at the same time, since it is the language that seizes desire at the very moment in which it is humanized by making itself recognized, it is absolutely particular to the subject" (Lacan, *Écrits* 81). As Lacan understands it, then, the process of interpretation is partly self-discovery, and the relationship between analyst and analysand (or reader and text) is on the order of echo or refraction: "The only object that is within the analyst's reach is the imaginary [in the Lacanian sense of pertaining to images and affects] relation that links him to the subject *qua* ego"; "Although he cannot eliminate it, he can use it to regulate the yield of his ears, which is normal practice, according both physiology and the Gospels: having ears in order not to hear, in other words, in order to pick up what is to be heard. For he has no other ears, no third or fourth ear to serve as what some have tried to describe as a direct transaudition of the unconscious by the unconscious" (45).

From all this it follows that study of the grammar of the unconscious is crucial not only for the analyst but for the Lacanian critic, whose task, as Ragland-Sullivan says, is not to "psychoanalyze a text" but rather to use Lacanian insights into meaning production in the interpretative enterprise: "Lacan holds out to semiology a fascinating theory of how meaning is produced and to semantics a theory of what lies beyond conventional meanings. A Lacanian poetics . . . would study the paralinguistic points of join between visible language and invisible effect" (382). Although the full details of Lacanian hermeneutics and interpretative strategies (or theories of reading) are still being worked out,[11] in what follows I identify a few key Lancanian "linguistic" principles applicable to the analysis of myth and literature and helpful in resolving the central problem of this introduction, articulating the relationships among baseball, its literature, and mythology so as to justify the claim that baseball is myth. The discussion will return us to the myth of the gap and its transactions, for I argue that both baseball field and text open out in the interstice that, as Ragland-Sullivan puts it, permits "points of join" between unconscious and conscious and the "grammars" appropriate to each; that, as Lévi-Strauss argues, this gap is the space of myth; and, finally, that here we must recall a crucial aspect of myth – called the sacred, the numinous, or the ineffable, among other things – that provides the necessary last aspect of the genre and transforms mythos to myth: a mythic text is structured like a Lacanian mind. It has both its surface topography – its words, sentences, and plot – and its linguistic underworld, its unconscious locus and source of images, symbols, and uncanny tropes beneath the gap.

THE SEMANTIC COMPONENT OF THE LACANIAN GRAMMAR

The meaning-producing component of the Lacanian (unconscious) *langue* has both nonverbal signs and verbal elements. Three Lacanian concepts relate to the semantics of the unconscious. The first concept, a nonverbal one, is "the imaginary," which denotes "the world, the register, the dimension of images, conscious or unconscious, perceived or imagined." The second, "the symbolic," belongs to language and refers to a group of Saussurean signifiers: "differential elements, in themselves without meaning, which acquire value only in their mutual relations, and forming a closed order" ("Translator's Note," *Écrits* 279). Ragland-Sullivan explains that Lacan means by "symbol" the "base unit of perceptual representation": "The symbols in question are neither icons, stylized figurations, or second meanings, but in other words, the rudiments of all knowledge" (385).[12] The order of symbols constitutes the subject, which is "an effect of the symbolic" ("Translator's Note," *Écrits* 279). Lacan puts it thus: "Man speaks, then, but it is because the symbol has made him man" (*Écrits* 65). The materials of these first two elements, the imaginary and the symbolic, belong to two types of experience, the imaginary relation holding between the unconscious ego and its perceptions and the symbolic holding between the conscious subject and language. One way of thinking of the relation between them is to suggest that the essentially nonverbal imaginary provides for the concrete (or material) revelation of the symbolic. The symbols are complex, linked together as "sound fragments, imagistic traces, and identificatory resonances" (Ragland-Sullivan 385). Lying beneath or prior to the symbolic, and serving as its ground and limit, is "the real," a biological/psychological X, an unknown that "remains foreclosed from the analytic [interpretative] experience, which is an experience of speech" ("Translator's Note," *Écrits* 280). As Lacan has it, analysis is forever barred from knowledge of the real, for it is "an essential encounter – an appointment to which we are always called with a real that eludes us" (*FFC* 53), the encounter of originary ground or motive over whose nature Lacan claims to stumble: What is it? It is not "*perhaps nothing*, but *not nothing*" (64).[13] "The gods," Lacan insists, "belong to the field of the real" (45). I return to this elusive "not nothing" when I consider the problem of myth and the sacred.

The symbols themselves are few and constitute a closed set of unconscious semantic primitives by which desire is externalized (*Écrits* 104). Symbols identified by Ernest Jones and accepted "as a fact" by Lacan are of five categories, those that "refer to one's own body, to kinship relations, to birth, to life, and to death" (82). Although assuming countless forms in texts, the symbols have "a *primary* character"; they are "like those numbers out of which all the others are composed"; they "underlie all the semantemes of a language (*langue*)" (82). Symbols are the closest Lacanian analogue of the Jungian archetypes (as innate, primordial, universal image, figure, or plot), but they have a linguistic character and, despite their "primary character," are subject to the same sort of linguistic determinism as the unconscious as a whole. Symbols are, moreover, the basis of all interpretation. Each possesses "the property of speech by which it communicates what it does not actually say"; in this sense, symbols are of the essence of language, whose function, Lacan asserts, "is not to inform but to evoke" (82).

In addition to including these imaginary and symbolic elements, and their mysterious ground, the real, the semantic component of the unconscious grammar has a third aspect, the rhetorical. As I already mentioned, one of the subjects Lacan finds to be useful in an analyst's preparation is rhetoric, by which he means the study of rhetorical figures, uses of language that involve indirection and polysemy, born in the grammar of the unconscious (according to Lacan) and filtered, often unnoticed, into narratives, dreams, and texts. Following Freud, Lacan arranges rhetorical tropes in two categories, one syntactic (displacement) and one semantic (condensation): "Ellipsis and pleonasm, hyperbation or syllepsis, regression, repetition, apposition – these are the *syntactical displacements;* metaphor, catachresis, autonomasis, allegory, metonymy, and synecdoche – these are the *semantic condensations* in which Freud teaches us to read the intentions – ostentatious or demonstrative, dissimulating or persuasive, retaliatory or seductive – out of which the subject modulates his oneiric discourse" (*Écrits* 58; emphasis added). Four years later, however, in "Agency of the Letter in the Unconscious," Lacan joins Jakobson in seeing metonymy as a form of *se-*

mantic displacement, so the categories of syntax and semantics do not entirely coincide with the Freudian concepts of displacement and condensation (*Écrits* 160). Lacan insists that we cannot dismiss these as "mere figures of speech," however, for "it is the figures themselves that are the active principle of the rhetoric of the discourse that the analysand [or the text] utters" (169).

Of the tropes listed by Lacan, the first in each category is of central significance – ellipsis, representing the syntactic gap, and metaphor, the master trope of resemblance.[14] Here Lacan identifies both as belonging to the semantics of the unconscious, having to do with condensation, which Freud claims to be a device through which dreamwork distorts the truths of the unconscious and reveals its meanings, even as it screens them from consciousness. Metaphor is primary, since "the operation of signifying condensation is fundamental to it" (*FFC* 247).

Two additional figures from Lacan's own rhetoric are pertinent to Lacanian semantics: desire, a prosopopoeia, a "speaking figure," whose mode of discourse is itself rhetorical, and law, another prosopopoeia. Desire speaks for the individual, and law, the Name of the Father (collective, authoritative precept), for society. Law is the Leviticus of internalized language, grounded on and elaborated from incest taboos whose best mythic revelation is found in the *Oedipus* of Sophocles. Law "sustains the structure of desire with the structure of the law" (*FFC* 34). Both desire and law, like and unlike Freud's id and superego, are voices of the unconscious, constituted of language, dressed in rhetorical garb, and admitted to the stage where the performance of the drama of the self ensues. Law, emerging later than desire, superimposes culture on nature (*Écrits* 66). Desire and law are by their nature opposed. They compete to be heard in texts, the one's passion and the other's vehement rage for order echoing in the rhetoric, the images, the symbols of the text.[15]

Rhetorical tropes are thus the grammatical modes or inflections of the unconscious, indirect, evocative, equivocal, and even haunting but capable, as I said, of disguising their import as well as their origin even from (or especially from) their speaker's understanding. Indeed, they are means by which the unknown, unsaid, and unsayable insinuates itself into speech or text, where it is available for interpretation.

THE SYNTACTIC COMPONENT OF THE LACANIAN GRAMMAR

Ellipsis is of special interest because it is the trope of omission, the eloquently and significantly unsaid. It and its rhetorical siblings thus belong, as Lacan said, to the syntactic component. The silence of ellipsis can be as brief as the gaps between words and sentences or as long as the censored chapter of one's life story: "The unconscious is that chapter of my history that is marked by a blank or occupied by a falsehood: it is the censored chapter. But the truth can be rediscovered; usually it has already been written down elsewhere" (Lacan, *Écrits* 50).

The function of a grammar's syntactic component is to provide the rules by which linguistic elements are combined to form sentences, the briefest forms of narratives. Following Freud, Lacan saw that the dream, for example, "has the structure of a sentence . . . the structure of a form of writing" (*Écrits* 57). Narrative (myth, plot, or story) is the product of the syntactic component and is the mode in which the self is constituted "as a fiction" (Ragland-Sullivan 386). When Lacan says that the truth of the unconscious has already been written down elsewhere, he directs attention to the syntax of the mental grammar, to symptoms inscribed in the "monument" of the body; to "archival documents," the narratives of childhood memories; to the linguistic evolution of the self as to matters of vocabulary and style; to mythic and literary traditions, "the legends which, in heroicised form [Freud's 'key narratives' or Gould's 'archetypes'], bear [the] history [of the unconscious]"; and to the syntactic distortions in the text of individual history necessitated by the "linking of the adulterated [censored] chapter to the chapters surrounding it, and whose meaning will be re-established by . . . exegesis" (50).

This narrative expression of unconscious meaning in the inherited metaphors and forms gives shape to the unconscious and joins the individual to the world of myth. It is as such narratives that materials of the semantic component find expression – the primordial ideography of the child, the phonetic and symbolic heiroglyphics of the adult (*Écrits* 57), and the rhetorical figures, all spread out syntactically, linearly, and diachronically to become plot. The imaginary, the symbolic, the real, and all the array of figures exist, like Lévi-Strauss's mythemes and Saussure's *langue,* in unconscious synchronic suspension until pushed into motion by the syntactic component to become narrative. Lacan makes these parallels explicit in a call for reclassification of the human sciences:

> Linguistics can serve us as a guide here, since that is the role it plays in the vanguard of contemporary anthropology, and we cannot possibly remain indifferent to it. . . .
> And the reduction of every language to a group of a very small number of these phonemic oppositions, by initiating an equally rigorous for-

malization of its highest morphemes, puts within our reach a precisely defined access to our own field. . . .

Isn't it striking that Lévi-Strauss, in suggesting the implication of the structure of language with that part of the social laws that regulate marriage ties and kinship, is already conquering the very terrain in which Freud situates the unconscious? (*Écrits* 73)

The parallel insists that speech (linguistics), myth (anthropology), and dream/narrative (psychology) are surface manifestations of deep linguistic structures – *langue* and mytheme in linguistics and anthropology and the imaginary, the real, and the symbolic in psychology. These deep structures occupy an unconscious terrain, the ground from which a "general theory of the symbol" might emerge; its basic principle would assert the linguistic nature of both reality and knowledge (*Écrits* 73–74).

The gap between the deeps of grammar and the dry land of discourse, like that between the plains of Shinar and heaven, is the space of language, of interpretation – both primary (myth, narrative, and plot) and secondary (analysis, exegesis, and hermeneutics) – where the tower builders work. This universe of language engages the concern of analyst and critic alike. Lacan's mythic caution to the analyst returns us to those plains and that tower: "Let [the analyst] be well acquainted with the whorl into which his period draws him in the continued enterprise of Babel, and let him be aware of his function in the discord of languages. As for the darkness of the mundus around which the immense tower is coiled, let him leave to the mystic vision the task of seeing in it the putrescent serpent of life raised on an everlasting rod" (*Écrits* 106).

Lacan's metaphors (the tower, the putrescent serpent of life, the everlasting rod) raised at the conclusion of his lecture "Function and Field of Speech and Language" are typically Lacanian, mythic, evocative, equivocal, and ironic, constituting both a message from the unconscious and a demonstration of its function. His readers are left to engage the text in an interpretative enterprise that threatens to reveal as much of themselves as of the meanings of the text, for the two are in some ways the same.[16]

APPLICATIONS: MYTH, LITERATURE, AND THE POETICS OF THE LINGUISTIC MODEL

Now, with the basic outline of the myth of the gap in view, I can specify its implications for the study of myth and the literature of baseball. These may be arranged under two broad categories, structural (how is it made?) and interpretative (what does it mean?). Structural investigation has two main concerns. It leads us first to ask about the structural primitives, or mythemes, their origins, their presence in the game itself, their variety of expression, their relation to the Lacanian symbols or topoi, and the system of binary oppositions, if any, to which they belong. Second, it prompts us to question typical plots composed of those building blocks: Are there key narratives or archetypes, compelling plots that insist on being retold in seemingly endless variety? Do those plots bear a necessary relation to the action of the game? Interpretative strategies likewise raise two sorts of questions, rhetorical (what are the tropes and figural processes of displacement and condensation?) and archetypal (in Gould's sense of the term) or intertextual (what networks of implications do we find, and again, are these tropes and networks in some way or ways prompted or necessitated by baseball itself?). Finally, there is the problem at the center of myth and hence of all mythic representation – that of the sacred – and the questions of whether and, if so, why and how the sacred (the numinous, the uncanny, the monstrous, or the profoundly mysterious) insinuates itself into the meaning-making enterprises of the modern and largely secular game, its writers and readers. In the remainder of this chapter I discuss such questions briefly (for they will continue to be of interest throughout this study); in chapter 2, again briefly, I apply them to one particular work, August Wilson's Pulitzer Prize–winning play *Fences,* whose protagonist occupies a figurative world defined by the metaphor of baseball, itself a bricolage of mythic rubble. First, then, a glance at the structural principles of mytheme and archetypal plot or key narrative and then at rhetorical and intertextual interpretative strategies.

STRUCTURE: BASEBALL AND MYTHEMES

The structural building blocks, or mythemes, of baseball literature presumably take their specific expression from the game, while referring to the universal concerns specified by the symbolic topoi – namely, the body, the family, birth, life, and death. For example, Western imagining, with its phallocentric emphases, finds its metaphor in the bat: the batter (with his phallic instrument of power, which appears to be a transform of Lacan's "putrescent serpent" and "rod") gets a hit or strikes out, the comic and tragic modes of the game and of sexual conquest. He[17] may even hit a home run and, Odysseus-like, make the long journey home. The action of batting is equivocal, however; the bat is also a weapon in a life-or-death struggle wherein all is at risk: the batter lives or dies. In the complexities and compromises of the symbols the two metaphors (phallus and weapon) merge. The batter gets a (sexual) hit so as inevitably to die. As Lacan puts it, "the link between sex and death . . . is fundamental" (*FFC* 130). Further, the "mystery of love" constitutes "a search by the subject not of the sexual complement, but of the part of himself that is lost forever, that is constituted by the fact that he is only a sexed living being, and that he is no longer immortal" (205). The lost part of the self, then, is life – immortality – and its accompanying felicity, the storied conditions of infancy, hence the compelling signification in a single narrative primitive focused on the metaphor of the bat. Put in terms of family relations, the situation is as follows: the batter is born from the batter's box–womb, onto the (base) paths of life, or childlike, he fails to set forth, remaining "at home." Within the figurative family of the team, the rookie-son defeats (or is defeated by) the veteran-father, or he joins the father to defeat an enemy. In the idealized world of the game, as in Eden and the Greek Golden Age, all men are "motherless," yet the very ground of their action is mother womb and tomb – Ge, Earth, who imposes her "mother-rules" or ground rules on the players and the game. As this study progresses, these and other mythemes, structural primitives dictated by the game, will manifest themselves in a variety of forms, revealing the game's mythic enterprise of attempting to bridge the gap or overcome a contradiction through language – whether in the primary ritual narrativity and signs of the game itself or in the secondary narrativity of the stories told about it.

STRUCTURE: THE KEY NARRATIVES

The great discovery of Freud and his followers was the constancy and universality of human psychology and its revelation in "texts," not only mythic and literary works but also the dreams and personal narratives of each of us, neurotic or not. They discovered "the textual unconscious" (Mellard, *Using Lacan* 5). The relative simplicity of the unconscious, its preoccupation with the five symbols or symbolic topoi (the body, kinship relations, birth, life, and death), and their infinite variety of expressions led, as Shoshana Felman puts it, to "Freud's unprecedented *transformation of narration into theory*": "In the constitution of the theory, however, the discovery that emerges out of the narration is itself referred back to a story which confirms it." For Freud, as for Lacan after him, the key narrative of this hermeneutic circle concerns the drama of Oedipus, out of which theory emerges and to which theory is referred for confirmation (Felman 1022).

Likewise, the first stunning demonstration of mythic structure by Lévi-Strauss focuses on the Oedipus myth in all its versions, including Freud's. The Oedipus is a "key-narrative – the specimen story of psychoanalysis" (Felman 1023) – because it meets three criteria: effectiveness, familiarity, and universality, revealed, as Felman says, by three questions that "support [Freud's] analytical interrogation":

1. *The question of the effectiveness of the story* (Why is the story so compelling, moving? How to account for the story's *practical effect* on the audience – its power to elicit affect, its symbolic efficacy?)
2. *The question of the recognition* (The story has power over us because it "is compelling us to *recognize*" something in ourselves. What is it that the story is compelling us to recognize? What is at stake in the recognition?)
3. *The question of the validity of the hypothesis, of the theory* ("a legend whose profound and universal power to move can only be understood if the *hypothesis* I have put forward in regard to the psychology of children has an *equally universal validity*"). (1023)

To borrow a phrase from Robert Graves, there was for Freud only one story that would prove worth the telling, that of Oedipus, "the love of the mother and the jealousy of the father" (cited by Felman 1022), a tale that focuses on one of the unconscious symbols, that of kinship relations gone wrong. Nonetheless, even in Freud's one story there are aspects that reveal what might be called the Laius complex (the father's fear and jealousy of the son) and the Polybus heroism (the father's love and sacrifice for the son), to which Freud was apparently oblivious.[18]

Addressing broader human concerns and other symbolic topoi of the unconscious, however, is a second key narrative that is observable through countless retellings and revisions and exemplified in *The Odyssey* of Homer. Both the Oedipus story and *The Odyssey* have their biblical counterparts as well. Oedipal themes, for example, work themselves out in the Old Testament story of David and Absalom and in the New Testament agon of the father (Yahweh) and the son (Jesus) – in both of which, incidentally, "Laius," rather than "Oedipus," prevails in the father-son struggle. Moreover, *The Odyssey* is enacted on a collective scale in the biblical epic of the Exodus, the story of a long journey from home (Canaan), through a series of trials, and a return home, which all along was the Promised Land, a journey lasting not nineteen years (as for Odysseus) but over four hundred years. *The Odyssey,* like the Oedipus myth, meets the Freudian criteria of effectiveness, familiarity, and universality; both reveal Lévi-Strauss's mythemic narrative primitives of the deep structure of myth; both reveal the grammar (the semantics and syntax) of the unconscious; both are stories in and of the gap; and both (as will become clear as this study progresses) supply their structures and themes to baseball and its literature.

INTERPRETATIVE STRATEGIES: THE TROPES

As already described, two types of trope dominate Freudian-Lacanian theory as techniques of unconscious discourse: tropes of condensation and displacement, both of which characterize the discourse of dreams (performing "dreamwork") and personal narrative, as well as literary texts. They conceal even as they reveal the meanings of the personal and textual unconscious. They are evasive, polysemous, and equivocal, yet at the same time they create a rich semantic texture that evokes, affects, and even haunts. They both invite and resist interpretation. We might ask of baseball what de Man asked of "the entire semantic, semiological, and performative field of language": is it "covered by tropological models" (28)? The answer – a resounding yes (already implied in the question) – takes us some distance toward understanding baseball's mythicity and what Klinkowitz called its "writability." Two examples of its tropological character will suffice here: ellipsis, a trope of displacement, and allegory, a trope of condensation.

The ellipsis I have in mind is primary and of the essence of baseball's mythic nature. It is the gap re-presented as the field itself, not abstract and mental but material and visible, a green pastoral opening in the urban ordinary. Homologous to the gap between conscious and unconscious, between mytheme and myth, the field is, in a sense, negative space and time, where the syntax of history (as it proceeds at a personal or collective level) is suspended, where, free of ordinary time and space, the fugitive language and imagery of the unconscious can erupt as figural feint and enigma. The field welcomes the projection of unconscious matters that are, as Lacan says, "inaccessible to spatio-temporal location and also to the function of time" (*FCC* 31), a matter explored at length in chapter 5. In its simple lines and empty expanses actions take on a clarity of outline, a definition, that they lack in the complex and cluttered world outside. They lend themselves to interpretation. Every individual, every act, and every image points beyond itself, means something more than itself, something spoken in play but intended in earnest – hence the tendency to see it all as an allegory whose basic system of reference is life itself.

The notion of baseball as an allegory for life is encouraged by the fact that baseball does not hide the individual in the society; each member of the team/society is spotlighted in turn, his degree of success or failure tracked unrelentingly on scorecards and in team statistics, texts that "tell his story." For example, each player comes to bat with a task to perform and a journey to begin; his course lies clear in the sun, and his progress can be charted from a god's-eye view as at each step of the way he encounters obstacles, challenges, and enemies. The narrativity of his enterprise is clear.

INTERPRETATIVE STRATEGIES: INTERTEXTUALITY, ARCHETYPES, SYMBOLS, BRICOLAGE

Intertextuality denotes the interdependence of texts and requires that the critic explore the effects on meaning of such overt signs of intertextuality as echo, allusion, and citation, as well as the covert intertextuality implicit in language itself. There are, therefore, intertextual implications in the notions I have already considered, both archetypal plots (key narratives) and symbols and their "universality" in texts. As Lévi-Strauss recognized, the mythmaker, the *bricoleur*, is necessarily and *essentially* an intertextual artist, using the debris of old myths to construct new mythological worlds. I have enclosed the word *universality* in quotation marks to call attention once more to the idea that once the signified becomes a signifier, it evolves, acquiring new implications and sometimes, as I show in chapter 9, ironically reversing or deconstructing the meaning of the archetype itself and hence calling into question any relevance it may seem to retain to the life lived in the present. These matters will continue to be of interest throughout this study. There is, however, the more pervasive intertextuality of language and its ancient shaping powers, constituting a network of implications that already exists at the moment of any individual's entry into it, that captures the individual and makes each one, as Lacan puts it, a "slave of language," of a discourse "in the universal movement in which his place is already inscribed at birth" (*Écrits* 148).

Although language enslaves us, however, it also provides the means for our manumission. The network determines that any signifier bear a relationship not to a particular signified but rather to a history (and prehistory) of representations that stretches so far into the past that no eye can see its origin and no mind can imagine it. This fact does not, however, preclude a remarkable amount of etymological investigation on the part of modern critics. For Lacan, each signifier is not merely a sign in a horizontal, linear utterance or text. Rather, each signifier forms part of a discourse that has depth as well, one that is "aligned along several staves of a score": "There is in effect no signifying chain that does not have, as if attached to the punctuation of each of its units, a whole articulation of relevant contexts suspended 'vertically,' as it were, from that point" (*Écrits* 154).

Each word, like the narrative it helps to constitute, is thus an invitation to interpret, to construct meaning, a kind of sirens' song that, as Blanchot describes it, is a "song of the deep which, once heard, reveal[s] the depths contained in every word, the depths into which the listener [is] inevitably drawn" (58). The chain of relevant contexts suspended vertically from each unit is, aside from ordinary, personal contexts, a depth of associations culturally transmitted as myth and archetype, as is apparent in Lacan's analysis of the word *tree:* "Even broken down into the double spectre of its vowels and consonants, it can still call up with the robur and the plane tree the significations it takes on, in the context of our flora, of strength and majesty. Drawing on all the symbolic contexts suggested in the Hebrew of the Bible, it erects on a barren hill the shadow of the cross. . . . Circulatory tree, tree of life of the cerebellum, tree of Saturn, tree of Diana, crystals formed in a tree struck by lightning . . ." (*Écrits* 154).

Lacan's tree is a meaning-laden signifier in which inhere ages of meanings and mysteries, as he says, "from an unnameable night" and endless chains of association. Nevertheless, Lacan says that "this whole signifier can only operate . . . if it is present in the subject" and that "what this structure of the signifying chain discloses is the possibility I have . . . to use it in order to signify something quite other than what it says," that is, to use language figuratively in the "search for the true" (*Écrits* 155), to evade the service of language that speaks the speaker and instead speak it for one's own ends – conscious or not.[19] Narrative (plot or novel), Blanchot says, is born in Odysseus's resistance to the Sirens' song, yet the Sirens "did not let [him] get away with it": "They lured him to a place he wanted to avoid and there, hidden between the pages of *The Odyssey* which had become their grave, they forced him – and many another too – to undertake the successful, unsuccessful journey which is that of narration – that song no longer directly perceived but repeated and thus apparently harmless: an ode made episode" (60–61). Blanchot builds an account of a monomyth on Odysseus's encounter with the Sirens, their song, language per se, every word of which contains the depths, abysses of meaning concealed beneath its light-hearted surface: "The narration heroically and ambitiously tells the story of a single event": "[Odysseus's] encounter with the unsatisfactory and luring song of the Sirens" (62). The song of language requires the endless journey of interpretation, mythicity (the intent to interpret), and narration of the story that will never be completely told (mythmaking).

BASEBALL AND THE SACRED

Baseball's special affinity with mythmaking encourages not only the production of mythic texts – a mythology – but also the representation of the sacred, that *given* of traditional mythologies, as is suggested in Hatab's generalization about myth: "A myth is a narrative which discloses a sacred world" (19). To address the problem of the sacred in connection with the modern game and its literature, and to understand its role, requires first of all analysis (and perhaps redefinition) of the term *sacred.* Second, I will explore the linguistic nature of the sacred and will need to go back to a point made earlier about the analogous, metaphor-made relationships among myth, the unconscious, and baseball, recalling in particular the epigraph by Jerry Klinkowitz, with his claim that baseball has a special affinity for *language as a system*" (emphasis added), a "distinguishing point in base-ball's fundamentally *writable* nature." In this respect I have shown that myth, the unconscious, and baseball are all said to be structured like lan-guage, as system – Saussure's *langue* – which supplies the metaphor, the heuristic model for exploring and discovering/creating their intricacies. In connection with this second task, of special interest are those areas where myth, the unconscious, and baseball overlap and converge in their linguis-ticality: metaphor in general and, in particular, the metaphor of the gap, the archetype (signified-become-signifier), the Freudian key narrative, the Freudian-Lacanian symbols, and touching on them all, Lévi-Strauss's notion of bricolage.

THE SACRED

Whatever our declarations to the contrary, the shades of the sacred have not been dispersed by science or displaced by facts. Harold Bloom says of Americans in particular that "we are a religiously mad culture, furiously searching for the spirit, but each of us is subject and object of the one quest, which must be for the original self, a spark or breath in us that we are con-vinced goes back to before the Creation" (*American Religion* 22). This ubiquitous modern quest need not surprise us, for it has been argued that the Enlightenment, with its guiding scientific light, resulted in a historical discontinuity that not only marked the boundary of the modern era but ac-tually produced a mutant species of the sacred, its forms subsumable under the term "uncanny" – Freud's *unheimlich*. Mladon Dolar argues that in premodern societies "the dimension of the uncanny was largely covered (and veiled) by the area of the sacred and untouchable" (7) but that the modern era introduced a free-floating, homeless species of the sacred: "The uncanny in the strict sense," that is, *das Unheimliche,* the alien, the frightening, the monstrous. The motto of post-Enlightenment humanity is captured in the statement of the contradiction between conscious denial and unconscious credulity: "I know very well, but all the same . . . I believe" (Dolar 22). The sacred that survived the Enlightenment has assumed a proliferation of forms, not many of them comforting. Maurice Blanchot's comment on the sacred reveals the modern consciousness confronting a modern form of the sacred, the numinous of absence: the sacred is a "something . . . approaching, standing not nowhere and everywhere, but a few feet away invisible . . . an ever more monstrous absence that [takes] an infinite time to meet" (cited in Taylor 1). Blanchot's allusion here is instructive. This sacred has a history, a form against which to be measured and judged. It is not, as was the divine of the premodern periods, a presence everywhere and nowhere (specifically, as Hermes Trismegistus described God, "a circle whose center is everywhere and whose circumference is nowhere") but a "something" – the ultimate equivocation – specifically unlike God, not nowhere and everywhere, but approaching, standing a few feet away invisible (with a play on the etymology of *absence* – "to be away"). Recall Lacan's attempt to describe "the real," a "field" to which the gods belong: it is not "*perhaps nothing,* but *not nothing*" (*FFC* 45, 64). Lacan's ever-elusive "not nothing" and Blanchot's terrifying, invisible "something" are both forms of the modern sacred. Evident in each instance is the presence of old myths and ancient meanings – Blanchot's everywhere-nowhere echo and Lacan's invocation of gods; that is, the modern sacred may be monstrous, elusive, and undefinable, but it carries historical baggage, old signifiers speaking equivocations in the modern text.

The Linguistic Nature of the Sacred.   A crucial point in Eric Gould's analysis is that the sacred, as it appears in both ancient and modern myth, arises at the call of language and *as* language, obedient to the linguistic principle of meaning that insists that *something* (a name for the absent, invisible, unknown signified), the *not nothing,* oppose the recognition of lack, absence, gap, or nothing.[20] The ruined tower eloquently attests the persistent attempt and foredoomed failure to fill the gap between the apparently absurd conditions of human life and the purposeful, permanent, and significant. In the gap between meaning and event, birth and death, in the face of cataclysm in nature or culture, in the face of nonbeing, language seeks through all its resources, both conscious and unconscious, to create coherence and intelligibility. When necessary those linguistic resources bring forth gods, the fates, providence, telos, spirit, manna, or ghastly, uncanny comfortless beings, powers, and *things* and provide them with the form and closure of plot. "In myth," Gould comments, "we enter the therapeutic of sheer inventiveness" (189). Language conspires with fear and desire, and the sacred is born in the insistence (or pretense) that beyond the realm of signs, beyond the sphere of signifiers and signifieds, beyond the reflecting, echoing, refracting pale of language, there is more than mere darkness and silence – a not nothing. It is, however, ironically and necessarily only within the pale of language (amid the rubble of the tower) and by its means that we find our probes into the darkness. As Gould says, "language makes the sacred possible" (172–73).[21]

Starting from the proposition that the sacred is born in the nature of language itself, from its desire to maintain the illusion of ground, coherence, and intelligibility through the figurative managing of incoherence, incongruity, and equivocation, we find that certain of language's resources are especially productive of the sacred. As I already mentioned, these resources include metaphor (especially the metaphor of the gap), the archetype, the key narrative, the symbols, and bricolage. I discuss each of these briefly here, because I will return to them in detail as this study progresses.

Metaphor and the Sacred. Eric Gould argues that myth and the sacred operate as metaphor, the trope in which there is both "substitution and statement": "Meaning is only possible because the two functions of language exist simultaneously in the act of predication. . . . Through the predicative assimilation, we are drawn in by metaphor's distinct attempt to *imply* an absent element, another signifier, a metonymical relationship where there is no hope of one" (51). This striving of metaphor to become metonymy involves the attempt to leave the vertical, diachronic plane of language (Lacan's endless chains of association or Blanchot's "depths" of meaning) and achieve the horizontal, synchronous plane, the "natural" condition of metonymy "defined simply by proximity in time and space" (52).[22] The mythic plot – its metaphorical knot pushed into predication and narration – similarly strives for some sort of identity between language and world, for ultrasignification; according to Gould, "A fiction never ceases trying to be real, even while it must always be largely metaphorical." Given this intention of myth, the job of myth criticism lies in "the attempt to follow the phenomenon of the writing of myth and fiction as each tries to suppress the void of consciousness, the failure to understand fully, which always lies behind the fictional proposal and its closed plot" (180).

The metaphor of the gap, which serves as the figural core of the myth of the gap and hence of our understanding of language, myth and myth-making (with its disclosure of the sacred), the relationship between the unconscious and consciousness, and the work of literary criticism, is obviously a spatial metaphor. This gap is an open space, a stage or arena for the meeting of all the contradictions, incongruities, equivocations, and dissimulations of language-made realities. I have said, too, that it is the site of the ruined tower (that sacred relic with its linguistic rubble – old myths and texts) and that baseball is peculiarly suited to mythic enterprises in that it presents in its scene a *real* gap and a *real* confrontation, that it forces on the spectator's attention an image, a huge visual representation, of the psycholinguistic gap where myth occurs, the border space where dark can commune with light. Of this same ilk is another architectural metaphor, the temple, to which baseball's space corresponds and which helps us to understand the gap and its relationship to the sacred.

The metaphor of the temple is a focus of Mark C. Taylor, a contemporary theophilosopher who, like Gould, takes an interdisciplinary approach to his subject, the intersection of literature, philosophy, art, architecture, and theology (all with a focus on the sacred), and who, also like Gould, places his exploration in the mainstream of structural and poststructural theory.[23] One of Taylor's pertinent claims is that although the sacred is subject to experience, it is *not* subject to cognition, and that art provides a stage for that experience (112), a space like a temple. The word *temple,* Taylor explains, derives from the Latin *templum,* which is in turn derived from the Greek *temnos,* meaning "that which is cut off," and "by extension *templum* is a 'space in the sky or on the earth marked out by the augur for the purpose of taking auspices; a consecrated piece of ground . . . a place dedicated to a particular deity, a shrine'" (112). The temple, what is "cut off," functions to open and maintain a space between dark and light, earth and sky, for the experiencing of the sacred; in the process of holding open this space, it also serves as a meeting place, a site of both "revealing and reveiling" (113). In this respect the temple is like the work of art that, as Heidegger says, "breaks open an open place," a tear. Both temple and open place of art are sites for the approach of the sacred, "the trace of the fugitive gods," a "mysterious proximity," the "non-absent absence of the Holy";

moreover, and similar to Gould's myth and its metaphoric openness, it is a place for evading through art, artifact, and language the seductions and the horrors of nihilism. Taylor presents and enacts the linguistic struggle to embody the sacred:

> The trace of the fugitive gods is the nonabsent absence of the Holy. This trace is a different trace, the trace of difference itself, which can never be expressed directly, revealed totally, or known completely. It is ever elusive, evasive, excessive. Irreducibly ex-orbitant, the Holy eternally returns to interrupt the circulation of knowledge and to disrupt every form of reciprocal exchange. To hear the "inhuman," "anonymous," "uncanny" murmur of the Holy is to become open to that which cannot be conceived, grasped, mastered, or controlled. To be "released" or "drawn" into the un-dis-closable openness of this rending difference is to overcome nihilism by no longer "giving a negative reading to that which is." (119; embedded quotations are from Heidegger)

All this is not easy, of course; the sacred pushes language to the limits of its resources. In fact, in *Blessed Rage for Order* David Tracy uses the term *limit language* to describe religious metaphors – linguistic lights shown into the darkness of that "which cannot be conceived, grasped, mastered, or controlled." "Limit situations," which trigger resort to limit language, include two sorts: boundary situations ("of guilt, anxiety, sickness, and the recognition of death as one's own destiny" – Heigegger's anxiety as "a fear of the No-thing") and ecstatic experiences ("intense joy, love, reassurance, creation" – "self-transcending moments"). Tracy explains: "All genuine limit situations refer to those experiences, both positive and negative, wherein we both experience our own human limits (limit-to) as our own as well as recognize, however haltingly, some disclosure of a limit-of our experience" (105). Both sorts of limit situations encourage the approach of or invoke the sacred, and it is here that Tracy, like Gould, finds metaphorical and symbolic language called on to describe the indescribable: "However helpful a later metaphysical language may be, all authentic limit-language seems to be initially and irretrievably a symbolic and a metaphorical one. Insofar as the hidden dimension of an ultimate limit is not merely hidden but not even expressible in the language of the everyday (as no-*thing*, no object in the world alongside other objects), that language retains the linguistic structure of metaphor and symbol" (108).

One is tempted to say that these limits, beyond which is darkness or the blinding light and where the sacred abides, open onto echo chambers that, of necessity, return our own metaphors, our language-made realities, back to us so that we may know them. What is clear, however, is that the fissure, cutoff, gap of temple and art, and the sacred realms beyond the boundaries of everyday experience are familiar holes, akin to the Lacanian gap at the border of the unconscious, near synonyms for the structuralist's gap between *langue* and *parole,* all insisting on the primacy of language and the linguisticality of being and Being. Consequently, when Taylor describes the encounter with the sacred, he might well be discussing the Lacanian other: "In the dark light of this nocturnal intensity [when waking mind opens into unconsciousness], the death of the metaphysical subject announces the monstrous birth of an other – a (w)hol(l)y Other that approaches as 'the origin of that which has no origin'" (120).

The language used for the sacred is paradoxical – Lacan's "not nothing," Blanchot's "nonabsent absence," and Taylor's "dark light"; hence, as Gould says, it involves an excess of language, like that Rudolph Otto refers to as the "clear overplus, excess or surplus" that resides in the word *holy* [*das Heilige*]. Otto thus names it, "the monstrous," "the uncanny," and "the numinous" (cited in Taylor 106–7). Taylor underscores this paradoxical nature when he observes that the holy or sacred is "both attractive and repulsive" (107). This is what sifts into the openness of temple, art, or gap. If we could depict this cut-off-ness, it might look like a baseball stadium, that pleasure dome, artifact, and gap where the language-made "(w)hol(l)y Other" comes to play and finds its way inevitably into the texts of the game. Play in the artifact-stadium is a form of the strife Heidegger poses as the condition in which truth "establishes itself in the work [of art]" – the "conflict between lighting and concealing" (62). Only such a thesis of the "dark light" of baseball's space and the centrality of the metaphor of gap, together with the strife-play of its action, can account for baseball texts' remarkable hospitality to the sacred, this *something,* this attractive and repulsive, terrifying and comforting, homey and homeless not nothing. (The specific features of baseball's dimensions and their attraction for the sacred are the subject of chapter 5.)

Archetype, Key Narrative, Symbol.   The sacred rides in on whatever vehicles it can commandeer – a structure, a plot, a figure, an intertextual allusion or echo, an image, or a mere word – bringing the sense of something approaching the space of the gap. Because the terms *archetype, key narrative,* and *symbol* are not always clearly defined, however, because they describe overlapping phenomena, and because they are all implicated in the expression of the sacred in myth, in this section I specify the senses in which I use these terms and describe both the relationships among them and their links to the sacred.

The term *archetype* has been used in psychology (especially that of Carl Jung and his followers, although it is implicit as well in Freud's mythic theorizing), in the comparative mythography of Joseph Campbell and others, and in traditional myth criticism (after Northrop Frye). In general, although there are slight and not-so-slight differences in meaning from field to field, *archetype* has been used to mean a universal psychological given or, to use a term to which Joseph Campbell is partial, an "elementary idea" preceding language and the shapings of culture – a plot (monomyth), figure (anima, shadow, terrible mother), or image (garden, mandala) – that singly and collectively with other archetypes determines the shape of human imagining and reveals the psychological "truths" of humanity.[24] From this perspective archetypes are said to be universal and changeless and to reveal themselves in myth, dream, art, architecture, and literature, bearing with them constant, readable meanings of enduring and crucial import in human life and its progress. From the theory of archetypes emerged, for example, the notion of "the hero with a thousand faces," the mythic Everyman whose tale is representative of all life stories, or the notion of constancy and universality of emplotments, with the quest structure of romance (based on the metaphor of life as a journey)[25] prior to all others.

Eric Gould's important and paradigm-changing shift in perspective in the field of myth criticism, made possible by an insight of Lévi-Strauss, arises from his reordering of the relationship between archetype and language. Archetype does not precede expression; rather, language precedes archetype. The archetype is not a "transformational process beyond language" (Gould 23). Archetypes are made in language and as language, a part of the speech each of us is born into (that captures us, as Lacan puts it), and for these reasons, they help to determine or create the reality of ourselves and our world. According to Gould, "We are not possessed by archetypes, but our fate is *transacted* in them." He elaborates: "My subjective interest in language, then, is never simply intentional as if what I want to do with language is sufficient to control it, for language has (as even thoroughly subjectivist critics admit) a certain dominance over me, a life of its own determined by its role as the *history* of my inherited metaphors" (68). Gould's point is that archetypes, although not part of our innate psychological apparatus, are nevertheless powerful "inherited" tools of language, speaking to fundamental human preoccupations, fears, desires, and all sorts of unconscious motives. Archetypes provide the approach to metonymy desired by myth's metaphors; they are "the rhetorical degree zero of metaphor" (69). They embody in language, Lacan's Name of the Father, the culture's sanctions of the fugitive language of the unconscious while at the same time providing solutions, compromises, and means of expression, the "natural" condition of metonymy. Archetypes are therefore border phenomena for the attempted rapprochement of "inside" and "outside," unconscious and conscious, nature and culture. Consequently, "there is no reason to discard the term 'archetype' as inappropriate. On the contrary, it requires a fresh definition. Signs can now retain archetypal significance for us, in both ancient and modern texts, because they re-enact continually, through the play between metonymy and metaphor, the alternative closing and widening in discourse of the gap between the inside and the outside. They thereby inspire our ratiocination, creative fantasy, and above all, our process of interpreting the world as a sign system" (68–69).

There are at least two ways in which the archetypes of ancient and modern texts invite the sacred. First, the unself-conscious metaphysical character of ancient texts and the apparently *literal* presence in them of the sacred or uncanny accompany the archetype and set up expectations or eerie, perhaps ironic suggestions of the sacred when the ancient archetype is invoked in modern texts, whether by re-presentation, image, echo, or allusion. Second, the inherited structure of the archetype as the site of meeting of inside and outside (as in Gould's analysis) provides a linguistic form for calling forth and expressing unconscious material, which of necessity takes its shape and its imagistic character from the mold provided by the archetype. Wordless, imageless, and hence parasitic, human fear and desire thus find hosts in these ancient verbal artifacts, these old signifieds-become-signifiers. Abstract, nameless fear may well become known only through an archetypal image (a signifier) – for example, as shades swarming from a pit filled with blood.

The previously discussed Freudian notion of *key narrative* is clearly a subspecies of archetype in Gould's redefinition. For Freud, *the* key narrative was the Oedipus story (I suggest in the course of this study that other tales and patterns likewise deserve the designation of key narrative), but the criteria he established for recognizing the Oedipus story as the key to understanding the human unconscious are useful in making the connections among the unconscious and mythicity and the sacred, as well as for understanding why some themes, figures, images, or plots are recognized as archetypal.

As I mentioned previously, for Freud the Oedipus myth is the key narrative because of its power to "elicit affect [fear and desire], its symbolic efficacy"; because it compels us to recognize "something in ourselves," a recognition in which much is at stake; and because its power to move is "profound and universal" (cited in Felman 1023). Gould's redefinition of archetype (in which the unconscious is seen as a product of language) will affect this Freudian notion of universality (which requires that the unconscious precede language, rather than the reverse). Nevertheless, from Freud's criteria it is apparent that a narrative is key when it specifically speaks to the unconscious by means of symbolic efficacy – a language spoken in the primary Freudian-Lacanian symbols relating to the body, kinship relations, birth, life, and death (the ultimate limit situation) – when it compels us to look inward, to recognize something in ourselves, something hitherto unconscious and therefore unseen, however deeply significant, something at the limit of being or beyond. We can add to these two aspects not the universality of which Freud speaks but a mythic character about the story, the Lévi-Straussian attempt to reconcile opposites, and mythicity as Gould defines it, insisting on the need for interpretation to narrow the gap between word and thing, inside and outside, metaphor and metonymy.

Lévi-Strauss's bricolage, recall, is a term for myth, understood as the product of the intellectual *bricoleur,* the worker who builds structures with whatever is at hand, building "new mythological worlds" from the shattered remains of the old, as well as other oddments lying about. And so archetypes, those old patterns, images, and figures (understood now as signifiers), are themselves bricolage, and the mythmaker, ancient or modern, has access to such verbal debris for use in constructing the new thing, the "new mythological world" at which he or she labors. Of special interest to me in the term *bricolage* is its applicability to recent art (literary, visual, and plastic) and current criticism. The postmodern work is itself frequently described as a pastiche, a hodgepodge of fragments, parts, themes, images, and so forth gathered from other works and assembled – usually with radically ambiguous effect – into the new poem, play, novel, sculpture, or painting. The product of the *bricoleur* need not be ironic or satiric (although it may be so), but it is always revisionary (in the senses both of remaking and reimagining) and unavoidably equivocal. The link between bricolage and the sacred lies in the fact that the parts of the bricolage are, by definition, mythological in their origins and so tend to bring their ghosts with them into the new work. The product of the *bricoleur* almost of necessity contains in its makeup the sacrality of outmoded, superseded, but still significant texts. An instance of what I have in mind can be seen in a Lacanian passage cited earlier in this chapter, in which Lacan cautions the psychoanalyst about the complexities of language and the difficulties of interpretation. I repeat it here for convenience: "Let [the analyst] be well acquainted with the whorl into which his period draws him in the continued enterprise of Babel, and let him be aware of his function in the discord of languages. As for the darkness of the mundus around which the immense tower is coiled, let him leave to the mystic vision the task of seeing in it the putrescent serpent of life raised on an everlasting rod" (*Écrits* 106).

This is a difficult text, to say the least: it consists of bricolage, the rubble of old myths. Metaphoric, mythic, and archetypal, it is at once a description of the analyst's task, an illustration of the interpretative skills required by the analyst, a demonstration of the sorts of material psychological "texts" present, and a revelation of the work of the *bricoleur,* the psychoanalyst as mythmaker. Paragraphs could be written, for example, simply on the use of the word *period,* its ambiguity and history. More obvious is the use of the old tale of Babel as archetype, now a signifier of the analyst's work. Coming into this text with the tale is the ancient sacrality of the mythic enterprise of building a tower to heaven; the sacred implications in the word *babel* ("gate of God"); the ancient and enduring effects of the divine presence, speaking, and confusion of languages; and the necessary, continuing attempt to achieve coherence, connection, and understanding – all through metaphor.

But the matter does not stop there. Other figures and images are drawn into the text, for example, Moses: the biblical patriarch or father (but also son in Freud's *Moses and Monotheism*) who lived long after the tower was reduced to rubble; an archetypal poet-prophet, ironically a man with a speech impediment (a victim of Babel) ordered by God to be his spokesperson; a man said to have received the law (the Torah) from God and recorded its unimpeachable language in the first five books of the Bible; a magician who inexplicably raised a bronze serpent on a magic rod to ward off a plague of serpents that had attacked his people in the wilderness; and a man ordered to lead the Israelites into the promised land but himself denied access to it. All these Mosaic complexities enter in, certainly, but there is more. Lacan's serpent is not bronze but a paradoxical *putrescent* (rotten and therefore dead, foul-smelling, physically or morally corrupt) serpent *of life.* And the serpent will not hold still even yet, for it becomes identified with the tower coiled around the darkness of the world. The ironic admonition to leave it to the mystic to see the serpent is a bit like telling someone to sit in a corner and not think about an elephant – an impossible and therefore a heroic task. Moreover, of course, the serpent and raised rod are phallic. The net effect is to connect through such images and their metaphoric equivalence what are clearly manifestations of the Lacanian symbols: the father and son (Moses), phallus (serpent, rod, coiled tower), language (tower), confusion of language (coiled tower, whorl, darkness), death (putrescence), and life (serpent).

This brief discussion does not exhaust the meanings implicit in the Lacanian text, but it is sufficient to demonstrate the process and effects of bricolage, mythmaking, its metaphoric center, its connections with the important terms *archetype, key narrative,* and *symbol,* and its hospitality to the sacred.

THE MYTH OF THE GAP: SOME SUMMARY REMARKS

The *Bedford Book of Hours,* a fifteenth-century illuminated manuscript, contains a miniature of the building of the Tower of Babel, the mythic enterprise that Lacan saw as metaphoric of the analyst's task and that I have called into my text as a metaphor for mythmaking in general and, in particular, as an image of the myth of the gap. In the miniature the tower rises in the space between ground and sky. Around its base workers fashion blocks (bricks), while another mixes mortar (slime), the materials for their linguistic structure leading to heaven. Coiled around the tower is a serpentine stairway on which people stand or climb. People appear to converse and labor, for the most part oblivious to (unconscious of) the fact that the confusion is already starting; as signs of confusion, shards fall from the precarious scaffolding at the tower's top, and one of the workers plunges head-first toward the ground. Only at the very top, at the point of closing the gap or achieving ultrasignification, are the workers aware of the tower's disintegration and of their own impending doom. Meanwhile, hovering on extended wings at the upper limit of the miniature, nearly out of the picture, are two uncanny beings in a night sky, the Lord and a companion. The tower itself appears to extend not only from earth to heaven, from mundane to sacred, but from day (consciousness) at its base to night (unconsciousness) at the top, the "dark light" where the uncanny abides. The miniature is a visual metaphor of the mythic enterprise of Babel and of the hard and continuing labor of the gap, which is itself based on a myth constructed by a master *brico-*

leur, whose tale, in turn, attempted to account for a massive ruined temple on the plains of Shinar.

Like the tower itself, the tale of the tower, and the miniature offering a visual depiction of it, the game of baseball is of the nature of bricolage – shards, rubble of old mythic worlds. Baseball's narratives, which grow out of the bricolage of the game, its archetypal scene (itself a gap, a place like a temple), its rules, and its peculiar progress, use that mythic stuff, those old signifiers, as building blocks in the ongoing, essential mythic enterprise, the intent to interpret, to bridge the gap. As Klinkowitz puts it, baseball has a writable nature. The game offers a space and a structure – a language, a system of signs – where the unconscious can make itself heard, a place friendly to interpretation and, at its boundaries, its outer limits, hospitable, even today, to the sacred in whatever forms it appears.

In the following chapters I use this theoretical ground to consider various aspects of baseball's myths, exploring the implications of theory for an understanding of the works singly and as a group – a mythology. I turn first to a Lacanian examination of August Wilson's extraordinary and moving play *Fences,* a work whose mythicity is apparent, a structure in which archetypes, the metaphors and bricolage of old narratives, combine with (or manifest themselves as) a system of signs from baseball, a system in which the destiny of the protagonist, Troy Maxson, is transacted and through which he attempts to find meaning.

2

AUGUST WILSON'S *FENCES* AND THE ART OF BRICOLAGE

Wilson's play *Fences* contains no ballpark, no game, no public heroics with bat or glove. Nonetheless, its system of reference is baseball, and its tropes are uprooted from the game and transported to the field of personal history, whose progress is reified in terms of the game. At the same time the game's ultimate reliance on archetypal plots provides thematic links between the play's protagonist and both Oedipus and Odysseus. In fact, in his kinship relations Troy Maxson is a man who plays by turns Oedipus, Laius, and Polybus and in the end may even achieve something of the triumph and dignity of Oedipus at Colonus.

Although he is caught in one ancient plot, however, and compelled to enact its roles, he attempts to make sense of his life in terms of another. Like Odysseus, he is a man who has made his life's odyssey, gone on an indescribably long journey and faced many bitter trials, seeking only to return home. At the center of both his stories is baseball – his own Trojan War (in which he, Troy, has fought on the losing side) – whose images, symbols, action, and scene provide the opening, the temple wherein he attempts to take auspices, to perform the linguistic magic of bridging, knowing, and being. There are gaps in Troy's personal narrative of the self – ellipses occupied by a falsehood, as Lacan puts it – for like Odysseus, Troy is a liar, a man whose lies, given proper attention, reveal truths of which he is himself unconscious. The opening words of the play are Bono's admonition "Troy, you ought to stop that lying!"

There is a single set for the play, at once baseball field and ironic Eden, a scene constructed by a master *bricoleur*; it is the partially fenced (and at last fully fenced) yard in front of Troy's house. Dominating the scene is a tree from which is suspended a baseball made of rags and against which a baseball bat leans. The scene and its emblems are archetypal (as that term has been redefined), carrying mythic significations and ironic equivocations into the modern scene. To understand the meanings of this scene and its emblems, and thus to read their message, it is necessary to recount the events of Troy's past as they emerge in the progress of the play.

Troy is the son of a sharecropper whom Troy describes as "just as evil as he could be" (148) and "the devil himself" (148). His mother left both husband and children when Troy was eight, telling Troy that she would return for him; she never does. At fourteen Troy engages his father in an Oedipal battle whose figurative stakes are possession of the absent mother, present now in the thirteen-year-old girl with whom Troy is "enjoying himself" (148) when interrupted by his father, who beats him with reins (an emblem of control and power), drives him off, and claims the girl for himself. Troy in turn picks up those same reins and begins to beat his father. As a result the two join in a combat in which Troy is beaten unconscious and rendered temporarily blind (the symbolic castration of Oedipus) by his father. In this first confrontation "Oedipus," the son, is bested by "Laius," the father.

At this point Troy is launched into a world that "suddenly got big" (149), exiled from home to begin the quest for home again. He will begin to reduce the immense world to manageable size only when he reaches a dim understanding that he and his father are one: "Part of that cutting down was when I got to the place where I could feel him kicking in my blood and knew that the only thing that separated us was the matter of a few years" (149).

Freudian-Lacanian kinship symbols here reflect an unconscious in which pathological father-son and mother-son relationships dominate. The emergence in Troy's psychic world – in his blood – of the father as object-self, or double, his "primordial being," is the harbinger of the death drive, as Lacanian critic Mladon Dolar explains:

> The double, retaining the object [the mirror image], also immediately introduces the death drive. The original function of the double (as the shadow and the mirror image) was "an insurance against the destruction of the ego, an 'energetic denial of the power of death' . . . and probably the 'immortal soul' was the first 'double' of the body." Yet what was designed as a defense against death, as a protection of narcissism . . . , turns into its harbinger: When the double appears, the time is up. One could say that the double inaugurates the dimension of the real [the field, according to Lacan, where the gods belong] precisely as the protection against "real" death. It introduces the death drive, that is, the drive in its fundamental sense, as a defense against biological death. (14)

The psychic double, originally the unrecognized image of the self, "keeps repeating itself . . . springing up at the most awkward times" (Dolar 14). For Troy Maxson, the father-double is a death-dealing, pleasure-spoiling incarnation of evil who stalks him inexorably. Troy meets him as Death, a figure in a white, hooded robe carrying a sickle (both weapon and phallus) that Troy seizes and casts away. (In the Greek tradition the first father-son conflict, that between Uranos and Kronos, was resolved when Kronos castrated his father with a sickle.) During a near-fatal illness Troy, Jacob-like, wrestles heroically with the figure for three days and nights and prevails. The father-double leaves with an unnecessary promise, "I'll be back" (114); the double always returns. Rose, Troy's wife, accuses Troy of fabricating the story of wrestling Death, a charge that, although perhaps accurate, does not mitigate the tale's psychological truth and figurative evasions. The double appears also as the spiritual form of the negative father – the devil – whose reality Rose likewise denies: "You ain't seen no devil. . . . Anything you can't understand, you want to call it the devil" (116). Troy's devil is identified with death through color symbolism: "devil standing there bigger than life. White fellow" (117). The concept of evil projected onto the father-double is refracted through the prism of Troy's unconscious into multiple, recurring images, all standing there bigger than life.

Troy's strategy for dealing with this personal haunt is to define his world and the inevitable confrontation in terms of baseball, a game that he learned in prison and that he has played in the Negro Leagues with extraordinary success, batting .450: "Death ain't nothing but a fastball on the outside corner. . . . You get one of them fastballs, about waist high, over the outside corner of the plate where you can get the meat of the bat on it . . . and good god! You can kiss it goodbye" (112–13). The nonabsent, uncanniest of pitchers throws death, the fastball, which Troy opposes through the only means he knows, the phallus-weapon-bat.

Looking again at the scene of Troy's drama, then, we may begin to read its significance and to understand its objects: the tree, the ball, the bat, the half-finished fence. The tree is ambiguously both tree of life and tree of the knowledge of good and evil (the tree of death, its fruit the suspended fastball) in a semi-enclosed and vulnerable Eden. It rises, like the Tree of Jesse as depicted in medieval representations, from the loins of the father. It is a family tree. The rag ball, the tree's ironic, poisonous fruit, hangs ever ripe for the plucking/hitting; the phallus-weapon-bat lies at hand. A peculiar pathos inheres in the scene, for baseball is the place both of Troy's triumph and of one of his bitterest defeats. All the might-have-beens are entangled in it and, in particular, in the fact that Troy has been excluded from major league play because of his race (he says) or because of his age (Rose says) (137–38). Like the baseball dwarf who suffers violence and exclusion, Troy is "physically wrong" for the game, and he too has suffered violence and exclusion, exiled from the game and its paradisiacal precincts as from his home; the pitiful parody of home-paradise-game, with its baseball-fruit and phallus-weapon-bat, provides a visual metaphor, a "sentence" in symbols, of Troy's resistance and quest, both of which are implicated in sexuality and death.

Troy's great period of sexual conquest coincided with his playing days, as his friend Bono recalls: "When you was hitting them baseball out the park. A lot of them old gals was after you then. You had the pick of the litter" (157). Now, however, in one of his true lies, Troy claims to go down to Taylors' (a local bar) to watch baseball games on television, but in fact he is having an affair with Alberta, a woman who works there, the embodiment of mystery, fecundity, and mother earth. This is a woman who, Bono says, just "showed up one day"; Troy says that she is from Florida, a land of "big healthy women" who grow "right up out of the ground," a primitive, autochthonous being with an ancient bloodline, "a little bit of Indian in her" (108). Bono cannot understand why Troy would jeopardize his long, loving marriage to Rose for an affair, and even Troy cannot really explain, but it is obvious that strong, unconscious currents move him. He says that it seems "like this woman just stuck onto me where I can't shake her loose"; in this respect she represents a reversal of the mother who would not stay. Troy says that he has "wrestled with it, tried to throw her off . . . but she just stuck on tighter" (158). Troy's clearly evasive explanation rings hollow. When we recall Lacan's understanding of the "mystery of love" as the search not for the sexual complement but for the lost part of the self, "constituted by the fact that [the subject] is only a sexed living being, and that he is no longer immortal" (*FFC* 105), Troy's actions are understandable and almost inevitable.

Troy himself, at some level, knows the truth: he describes his lovemaking with Rose as falling down on her and "try[ing] to blast a hole into forever" (138). When he finally confesses the affair and Alberta's pregnancy to Rose, he tries again to explain, this time abandoning the "stick-tight" story: "She gives me a different idea . . . a different understanding about myself. I can . . . be a different man. . . . I can just be a part of myself that I ain't never been." The lost part is joy, a capacity for "enjoying" interrupted all those years ago in the woods by his father and even earlier damaged, effaced, by the abandoning mother: "I can sit up in her house and laugh. Do you understand what I'm saying. I can laugh out loud . . . and it feels good. It reaches all the way down to the bottom of my shoes. . . . Rose, I can't give that up." Troy's laughter reaches not only to the bottom of his shoes but to the ground of his being, to a forgotten time, forgotten images and feelings: "I done locked myself into a pattern trying to take care of you all that I forgot about myself" (163–64). The self that returns with Alberta is still forgotten, unconscious, and therefore more compelling. Troy quite literally cannot give that up.

The partially fenced yard, the tree, the ball, and the bat represent the symbols of the unconscious and the enigmatic message Troy is compelled to heed. Troy comes to understand that his wife, his son (Cory), and his job (as a garbage collector) are a compromise that has stalled his quest and mitigated the integrity of the self. These eighteen years are like the seven years Odysseus spends on Ogygia with Kalypso – safe but stagnant, without progress toward his goal. As Troy sees it, a man is born "with two strikes on [him] when [he] comes to the plate." Knowing this, when the crucial pitch was thrown – the potential strike three – Troy has not swung from the toes but has "fooled them" and bunted: "When I found you and Cory and a halfway decent job . . . I was safe. Couldn't nothing touch me. I wasn't gonna strike out no more. . . . I was on first looking for one of them boys to knock me in. To get me home. . . . Then when I saw that gal [Alberta] . . . she firmed up my backbone. And I got to thinking that if I tried . . . I just might be able to steal second. Do you understand after eighteen years I wanted to steal second." Troy, like Odysseus, leaves the safety of Ogygia, of first base, to make progress toward home. Rose objects, "We ain't talking about no baseball," and Troy, quite correctly, accuses her of not listening, which means not hearing (164–65).

Whereas the absent mother, imaged both in Alberta (who grows from the ground) and in the yard itself, exerts her power across time, the brutal, unloving, sexually competitive father – "Laius" – is there in the tree, the ball, and the bat, and his influence is equally compelling. His power – his law – is manifest and reenacted in Troy's relationship with his son Cory. In this relationship Troy enters his "Laius" phase, where he and his father are one. Troy uses figurative reins to attempt to control Cory, to keep him from playing football and attending college on a football scholarship, to keep him working. Troy has said of his own father, "He ain't cared nothing about no kids. A kid to him wasn't nothing. All he wanted was for you to learn to walk so he could start you to working" (147). Like Troy, his father was trapped with his children and felt a responsibility, a fact that earns Troy's grudging respect (147). If Troy's father substituted responsibility for love, however, and power relations for family diplomacy, so does Troy. The "family tree," the father "kicking in the blood," is a fierce determinant of Troy's own behavior. It is intriguing that Wilson provides as an epigraph to the play some lines from one of his own poems: "When the sins of our fathers visit us / We do not have to play host," lines whose message appears as a conscious filter for the counter-messages enacted in the drama and symbolized in the scene. Troy in fact reenacts the sins of his father, and as a result Cory fears him and suffers an unending barrage of verbal and psychological abuse. Cory asks, "How come you ain't never liked me?" Troy replies, "Who the hell say I got to like you?" (135–36). Like the elder Maxson, Troy provides a home and food and a model of work not out of love but out of responsibility, which was his father's only virtue: "It's my job. It's my responsibility" (137).

The battle goes on until a moment when Troy and Cory reenact the scene in the woods, with Troy in the role of Laius and Cory as Oedipus.

The symbolic struggle focuses on the bat, which Cory takes up to ward off Troy's menace. Troy, like his father before him, is attempting to drive his son from home. He shouts, "That's my bat!" and "Put my bat down!" The phrase "my bat" echoes here, and Cory swings the bat at Troy as he advances. Troy makes the desperate nature of the agon clear: "You're gonna have to kill me!" (181). After a fierce struggle Troy wrestles the bat away from Cory and stands over him ready to swing. Like Laius and like his own father, he stops short of killing his son, but he finds in Cory another transformation of the double; the boy, he says, has the devil in him (180), the claim he has made about his father. After Cory has left and as the scene closes, Troy stands beneath the tree wielding the bat, facing an advancing menace – death, the devil, his father, his son, himself: "Come on! It's between you and me now! Come on! Anytime you want! Come on! I be ready for you . . . but I ain't gonna be easy" (182). This is our last view of Troy. The next scene takes place seven years later on the day of Troy's funeral. The fence he has promised first Rose and then Death to build is complete: "I'm gonna build me a fence around what belongs to me. And then I want you [Death] to stay on the other side" (171).

The scene of horror involving the confrontation of Troy and Cory is in some ways balanced by another, one equally stark but strangely comforting, occurring just before the fight with Cory. Here, large and awkward, Troy brings home to Rose the daughter whose birth caused Alberta's death: "She innocent," Troy tells Rose, "and she ain't got no mama" (172). In these respects the baby is like Troy all those years ago when abandoned by his own mother. For a while Troy sits with the baby on the porch, frightened and, as he says, homeless, before asking Rose to help him take care of her. In some respects the most admirable figure in this mythic universe, Rose says that she will mother the child, agreeing that she is innocent and that "a motherless child has got a hard time" (173). Significantly, however, Rose is transformed at that moment from wife to mother: "From right now . . . this child got a mother. But you a womanless man" (173). One wonders whether through this infant surrogate (double?) Troy has at last come home.

Like Oedipus Troy dies off-stage, and like Oedipus he leaves his family under a curse. Lyons, his older son, has followed Troy to prison; Cory, his younger son, seems condemned to repeat Troy's grief, error, and homelessness. He has returned on the day of Troy's funeral only to say that he will not attend. After seven years his bitter resentment is intact: "Papa was like a shadow that followed you everywhere. It weighed on you and sunk into your flesh. It would wrap around you and lay there until you couldn't tell which one was you anymore. That shadow digging in your flesh. Trying to crawl in. Trying to live through you. Everywhere I looked, Troy Maxson was staring back at me . . . hiding under the bed . . . in the closet. . . . I've got to find a way to get rid of that shadow, Mama" (188–89). Cory's double has appeared, and as is the nature of doubles, it will return and return, interrupt and disrupt. Rose sees the identity: "You Troy Maxson all over again," but she adds that Troy "meant to do more good than he meant to do harm" (189).

Troy's life and its progress are metaphorically determined. The Oedipal and Edenic archetypes, channeled through the emblems of baseball, its objects and progress, merged in Troy's symbol-laden space, and re-enacted in his life, predictably carry into the ironic tale of Troy Maxson eerie significations. The uncanny, unavoidable fate of Oedipus, the determined fall of Eden, the powers of the Moirai and of the creator-father-God of the Old Testament, combined with the pitcher death and his fastball, the ubiquitous devil, the ball and the bat, the bunt, the tragic attempt to "steal second," to get home, and the hellhounds that tear through Troy's brother's world, Gabriel's obsession with finding Troy's name in the book of life – all these constitute the mythic rubble of Troy's tale. These shards make up the new mythic world, but they are equivocal; they scrape against one another, speak against one another. Nevertheless, the tale uses them to make sense of Troy's life, to bridge the gaps in understanding. Taken together they bespeak the presence of the uncanny, the approach and the lingering near of something, the "not nothing" of an ironic and comfortless sacred.

As the time for Troy's funeral approaches, Gabriel's mad vision expands to encompass both players and their tale, becoming the play's reality. Troy's brother (with half his brain blown away in World War II) thinks he is the archangel Gabriel. He has talked to Saint Peter and has seen Troy's name in the book of life. Now, in a terrible moment, as he blows into his trumpet and no sound comes out, the stage directions call for him to perform a strange "dance of atavistic signature and ritual. . . . He begins to howl in what is an attempt at song, or perhaps a song turning back into itself in an attempt at speech. He finishes his dance and the gates of heaven stand open as wide as God's closet" (192). The reader/audience is at this last moment left disoriented. The mad delusions of Gabriel, his "lies," are in fact reality. The numinous, lurking always, menacing Troy, has, through Gabriel's madness, revealed itself as there and yet not there (Derrida's *fort:da*) all along. Heaven with its opening gates, verging on the symbolic yard and perhaps overlapping with it, and like the yard, a fenced place, is, it seems, accessible from Troy's ironic Eden. In the end we understand that from his parodic baseball paradise to God's insanely conjured closet, Troy's life, his unending quest, and his death transpire in the most homely and *unheimlich* of temples.

I have mentioned the Oedipus tale and *The Odyssey* in connection with Troy Maxson's career and have pointed to their presence as archetypal plots in baseball. In the next chapter I want to elaborate on these claims, examining the game and some of its narratives to explain how a game can evoke and, indeed, imitate ancient mythic structures and use these structures (archetypes, mythic signifiers) in the mythology of the game.

3 THERE ARE ONLY TWO STORIES. ONE IS, SOMEONE WENT ON A LONG
JOURNEY; THE OTHER IS, A STRANGER CAME TO TOWN.[1]

GENERATIONS OF MEN, THROUGHOUT RECORDED TIME, HAVE ALWAYS
TOLD AND RETOLD TWO STORIES – THAT OF A LOST SHIP WHICH SEARCHES
THE MEDITERRANEAN SEAS FOR A DEARLY LOVED ISLAND, AND THAT OF A
GOD WHO IS CRUCIFIED ON GOLGOTHA. Jorge Luis Borges (cited in
Frye, *The Secular Scripture* 15)

PATHS OF GLORY

BASEBALL, KEY NARRATIVES,

AND THE MONOMYTH

As I said in chapter 1, I have followed Eric Gould's lead
on the question of archetypes, or archetypal plots, in finding such plots,
with their metaphoric knots, to be linguistic signifiers that offer their forms
for the transactions of the gap and the communications between, as Gould
puts it, "inside and outside." Two forms of structuralism contribute to our
understanding of such forms. Thus far I have emphasized the work of the
French structuralists, but the notion of the literary archetype really emerges in another tradition of criticism, that of the American structuralists,
whose work illuminates another aspect of structure and is thus comple-

mentary to that of the French. American structuralism is the sort that Tzvetan Todorov recognizes as pioneered by Northrop Frye. Todorov finds that both French structuralists and Frye and his followers belong to the poetic tradition "as it has existed since Aristotle," that is, a tradition that seeks to be "scientific," or both "internal" and "systematic." Todorov finds it ironic that while French structuralists worked with knowledge of the Russian formalists, they had no awareness of Frye, whose earliest important writings preceded those of the French structuralists by some ten years. Nevertheless, Todorov shows that the two varieties of structuralism are complementary rather than contradictory, and he describes their different approaches as regards rhetorical figures, plot, and what may be called the isolating tendency of the French structuralists versus the comparative or encompassing view of Frye:

> In France, the study of metaphor and rhetorical figures was undertaken in order to describe a linguistic mechanism; when Frye studies them, his aim is to catalog the most persistent metaphors in the Western tradition. French poeticians have studied narrative in order to understand how a plot is formed or presented to the reader; Frye on the other hand records and classifies the favorite plots of two thousand years of European history. . . . We may say that Frye is more interested in substance, while the French "structuralists" are oriented toward form; he writes an encyclopedia, they produce a dictionary in which the definitions are cross-referenced, referring to each other rather than to an object that remains external to them (namely, literature); he is panchronic, in that he perceives . . . the simultaneous presence of all literature, whereas they are achronic, since in the last analysis they are studying the faculties of the human mind (the capacity to symbolize or to narrate). (92)

Returning to the tower metaphor, one might say that the French are more interested in the bricks and slime, the bricolage; Frye, in the configuration of the tower itself and its major architectural features, its stories and *stories*. Alternatively, we could use Frye's own metaphor and say that he is interested in the *body* of literature, hence his *Anatomy of Criticism*. What Todorov refers to as the favorite plots of two thousand years of European history (actually at least *three* thousand years) I call archetypal plots or, in Freud's terminology, key narratives, again stressing the fact that these are not mental givens but signifiers in which the unconscious has found and continues to find shape and expression but that, like other signifiers, are equivocal, subject to change and decay. These archetypal signifiers are a part of the language we inherit.

In this chapter, then, emphasis will shift from the work of the French structuralists to a Fryean approach, one likewise valuable to a study of the intersection of myth and literature. The epigraphs reveal Frye's influence, or a similar structural impulse, in their recognition of recurring plots in literature, grounded in myth. There are, it seems, only two stories. One is that of Oedipus, the tale that obsessed Freud, yet the story also of Jesus – that of a stranger-son who comes to town, with dire, if redemptive, results for himself and society; the other is the tale of Odysseus, representative of all wanderers and seekers who set out on a long journey and attempt the difficult passage home. The intriguing fact of baseball – its progress and scene – is that it is peculiarly crafted to reflect and imitate such plots and to provide a space for apparently endless transformations, visions, and revisions of them.

THE CLASSIC MONOMYTH

Of particular relevance to this chapter is the practice of Frye's form of structuralism in the field of comparative mythology (and returning by that route, in a spiraling course, to literature, what Joseph Campbell calls "creative mythology"). A central idea in Campbell's work (which was influenced by both Freud and Jung) is that of the monomyth ("one story"), a term borrowed from James Joyce. The term is a misnomer, however, because as I will show, there are two monomyths corresponding to the two archetypal plots or key narratives already examined and identified again in the epigraphs to this chapter. Whereas Freud focuses on one of them, the tragedy of Oedipus, Campbell, like Jung, focuses on the other, the quest pattern epitomized by *The Odyssey*. Unlike Gould, Campbell accepts the notion of the shaping force of the inherited image or archetype in the Jungian sense; that is, he puts mind before language. But his observations are nevertheless valuable for my purposes. He examines the structures of hero tales from diverse times and cultures and announces that there are not many heroes; there is only one hero with a thousand faces, and his is the one story (monomyth) "of the soul's high adventure," whose outlines Campbell sketched as follows: "A hero ventures forth from the world of common day into a region of supernatural wonder: fabulous forces are there encountered and a decisive victory is won: the hero comes back from this mysterious adventure with the power to bestow boons on his fellow man" (*Hero* 30).

The hero's journey is a structural analogue of human life, its challenges, threshold crossings, and inexorable movement from birth to maturity to death. The goal of the hero's journey is to return, like Odysseus, to find the place where he started and, as Eliot says, to "know the place for the first time" (*Four Quartets*, "Little Gidding" V). The structure of the monomyth, this archetypal signifier, is foundational and persistent, and it is the pattern as well of quest romance, a form that Frye calls "the structural core of all fiction": "being directly descended from folktale, it brings us closer than any other aspect of literature to the sense of fiction considered as a whole, as the epic of the creature, man's vision of his own life as a quest" (*Secular Scripture* 15).

Not surprisingly this structure appears in the oldest of Western hero tales, *The Epic of Gilgamesh,* whose protagonist, the king of Uruk in ancient Sumer, ventures forth on a journey that will eventually take him to "The Far Distant" and beyond in search of the secret of immortality. Having found and lost the plant of life, Gilgamesh returns to Uruk with new wisdom to accept both the limits and the rewards of human life. Odysseus, after nineteen years, comes home – older, sadder, wiser – for the reunion long sought, nearly always in doubt, and miraculously achieved. On returning, the romance hero brings boons – the secret of life, for example, or greater wisdom and knowledge to enrich his home and society, into which the returning traveler is reintegrated. Along the way, as the stories of Gilgamesh and Odysseus illustrate, the usually masculine hero will often confront and defeat death (thus providing a form for expression of the most basic of human fears and desires), suffering in the process an actual or symbolic death. At the same time, however, he may lose or reject immortality. Thus Gilgamesh descends into the bottomless abyss and surfaces with the plant of life, which he loses to the serpent (a transform of Lacan's "putrescent serpent of life"); Odysseus travels to the underworld and returns, "twice born," but he rejects Kalypso's offer of static, dependent, childlike immortality. The structure of both tales is a circle that returns the traveler home, or as Frye prefers, it is a spiral, "an open circle where the end is the beginning transformed and renewed by the heroic quest" (*Secular Scripture* 174). This circle or spiral is fundamental as well to baseball, which has incorporated into its rules the ancient archetypal plot, for within the action of the game the goal is to travel out and back, to come home. Christian K. Messenger has observed that "the psychological theme of 'coming home' . . . takes its primary structure from baseball's journey around the bases." The game has, he says, "provided the strongest of sports meditations on questing, exile, and return" (*Sport and the Spirit of Play* 322). This return brings the traveler home, figured in home plate. As Giamatti puts it, "Home plate has a peculiar significance. . . . Everyone wants to arrive at the same place, which is where they start" (87).

Home is a concept rife with feeling, separable from the vagaries and strifes of individual houses and cities with names. It is the place of departure but equally the place of arrival, of return; it is thus both beginning and end, ambiguously comforting and ominous, womb and tomb. Giamatti has offered a meditation on the positive connotations of the word *home*, an English word that, he says, is "impossible to translate into other tongues": "*Home* is a concept, not a place; it is a state of mind where self-definition starts; it is origins. . . . Home is when one first learned to separate and it remains in the mind as the place where reunion, if it ever were to occur, would happen" (91–92). Seen in this light, home is perhaps the primary destination of all quests, in and out of baseball, "the goal – rarely glimpsed, almost never attained – of all the heroes descended from Odysseus" (92).

BASEBALL AND THE CLASSIC MONOMYTH

The structure of baseball, the game, thus enacts the plot of the first story: someone went on a long journey, the quest in the classic monomyth. In baseball the batter-warrior-hero begins at home and may "die" there, never having begun the journey. If he is skilled and fortunate, he starts out, only to encounter a host of adversaries who attempt to block his progress. Enemies await him at first base and second, where he may die, perhaps with a brother-comrade-teammate as part of a "twin-killing." Third base may be a nearly impossible threshold crossing attempted (and as likely as not failed) even in sight of home, of Ithaca, whose watchfires beckon home Odysseus, the traveler, the hero, the batter. Finally, the traveler reaches home only to find usurpers in the great hall: "The catcher bars fulfillment, . . . the umpire-father is too strong in his denial" (Giamatti 93). As a result the batter is "out," a type of Agamemnon struck down after years of war and wandering only as he reaches home: "The impossibility of going home again is reenacted in what is often baseball's most violent physical confrontation, swift, savage, down in the dirt, nothing availing" (93). When successful, the traveler's quest brings him home with Phaeacian treasure for reunion with Penelope and Telemachus, his teammates and true family.

Home and going home are the stuff of myth and its work. Home itself is a gap, a space where notions of sanctuary and bondage, love and hate, vie for supremacy. Home is both haven and prison, place of reunion and life but also of isolation and death. One of the most basic of conflicts – the Oedipal conflict – is engendered and enacted at home. Messenger notices that "a clash in Oedipal terms" may be involved in the "psychological theme of 'coming home' which takes its primary structure from baseball's journey around the diamond" (*Sport and the Spirit of Play* 322), as does Giamatti ("the umpire-father is too strong in his denial"), and thus is raised a tragic specter to haunt the most innocent and universal of labors. If reunion is ever to occur, it will be at home, and yet it cannot take place: "the impossibility of going home again is reenacted" (Giamatti 93).

In *The Universal Baseball Association* Robert Coover humorously expresses the act of batting, circling the bases, and returning home in terms of the Freudian family romance, but he changes the metaphoric roles. Now Laius is the pitcher; Jocasta is the catcher "in a protected crouch, holding up her big padded womb"; Oedipus is the batter, "standing there in the box. Frustrating old Dad by poking his own stick out there in the way. Of course, the old man wasn't alone: the other seven were in their places, out there behind him, backing him up, protecting Mom's chastity and the way things were, putting down that rambunctious boy with the big rebellious bat." When Junior "explodes one off his piece of lumber" he can "upend the whole system," but "he's still got to make the full circuit," and "it's a long run around there, lot of ground to cover, and a lot can happen on the way, but he hopes, and the minute he leaves it that old home plate starts exerting a tremendous pull on him, and the good ones, on the good days, they do get around there, they do make it back" (34). In this Oedipal comic allegory home plate (with Mom waiting) exerts a tremendous pull; the good ones make it back. Thus both theorists and fiction writers find that Oedipal themes from the second story are implicit even in the first, to which the narrativity of baseball's action corresponds. The same conflict and quest are, as I have shown, likewise apparent in Troy Maxson's life; the scene portrayed humorously by Coover is in *Fences* enacted in dead earnest between Troy and Cory over possession of the phallic bat, home, and "Mom."

Whether or not pervaded by Oedipal elements, the first of the two stories, the archetypal plot of the classic monomyth, is baseball's plot, reenacted countless times with infinite variation. This action underlies the movement of much baseball literature, and Robert Coover's protagonist, J. Henry Waugh, meditates on it as he observes a New York scene:

Motion. The American scene. The rovin' gambler. Cowpoke and train-man. A travelin' man always longs for a home, cause a travelin' man is always alone. Out of the east into the north, push out to the west, then march through the south back home again: like a baserunner on the paths, alone in a hostile cosmos, the stars out there in their places, and him trying to dominate the world by stepping on it all. Probably suffered a sense of confinement there in the batter's box, felt the need to strike forth on a meaningful quest of some kind. Balls hurled down to him off the magic mound, regularly as the seasons: his limited chances. (141)

Why does the hero begin the quest? The Coover passage suggests that a sense of confinement pushes the traveler into motion – confinement at home, the place one must leave to find again. This is the internal motive, but external motives may operate also. Both Odysseus and Troy Maxson are forced from their homes (Odysseus by Agamemnon's draft and Troy by his father), later to become stalled in their quests, confined in safe but false homes, before they set forth again. Joseph Campbell likewise claims that a sense of confinement prompts the journey: "The familiar life horizon has been outgrown; the old concepts, ideals, and emotional patterns no longer fit; the time for the passing of a threshold is at hand." When it comes, the setting forth "rings up the curtain, always, on a mystery of transfiguration . . . which, when complete, amounts to a dying and a birth" (*Hero* 51). The archetypal plot, in this sense, provides a model for psychological growth.

Douglass Wallop presents this first story in his now classic novel *The Year the Yankees Lost the Pennant* (1954). Its quest involves Joe Boyd, a fifty-year-old real estate salesman and "grimly devoted" follower of the perpetually second-division Washington Senators. As the novel begins Joe's life is stalled; he is psychologically ready for a threshold crossing. One hot July night Joe is called from his home to embark on a perilous journey from which he likely will never return. His herald, guide, and antagonist is Mr. M. Applegate, a dark-clad representative of the uncanny who emerges from a manhole at a Washington intersection to offer Joe Boyd a contract to become "the finest baseball player in the world" (19), in order to redeem the Senators. All he must do is make an eternal commitment of his soul and a long journey, in time, not space, and leave his home and his wife, Bess, to become Joe Hardy, a twenty-one-year-old "phenom" who bats over .500 and fields his position impeccably – even miraculously.

After insisting on an escape clause, Joe Boyd agrees to become Joe Hardy, writes a note to his aging wife, and leaves his troubled home for he knows not how long – until September 21, when the escape clause may be exercised, or (as Applegate believes) forever. The "region of supernatural wonder" into which this twentieth-century hero ventures is coextensive with the world of baseball, a space of art where, at first with the help and at last with the hindrance of Mr. Applegate, Joe wins a decisive victory (through an inside-the-park home run), defeating Applegate's team of choice, the New York Yankees, to capture the pennant for the hapless Washington Senators.

Suitably displaced Oedipal themes recur in this novel, for in undergoing his metamorphosis Joe Boyd figuratively becomes his own son, returning home as Joe Hardy, a youthful boarder in his wife's home whose presence there causes talk in the neighborhood. An intriguing tension results from the situation wherein Joe Boyd knows that he is Bess's rightful husband, yet as young Joe Hardy, he is required to occupy the guest room. The age difference creates a poignant situation, one in which Joe Boyd must view his home and wife from the perspective of youth. Like Oedipus in the palace of Queen Jocasta, Joe Boyd is both son and husband, but unlike Oedipus, he is aware of the irony.

In the end Joe Boyd grows up, gains wisdom and a new appreciation for his life and his wife, and loses his obsessive passion for baseball. Having reassumed his middle-aged body and limping a little from the collision at the plate (repeating the walk of Oedipus, whose names means "swell foot"), Joe Boyd returns home, no longer son but husband.

Joe Boyd is one of baseball literature's classic protagonists, and his story is the one Campbell describes; he wears one of the thousand faces of the hero. In his quest romance good and evil collide in their largely unambiguous forms, and good prevails. The scene not surprisingly makes room for the sacred or uncanny, invites mystery and miracle. The time of the novel, fluid like dream time, spirals the hero down and back to youth and up and forward to middle age, returning him, utterly transfigured after having undergone death and rebirth, where (and almost when) he started. Joe leaves home in the night, literally and figuratively circles the bases, and returns at night: Joe "approached [his home] slowly, with an eerie feeling. Except that there was no sound of Old Man Everett watering his azaleas, this might be the same night in July [on which he began his journey]" (250). Like Odysseus, Joe Boyd has come home, and also like Odysseus, he has matured, in the process rejecting a brand of immortality and eternal youth for life – trial, toil, and eventual death.

The language and structures of traditional hero tales clearly manifest a masculine perspective and the intimations of a masculine unconscious, the hero most often performing the mythic work demanded by the office of sonship, especially in expressing the need to leave home to find it again. It follows that feminine protagonists caught in masculine structures of baseball and its texts will encounter some problems of adjustment. Christian K. Messenger has observed that "baseball novels by women have become a flourishing subgenre in recent sports fiction." Messenger notices some interesting differences between women's and men's baseball narratives, women's fiction "center[ing] on the mode of cooperation, of interaction and support among teammates," rather than emphasizing individual action and achievement. He continues: "Baseball appears to be the team sport most congenial to women athletes, with its lack of aggressive physical contact and premium on attributes other than size and strength. Competition and heroic striving are present in the fiction but are integrated with the team's other potentials: nurture, family, growth" ("Expansion Draft" 70). Messenger marks an important shift and a very late-evolving congeniality. As recently as 1969 Deena Metzger, in her poem "Little League Women," portrayed the women on the periphery of Little League baseball as cows, "Herding in dumb bulk, . . . eating grass and men." She later says of the poem that it was written at a time when "it was difficult to establish the self without dissociating oneself from other women and women's roles" and that since then she has come to see that the poem "is a lie" (in Chapin 63). Another way of putting the matter is to say that the poet wrote of women from the perspective of the masculine myths. If the game (or some version of it – usually softball) increasingly permits female participation, and sports fiction increasingly admits novels in the feminine subgenre, we might well ask whether Metzger's sort of dissociation is present in these texts. If a mythology capable of admitting female protagonists is emerging, does it acknowledge that the face of the hero may be feminine? Or does the feminine subgenre present an entirely distinct sort of figure and plot?

Part of the answer is advanced by Messenger, who is correct in finding in women's baseball narratives a shift of emphasis from individual to group. At times the shift is subtle, for the team, the group, "society," has always figured importantly throughout the plots of baseball's largely male myths. What does appear different in women's narratives is that the venue of the group emphasized has changed from the scene of field and team to what may be called the broader "domestic" scene of home, family, and neighbors. This shift of emphasis is figured in a shift in focus on the game played, broadly seen as a shift from offense to defense. The journey out and back figured in the running of the bases is baseball's offense and the most obvious highlighting of the individual, a matter central to the content and form of masculine texts. This offense is for feminine writers and feminine protagonists pushed toward the periphery of the action. The feminine text is likely to foreground defense, the teamwork of the field, not the batter and bat. The protagonist is often a pitcher or catcher, roles associated with a static aspect of the field – the center, imaged as either pitcher's mound or home plate. The makeshift team of substitutes – mostly mothers – who take the field against the Dead Knights in Nancy Willard's *Things Invisible to See* look not like themselves in their slacks and shirts but as if "they work in a *defense* plant" (253; emphasis added). In Sara Vogan's *In Shelly's Leg* Margaret is a pitcher for a women's softball team whose lover, Woody, wants her to embark on a musical tour with him – in a way, to run the bases, to travel out and back. Margaret wants to stay at home, however. Her house is a crucial space, the place of self, and the pitcher's mound is a metaphor for it. In his last conversation with Margaret, Woody tells her, "I want to take you to the ends of the earth," to which she replies, "I'm staying at the center. . . . You can always come back" (221). Her decision is based on her understanding that "women never had anywhere to go and men surely and always did" (203). Such a representation of gender roles and possibilities of necessity bars this protagonist from embarking on the hero's journey. Nonetheless, the condition of never having anywhere to go seems to be generalized in women's tales and is frequently represented figuratively by various kinds of mutilations and handicaps. The bar (Shelly's Leg) that sponsors Margaret's softball team is named for its former owner, Shelly, a one-legged woman who coached the team before she died of cancer. Ellen Cooney, in *All the Way Home,* presents an array of female protagonists, one of whom, Gussie Cabrini, is a "natural," formerly a great player and now a coach, who has a mutilated leg and who pitches in the big game braced against her crutch. She cannot run either literally or figuratively, even if she wanted to, for like Margaret, she is fixed at the center. Similarly, in *Things Invisible to See* Nancy Willard depicts a female protagonist who throughout most of the narrative is unable to walk at all and who learns to pitch from a wheelchair. Missing, mutilated, or useless legs recur with such frequency, and players are so often "fixed" at either the center or the edge, that we ought not ignore this important signifier. We may be justified in seeing the missing or useless legs and the shift of emphasis away from batter and bat, from offense to defense, as unconscious representations of female anatomy and female behavior, a kind of biological determinism embraced by this emerging mythology. (Nancy Willard's crippled pitcher plays for a priest-coach named Father Legg.) We may also see in the defective leg motif mythological intimations of inherent deformity or impotence against which the feminine protagonist struggles.

Even so, it is appropriate to ask whether there is in baseball's narratives a feminine counterpart to the classic hero. Messenger has observed that even with the shift of emphasis in women's baseball fiction, "competition and heroic striving" are still present. The heroism that is present, re-presented, in women's baseball narratives does seem often to be the sort previously described, the struggle against absence, deformity, or impotence, but even so, it at times mimics the structure of masculine mythology, an imitation due in part to the bricolage at hand, the mythological debris of the tradition with which the mythmaker works, but also in part (and perhaps the larger part) due to the shape and progress of the game itself. It is impossible to win a game by defense alone. A case in point is seen in Ellen Cooney's *All the Way Home*, which, as Messenger notices, focuses on the strange assortment of women who constitute the group; it is "really an anatomy of a team" (72). Within that team, however, one apparently classic hero and her tale may be discerned. The hero is Avis Poli, a protagonist in several ways like Joe Boyd. In a narrative more realistic than Boyd's, Avis is nevertheless like Joe in that she enters the game (softball) "too old" to play (fifty-two), and once in the game she sheds years and regains a youthful body with conditioning and the loss of thirty-four pounds (15). Like Joe, she embarks on her hero journey for a cause – in her case the "salvation" not of the Washington Senators but of Gussie Cabrini, a crippled, despairing former athlete. Although her motives and quest initially have nothing to do with softball, on the day of the crucial game she realizes that "for the first time in her life, the thing she wanted more than she had ever wanted anything was the thing she was now calling victory" (41). A similar intense desire for victory for his team drives Joe Boyd to sell his soul, but that desire is where his story begins; Avis Poli gains the desire for victory almost at the end of her story. At last she realizes that she wants the thing called *victory*, a concept from heroic legends and a word from the lexicon of combat. Her enemy, and the team's, is embodied in the coach of the other team, a sinister, mannish woman with the suggestive name of Linda Drago (a man disguised in drag?). Avis does achieve victory, and that victory comes through mythic means, for Avis's tale ends as Joe Boyd's ends, with a two-out, last-inning, game-and-cause winning, inside-the-park home run (207); in both cases the image of the middle-aged hero running with great difficulty all the way home (Cooney's title) reiterates the ancient, often-told hero tale of the journey out and back, the hero returning, reborn and transformed, to Ithaca.

Despite these similarities, the triumph of Avis's moment is mitigated somehow by a psychology at odds with such concepts as heroism or victory: "Madly, violently, she heaved herself forward and dove, sprawling across the plate on her belly as Drago stood above her begging for the ball. She felt herself sinking. She let her arms and legs flatten out against the earth. She turned her face away from the crowd that was gathering all around her. She had had enough. She wanted only to be still. She would not have minded it at all if they left her alone, and let her stay where she was forever" (207). This victory is a queer one, for it shades into sinking, flattening, turning away, having had enough, wanting to be still forever, to be *hors de combat* in a final and ultimate sense, indeed, to be dead. Avis's victory marks a crucial departure from the triumphant return of the classic hero.

Nancy Willard's echoing metaphysical fantasy, *Things Invisible to See,* also presents what at first appears to be a classic plot, with the kinds of baseball themes, figures, and images seen in Wallop's narrative. The pertinent aspect of Willard's narrative concerns not the female but the male protagonist, Ben Harkissian, a World War II serviceman adrift on a raft in the Pacific. In a distinctly Coleridgean episode Ben makes a wager not with the Devil (as does Joe Boyd) but with Death, a minion of the tale's pitcher-God. Harkissian agrees to play with his boyhood team, the South Avenue Rovers, against Death's team, the Dead Knights, and wagers on which team will win. The stakes are life or death. As in Joe Boyd's agreement with Mr. Applegate, Ben's wager is put into contract form: "The game shall be played for three innings. If the Dead Knights win, Death shall take the South Avenue Rovers. If the South Avenue Rovers win, Death shall give the members of this team a new lease on life. They shall live through the war and beyond it. If any of the South Avenue Rovers shall be unable to play, their places shall be taken by their next of kin" (195).

Because of a bus accident arranged by Death and his freshly recruited minion, Willie Harkissian, the game is played largely by the next of kin, mostly women, an assortment of maladepts. It is the bottom of the third and last inning, two are on, one is out, and a home run would tie the game. None of the women steps up to save the day and the lives of the South Avenue Rovers. Instead, Ben Harkissian comes to bat straight from his hospital bed. Unlike Joe Boyd or Avis Poli, however, Ben cannot win the game; he can only tie it. What a tie means is mysterious. The announcer says, "Here's the windup . . . and the pitch." The scene shifts, and the narrative ends with a cosmic perspective on an ambiguous event: "In Paradise, the Lord of the Universe tosses a green ball which breaks into a silver ball which breaks into a gold ball, and a small plane lands safely at Willow Run and Hal Bishop climbs out, singing for joy. He is too far away to hear the crack of the bat. . . . But he hears the distant cheering. Clare starts running and Ben runs after her as they round the bases, past the living and the dead, heading at top speed for home" (263).

It takes readers a while to notice that this resolution resolves nothing. The tie means only that the home team has not lost yet. Ben and his fiancée have made it home. What will happen next? Will one of the "mothers" belt one out? One ominous possibility is that the game against the Dead Knights will go on forever, with the baseball game a metaphor for life, the home team in an unequal battle against Death and its team of baseball "immortals." Death suggests this possibility to Ben's brother, Willie, when he claims that the Dead Knights, all former baseball greats, would "go extra innings into infinity for the chance to be alive again" (261). Does "be alive again" mean remain in the game? While we cannot resolve such issues, we can notice that not only is the classic plot of traveling out and back, as imaged in the game and the home run, given an ironic twist here but also that whatever victory is achieved is won by the male protagonist, a man with two good legs and a bat.

In both these cases of seemingly classic hero journeys, the triumphant return shades into defeat. Perhaps this is an aspect of an emerging feminine subgenre of baseball's mythology. By contrast, there is nothing ironic or ambiguous about the plot of the film *The Natural,* whose protagonist, Roy Hobbs, wears another of the classic hero's thousand faces. The filmmakers have bowdlerized the novel, stripped the protagonist of complexity, and transformed the novel's essentially tragic-ironic structure into a quest romance. In the film Roy Hobbs leaves home at eighteen and returns sixteen years later. The filmmakers have provided Roy with an idealized home (midwestern farm, golden fields, close relationship with his father and his fiancée) from which he sets out, thus establishing from the outset the conditions for the classic monomyth. Like Joe Boyd, Roy Hobbs confronts evil in the persons of Harriet Bird, Memo Paris, Gus Sands, and most powerful of all, the Judge (Goodwill Banner), owner and manipulator of the New York Knights' baseball team and the film's counterpart of Mr. Applegate or Death.

After a rocky start Roy Hobbs, who like Joe Boyd is an "old" player, stalwart and honest, resists temptations of the world, the flesh, and the devil and wins the pennant for Pop Fisher, the Judge's virtuous adversary and manager of the Knights. Like Joe Boyd, too, Roy achieves his miraculous feat in a brief time (three months, rather than two) in a career that ends, like Joe's, in a game- and season-saving, pennant-winning home run. And again like Joe Boyd, the film's Roy Hobbs moves from heroic act and decisive victory immediately to his home. In Roy's case the final scene transports him miraculously from night to day, from lightning-illuminated ball field to the sun-flooded, golden fields of his farm. Now thirty-four years old, he is father of Iris Lemon's son, playing catch with the boy, as Iris fondly watches her reintegrated family. In each of the cases of Joe Boyd and the film's Roy Hobbs, the last at-bat is a re-presentation of the archetypal plot, mirroring the structure of the work as a whole.

THE AMERICAN MONOMYTH

Someone went on a long journey. This is the archetypal plot, the one of the only two stories, corresponding to the classic monomyth. There is that other story, however: a stranger came to town. As will become clear, this plot corresponds to what has been called the American monomyth. This second story, however, often proves to be the first story viewed from another perspective. Sometimes the stranger who comes to town is the hero returning unrecognized to his home. Odysseus, the beggar at the door, proves to be the true king of Ithaca; arriving in Thebes, Oedipus is, unknown to all, the son of the dead king and heir to the kingdom; Jesus entering Jerusalem as a wandering teacher is the true scion of the ancient line of kings; Joe Hardy goes unrecognized in his own house. Alternatively, in the course of his journey the traveler of the first story may perform the deed of the stranger by entering another kingdom or village beset by evil and heroically engaging and defeating the enemy before resuming his journey.

The second of the two stories is likewise enacted in baseball, where its emphasis shifts from home as origin and destination and the landscape of the journey to the scene of arrival – the park, field, or walled garden, the troubled paradise into which the hero moves, the town into which the stranger comes. Jewett and Lawrence describe this second pattern of the monomyth: "A community in a harmonious paradise is threatened by evil: normal institutions fail to contend with this threat: a selfless superhero emerges to renounce temptations and carry out the redemptive task: aided by fate, his decisive victory restores the community to its paradisal condition: the superhero then recedes into obscurity" (xii). These authors find the troubled paradise redeemed by the hero peculiarly American, stating that "the American monomyth begins and ends in Eden" (169).[2] From the beginning immigrants to the Americas felt that they were coming to a new world, a land unsullied by sin and sorrow and identified with mythical perfections – Eden at the beginning of Western history or the "new earth" of Revelation. Thus, according to Jewett and Lawrence, "The action of the American monomyth always begins with a threat arising against Eden's calm" (174). Naturalized American or not, however, the pattern itself is ancient, appearing even in Freud's key narrative: Oedipus arrives in Thebes, a city terrorized by the Sphinx, solves her riddle, and thus rids the city of her presence, restoring order and calm. In *The Faerie Queene* the Red Cross Knight performs a similar function, killing the dragon that threatens Una's land, a troubled paradise. That is, this second archetypal plot, this signifier, is not less ancient than the first; that it finds such frequent re-presentation in American plots may suggest that it is a more active signifier in U.S. culture, fostered by America itself as signifier and thus having become a part of its narrative idiom, a peculiarity of the "American dialect."

Baseball's pristine walled garden, too, is archetypal with an ancient etymology. It is an image of the garden of origins and hence of the American Eden threatened by evil forces. Its confines are an artifact, an idealized representation of both nature and life, in which mind has apparently subdued matter, culture has tamed nature to human uses, and the human and the natural are reconciled, or (as Frye puts it) "nature itself has become home" (*Secular Scripture* 54). Thus, in this space of art we find a metaphor for human society and culture expressed as a form of unfallen nature, including human nature. As the character Christy Mathewson argues in *The Celebrant*, "There is nothing real about [baseball]." It is "all clean lines and clear decisions" (Greenberg 86). The point he makes is that baseball provides a model from which the ills of ordinary life are missing, especially its injustice and ambiguity. As I have shown, however, the space of art is a gap, here providing room for representation of an idealized nature (after the romantic model), but such space is likewise a place of collision, of conflict, as Heidegger said, "between lighting and concealing." As such, to borrow a phrase from Camille Paglia, it is "the uncanny crossroads of Hecate, where all things return in the night" (3). Thus nature can be idealized only by repression of the unconscious, material, violent, and lustful conditions under which it operates with its "universal law of creation from destruction" (Paglia 2). Paglia assigns to nature (and hence the "outside") what appear to be human impulses, motives, fears, and desires. It is precisely by such means, however, that the unconscious and therefore the unknown can be encountered – when it is embodied or imaged in the archetype. Consequently, even when imposed on by mind and art, nature will retain its ability to image the repressed, the dark, the sacred. Any complete representation of nature, the outside onto which inside matter is projected and by which it is signified, must of necessity include the shadows; it must leave the gates open to permit uncanny things to enter into the openness – the gap of Edenic scene – not so much to reveal the illusion of that perfection as to *perfect* that perfection by initiating the strife through which the truth of both art and the unconscious may be revealed.

It is this scene into which the stranger, the selfless superhero, steps to enact the age-old contest against evil, however defined, and his willingness to enter the contest is the American hero's distinguishing trait. Jewett and Lawrence speculate that the telling distinction between the classic and the American monomyth must lie in the differing ritual origins of the two plots: the classic monomyth, they claim, is based on rites of initiation wherein the young hunter-warrior-hero departs on a first, solitary journey to kill a wild animal, confront an enemy, or experience a wonder vision, after which he returns with full status to his community. By contrast, they say, the American monomyth is based on Judeo-Christian tales of redemption in which the hero is a composite figure, part "selfless servant who impassively gives his life for others" and part "zealous crusader who destroys evil" (xii). Although the speculation is suggestive, it begs the question of the relationship between ritual and mythos, a relationship by no means clear or settled. If language precedes archetype, as Gould argues, then it likewise precedes ritual (especially as ritual reveals a narrative structure). Seen in this light, the wonder journey is not a signified but a signifier, an enactment of a linguistic form, an archetypal plot; ritual and narrative are not parent and child but siblings, the children of language. Baseball's ritual circling of the bases is a reiteration of both the initiatory journey and the mythic plot or archetype.

Again, we should recognize that although the American monomyth may show a preference for the Edenic scene and the suffering, self-sacrificial, crusading hero, the patterns are by no means exclusively American, nor are American fictions exclusively based on this model. The American hero may be a type of Odysseus, as I said, or linked to the universal ironies of Oedipus, as well as to Jesus and the suffering servant. Further, representatives of this last type may be found also in the chivalric tradition of medieval Europe, whose knights undertook to protect innocence and oppose evil. Thus we find figures like Sir Lancelot and Spenser's Red Cross Knight among the literary ancestors of heroes seen as peculiarly American – Superman, for example, or Captain James T. Kirk.

There are, however, significant differences between classic and American heroes resulting from their respective plots. The effect of plot imitative of initiation is to reintegrate the hero into society, whereas the effect of the plot of sacrifice and confrontation is to exclude – to exile, as with Oedipus, or to sacrifice, as with Jesus. The two plots thus call for two types of hero, one a social man and one a loner. This fact suggests that it is unlikely, given Messenger's discovery of themes of cooperation, interaction, and support in women's narratives, that the subgenre of women's fiction would present versions of the American plot. The two stories are suited to two modes of literature, the comic and the tragic. That is, as regards the fortunes of the hero, a narrative will strike us as classic or American, as predominantly comic or tragic, depending not only on the protagonist's success or lack of it but also on his integration into or exclusion from society.

In its pure form the American monomyth presents a hero who is to some extent socially dysfunctional, that is, one who is isolated or shunned or who refuses to participate in society's normal human relationships. He is often essentially uncivilized. One thinks of such figures as the Lone Ranger or Shane, Dirty Harry or Rambo. As Jewett and Lawrence remark, the American hero's mission prevents permanent communal or familial relationships (212). A corollary of his outsider status is the fact that the American hero's personal and sexual relationships, like those of the archetypes, are abnormal. Typically, too, the American hero is a silent man; his speech is guarded, rationed, or uneasy. He may, in fact, be nearly inarticulate, unwilling or unable to tell his story or reveal his true identity. He is silent about both his past and his present. The text of his life is largely ellipsis, evasion, Lacanian censorship – that is, largely unconscious, revealed ambiguously in symbol and metaphor: a silver bullet, a mask, a special suit of clothes, a revealing name. One feels that the nameless, masked, or mysterious stranger is himself a metaphor, the walking rhetoric of the unconscious, the other. As the embodiment of the linguistic unconscious, the American hero appears as type, not individual. Joe Hardy, the persona who comes as a stranger to save the Washington Senators, has no past and very little present; attempts to find his home fail. The unanswered and unanswerable question, Who is that masked man? is fundamental.

As is clear by now, the American literary tradition, including its baseball literature, reveals both classic and American versions of the monomyth, or archetypal plot. Like the classic tales of Odysseus or Sir Gawain, *Shoeless Joe*'s Ray Kinsella departs from home (farm–ball field), journeys far through time and space, encounters dangers, and returns to cast the usurpers from his house and field and bestow boons on his small society. Like the selfless crusader of the American plot, Roy Hobbs of the film *The Natural* comes from obscurity to the troubled paradise of the New York Knights' home field, a scene over which evil, personified in the Judge, broods in a darkened tower. Roy confronts and defeats this evil, redeems the team, and restores harmony to the troubled paradise.

As I have shown, however, these two stories often form a composite structure with aspects of both classic and American plots. Moreover, a slight shift of perspective may transform one into the other. As was already suggested, viewed from the perspective of the ball team, the figures of Joe Hardy and Roy Hobbs appear not classic but American. Both men join their teams, and thus "society," from obscure origins. Both are mysterious, silent figures who confront evil (Mr. Applegate and the Yankees or the Judge) and score a decisive victory (win the pennant) that restores the community to its paradisiacal condition, after which they recede into obscurity, Joe Hardy returning to his home as Joe Boyd and Roy Hobbs returning to the anonymity of his boyhood farm. Even though the two stories often seem to be two sides of a coin, they nevertheless tend to produce different heroes, different plots, and different moods. Based on such gross features of plot and character, any work will likely strike us as classic or American. Mark Harris's *Bang the Drum Slowly* is remarkable in this respect, for the novel performs a rare feat of balance in finding room for both sorts of hero, together with their appropriate plots and moods. It is to that work that I now turn my attention.

4

MARK HARRIS'S *BANG THE DRUM SLOWLY* AND THE TWO STORIES

Mark Harris's novel *Bang the Drum Slowly* exemplifies the thorough merging of the archetypal plots of the two basic stories through its doubling of protagonists, one classic and one American, and its delicate balance of comic and tragic structures and moods. When compared with a work like Wilson's *Fences,* the novel's fictional world strikes us as wholly different in atmosphere. For one thing, the scene seems realistic, inhabited by ordinary characters who do not live in symbolic yards coextensive with or adjacent to God's closet and who have no truck with death personified or the devil. The progress of calendar and movement of plot are congruent, without apparent ellipses, although the latter is marked by a fair amount of coincidence. Such realism includes a matter-of-fact acceptance of life as profane (in the old sense of "outside the temple"), proceeding without divine direction or purpose. In the novel life is TEGWAR, "The Exciting Game Without Any Rules," a cosmic card game with a capricious dealer who makes up the rules as he goes and all of whose players are, in Henry Wiggen's vernacular, "clucks" and "doomeded." Life is contrasted with baseball, the other game, wholly rule governed and purposeful. Commerce with the sacred is limited to attempts by various characters to comfort the bereaved with religious platitudes in which few believe. When Joe Jaros tells Mr. Pearson that heaven "will be a better place than Chicago," Henry, the narrator, thinks to himself, "Lay it on thin" (212). The true representative of the sacred or uncanny is elided in the grammar in which characters describe Bruce's fate, always expressed in the passive voice with the agent omitted: "I been handed a shit deal," Bruce says to Henry, and "I am doomeded" (61). These two passive sentences are spoken over and over by various characters throughout the novel: "It is some shit deal Pearson been handed," Red translates for the Spanish-speaking George, and "We are all doomeded" (241, 243). The agent of the dealing and the dooming is, one might say, a "monstrous absence," a not nothing lost in the passive transformation.

Within the novel the two stories are told through a doubling of protagonists – Henry Wiggen, "Author," who narrates the story, and Bruce Pearson, whose illness and death are chronicled. In telling Bruce's story Henry works as a *bricoleur,* a mythmaker who uses the materials at hand – including other texts (his own earlier novel, newspaper reports, receipts, letters, scorecards, and calendars), his own selective and flawed memory, and most important, the forms and figures of baseball – to create a structure that will bridge the gap between his own fate and Bruce's, that is, between the comic and tragic, life and death.[1] He constructs his own story on the pattern of the classic monomyth. His long journey is a spiral through a nine-month period that begins in January 1955 and ends in October, just after his team, the New York Mammoths, wins the World Series. His journey takes him from his home in Perkinsville, New York, to Minnesota, Georgia, spring training in Florida, the scheduled wanderings of a season, and finally back home, changed, humanized, and wise in the ways of life and death.

Within this larger circle is a smaller, linear structure framed by two scorecards (the figurative equivalents of birth and death certificates for a man and a season) – one dated April 12, 1955, opening day, and reproduced just before chapter 1, and the other from the final game of the series early in October 1955, which Henry saves for Bruce but fails to send him as promised. Its omission from the text is an ellipsis, a silence that absorbs the silence of death. The scorecards define the season, the scene, and the society of Bruce's influence. The season itself is emblematic of a life, a season of youth, light, clement weather, and achievement. Outside this frame are the cold and dark, Bruce Pearson's illness, diagnosed in January, and his death, occurring October 7.

Bruce Pearson's story is essentially that of the American monomyth, the tale of a selfless hero who emerges to defeat the evil threatening a troubled paradise, redeem the small, contained society of the team, and then retreat into obscurity. As I noted in chapter 3, both monomyths are forms of romance, the classic essentially comic in its structure, mood, and rhythms and the American potentially tragic, although not necessarily so. Romance in the comic mode tends to be propelled by guile; romance in the tragic mode, by violence.[2] Within the novel Henry Wiggen is one who survives and triumphs through guile, trickery, and deceit. He manipulates language to his advantage. Known as "Author," he is wily, evasive, clever, and brash. By contrast, Bruce is utterly without guile. Whereas Henry is smart, Bruce is, as most everyone agrees, dumb. Although *dumb* as applied to Bruce is intended to mean "stupid," it means "mute" as well. His is the silence of enigma. Bruce is, in fact, like the type he represents, nearly inarticulate, speaking single sentences in pieces over a period of hours, sending postcards home without messages, asking Henry to speak for him. He is the helpless butt of jokes and the victim of his teammates' ill-natured ragging.

As may be predicted, the two protagonists create complexities as the structures of the two stories intertwine. Despite their apparent differences, Henry and Bruce are in some ways like photograph and negative, that is, apparently opposite but fundamentally alike. One is tempted to see in Bruce the very mundane (yet psychologically devastating) appearance of Henry's double, the embodiment of the unconscious and hence the harbinger of Henry's own death. His language, like his plight, serves to interrupt and disrupt the smooth running of Henry's existence and shows Henry his own mortal face. In any case, Henry and Bruce are inseparable. They are battery mates and roommates but are linked as well by closer bonds. Their shared secret of Bruce's fatal illness has isolated them and made Henry responsible for the quality, if not the length, of a life now defined as a single baseball season. The symbol of this bond and Henry's obligation is the clause that Henry insists be put in his contract, tying him, as he says, "in a package with Pearson": "If he is sold," Henry says, "I must be sold. . . . Or if he is traded, I must be traded the same place. Wherever he goes I must go" (88). Henry's often awkward, humorous language here takes on an atypical dignity, echoing the words of Ruth, that biblical personification of selfless love, to her mother-in-law: "Whither thou goest, I will go; and where thou lodgest, I will lodge: thy people shall be my people, and thy God my God" (Ruth 1:16).

Dutch, the manager, cannot understand Henry's insistence on the clause. He responds, "A roomie is a roomie, Author, not a Siamese twin brother fastened at the hip. . . . Are you a couple fairies, Author?" (89). He reminds Henry that there were days when Henry hated Pearson, that he had seen Henry get up from a table and just walk away from him. Henry replies that it was "because he laughed without knowing why." One of the owners, Patricia Moors, observes, "Such a thing can be not only hate but also love." When Henry denies that it is love, she explains, "I do not mean fairy love" (90). Part of the wisdom that Henry will gain concerns just this inexplicable nearness of love and hate for the other – brother, twin, double, shadow, self.

In line with this joining, Henry insists to Joe Jaros that they include Bruce in the card game of TEGWAR, which is not only a metaphor for life but a vehicle of elaborate jokes played on unsuspecting outsiders ("clucks"). Joe refuses, saying that Bruce is "too damn dumb" to play (79). He gets angry when Henry persists, reiterating not only the suggestion of homosexuality but also, in his choice of simile, the themes of love and death, subjects about which Henry must learn: "What are you 2 anyway? Are you Romeo and Juliet?" (142). Team members pick this up, along with other forms of verbal harassment, aimed for the most part at Bruce. A favorite subject of their ragging is Bruce's desire to marry the prostitute Katie, a liaison indicative of Bruce's outsider status. In his lack of verbal skill and his essential good nature, Bruce passively accepts such insults. He is, Henry says, "easy pickings, like punching a punching bag that can not punch back" (146).

Bruce's passivity manifests itself in his habit of listening to others' conversations rather than talking, in his doing what others tell him without question, and in his accepting others' assessments of him, almost without ego. For example, Bruce, accepting the common judgment, concurs that he is dumb: "I never been smart, Arthur" (100). (Bruce is the only one who calls Henry "Arthur" and perhaps unconsciously sees him as kingly or chivalric.)

As part of his care for Bruce, Henry argues at length that Bruce is really not dumb, his final point being that ball players room "like with like," and he thus reiterates the doubling motif of their relationship. Henry asks Bruce, "would a smart fellow like me room with a dumb one?" (102). Malleable as always, Bruce agrees that he would not. Although Henry mistakenly is unconvinced by his own argument, concluding, "He always believed me, dumb as he was" (102), he will eventually learn that Bruce is indeed a man like himself.

Henry's somewhat flawed facility with language and its uses in jokes, lies, insults, and arguments must be contrasted with Bruce's terrible inarticulateness. As I already suggested, this is the real meaning of *dumb* applied to Bruce. Language is thus central to the irony of the work and its lessons, as well as being the means of balancing and indeed merging its comic and tragic elements. Henry's story and its essentially comic mode (the pattern of *The Odyssey*) in the end prevail by encompassing and integrating Bruce's story (which Bruce is incapable of telling), the tragic within the comic. Desire is realized within the comic structure. Life and its celebration prevail over death, love over strife, laughter over tears. It is by means of language that Henry successfully lays to rest his mortal double, incorporating Bruce's tragedy in the comic structure of his own autobiography. Finally, however real the suffering of Bruce, Henry, and others, however isolated, angry, and frightened Henry may be, however imminent Bruce's death, Henry's language is the vehicle wherein life's story continues. Success and triumph accompany one on the way; laughter lurks always just beneath the surface to interrupt, negate, or deconstruct the tragic plot as it moves inexorably to its conclusion. This humor emerges from the unconscious as a psychic defense against mortality. An exchange between two coaches, Mike Mulrooney and Red Traphagen, just after the onset of Bruce's final illness illustrates this juxtaposition of the tragic and comic and the ascendancy of the comic: " 'It is sad,' said Mike. 'It makes you wish to cry.' 'It is sad,' said Red. 'It makes you wish to laugh' " (279).

Henry, whose language is the mechanism for balancing the comic and tragic, has earned his nickname, "Author," by writing an autobiography, *The Southpaw,* a book of which he is both the author and the hero, to which he often alludes, and from which he quotes, sometimes at length. The irony in the situation is that, as the reader notices immediately, Henry is a more exuberant than eloquent writer. All his characters talk as Henry does, in a semiformal style without contractions (one of Henry's rules for writing) that arranges itself into fractured patterns of prose. Physicians, farmers, prostitutes, ball players all use this flat and funny style. To increase the comic pull of language, Henry is cast as a casual speller at best, and he produces such sentences as "I went up to the Moorses sweet, feeling sorry for Joe and yet also laughing" (83); he has Dutch, the manager, say, "I am libel to wind up using my catcher that is just plum dumb more and more" (91); Bruce, Henry says, can run "like a dear" (46). It is interesting to notice that Henry's creative misspelling is likely to substitute (unconsciously) the language of endearment (sweet, dear) for more objective terms (suite, deer). Henry's grammar is all his own, too, and as filtered through Henry's consciousness, even ordinary idiomatic expression undergoes a sea change: "It was Joe's wife later left the cat out of the barn" (19), or "He was the greatest reliefer in baseball down the stretch, fat old Horse, a rock of strength all September" (241).

Even as Bruce's story and the novel close, the humor lurking in Henry's language continues its work of opposing and partially neutralizing the pathos of Bruce's early death: "And he was dead. That was October 7. In my Arcturus Calendar for October 7 it says 'De Soto visited Georgia, 1540.' This hands me a laugh. Bruce Pearson also visited Georgia. I was his pall-bear, me and 2 fellows from the crate and box plant and some town boys, and that was all. There were flowers from the club, but no person from the club. They could of sent somebody" (283–84). The unconscious, psychic defense mechanism of humor accounts for the strange fact that people often feel an almost irresistible impulse to laugh during funerals. Harris represents this impulse through Henry's language. No matter how stark the statement "and he was dead," following this with "I was his pall-bear" calls up that shameful yet utterly natural desire to laugh. Henry's language (which speaks the man) thus usurps the horror of death, speaks away its unspeakability, and dominates it by linguistic play.

Bruce's story, which is contained within Henry's and representative of the American monomyth, is the simpler of the two. The first point to notice about the American monomyth is that the emphasis is often on community rather than on the silent sufferer. The hero confronts and defeats a threat not so much to himself but to the potential paradise. The society was there before the hero's arrival and continues beyond his departure or death. The selfless hero's task is one of redemption, but as the Christ archetype reveals, not necessarily one of survival. His deed and sacrifice restore life to the community by overcoming whatever threatens its harmony and well-being. As I suggested in the previous chapter, such a hero hardly needs a name, and indeed he may have only a title (e.g., the Lone Ranger or the Red Cross Knight), or he may have a single name that suggests a title (e.g., Oedipus, Shane, Paladin, or Dirty Harry). Bruce Pearson has a name, but he is so self-effacing that almost no one notices him or learns his name. Henry comments, "There are writers that don't even know he is with the club, and ballplayers on other clubs the same that call everybody by their name but Bruce because if they once knew it they keep forgetting, shouting at him maybe for a stray ball, 'Hey, catcher.' There was never much to keep them remembering. He been up there a long time, yet nobody ever really knows him. I doubt that anybody even keeps a book on him" (58). It will be Henry's job to learn to know Bruce and to keep such a book. Bruce does not keep a book on himself. After learning of his disease and before joining the team for his final season, Bruce burns his papers, the text of his life. Now, just as he has no future, he has no past. He is in all respects a stranger. Henry comments that the image of Bruce destroying his papers remains his "best picture of him, standing there all black against the light of the fire" (68). In this image Bruce is the mere form of a man visible against the fire that consumes his papers, text, and identity; he is a human template, a pattern, a shadow image of mortality, that is, of everyone. Bruce's malady is Hodgkin's disease, second cousin to the malady from which all suffer.

The selflessness of the American hero is characteristic of the redeemer/sacrifice figure wherever he or she is found in ritual or myth. Among primitive planting peoples the one singled out for sacrifice to renew the life powers of the group is frequently not only feasted and treated with honor but also tortured before death (Campbell, *The Sacrifice* 37–43), as were Christ and a host of Christian martyrs. This figure is particularly prominent in American literature. The "punching bag" simile Henry uses for Bruce thus may be seen as a realistic displacement of this ritual treatment of the redeemer/sacrifice. Certainly the team that Bruce "saves" suffers from an inexplicable malaise threatening its collective life.[3]

Under Henry's protection and tutelage Bruce's playing improves, but relations among coaches and teammates disintegrate. The club, as Dutch phrases it, has become suicidal (151). The problem is discord and various sorts of in-fighting. The men cannot cooperate for their common good, and it is only as news of Bruce's impending death gets out that things begin to change. Goose Hill, the aging, derelict, despairing catcher and one of the most vehement of Bruce's tormenters, is the first team-mate Henry tells and thus the first to be redeemed. Goose is prompted by this knowledge to reexamine his own life, mend his fences, and plan for the future. He even begins to play better baseball and writes, with the help of a ghost writer, an article entitled "How I Hit the Comeback Trail at 35" (171). The team's general redemption begins on August 26, Goose's thirty-fifth birthday, when the other team members learn of Bruce's illness. They mark their transformation and new-found life with a communal rite, a party in Bruce and Henry's room. Afterward, as Henry sees it, the winning of the pennant and the World Series is a foregone conclusion. "There was plenty of scrap left in Washington yet. They did not know they were beat. You probably could of even found a little Washington money in town . . . for the town did not know what the Mammoths knew, not knowing the truth, not knowing Washington was beat on August 26, which I personally knew, . . . knowing what it done to a fellow when he knew, how it made them cut out the horseshit and stick to the job. . . . We thought, 'Washington, you are dead and do not know it'" (273).

Bruce's last game is on Labor Day, a game appropriately shortened by rain that coincides with the onset of his last illness. Henry pitches that game, and Bruce catches. Henry throws one pitch in the top of the seventh inning as the downpour begins: "The rain come in for sure now, and [Bruce] seen everybody running, but he did not run, only stood there. . . . I seen him standing looking for somebody to throw to, the last pitch he ever caught, and I went back for him, and Mike and Red were there when I got there, and Mike said, 'It is over, son,' and he said 'Sure' and trotted on in" (278). Mike's statement that it is over, with which Bruce concurs, is familiar: *consumatum est*, "it is finished," are the last words of Christ. And for Bruce it is finished – the game, his career, his life, his redemption of the team. Bruce will not play again, although he will remain with the team through part of the series before he goes home to die. Having achieved unaware the redemptive task, he recedes into the obscurity from which he has briefly emerged, a stranger come to town.

As I mentioned, Bruce's story is contained within Henry's, which is that of someone going on a long journey. Henry is indeed a distant descendant of Odysseus, and like that hero, Henry is a master of stratagems. He survives and triumphs through guile and trickery; he is one who travels out and back, one who comes home. Henry's character, like his story, stands in stark contrast to Bruce's. He moves smoothly through life, at ease with people, confident, humorous, a social man integrated into family, home, and team. He is not nameless and faceless like Bruce but is known, liked, and valued as friend and ball player. He is "Author" to the baseball world and "Arthur" to Bruce; most important, he is Henry W. Wiggen, a man who, he believes, knows who he is. He loves tricks and jokes and stratagems, as is evident in his telephone games, his skill at TEGWAR, and his battles with and subterfuges against the IRS. But all his skills of deception are required in his journey toward wisdom. He must keep Bruce's illness secret, and he must keep Bruce nearby where he can watch out for him, hence his great strategy involving the contract clause linking Henry and Bruce in a package. In a sense Henry's personal risks on Bruce's behalf enable Bruce to redeem the club.

On his own journey toward Ithaca Odysseus learns important lessons. He experiences grief over dead comrades; he discovers in the underworld the absolute finality of death; he learns to survive through strategy and guile. In the process he sheds his brash, destructive, soldierly persona and learns kingcraft. He comes to recognize the value of life and the importance of family and home. He matures from boy to man.

Henry learns similar lessons. Through the early chapters of the novel he is a man obsessed by money, self-centered and lacking empathy. When Bruce's call for help comes (collect), Henry at first refuses to accept it. When he learns that Bruce is in the hospital, his first thought is that he has sold Bruce a total insurance policy. He refers to his unborn child as "600 Dollars," the amount of a tax exemption. He takes his Arcturus Insurance kit along on the trip to see Bruce so as to make the trip deductible. Arriving at the hospital, he berates Bruce for calling him Arthur. Bruce says, "Do not be mad. . . . They do not wish me to leave without a friend." Henry responds, "Then stay" (23).

To his credit, however, Henry is visibly shaken by the news of Bruce's disease, and he assumes immediate responsibility, taking from the doctors the instructions for dealing with a crisis, a text that he will carry with him until Bruce's final illness. With this text will come the beginning of insight and a certain human-heartedness that have been lacking. Henry soon is able to see, looking back at his own earlier book, that Bruce has been lonely and desperate for a long time and that Henry had not been wise enough to recognize, let alone empathize with, Bruce's pain: "If I had the sense to look in my own goddam book I would of seen where his guts and his heart were being eat away. I should of knew it the first time I ever took any notice of him, in the spring of 52 at Aqua Clara" (49).

With the arrival of his double he begins to notice, too, how omnipresent death is in the world. It pervades the realm of everyday language. "You would be surprised," Henry says, "if you listen to the number of times a day people will tell you something will last a lifetime, or tell you something killed them, or tell you they are dead" (26). Henry begins to realize that he too is mortal. As he runs down the roster of players, he finds that he is older than nine others, whereas three years before he had been the youngest man on the team. For the first time he feels vulnerable and calculates for himself a wonderfully long life. On July 4, Henry's twenty-fourth birthday, he claims that it is "25% of the way along for me, for I believe I can live to 96 if I keep in shape and don't come down with a fatal disease and if the son of a bitches don't blow up the place with their cockeyed bomb" (187).

For much of the season Henry, keeping the secret, suffers a consuming anger. "Dying old," he says, "is in the cards, and you figure on it, and it happens to everybody, and you are willing to swallow it. But why should it happen young to Bruce? It made me mad" (108). Because he cannot share his anger, it continues to build until the All-Star break, when two crucial events happen at once. Henry earns his first All-Star win, and he learns that his wife, Holly, has gone to the hospital to deliver their child. Getting this news from his father, Henry realizes that his father (who knows of Bruce's illness) also carries "this mad around inside him." Henry says, "It really hit me, and I done a crazy thing" (195). What he does is destroy his room and, for the first time, cry, permitting himself at last to grieve. He says that he will deduct the damages to the room as medical expenses, "because somewheres along the line you have got to blow your fume little by little or else blow it all in one blow later" (195–96).

The grief and anger are humanizing Henry, giving him the ability to hear, in a sense, the still, sad music of humanity. Later in the evening Henry is at dinner with "many old-time ballplayers," listening to their stories, which he recognizes are largely fiction. He says, "I used to correct people a lot when they lied, but I cut that out . . . because why in hell snag old men on their lies. Who cares anyhow?" (195). He no longer cares that they lie because he has recognized a more important truth: "Every year they die. You see an old fellow at the All-Star Game, or at the World Series, or in the South, or hanging at the winter meetings, and they lie to you, and the next thing you read in the paper where they are dead, old fellows not so many years before so slim and fast, with a quick eye and great power, and all of a sudden they are dead and you are glad you did not wreck their story for them with the straight facts" (196). Henry is beginning to learn the difference between history and myth. The old men's stories are a means of constructing their lives as fictions; they are plots imposed on the straight facts and thus means of shaping and reshaping life, for making sense of it by giving it structure and meaning and thus making it endurable. In other words, these are not lies but myths, doing the mythic work of attempting to bridge the gap between desire and straight fact, or put another way, to rescue significance from the absurdity of events.

Within a few hours Henry's daughter is born, no longer "600 Dollars" but Michele, who, as Holly says, is "a human person already" (197). Holding the child for the first time, Henry is ready to cry again: "The sun was first coming in the window like it was that morning when Bruce had the attack . . . , and I was about ready to bawl again after just getting through bawling in Milwaukee, sitting there with this little bit of a human person in my hand" (167). Like the old men, Henry is a mythmaker, imposing a pattern on human life, a linguistic structure crafted of the bricolage of event, image, and desire. Two moments of intense emotion are linked through language; two dawns are retrieved from the shards of time and juxtaposed, one associated with life and one with death. The impossible but necessary task of reconciling them requires the mythmaker's craft (art, craftiness, lies). On that earlier morning Henry had held a man whose life was ending; on this morning he holds a child whose life is beginning. On that earlier dawn Bruce was ill and frightened, as he and Henry were waiting for Goose to bring the doctor. Surprised that Goose is willing to go out of his way to help him, Bruce suspects that Henry has told him the secret and remarks, "Probably everybody be nice to you if they knew you were dying." Henry's response reveals a new-found wisdom: "Everybody knows everybody is dying. . . . That is why people are nice" (168). When Bruce asks Henry to hold onto him, Henry says, "I took his shoulder and held it, and he reached up and took my hand, and I left him have it, though it felt crazy holding another man's hand. Yet after a while it did not feel too crazy any more" (168). Now, on this dawn, Henry's impulse to cry reveals the connection he has made: his child, too, is a human person, and Henry knows that everybody is dying.

Henry's story is a spiral following the rhythms of the year. It begins in winter and returns to winter and the writing of Bruce's story. It has been, for Henry, a season of achievement: he has pitched in and won the All-Star game, he has been a pivotal member of a pennant- and World Series-winning team, he has won twenty-plus games and earned his bonus, and he has become a father. For Henry the year will circle around; a new spring will come, and with it a new baseball season, new contract negotiations, new feats to be performed. For now, however, Henry, like Odysseus, has come home. What he has learned on his journey has changed him. It is something about life and death, about love and his own ephemeral condition. He acknowledges his kinship to Bruce, of whom he can say, "He is my friend" (203), and about whose existence he declares, "He was not a bad fellow, no worse than most and probably better than some" (284), a modest but appropriate eulogy for a mere man – in the end, Everyman, nameless, faceless, speechless, unknown.

Writing Bruce's story is an act comparable to the old men's lies. That is, the "book on Bruce" is a myth that imposes meaning and structure on an otherwise unremarkable and typically absurd human life. It is myth gathering and constructing from shards of language a form that will bridge the inevitable gap between the living and the dying. Baseball and its forms are some of those shards. It is not Bruce's "doomeded" condition that gives meaning to baseball but baseball – its triumphant season and Henry's manipulations and shapings – that gives meaning to Bruce, the man without language or text whose story Henry tells and whom Henry will remember best as a form "standing there all black against the light of the fire," friend, brother, self.

The artful realism of Harris's text veils the complex interweaving of two hero tales and the mythmaking endeavor of its fictional and archetypal Author, although it does not obscure the attendant traditions. The novel's fiction is that it stands firmly on mundane ground, its rhythms conforming to the ordinary movement of clock and calendar. Whatever miracle and meaning grow among the players spring from earthly soil. By contrast, the next chapter concerns itself with baseball's time and space, dimensions often unconstrained by physical law – the sacred, uncanny, wonder-plagued dimensions of the field of play.

IT SEEMS CLEAR THEN THAT LIFE, AT LEAST AS WE KNOW IT, CAN EXIST ONLY IN REGIONS OF SPACE-TIME, IN WHICH [THERE ARE] ONE TIME AND THREE SPACE DIMENSIONS. Stephen Hawking, *A Brief History of Time* 165

BASEBALL EXISTS IN FOUR DIMENSIONS: HEIGHT, WIDTH, DEPTH AND MEMORY. THE DIAMONDS IN OUR MINDS, THE FIELDS OF REVERIE, OFTEN RIVAL REALITY. Thomas Boswell, *Why Time Begins on Opening Day* 247–48

BASEBALL . . . IS TOTALLY ARTIFICIAL, CREATING ITS OWN TIME, EXISTING WITHIN ITS OWN SPACE. Eric Rolfe Greenberg, *The Celebrant* 85

BASEBALL DOES WONDROUS THINGS TO TIME AND SPACE THAT MAKE IT AN AUTHOR'S DELIGHT. BASEBALL'S TEMPORAL DIMENSION IS ALWAYS IN THE DOMAIN OF GAME TIME AS IT UNFOLDS IN PURE POSSIBILITY. Christian K. Messenger, *Sport and the Spirit of Play* 316

BEING DEAD HERE WOULD SITUATE A MAN IN PLACE AND TIME. William Kennedy, *Ironweed* 13

DIMENSIONS OF THE FIELD OF PLAY

Mythic time and space, or what may be called the space-time continuum of the gap, constitutes the world of baseball and its texts. Indeed, baseball is not only a visual representation but a working model, a concrete metaphor, of both the stasis and the dynamics of the mythic dimensions. Addressing these dimensions we may become interested not in the physics of the matter but in the metaphysics, the world and plot of narrative (as encompassing not simply fictions and myths but also visions, dreams, and other plots that take shape in the gap), which is in some sense the space and progress of desire and fear, "sacred" time and space as they appear, rebuslike, in image, symbol, metaphor, and archetype. As I have shown in chapters 3 and 4, the structures and progress of baseball help to create the game's own forms of mythic narrative. In earlier chapters I have also introduced the subject of mythic space as being coextensive with the gap, and I explore this overlap further in a later section of this chapter, but now I need to specify what mythic time is, identify some of its peculiarities, and show how baseball re-presents such mythic temporality.

The first thing to notice about time is that it is not one thing. We can speak of cosmic time, for example, that view of time suggested in the first epigraph from physicist Stephen Hawking, the dynamics of the universe. For Hawking, time obeys the laws of physics, especially Einsteinian physics, and life as we know it can exist only in regions of space-time. These are regions regulated by the cosmic clock, the mechanism of the physical universe, a clock that may work by complex rules, but work it does, and nothing human beings do or imagine can alter its running. So far as the individual is concerned, cosmic time is unidirectional, a principled progression within whose workings human beings are born, live, and die; thus cosmic time is ultimately time the destroyer.

When we turn our attention away from the sweep of cosmic time, it is possible to discern another form of temporality, to which certain philosophers refer as phenomenological time – time as experienced, whether as "objective" or "subjective" progression. Human beings, David Wood says, are subject to both forms of time, which can be considered "two discrete and autonomous dimensions of the real." Confronted with the twofoldness of temporal reality, the individual may "suffer diremption," a wound that may "never finally be healed" (9). Wood points out that time "is near to the surface of most of the central problems of philosophy and has a major impact on how we think of identity, of truth, of meaning, of reason, of freedom, of language, of existence, of the self" (2). The problem of time is thus built into the human condition and, by its very nature, will continue to call forth attempts (philosophical, fictional, and mythic) to reconcile its contradictions.

Time is not only a complex philosophical issue but also a central concern of narratologists and historians, the many who turn their attention to the story, whether as myth, literary fiction, or history. Explaining Ricoeur's understanding of time and narrative, historiographer Hayden White points out that, for Ricoeur, all narratives are "symbolic discourses" and are alike in terms of their reference to time:

Ricoeur does not erase the distinction between literary fiction and historiography . . . , but he does scumble the line between them by insisting that both belong to the category of symbolic discourses and share a single "ultimate referent." While freely granting that history and literature differ from one another in terms of their immediate referents . . . , which are "real" and "imaginary" events, respectively, [Ricoeur] stresses that insofar as both produce emplotted stories, their ultimate referent . . . is the human experience of time or "the structures of temporality." ("Metaphysics of Narrativity" 146)

Although centrally concerned with time (as "ultimate referent"), narratives have their ways of working against cosmic time, as is indicated by the fact that narratives are often seen as "time frames," "time shelters," or as David Wood puts it, "little bubbles of narrative order" blown in the cosmic winds of time (10). One of the claims made about narrative in general is that it is a means of mending the aporias, contradictions, and "double-binds" of time as experienced. Paul Ricoeur, writing on the subject of narrative and time, explains that plot is characterized by "the competition between succession and configuration." One of the operations of emplotment thus is to seek to neutralize or control cosmic time, the open, potentially infinite, and therefore meaningless sequence of incidents, by means of a closure or configuration, and hence significance, imposed on this succession by plot. Ricoeur says, "In this sense, composing a story is, from the temporal point of view, drawing a configuration out of succession. . . . The temporal identity of a story . . . [is that which] endures and remains across that which passes and flows away" ("Life in Quest" 22). In Ricoeur's sense of the term, plot keeps cosmic time at bay, admitting temporality only to hold it still, to make it endure. Narrative, like the limiting shore, thus lets time sing like the sea in its chains, the bindings of plot.

When we narrow our focus from all stories to mythic stories, we find that myth is in some ways like narrative in general in its means of addressing the time problem. For one thing, myth, like other narratives, erects "time shelters" against cosmic time and its terrors. Also like other narratives, myth is preoccupied with the past. Its vision is essentially retrospective. "Once upon a time," our stories begin, or "In the late summer of that year," or "There was a time," or "In the beginning." The mythic presentation of time, however, differs from that of other narratives in a crucial awareness: the sense that the edges of time are just "there," that the origin, the beginning, is accessible and recoverable, or that the end may be located and even colonized by human travelers. For this reason myth differs from narrative in general in its map of the space-time continuum and the expanses of the past or future to which its roads lead. Its destination is often the deepest past, the beginning, the origin, which as Mark C. Taylor says, is the "temporal correlate of the spatial center" (2), a point, a timelessness, when a different order of temporality enfolded humanity. Curiously, on the mythic map this point of beginning may well be also a point of ending: we may find in the golden city of the apocalypse the tree of life from the first garden; "In my end is my beginning," as T. S. Eliot has it.

Explaining St. Augustine's view of the distinction between the two orders of time, Ricoeur says that for Augustine, time is "a distention of the soul" in which a dissociation occurs: "It consists in the permanent contrast between the unstable nature of the human present and the stability of the divine present which includes past, present and future in the unity of a gaze and a creative action" ("Life in Quest" 31). The phrase "divine present" aptly describes not only mythic time but also baseball's temporality. Mythic time can and often does swim against the flow of cosmic time. Taylor explains that in myth, "the presence of [the] origin is not lost in the past but can return again and again" (2). As Augustine's notion of the divine present and Taylor's notion of the presence of the origin suggest, mythic time is not only mental but sacred, the ultimate time shelter, contrasting with "the unpunctuated monotony of profane time" as well as with the evasiveness of the human present. Mythic or sacred time is reversible in that "it is *a primordial mythical time made present*" (Eliade, cited in Taylor 2). Mythic time and its presence are thus ancient forms of phenomenological time, archetypal signifiers of enduring utility and, as such, endlessly speakable, repeatable, transformable modalities of plot.

BASEBALL AND THE FOURTH DIMENSION: ANNULLING THE WORK OF TIME

Baseball has transformed and incorporated into its very structure these ancient temporal archetypes. The game shares with narrative an ability to display the modes of phenomenological time. Both the field (its plot of ground) and the rule-governed progress of the game (its narrative or plot),[1] as well as the plots (the narratives) based on those plots, re-present what

Ricoeur termed "that which endures and remains across that which passes and flows away." Like Ricoeur's Aristotelian notion of plot, the game is a "discordant concordance" ("Life in Quest" 31) that can impose order on mere succession, create its own time, and exist within its own space, as the Greenberg epigraph claims; it has its means of presenting – actually making present – not only a form of phenomenological time, time as experienced, but also the *presence* of mythic time, and in so doing it allows the coexistence of past, present, and future (a characteristic found not only in narrative and memory but also in language in its verb paradigms, which by forms of linguistic legerdemain render all times here and now). Consequently, and also like narrative, baseball can hold event, character, affect, word, and symbol in achronic suspension. Boswell's notion that the fourth dimension of baseball is not time but memory points to the ways in which the game substitutes mental time for cosmic time. The game, like memory, language, narrative, dream, and myth, operates under nonphysical laws of space and time. In brief, in baseball one finds a means of presenting a concrete model of the mythic space-time continuum, of the gap as time shelter, where archaic mind stuff, archetype, metaphor, image, and conscious and unconscious symbol can speak to, with, and through the material of the moment. Baseball, by creating a context, a plot in both senses of the term, its own space and time, provides a hospitable environment for evading the determinisms of nature's time and space and for producing transformations of the ancient, often repeated, backward journey to the beginnings. The progress of the runner on the base paths is counterclockwise, and his end, his destination, is his beginning.

Throughout his work mythologist Mircea Eliade has explored the centrality of time in the world's myths, rituals, religions, and philosophies, and he finds the backward journey a typical response, an "archetypal plot," a crucial signifier in which human imaginings find a means of evading or curing the workings of cosmic time: "It is interesting to observe a certain continuity of human behavior in respect to time, both down the ages and in various cultures. This behavior may be defined as follows: *To cure the work of time it is necessary to 'go back' and find the 'beginning of the world'*" (87–88). This focus on "the pain of existence in time" (85), or what I have called cosmic time, accounts, Eliade says, for innumerable facts of myth, which often seeks to explain, justify, cure, or empower one to transcend the pain of time, to bridge the gap between time the destroyer and the eternity of desire. Consequently, countless metaphysical announcements and ritual acts express the theme of return. Humans have sought in myth, as in dream, to go back to a moment just before ordinary time began, to the "'strong time' of myth . . . the prodigious 'sacred' time when something *new, strong* and *significant* was manifested" (19). It is clear that mythic time, as signifier, represents the temporal mode of the Lacanian unconscious; profane time, the mode of consciousness. As the rhetoric, images, and symbols of the unconscious well up into the gap, they come with their own archetypal timepiece, a clock stopped at a crucial moment, a clock whose hands move counterclockwise, or a clock with no hands at all.

Indeed, strong or sacred time seeks the condition of timelessness, at least with respect to human beings, hence the widespread archetypal theme of a sacred time before time when human beings lived and played untouched by time, a theme reiterated throughout the world's myths and present in two foundational texts of Western literature, one classical and one biblical. Both tell of an alternate reality exempt from the killing effects of time and labor that was once enjoyed and is now irrevocably lost. One of these tales is found in Hesiod's *Works and Days,* a composite Greek text, part book of proverbs and part farmers' almanac, exploring the theme of labor in time. The other is found in Genesis 2–3, an account in part of the beginning of cosmic time for the first humans and the curse of unending labor and death for the children of earth.[2] The image of the prelapsarian paradisiacal garden in Genesis, a place untouched by time, is particularly evocative and enduring in the archetypal lexicon of the Western imagination. It is a nearly indispensable signifier, undergoing endless transformations as *the* domestic signifier of signifiers.[3]

This mythic, collective home – this timeless space, this walled garden – has through our inherited language and its linguistic archetypes attained a certain microcosmic existence in the psyche of each individual. As Eric Gould puts it, it is one of the archetypes in which "our fate is transacted." The garden and other similar places provide forms for imaging the temporality of desire. This linguistic legacy determines that the individual past, infancy and childhood, is homologous to the strong or sacred time at the beginning, the infancy of humankind. Just as life in the garden was said to be free of labor and overt consciousness of time, so is childhood (at least in the unconscious and in memory) a time of comfort and ease, impervious to the destructive advance of time. The mythic collective home and time before time are thus metaphors for the individual home and early childhood. This fact provides another reason for the existence of a psychological aspect to every individual quest against time.

It is the attempt to go back and find, as Eliade says, the "mythical, paradisal time" where the child lives: "For psychoanalysis . . . the truly primordial is the 'human primordial,' earliest childhood," or in Freudian-Lacanian terms, the image realm and primitive symbology of mirror stage and pre-Oedipal development. For Eliade, this psychological beginning holds strong or sacred time in suspension in the unconscious, stored in what he sees as a mythic mode, which "is why the unconscious displays the structure of a private mythology. We can go even further and say not only that the unconscious is 'mythological' but also that . . . modern man's only real contact with cosmic sacrality is effected by the unconscious, whether in his dreams and his imaginative life or in the creations that arise out of the unconscious (poetry, games, spectacles, etc.)" (77n). In finding the source and repository of the sacred (and mythic expressions thereof, including literature and games) in the unconscious, Eliade aligns himself with other theorists whose ideas I have examined in this book. What Eliade's work supplies is an emphasis on sacred time and space as expressed in the world's myths and religions, and his work is therefore of particular interest here.

Literary expressions of the sacred time and space of the archetypal garden (and other such enclosed or isolated structures) are the focus of much of A. Bartlett Giamatti's traditional scholarly work, and he finds the image replicated in playing fields.[4] Among games, baseball is the most reflective of the central mythic concern with time and with going back. Its dimensions and dynamics have a character that was already archaic even as the game came into being. Evolving in a post-Newtonian age,[5] the game is a throwback to a time before modern science (itself signaled by the Newtonian revolution) "deconsecrated" (Dudley Young's term) both time and space and in so doing released into the world, as Dolar claims, the homeless species of the sacred, *das Unheimliche.* Baseball thus preserves aspects of a pre-Newtonian universe, which is typically a circumscribed, closed system in which action is highly ritualized (Young 7). The walled garden, whose timelessness is perhaps its most definitive aspect, is a sort of microcosm not only of the beginning but also of the pre-Newtonian universe, for which baseball's field is a model or metaphor. Baseball presents the dimensions of the gap (the unconscious, the human primordial, the space of art) in a form that reveals both their archetypal nature and a pervasive intertextuality. As discussed previously, archetypes as signifiers tend to bring along their semantic freight, their sacred implications, and traces of their plots. Therefore, in evoking this ancient signifier (this archetype, this bit of intellectual bricolage) of sacred time and space, baseball is itself laden with significance; a myth in game form, baseball both interprets and demands to be interpreted.

I have called baseball "timeless," for one of the truisms of the game is that, unlike almost all other team games, it is not limited by a clock. (Like other truisms, this one is subject to review, but for the moment let it stand.) Baseball's mythology includes the claim that here is a realm, theoretically free of the negative effects of time, where play may last forever. Its units are, as Gail Mazur puts it, "the soothing, unclocked unrolling of . . . innings" (quoted in Gordon, Waller, and Weinman 62), and Roger Angell concurs that inside the park "time moves differently, marked by no clock except the events of the game" (303). Since the progress of the game is measured not by machine but by deed, its participants maintain a measure of control over time. In other words, as in myth, in baseball the laws of nature are superseded by the rules and acts of the game, human constructs enacted on the field. Camille Paglia claims that all culture is "an artificial construction, a defense against nature's power" (1); even so, the astonishing fact of baseball's opposing and maintaining its own temporality against natural or cosmic time remains unique among culture's secular defenses. Baseball's uniqueness lies in the fact that, like a Chomskyan grammar, the game has a built-in recursive rule. In the grammar of the game, when the score is tied at the end of the ninth or any subsequent inning, the rule kicks in, telling the participants to begin again. Baseball's grammar specifies that the game has a potentially infinite number of innings embedded within it. In this way baseball differs not only from other team games but also from ritual, religious or secular. Ritual may proceed more or less slowly, but finite it is, and once done is done. By contrast, there theoretically is no longest game in baseball; as long as its conditions are met, the recursive rule will extend the game into eternity. Of course, in practice a game must end when its players die, just as a sentence must end when a speaker runs out of breath. In both cases there is a discrepancy between the Chomskyan notions of competence and performance. Baseball thus changes the universe with this recursive rule, producing the "feeling that time could be stopped" (Angell 303). In *The Iowa Baseball Confederacy* W. P. Kinsella gestures toward an endless game, a game out of time, when he permits his apocalyptic contest to continue for forty days and over 2,000 innings.

If baseball's rules make limitless future time (eternity) a potential aspect of any single game, however (and therefore of *the* game – "I don't care if I ever get back"), as in Augustine's "divine present," so is past time made accessible or present in numerous implicit ways. The field itself, each game, the players, and all their acts are by nature ritualistic, haunted by the fields, games, players, and deeds that have preceded them, against which they are measured and by which they achieve significance. These old fields, persons, and deeds, carefully preserved as "records," are a past that remains always present. Complementing this notion of a present past is the fact that the men of the game are relatively youthful (they are often called "boys") and appear to live their own pasts in an extended childhood, "playing" rather than "working." Not for these youths the doom of tilling and toiling and eating bread in the sweat of their faces. George Will seems to deny this notion of boys at play with the title of his book *Men at Work,* and although admitting that "ballparks are pleasant places for the multitudes," he finds that the field of play is really a workplace: "For the men who work there, ballparks are for hard, sometimes dangerous, invariably exacting business. Physically strong and fiercely competitive men make their living in those arenas" (5). Nevertheless, he recognizes that this work may not exactly be work: "Most of these men have achieved . . . the happy condition of the fusion of work and play" (5).

It may well be that we make a false distinction between work and play. In ideal circumstances (that is, in sacred time and space, which may obtain for some in the game) work would be play, and play could be significant work. The Greek word for "labors" (including in the term the senses of "tests," "trials," "contests," and "battles") is *athloi,* from which we get our word *athlete,* one who plays or competes. For the Greeks, however, these *athloi* were activities of the warrior aristocracy, skills useful in both battles and friendly games or competitions. As a class such warriors were exempt from labor in its everyday, life-long forms engaged in by the rest of humanity. Perhaps Giamatti suggests a useful distinction between work and play when he associates freedom with the latter term and with the timeless garden: "It is the condition of freedom that paradise signals, and that play or sport . . . wishes to mirror, however fleetingly. . . . [I invoke] paradise as a general condition. . . . The condition is to live in a physical and mental world of choice, where every choice is free of error" (43–44). To go back to the distinction between time and eternity as associated, respectively, with cosmic and mythic time, nature and culture (art, game, narrative), one can say that freedom is realized only through culture, never through nature. Work lines up on the side of nature; play, on the side of culture.[6] Clearly for many the work of baseball is play, an attitude implicit in the declarations of both fictional and real-life folk. Kinsella's Shoeless Joe, for example, says, "I loved the game. . . . I'd have played for food money. I'd have played free and worked for food" (*Shoeless Joe* 15). Pete Rose was reported to have said, "I'd walk through hell in a gasoline suit to keep playing Baseball."[7]

The "game" waged by the warriors at Valhalla provides a useful analogue. One can imagine that paradise – any paradise – with all its advantages, its freedom from time and toil, must eventually grow tedious. (This was a lesson learned by Odysseus on Ogygia. Even Kalypso's granting Odysseus eternal youth and life could not compensate for the lack of meaningful activity. "Let the trial come," he says [Homer 5:87].) Boredom is not a problem in Valhalla, the "home of the slain," however, because the dead warriors continue to do what they did in life. They arise each morning and engage in a no-holds-barred battle among themselves, after which winners and losers alike repair to the meadhall for an evening of feasting, drinking, and retelling the tales of their exploits. Surely the warrior's "work" is not work at all but play. Here is something to do that one does well, and something at stake – winning or losing, living or "dying" – but as in baseball, in these daily contests losing is not final nor mistakes fatal. To put the matter in Giamatti's terminology, each choice is free of error. There is always tomorrow.

Nonheroic work, hard and unremitting, with unforeseeable failures and natural disasters, is the work of time and the fallen world. The contrast between the play of paradise and the work of the world is apparent in Kinsella's *Shoeless Joe*. Ray Kinsella, Adamic protagonist, has Adam's profession. He farms the land – the dust – from which he has been crafted. Unlike Adam, however, from his fallen farm Ray audaciously reclaims Eden, constructing in his cornfield a walled garden of eternal youth. Into this space step long-dead ball players (and in one case an antique never-was ball player) through a mysterious time door in center field. They enter not middle-aged or elderly, as they were at their deaths, but young, as they were at their moments of peak performance. They occupy the mythic present.

Outside the field nature's time proceeds, work goes on, children grow up, and men and women age. Ray Kinsella grapples with this universal human fact: "The process is all so slow. . . . I want it all to happen now. . . . I want whatever miracle I am party to to prosper and grow; I want the dimensions of time that have been loosened from their foundations to entwine like a basketful of bright embroidery threads. But it seems that even for dreams I have to work and wait. It hardly seems fair" (Kinsella, *Shoeless Joe* 25–26). Ray will continue to labor and age, while within the confines of his artifact field, his mythic time shelter, all is play and youth. There the past is present; even his own father is younger than he is. At one point, accentuating this contrast between cosmic and mythic time, nature and art, Eddie Scissons, the "Oldest Living Chicago Cub," watches from Ray's left-field bleachers as the youthful "Kid" Scissons down on the field, in the gap, the timeless realm, takes the mound. This version of the ancient prevaricator is a young man with "a swath of blond hair cascading over his forehead, his body solid, pure, and hard as birch" (224). A similar contrast is noticed imaginatively by Henry Wiggen in *Bang the Drum Slowly*: there is youth on the field and age in the world. The old men hanging at the edges of the game, telling lies, were only yesterday "slim and fast, with a quick eye and great power" (Harris 196). In *The Year the Yankees Lost the Pennant* Joe Boyd drops twenty-nine years as he steps across that curious boundary between the world of ordinary time into the timeless, ever-young field of play. Robert Parker, in his "Spenser's a Fan, Too," draws a similar distinction between inside and outside, the timeless and the timed, culture and nature: "Outside [Fenway Park] there were fathers and sons and overweight women in plastic mesh baseball hats, and scalpers, and pods of young white guys already half gassed, and a couple of old cops with sunburned arms. Inside was eternity. Through the darkness under the stands and up and into the bright green park, bathed in light, changeless and symmetrical, contained, exact, and endlessly different, like water in a stream" (in Gordon, Waller, and Weinman 21). The unidealized scene of the world outside the park, with all its processes and variety (the good, the bad, and the ugly; the orderly and the disorderly; spenders and makers of money; the young and the old; and the male and the female), stands in stark contrast to the idealized bright green park, changeless, symmetrical, and eternal.

Whereas the old of the world frequently become young as they pass into the "bright green park," the process is also reversible. A rapid aging process begins for Joe Boyd even as he thunders down the third-base line on his way home. In *Shoeless Joe* a stunning reversal of the sudden emergence of youth on the field occurs as Moonlight Graham leaves it. Ray describes the transformation: "I see . . . Moonlight Graham loping in from right field, lithe, dark, athletic; the same handsome young man who played that one inning of baseball in 1905. But as he moves closer, his features begin to change, his step slows. He seems to become smaller. His baseball cap is gone, supplanted by a thatch of white hair" (247). Reinforcing the connection between past time made present, youth, and the game is the uniform. Here the boyish cap of the timeless realm is replaced in the world by a thatch of white hair as the player steps from the field. The knickers and knee-length stockings are reminiscent of the garb of boys in an earlier age.

The sense of a realm of eternal youth is enhanced by the seasons and cycles of play. Metaphorically, spring is the season of childhood, summer that of youth, autumn of maturity, and winter of age and death. Baseball's season extends from spring through summer and into early fall. Part of the tradition of perfection is that fall never comes to paradise. For instance, Homer's vision of Elysion "at the world's end" – in sacred time and space – reveals a place where "all existence is a dream of ease" and where winter is unknown:

> Snowfall is never known there, neither long
> frost of winter, nor torrential rain,
> but only mild and lulling airs from Ocean
> bearing refreshment for the souls of men –
> the West Wind always blowing. (4:69)

In the biblical tradition, too, autumn and winter are seasons initiated by the Fall; they are not relevant to mythic or perfected time. It is perhaps psychologically appropriate that in English *fall* (autumn) and *Fall* (the descent from perfection into profane time and space) are homonyms. Karl Shapiro, retelling the story of the Fall in his poem "Adam and Eve," imagines the first humans moving away from Eden, looking back to find the garden burning in fall colors:

> They turned in dark amazement and beheld
> Eden ablaze with fires of red and gold,
> The garden dressed for dying in cold flame,
> And it was autumn, and the present world. (202–5)

So pervasive in baseball is the image of the youthful seasons of clement weather that one often feels the six months that elapse between the final game of one year and the first game of the next to be a period of suspended animation, when nothing consequential happens, or worse, when the laws of cosmic time reassert their sway. So antipathetic is baseball to inclement weather that it suspends play for rain, picking up the action after the delay, as if no time had passed. Although the explanation for this custom is that it is dangerous to play in the rain, no similar argument is advanced in football or soccer. In baseball, then, winter often seems to be an extended rain delay. Like the activities in paradise, baseball is a summer game (as the title of a Roger Angell book declares); the season ends when summer ends, and something is lost.

Giamatti felt this devastation as he contemplated on October 2, at the age of forty, the end of a baseball season and the end of youth: "It breaks your heart. It is designed to break your heart. The game begins in the spring, when everything else begins again, and it blossoms in the summer, filling the afternoons and evenings, and then as soon as the chill rains come, it stops and leaves you to face the fall alone. You count on it, rely on it to buffer the passage of time, to keep the memory of sunshine and high skies alive, and then just when the days are all twilight, when you need it most, it stops" (in Gordon, Waller, and Weinman 142). Giamatti's claim is not that baseball is a season of sunshine and high skies but that one counts on it to keep alive *the memory* of sunshine and high skies, the internalized springs and summers stored in the unconscious, in the realms of desire, the garden, one's youth, and thus the ambience of primordial inner temporality. But the season ends. The sense of timelessness inside the summer fields fails, and each autumn humankind reexperiences the Fall, exile, and exclusion. There may be no cherubim with flaming sword barring the gate, but the garden nevertheless is closed, and it *is* autumn and the present world.

We thus are back in profane time, in nature, with its meaningless rounds, its mere sequence, its progress that kills all persons, just or unjust, and as the Preacher says, where "there is nothing new under the sun" (Eccles. 1:9). Profane time does not give way easily to strong or sacred time; it is always already there, outside the temple, the field, the space of art. For centuries the response to the Preacher's weary cynicism was to say that the broken circles of time are perfected elsewhere, in heaven or in the new earth of Revelation. In the post-Newtonian age, however, one is more likely to understand that the crafted perfection of eternity is always broken by the progress of time. Ironically, the Preacher claims that eternity is an idea that God has "put into man's mind, yet so that he cannot find out what God has done from the beginning to the end" (Eccles. 3:11); that is, for the Preacher, eternity is not a human artifact but a divine deception intended to shield from human awareness the essentially linear progress of things.

Nevertheless, baseball is a similar deception, craftiness, or shield. Its imagined perfection and timeless mode are also broken by the progress of time and made subject to its rhythms. Like it or not, baseball is designed to break your heart. What remains is the sense of (broken) cycle, of eternal return. Chicago television sports announcer Steve Stone closed his last *Tenth Inning* show for the 1991 season – a season of frustrated expectations for the Chicago Cubs – with words of comfort: "There are only 184 days to Opening Day." If we cannot have eternity, we will settle for the eternal round that makes all things new again and, when the time is ripe, reopens the gap for the return of strong or sacred time: "In the game, a new world begins every spring" (Greenberg 90). We will go back to the "beginning of the world."

The artifact of baseball presents desire's attempt to realize perfected time as present, as ritualized, creative repetition, and hence cyclical, not as the linear advance of devouring tide and inevitable extinction. Frye says of the experience of time "in the unfallen state" that it "would be the kind of experience represented by the dancer, whose world is not timeless but where time is the effect of exuberance" (*Myth and Metaphor* 159), or as in baseball, where time is the product of play whose patterns and rounds, like the advent each spring of Opening Day, present opportunity, variation, and return.

Baseball and its texts attempt the mythic task of reconciling time and timelessness. On this point Christian Messenger remarks, "'Creating the field' is expressly linked to 'creating the book' in many baseball novels. . . . An 'interior stadium' [Roger Angell's term] exists where one may defeat time in memory of games and teams, in one's own personal history in relation to the game" (*Sport and the Spirit of Play* 320). Through ritual and word-craft, baseball and its texts, the field and the book, seem, at times, for a while, to succeed.

Such is the complexity of the game, however, that it can manifest not only these timeless and expansive time-as-creative-cycle aspects but also its own stern, unforgiving acceleration of time, its chronometer speeding faster even than clocks in the ordinary world, for its domain is one where men grow old quickly, and like Adam's, the individual's tenure in the garden is brief. As Donald Hall puts it, baseball exaggerates "the rainbow arc all living makes": "When you are in sixth grade, the rook has fuzz on his face and throws to the wrong base; before you leave junior high school, he is a seasoned regular, his body filled out, his jowl rippled with tobacco; when you graduate from high school, he is a grizzled veteran – even if you are not certain what *grizzled* means. In a few years the green shoot becomes the withered stalk, and you learn the shape of the hill all beings travel down" (in Gordon, Waller, and Weinstein 147). Baseball texts can enact this sort of rapid aging or depict the acceleration of time, both of which are common mythic themes. For example, the Irish hero Finn spends three years in Tir na n-Og, the land of youth, but on returning to Ireland finds that, measured by ordinary time, those three years are a life-time, for on touching profane soil he immediately ages three hundred years. The mythic binary opposites of ever-young and soon-old, the hu-man forms of eternity and cosmic time, collide and seek reconciliation in the artifice of the game and its texts.

SPACE: BASEBALL AND THE TEMPLE OF BEING

Being, as itself, spans its own precinct, which is cut off (temnein, tempus) by Be-ing being in the world. Language is the precinct (templum), that is, the house of Being. . . . It is because language is the house of Being that we reach what is by constantly going through this house.
—*Martin Heidegger,* Poetry, Language, Thought *132*

I have called the space of baseball a model or re-presentation of the gap, that is, the temple, the place of language and place where the language of conscious and unconscious meet, the space of art, the text, and the field of contested and colliding meanings. It is here, whether they know it or not, that the mythmakers of baseball dig their pits and fill them with blood for the shades – uncanny denizens of the depths – to drink so as to be able to speak. When they talk, they mention simple subjects named in the Lacanian primary symbols – the body, family relations, birth, life, and death – expressed with infinite variety and complexity. Although they may not know the language of baseball, the shades know the gap, and the di-amond-shaped space into which they step feels familiar; it is archetypal, metaphoric ground, figurative expanse, receptive to their own disrupting, ambiguous rhetoric.

Mythically aware writers assume that they are using myth for their own conscious ends, but myth emerges from the deep, and the space of those texts assures us, whatever conscious filters are applied, that the mythic unconscious will have its say. Secrets will be whispered insidiously through the screen of conscious intent: hatred and terror coexist with love and courage; lust and militant aggression drive the most innocent acts of the game; the field is soul, and soul is not only fountain but cesspool; beneath the manicured, green symmetry (nature dominated and civilized) is a graveyard; the timeless world is the world of both the ever-living and the dead.

The most powerful of conscious filters is the field itself, baseball's plot, the garden paradise with its deceptive claim of eternity. To begin with, the garden of delights is the manifest face, the mask. Other faces, other scenes, are hidden, for as I have shown, it is also world, the place of journey and quest. Behind the masks of garden and world, however, there is also battlefield; behind that, through metaphoric condensation, is the self, one's own inner reaches, and among those inner reaches there is (in a special sense) a primal scene. To change metaphors, the archaeology of the terrain runs deep, layer after layer.

BASEBALL'S FIELD AS BATTLEFIELD

At a relatively shallow level of our dig is the discovery of baseball's space as battlefield. The notion of both Edenic garden and battlefield overlapping in baseball's space raises what Robert J. Higgs sees as a distinction between play and sport. He says that there are two sides to play theory in general, the "Edenic" and the "agonic": the Edenic side of play is "simple, free, nonegalitarian, and noncompetitive"; the "less conspicuous side of play theory," Higgs finds, is agonic, "a competitive or scorekeeping aspect that is analogous to the idea of contests (agon) that lies at the heart of the sport literature tradition." In making this distinction Higgs paraphrases Melville, "in no world but a fallen one could sports exist." Play, Higgs suggests, takes a retrospective view, looking back to "an undifferentiated world of green pastures and murmuring brooks"; by contrast, sport gazes toward a future apocalyptic city "where the winners walk eternally on streets of gold" (148). Of course, the green pastures, the Edenic garden, may be there too in the heavenly city. Characterized in Higgs's terms, baseball is both play and sport, both Edenic and agonic.

In this dual character baseball is in line with mainstream Western mythology, for it is common to find mythic depictions of paradise – either as origin or destination – as places not only of ease and immortality but also of contests and battles, what I call the "officers' club heaven." Baseball's space as battlefield invites a narrative of conflict and redemption through forms of significant, ritualized confrontation. In this respect the mythic archetype of baseball's space is reserved for the elite, the masculine, the bravest and best. The fullest classical depiction of the haven for heroes is found in *The Aeneid*, the description of the "Groves of Blessedness" in the underworld. In its "generous" air and "dazzling light" the heroes of old engage in athletic contests surrounded by the accouterments of their profession: their "phantom armor and chariots" are there; their spears are planted in the ground; and their horses graze nearby. Their pleasure in such activities has been preserved in eternity, or the thousand years it takes to reincarnate souls in Virgil's system (6:846–68).

Another example of the officers' club heaven, and an even closer model of baseball's eternal battlefield and unending battle, is found in the previously discussed northern European tradition. The Nordic *Grimnismal* relates that in Asgard, realm of the gods, near the home of gladness, stands Valhalla, "vast and gold-bright," home of slain warriors. At Valhalla "every morning they arm themselves and fight in the great courtyard and kill one another; every evening they rise again, ride back to the hall and feast" (Crossley-Holland 61). According to tradition they will continue in this way while the world lasts, until the metaphysical winter of winters falls, when in one last battle (a sort of ultimate World Series wherein the forces of order will confront the forces of chaos) all the nine worlds will be destroyed. Baseball's resemblance to this sort of daily, nonfatal battle is emphasized by the character Christy Mathewson in *The Celebrant*: "Baseball is all clean lines and clear decisions. Wouldn't life be far easier if it consisted of a series of definitive calls: safe or out, fair or foul, strike or ball. Oh, for a life like that, where every day produces a clear winner and an equally clear loser, and back to it the next day with the slate wiped clean and the teams starting out equal" (Greenberg 86–87). As at Valhalla, so on the field of play – but not in ordinary life. The ritualized aggression of both Valhalla and baseball field is rule governed (all "clean lines and clear decisions") and endlessly repeatable.

The mythic tendency to build heavens, those ultimately civilized spaces, for warriors and their activities links in the "grammar" of the Western unconscious a paradoxical pair – civilization and combat – in an archetypal signifier of perfected space and time. Baseball, that mythic and most civilized game, reveals this paradox: the battlefield and its violence are clearly there in the serene perfection at the heart of baseball, often displaced, disguised, and rendered symbolic. The nature of bat and ball as weapons has long been acknowledged but treated lightly. For instance, Thomas Boswell, in *How Life Imitates the World Series*, observes that "ever since the first caveman picked up the first cudgel, . . . mankind has known the atavistic power and pleasure of the bat"; as he explains, "from

Robin Hood's quarterstaff to Paul Bunyan's ax, men of myth have loved the taper of a handle, the texture of wood grain, the centrifugal surge in the end of a whirling mass. Axes and stout staves have dwindled in everyday use. Now, that ancient inherited desire for thudding force, for an instrument that will deliver a satisfying blow, has descended to the baseball bat" (in Gordon, Waller, and Weinstein 37). Boswell humorously asserts that the desire to strike a satisfying blow is innate and that although history has provided numerous occasions to realize the "desire for thudding force," now opportunities are few, limited largely to the swinging of a bat and the striking of not flesh and bone but a ball. Boswell uses the term *descended* to describe this evolution, suggesting ironically that baseball is not refined but fallen violence. In any case, Boswell's implication is that a displacement has occurred, wherein the desire to strike has been redirected, the target being no longer other humans but an inanimate object, a point to which I shall return below.

Similarly, in *The Celebrant* Mathewson speculates that the ball and bat originated as weapons and further, that one of these, stone or stick, was the first murder weapon: "Throwing and clubbing. What could be more ancient? . . . We have to grant that our prehistoric forebears employed those same arts against the creatures of nature – indeed, against one another. Even in holy writ, mustn't we imagine that Cain slew Abel with a stone guided by the bare hand, or a club wielded as a bludgeon? Think of it. I stand on the pitcher's mound, the batter at home plate. We are surrounded by every manifestation of civilization. . . . Yet my action in throwing and his in swinging are echoes of the most primitive brutality" (Greenberg 85–86). These ancient impulses are played out in William Kennedy's *Ironweed* when Francis Phelan's throwing skill with a baseball easily reverts to "primitive brutality" and he lets fly a "smooth round stone the weight of a baseball, and brain[s] the scab working as the trolley conductor" (25).

Boswell's and Greenberg's suggestions of a sublimated and displaced aggression at the center of our civilized national game ring true, finding support in an example cited by cultural historian Bill Brown. He reminds us that in the early years of the twentieth century the indigenous inhabitants of Truk were notoriously violent, waging constant battles among themselves. This went on until 1914, when the Japanese, intent on eliminating this threat to commerce, "gave the Trukese a satisfactory substitute for war. They introduced American baseball." Brown comments that "As a mimetic representation of war, the game facilitates both the expression of violence and its restraint, its restraint within the limits of representation, within the regulations of the game." Maintaining many of the preliminary rituals for war, "the island games, substantively different from war, are nonetheless its structural equivalent, leaving the native culture virtually unchanged." Brown points out that an early report of this affair had concluded with the sentence "The natives don't play baseball, they wage it" (51–52).

Part of the conscious appeal of the eternal battlefield, of Valhalla and of baseball, appears to lie in the fact that primitive instincts ("that ancient inherited desire for thudding force") are here permitted expression but are restrained, rule governed. The violence of even the most ruthless and skilled warriors and players is ritualized, made to conform to the rhythm of the day and rules of the game and integrated into a changeless pattern of behavior. The natural consequences of violence – wounds and death – are neutralized in the eternal setting, while winning and losing remain necessary conditions of participation. Nothing is unpredictable, yet infinite variety is possible. Disguised in the punctuated serenity of the game is the combative "play" of Valhalla or the action of baseball as ritualized war of the Trukese. The game is a "satisfactory substitute for war." The players, like the dead and deathless heroes on their eternal battlefields, do not wage war; they play it.[8] Nevertheless, the field can revert quickly and at any moment from playing field to battlefield. A knockdown pitch thrown at the right man at the right time can result in a bench-clearing brawl. In "The Perfect Garden" Tommy Neil Tucker depicts the swift and stunning transformation of garden to battlefield in a scene in which Giller, a batter, attacks Cary, the umpire, with a bat: "Anger suddenly flared across [Giller's] face, and so quickly that you could hardly follow his actions, he rushed the mound and swung his bat at Cary, hitting him across the forehead. Cary fell, pitching forward into a collapsed mass on the ground" (62). The transformation on the field flashes to the stands and reflects the ominous lightning from the heavens. A flooding rain begins to fall "at that moment," and "Equally as suddenly, with the abandonment of something held in too long, the crowd [breaks] loose from the benches and stream[s], yelling and shouting, toward the plate" (62). The "perfect" garden is thus revealed for what it is, an easily and suddenly removable disguise for the battlefield.

The timeless fields of baseball thus avoid the tedium of Ogygia and Eden by incorporating the battlefield within the garden. It is necessary to keep both figures in mind to account for much that is intriguing in baseball literature. Recalling Jewett and Lawrence's claim that "the American monomyth begins and ends in Eden" (169), we must recognize that, as baseball's scene, this is an Eden that not only permits the intrusion of evil but provides space for its ritualized, violent confrontation.

Having uncovered garden and battlefield, however, I am still at a relatively shallow depth in my archaeological exploration of baseball's space. Beneath are deeper levels often camouflaged through authorial or readerly deceptions. The next deepest level discloses the ruins of inner space, clues to whose presence are offered in the configuration of the field itself. This aspect is most apparent when one looks down on the field, seeing it whole, observing its suggestively mystical configurations, an enclosed and squared circle shining in the sun, green, clean, and bright as Dilmun in Sumerian mythology (Kramer 55), its geometry at once contained and yet testing its constraints as its foul lines stretch into infinity. It is a gigantic transformation of the mandala, one of the oldest and most ubiquitous metaphors for both cosmos and self, outer and inner space. Of this symbol Eliade says, "the *mandala* is primarily an *imago mundi;* it represents the cosmos in miniature and, at the same time, the pantheon [assembly of gods]. Its construction is equivalent to a magical re-creation of the world" (*Myth and Reality* 25).

As *imago mundi* the circle of the mandala represents the cosmos, and the square represents the four compass points. It is common to find mandalas depicted wherever space is assigned special significance, especially in places of worship, homes of sacred kings, temples of the gods, and the like. Mark C. Taylor, following Eliade, points out that, psychologically, sacred space differs from profane space in seeming to be "real" or "really existing." Even secular, modern folk, on entering a cathedral, temple, cave, or other such enclosure, may sense a difference. As the only "really existing" place, sacred space constitutes a center (world axle, navel, omphalos) around which profane space spreads out, formless and banal. Sacred space is often felt to be characterized by the potential or actual presence of the supernatural, and sacred time, as experienced within sacred space, is that of the creative moment of origins, when divine presence is most fully realized, when "primordial mythical time is made present" through myth and ritual (Taylor 2).

The configuration of sacred space as mandala is repeated in the baseball field, a transformation of the ancient archetype, which then necessarily carries semantic luggage, appearing itself as an *imago mundi,* an image of the world rendered sacred. The potential implicit in this sort of identification is often exploited in the literature, especially as regards the ballpark at night. A baseball stadium at night may be "more like a church than a church" or "like the inside of a pyramid" (Kinsella, *Shoeless Joe* 160, 161); it may simply be "something awful" – that is, full of awe, the terrifyingly uncanny (Coover 122). Even more holy, sacred, or uncanny is a ball field on a moonless night, as is the case in William Heyen's poem "The Stadium." Fans are forced to light candles, and torches illuminate the diamond. One hears prayers, hymns, and moans, and notices that "makeshift communion rails" line the infield grass. All such evocations of the sacred lead in the closing stanzas to a collective experience of awe or fear and an overwhelming sense of the presence of a modern form of the sacred, the *Unheimliche:* "We've known, all our lives, / that we would gather here in the stadium / on just such a night." Just as winter never comes to paradise, so night, in normal circumstances, never comes to the ballpark; when it does – when the lights go out on a night game, when the moon fails, when the park is empty – one is left with sacred space that fills up with its own uncanniness. It is enough to make "even the bravest" among us "draw [our] difficult breath" (in Johnson 45). Usually, however, the field is flooded with light, and its sacred casts no shadows. Like the holy city, New Jerusalem, it is most often the case that "its gates shall never be shut by day – and there shall be no night there" (Rev. 21:25).

The mandala/field is, however, even more significant as an *imago anima,* representing not the macrocosm, the world rendered sacred, but the microcosm, inner space, soul, self, gap. Sidd Finch, Buddhist monk and fastballer of *The Curious Case of Sidd Finch,* notices this aspect of baseball's space: "A baseball field is something like a mandala – in which the focal point is in the middle of the diamond of the base paths – the pitcher's mound. When I see a pitcher walk across the base paths, on the way there I feel as if he were walking across the silks of a mandala to the center of consciousness" (Plimpton 79–80). In Sara Vogan's *In Shelly's Leg* Margaret, also a pitcher, identifies herself as center, the figurative pitcher's mound, the immovable focal point (221). Giamatti, too, sees the field as a mandala, but for him the center of consciousness is not pitcher's mound but home plate, "the center of all universes, the omphalos, the navel of the world," which "radiates a force," beginning "the dance of line and circle, the encounters of boundary and freedom" (86–87). The field as mandala, then, invites meditation and projection. As *imago mundi* or *imago anima,* this stadium/temple, this space of art, is a place of tension, of opposites in conjunction, of contested meanings. It is in such inner/outer space that myths are told and the shades speak.

BASEBALL'S FIELD AS PRIMAL SCENE

But something is still missing in my exploration of baseball's space. So far in my dig I have found layer after layer of high culture prevailing over nature, artifact over instinct. I have found, for the most part, pleasant, well-intentioned tropes representing this space: the garden, the rule-governed battlefield "surrounded by every manifestation of civilization," and the serene geometry of mandala world and soul. I have yet to uncover any crude, primitive level in this ground, this plot. Although the uncanny may visit, there are no real horrors in all this ordered beauty and controlled play. Does this mythology of baseball indeed control the compelling bioenergies that drive one to feed, to procreate, to plunder, and to love?[9] Where is the Nietzschean night, the pulsing will to power? What, if any, Lacanian ellipses, what significant silences, haunt this idyll? What sort of garden is this? What manner of battle? What manner of soul?

In his poem "The Garden" Andrew Marvell, speaking of another figurative garden, proclaims, " 'Twas beyond a mortal's share / To wander solitary there: / Two paradises 'twere in one, / To live in Paradise alone" (ll. 61–64), that is, without "the woman." In Genesis the human female is generic at first (simply called "the woman"), unnamed until after the Fall, but we know who she is because her son is named for her. She is *Adamah,* ground, earth, the mothering dust from which Adam is crafted, and the mortal part of him, as opposed to the animating breath of the divine father. After the Fall she is transformed, from mother to wife, but named to reveal her origins – Eve, "Mother of all Living," an epithet for the Great Mother, Earth, and the biblical counterpart of the Greek Ge ("Earth"); as Eve she is also like the Greek Pandora, "Giver of All Gifts" (another epithet for the Great Mother), the first woman, *kalon kakon,* "beautiful evil." By a stunning and apparently irreversible metaphoric maneuver, occurring sometime in humankind's prehistory, woman is nature, earth, dust: "You are dust and to dust you shall return" (Gen. 3:19), or in the words of Paracelsus, sixteenth-century alchemist and physician, "Woman . . . is also a field of the earth and not at all different from it. She replaces it, so to speak; she is the field and the garden mold in which the child is sown and planted" (cited in Griffin, *Pornography and Silence* 26). She is mother, bride, origin and destination, womb and tomb. Hers are the ground rules we call nature; hers the inexorable laws against which we construct plots, culture, our shield, our bricolage of myth: "A garden inclosed is my sister, my spouse" (Song of Sol. 4:12).[10]

Nina Baym, remarking that "nature has been feminine and maternal from time immemorial," asserts that nature ("landscape") in the narratives of American authors "has the attributes simultaneously of a virginal bride and a nonthreatening mother; its female qualities are articulated with respect to a male angle of vision: what can nature do for me, asks the hero, what can it give me?" (75). Clearly Baym envisions a benign, helpful nature in male texts, but in the mythology of baseball, at least (and elsewhere as well), the hero is unconsciously concerned with the rhetorical management of a terrifying nature – with the question being not "what can nature do for me" but "what will nature do *to* me," not "what will she give me" but "what will she take away?"

Marvell's speaker's desire to live in paradise alone and his description of his own replica of Eden (the enclosed place to which he retreats) are instructive. He wants to avoid competition and sexual aggression in the world (indeed, to renounce sexuality altogether), and he wants to live forever. Traditional Christianity's view is that sexuality, being "of the flesh," of nature, and therefore associated with woman and death, is dangerous to the immortal soul. Marvell seeks to create a sanctuary from nature by putting on it a mask of culture. Marvell's nature civilized, made artifact, seems almost safe from the woman, yet it is still obviously feminine and sensuous.

As a transformation of the Eden archetype, baseball's garden, like Marvell's, echoes with connotations of this ancient signifier. The ball field's dangers are the dangers of Eden, primordial motherland. The masculine havens of garden and ballpark must exclude the feminine, because the female means death: as a source of sin, woman is death to the immortal soul for Marvell; as the embodiment of raw nature, she is the mothering dust to which all return, and hence death to the individual. As William Irwin Thompson points out, social scientists, artists, and mystics agree that there is an "inseparable relationship between sex and death" (53). The association springs from the identification of woman with nature, the recognition that sexual generation is the problem (asexual generation is a form of immortality),[11] and the resulting vision of woman, as Camille Paglia says, as "the black maw that has spat [man] forth and would devour him again." As a result, "Men, bonding together, invented culture as a defense against nature" (9). Unlike Paglia, I insist on the linguistic foundation of both the archetype and the metaphoric claim that nature is feminine. Nevertheless, its linguisticality does not diminish the impact on Western civilization, on both men and women, of the identification, because metaphoric reality, that is, language-made reality, is most of what we "know," and our judgments about our nature, possibilities, and limitations are based on that language-made reality. Paglia clearly "knows" woman and nature as they have come to her through language, with its ancient, meaning-laden signifiers and archetypes. She says, "The identification of woman with nature is the most troubled and troubling term in this historical argument. Was it ever true? Can it still be true? . . . *I think this identification not myth but reality*" (9; emphasis added). A bit later all tentativity is gone from her pronouncement: "Mythology's identification of woman with nature is correct" (12).

Given the resistance to and arguments against such identification by feminist critics,[12] Paglia may seem simply wrong. The matter is complex, however, and in a profound psychological sense, saying (and the repetitions of millennia) does make it so. As long as language intervenes between us and "reality" (as it must), that reality can be known only through its signifiers, its archetypal and metaphor-made truths, the language into which each of us is born and that, as Lacan says, traps us at birth.[13] In her *Things Invisible to See* Nancy Willard represents an image of such a Lacanian linguistic trap that affects Eve and all her female descendants, including in particular the novel's female protagonist. This linguistic determinism comes in the form of ancient language, paralyzing "spells," "slow, traveling spells," that "come from the darkness that moved on the face of the waters" (246). These primordial waters are waters of life, birth waters through which each of us swims into the world of language. Curiously, Paglia's pronouncement of identity between woman and nature describes a seemingly genderless, language-made reality, one that has imposed and continues to impose on men and women alike. After noticing the tendency of male writers to cast nature as "virginal bride and nonthreatening mother," Nina Baym claims that there are situations in which a woman writer will put "a female construction on nature – as she certainly must from time to time, given the archetypal female resonance of the image" – but asserts that women writers, experiencing a "lack of fit between their own experience and the fictional role assigned to them" are most likely not to "cast themselves as virgin land" but instead to present a female nature as "more active, or to stress its destruction or violation" (75–76).

That women writers do identify women with nature is explicit in Paglia's criticism, however, and that women's baseball fiction does present protagonists identified with nature and field (if not necessarily virgin land) is demonstrated by the works by women I have examined. I have already noted, for example, that Vogan's protagonist, Margaret, identifies herself with the home field, the mound, the "center." Cooney's Gussie Cabrini is "fixed" to the mound, propped on a crutch to pitch, and Cooney's Avis arrives at home plate and figuratively sinks into the ground, wishing only to "be still," and to "stay where she was forever" (207), a permanent fusion of woman, home plate, and the mothering earth, the dust of the ground. The tendency of women writers to present a crippled, one-legged, or paralyzed protagonist as spatial center or ground may suggest something not about actual legs but about the missing figurative third leg, a term for the penis. To be both legless and fixed in place is, it seems, to be woman and nature.

In a more complex identification of woman and nature, Willard's Clare Bishop, paralyzed, confined to a wheelchair, and permanently "at home," is led on spiritual journeys by what seems to be the spirit of nature, a figure known as the Ancestress, a revised form of the Great Mother. When in her journeys Clare visits Ben (who is adrift, in mortal danger, on a raft in the Pacific Ocean), he knows that she is near "by the scent of leeks, and clover, and new-mown grass" (188); that is, she smells like turf, the native land (Cooper 76), and specifically like a baseball field. The grass, however, is Bible grass, a recurring emblem of nature's cycles, the swift running of time, and the brief span of human life: "Ben knew she was near by the scent of leeks and grass (tall grass, tall in the morning, cut down in the evening)" (190), an echo of Psalm 90, for example, where the psalmist declares that "men . . . are like a dream, / like grass which is renewed in the morning: / in the morning it flourishes and is renewed; / in the evening it fades and withers" (ll. 5–6). At one point Clare comes with a shark (a most sinister image) to feed the stranded men; at another, she comes as an albatross, which is shot by Ben's companion and eaten (191). Willard's female protagonist is associated not only with nurture and life and land but with sacrifice, violence, and death.

Clare's traveling "in the spirit" is a way around her paralysis, the immediate cause of which is a baseball batted into the darkness by Ben that hits her on the head. The hidden cause, however, is ancient and linguistic, an archetypal spell-speaking from the beginning of the world. Cold Friday, a medicine woman, identifies and explains the source of Clare's paralysis: "You is conjured with one of the old spells the devil sent out when he took his third of the earth. Them is slow, traveling spells. They come from the darkness that moved on the face of the waters 'fore the earth *was*. And them no-words hid in the water and that no-voice talked it in the water, and it done traveled from water to water, and it done entered the body of Eve. . . . And that spell got itself handed down, hand over hand, 'cause that spell is so evil. The hand that worked the spell on you didn't make it" (246). Cold Friday's claim is that an ancient spell spoken by some primordial uncanniness (a "no-voice") in "no-words" is responsible for Clare's paralysis, a spell that found its first embodiment in Eve, first and archetypal woman, the "mother of all living" and inhabitant of the first garden. Ben, the male protagonist, is only an instrument of the spell. By these figurative means Willard is here advancing a Lacanian theory of language, its antiquity, its lost beginnings, its signifiers and archetypes, and their continuing force in the world of men and women.

Throughout the novel God, baseball, paradise, and time are associated. The baseball is God's instrument for accomplishing events on earth, but it is also the carrier of an ancient spell that infects "the woman" – Eve – and the novel's female protagonist, Clare Bishop. God is pitcher of this baseball: "In Paradise on the banks of the River of Time, the Lord of the Universe is playing ball with His archangels. Hundreds of spheres rest like white stones on the bottom of the river, and hundreds rise like bubbles from the water and fly to His hand that alone brings things to pass and gives them their true colors. What a show!" (3). The one who can hit the pitch out of the park is not Clare but Ben. In her representation of baseball's mythology, Willard has apparently seen its seams, the curious affinity of baseball and language, and something of the ways in which gender relations in the garden rest on ancient rhetoric (speakings, spells, curses) and the ways in which baseball's feminine space is governed by the most complex of ground rules. The ball field/garden, nature prettified, cultured, is a disguise on Earth, Ge, Adamah, Mother Nature, creating a place for bonding and play but carrying an ancient curse. The beauty of Mother Nature is only skin deep. Scratch that skin and you smell Bible grass; you find what Paglia calls "nature's daemonic ugliness" (5), the Great Mother, the female body of death, a woman whose invisible presence is signaled by the smell of a ball field. Woman's body, says Paglia, "is a labyrinth in which man is lost": "It is a walled garden, the medieval *hortus conclusus,* in which nature works its daemonic sorcery. Woman is the primeval fabricator, the real First Mover. She turns a gob of refuse into a spreading web of sentient being, floating on the snaky umbilical by which she leashes every man" (12). Thus, in patterning its space on the ancient archetypes of garden, mandala, and the associated labyrinth, baseball and its mythology enter an enduring archetypal/intertextual realm of signifiers whose truths include the sinister face of Mother Nature, wherein, as in Marvell's "The Garden," one strives to overcome nature by culture so as to live forever in a society of men. If the signifiers reveal an ancient and enduring misogyny, it is a linguistic human bias, apparently shared by both male and female authors, by Paglia and Vogan and Willard no less than by Coover and Kinsella. If, as Lacan believes, language offers its own ways out of linguistic traps, both women and men need to set about reimagining and reshaping this most ancient of metaphors, Mother Nature. Seen from the perspective of long-entrenched figurative truth, Ray Kinsella's making of his ballpark, his walled, masculine playground in the cornfield, is heroic, desperate work. Courage and imagination are needed to transform feminine nature's fatal ugliness so as to raise from the mother mold those with whom she has had her way – Ray's Black Sox, for example. Given the power of the metaphor, Ray's field, like Marvell's garden, "logically" excludes "the woman."

Baseball's mask on the face of nature seldom slips, but occasionally the myths offer a glimpse of the unadorned field. In Coover's *Universal Baseball Association,* for example, Flynn (one of Waugh's "creatures") becomes lost in a pitch-black labyrinth of the sort Paglia has in mind (118–23). It is under the field, and eventually Flynn emerges from it onto the dark, "lifeless" field occupied by phantom players, fixed shapes in frozen postures; in the dugout are spooky benchwarmers. This natural behind the cultured becomes perceptible by night, when the inherent uncanniness of the field is revealed in a dark light. There may be a way out, Flynn thinks, past home plate. If one could just get home, escape might be possible, but the garden/labyrinth is a genuine prison, its shape that of the Great Mother, the female body of death, and Flynn's terror at this recognition is palpable. What Flynn now knows is a version of an ancient vision that prompted the building of both temples and burial grounds in the shape of the Great Mother, the entrance (and exit) made to correspond with the vagina of the goddess (Thompson 263–67), like Paglia's vision of the black maw that spews forth and devours. Elsewhere in the *Universal Baseball Association* the feminine form of the field is underscored when Hettie (Greek *hetara*, "prostitute"), in a sexual analogue of a baseball game, "stretch[es] out as the field, left hand as first base" (206).

Because the secret of baseball's space is that it is feminine, nature disguised as garden, it is often crucial to exclude women from the field to preserve the crafted illusion. Although the women's narratives I have examined are exceptions, in the men's narratives the intrusion of a woman into baseball's sacred space will signal some sort of disaster or inspire some unspeakable act tied in some way to sexual or sexually motivated violence. Coover parodies this grim pathology in an archetypal event celebrated in song: Long Lew Lydell's rape of Harriet Flynn in the visitors' dugout as the "fans" watch. In David Small's *Almost Famous* Noona, spurned by her pitcher-lover, Wally Shaw, charges the mound to "play her particular version of the game," that is, shooting Shaw three times before "the first baseman and the umpire tackled her and threw her out of the game, as it were" (69–70). It is not coincidental that Robert Parker's overweight women (representatives of the well-rounded Great Mother), in their obvious disguises ("plastic mesh baseball hats"), are left outside Fenway Park and its eternal green serenity. These women are perhaps the same group Deena Metzger portrays in "Little League Women" as huge, cow-like figures who eat "grass and men": "What cud there is / once chewed / is spit" (in Chapin 83).

So strong is this theme that we know to expect trouble when a woman enters a player's life. It may come as to Wally Shaw, shot by a woman with a (phallic) gun, as Roy Hobbs is shot first by Harriet Bird and then by Memo Paris. In these three cases the shooting is fatal not to the man but to *the player* and to his tenure in the timeless realm. By her mere presence the woman will complicate the clear patterns of the sporting life, distract the player, jinx him, or otherwise interrupt the progress of his career and the game. Inevitably, by introducing sexuality into the monastic garden, she brings the processes of sexual generation and death. As Paglia puts it, "The serpent is not outside Eve but in her. She is the garden *and* the serpent" (11). Jerome Charyn's protagonist encounters not one but two serpent-Eve figures in the Cottonmouth ladies, mother and daughter, Marylou and Iva (a name pronounceable as "Eve-a"). At one point Babe Ragland encounters "Mama Cottonmouth" in the Fens of Boston, where she desperately searches for a man – "Harvard Jack" – or indeed any "innocent" passer-by. When Babe first spots her through the bushes, he thinks that her hair is "a bushel of snakes: red snakes about to uncoil," and she seduces the Babe on the spot (59–60). So closely is Mama Cottonmouth associated with this sinister swamp, these Fens (the dark underside of the timeless garden, Fenway Park), that she will commit suicide here and continue to haunt the fallen garden wherever it may be encountered (her ghost, "dressed in swamp weeds and a torn blouse," rises at the call of the magician Samuel and appears to Babe Ragland in a Tennessee woods [230–31]).

Nancy Willard's ancient, paradoxical "no-word" spell, infecting the primordial waters and settling first in the body of Eve, is in a sense such a serpent. Clare has inherited that spell, she suffers from a language-made debility, and she smells like a ballpark, a garden. Despite her self-sacrificial, Christlike feeding and healing, despite her humanity, she cannot evade the implications of the textual unconscious: the serpent is inside her; she is the garden *and* the serpent. A similar case involves Lola, Mr. Applegate's minion in *The Year the Yankees Lost the Pennant.* She is a representative of Hecate, the Great Mother in her crone or underworld phase, but appears to Joe disguised as young and beautiful, the Great Mother of the garden. Her purpose is to prevent Joe from exercising his escape clause. "Escape clause" is an interesting term, however, because as Coover's Flynn discovers, there is no way out; there is only the illusion of freedom. Joe's escape would be from youth and eternity (which he enjoys as Mr. Applegate's minion) into the outside world, into profane space, with its process of aging and death but with the implied Christian promise of life after death. Retrieving his soul through the escape, Joe becomes eligible for the other eternal home, heaven. In a way, though, Lola offers within this complex of ideas the Ogygia choice: on the one hand, eternal youth, the sexual favors of a sinister but beautiful immortal, and unending ease; on the other, a life of trial, toil, and death. What is lacking in the first alternative is any real contest. Joe Boyd/Hardy's game is fixed, just as was Odysseus's on Ogygia. Like Odysseus, Joe will choose contest and death, a death whose horrors are attenuated by the implied promise of life after death.

In Joe's case the fatal woman is aligned with baseball, and eternal life beckons from beyond the grave. His choice is complicated because baseball is polluted by association with the woman Lola. When the choice comes down to the woman (death) or baseball (life), however (as it usually does), the choice is simple. As Ward Sullivan, protagonist of *Almost Famous,* considers Blue's demands, he thinks to himself, "She's trying to force me to choose between her and baseball. By God . . . if she pushes me I know what my choice will be" (130). In some respects Ward's girlfriend is the most sinister lady ever to step foot onto a baseball field, but she is sinister in a sort of no-fault, fated way that will lead to her own death and Ward's demise as a player. In fact, Ward, forced to take baseball *and* Blue, ends up killing her (accidentally, it seems), smashing himself up, and retreating to an uncomplicated life of dice baseball, a game into which no woman may intrude and in which the will to power is given free figurative rein.

A common effect of woman's invasion of the player's life is a prolonged, inexplicable slump. Ward Sullivan suffers one and knows that it is Blue's fault (123). Roy Hobbs suffers a slump after his first date with Memo Paris. Both heroes are warned by wisdom figures against involvement with the woman (Pop Fisher tells Roy that Memo is a jinx who "will weaken your strength" [97]; Blue, Wally Shaw suggests ominously, is a peril: "Be careful of your talent" [97]). The dangerous connection between sex and batting is perhaps suggested by Boswell: both are expressions of the "desire for thudding force." The Anglo-Saxon word for intercourse originally meant "to strike" or "to hit," and certainly Coover's Oedipal analysis of pitching and batting recognizes the metaphoric identity. The implication is that sexual contact with a woman drains off the energy of the bat as both object and metaphor. Hence batting within the sacred confines of the field is the figurative or ritual enactment of the dangerous, death-bringing activity in the profane realms outside. It is safe, a satisfactory substitute not only for war but for sex. At the same time, batting in an all-male world deflects sex toward violence and heterosexual activity toward homoerotic, tropological realization; battle may become a sadomasochistic form of sexuality, sanitized, disguised, approved, and innocent. When in *Ironweed* William Kennedy moves the battle and "batting" outside the park, the suppressed implications become manifest. Francis Phelan, armed with a bat and battling the "cops and Legionaires" that constitute "the other team," experiences that thudding force and its sexual associations: "He stepped forward as into a wide pitch and swung his own bat at the man who had struck Rudy. Francis connected with a stroke that would have sent any pitch over any center-field fence in any ball park anywhere, and he clearly heard and truly felt bones crack in the man's back. He watched with all but orgasmic pleasure as the breathless man twisted grotesquely and fell without a sound" (218).

William Irwin Thompson cites a phalanx of social scientists who have argued for the connection between sexuality and male competitive aggression, whose ultimate expression is war and whose cultured equivalent is game. Predictably, Thompson takes us back to the garden to find a "plot": "The fact that the female offers the male a red, attractive apple may express the situation that I am arguing for – that the female first shifts from estrus to attract the male into the new human culture. Out of this seduction, Adam loses his old companionship with the angels and the male god, Jahweh; he responds to his attraction to Eve by resenting her and longing for the good old days of the prelapsarian steady state" (73). Furthermore, he adds, "Sexuality becomes the force for disrupting the old camaraderie of males in groups" (75).

Such forms of speculation are, I believe, more interesting as mythic than as scientific explanations of the lines of human or social evolution. And why this myth? Clearly here we are dealing with an archetype, a signifier, of uncommon persistence and psychological utility. What language-born reality has it produced and perpetuated, and how has that reality encouraged it to proliferate as it has? What language-born reality does it continue to sustain? What intertextual forces are here at play? The application of this tradition of storytelling to the matters at hand reveals a family resemblance. Thompson claims that prelapsarian play and male camaraderie in the presexual gardens were disrupted by the entrance of the first females to abandon estrus and present themselves as always sexually available. Such a female, Thompson claims, exerted a powerful, disruptive force that triggered male aggression: men who had been chums began competing for women and space; male bonds were torn asunder; the social unit of family (mother, father, and child) was established (and with it all the romance and tragedy – Freudian and other – implicated in that institution); and play was displaced by labor as the activity of life outside the garden. The parallels between Thompson's and baseball's myths are apparent. The game returns us to those felicitous days "before," at the beginning, to a collective youth when relations between the sexes and issues of labor, sexuality, generation, and death were still matters of an unregarded and unforeseeable future. I return in chapter 11 to discuss some related matters. For instance, both Thompson and Paglia claim that sadomasochism is an inevitable result of the kinds of reality crafted by such mythic assumptions. Whether sadomasochism typifies the mother-son relationship and, generally, relations between the sexes within baseball's mythology will come into consideration there.

For now, however, I have defined the dimensions of the field of play, its time and space and the kinds of consideration such dimensions render crucial in the stories of the game. For baseball's protagonist, these realities present both opportunities and dangers. His choice often comes down to a heartbreaking, desperate decision: to inhabit the motherland, a garden-seeming space, an archetypal place made of the bricolage of other, failed mythic sites, the scene of innocent ritual, youth, and life, or to attempt the compromises required by life "outside," in profane space and time, with the goddess's often sinister representative, who offers the suspect pleasures of sex, the fruits of generation, and their mythical corollaries of toil, grief, and death.

To demonstrate the working out of typical themes of baseball's time and space, I turn in the next chapter to a consideration of them in W. P. Kinsella's *The Iowa Baseball Confederacy,* a novel more complex and darker than at first appears, and in William Kennedy's *Ironweed.* Both authors are mythmakers, *bricoleurs,* crafting their works from shards and fragments, the materials at hand, transforming old signifiers for service in the present moment. Both test the limits of baseball's dimensions until cracks and seams appear, basic flaws in the design, and then leave their protagonists, travelers both, uncertain residents of the largely uncharted geography of the gap.

6

GOING BACK TO THE MOTHERLAND

W. P. KINSELLA'S *THE IOWA BASEBALL*
CONFEDERACY AND WILLIAM KENNEDY'S
IRONWEED

In Joyce's *Portrait of the Artist as a Young Man,* when Stephen Dedalus's friends ask him whether he loves his mother, he knows that there is no right answer he can give them, and readers know that there is no accurate answer he can give himself. One of the great tensions in the space of art, of which the ballpark is a representation, is the tension between love and hate in male-female relationships, a tension that finds expression in the ancient, ubiquitous, endlessly repeatable archetype, or signifier, of the mother and her relationship to the son. The problem with going back and going home (a preoccupation, as I have shown, of myth and the literal and figurative plot of baseball and much of its literature) is that one is forced to confront that tension and an ambivalence sometimes so severe as to be pathological. On the surface the novels that are the subject of this chapter (Kinsella's *Iowa Baseball Confederacy* and Kennedy's *Ironweed*) seem very dissimilar, and indeed, their differences are legion, not least of which is the greater reach and resonance of *Ironweed*. Nevertheless, they are alike in their focus on going back to the beginning to cure the work of time and in their exploration of the motherland, the universe of their actions – Mother Nature, she who spews forth and devours, that ancient and perhaps least transformed of archetypes and most equivocal of signifiers. The archetype has two faces, space and person. In baseball's mythology this feminine space is baseball field, garden, graveyard, and temple all at once; in her human embodiment she is maiden, mother, and crone. Each protagonist must confront this figure (and her space) in all her ambiguity as beloved and despised, life-giver and destroyer, and resolve, to the extent possible, his conflicting emotions of love and hate, anger and longing, guilt and pride.

Each work provides a theater for an overt reversal of the Oedipal themes of love for the mother and violence against the father, these transformations apparently directing violence against the mother while reconciling fathers and sons. In this way they invoke another archetype, that represented by the *Oresteia,* works that address the kinship preoccupations of the unconscious in ways quite different from the Oedipus myths. At the same time the covert and suppressed Oedipal message nevertheless manifests itself in a palimpsest of conscious and unconscious texts. Within such complexity each novel provides a stage for the equivocal and compelling speech of the uncanny.

GOING BACK TO THE BIG INNING OF THE WORLD

Kinsella's protagonist, Gideon Clarke, inhabits a world in which time is vertically aligned, with past, present, and future stacked up like a three-story building. Transport between present and past is by way of a diamond-shaped elevator, the ball field at Onamata, with access to all levels. Gideon abandons an intolerable present (1978) to return to Big Inning (beginning), the former name of the town Onamata, so as to prove the factuality of a game between the Iowa Baseball Confederacy All-Stars and the Chicago Cubs, a game played seventy years before that has passed from human memory and written records without a trace. This ostensible reason for the journey masks the real purpose, which is to grapple with the mother question.

Kennedy's Francis Phelan (*felon,* "evil, cruel"), the protagonist of *Ironweed,* is likewise one who flees an intolerable situation at home for a journey even longer than that of Odysseus – twenty-two years. His story begins with an epigraph from Dante's *Purgatorio* introducing the theme of flight: "To course o'er better waters now hoists sail the little bark of my wit, leaving behind her a sea so cruel." Francis is a former professional baseball player, a third baseman, "a damn fieldin' machine, fastest ever was" (50), whose skills of fielding and throwing (and his errors) are implicated in key events in his life. The man with a third baseman's sure hands has dropped and killed his infant son, Gerald; the man who unerringly threw to "first or second base, or wherever it needed to go and you're out" (50), also threw a baseball-sized stone with deadly accuracy at a man's skull, killing him (26). Francis has run many times in his life. He thinks of himself as a man "who abandoned his own family . . . every spring and summer . . . when baseball season started" and then abandoned them permanently in 1916, not returning for twenty-two years (26). As Francis explains to the shade of Harold Allen, the man he killed with the stone, there are reasons that he ran: "That stone. The soldiers would've shot me. And I had to play ball – it's what I did. Then I dropped my baby son and he died and I couldn't face that" (26). It is this last "error" and the resulting grief and guilt that have been most devastating. This terrible failure of the fielder's hands has sent him off.

Francis likens his flight to running the bases: "Francis began to run, and in so doing, reconstituted a condition that was as pleasurable to his being as it was natural: the running of bases after the crack of the bat, the running from accusation, the running from the calumny of men and women, the running from family, from bondage, from destitution of spirit through ritualistic straightenings, the running, finally, in a quest for pure flight as a fulfilling mannerism of the spirit" (75). Ironically, though, Francis's own baseball metaphor betrays him, for in his quest for pure flight he embarks on the journey that will return him home, where he began, to face all that he has fled in the first place. This is the situation in which Francis finds himself at the opening of the novel. After twenty-two years of flight and wandering and violence, he has come home, to his city (Albany), his neighborhood, and specifically to the family plot, the home graveyard. Here are buried his father, mother, and infant son. Like Gideon Clarke, Francis has returned to the beginning.

Gideon Clarke's space is charged with the currents of mind and dream, with no clear distinctions to be made between inner and outer space. "Onamata," the name of Gideon's town, illustrates something of the multivalence of the novel's "plot." The official etymology records that the name is "possibly a corruption of the Black Hawk Indian word for magic" (Kinsella, *Iowa Baseball Confederacy* 24), an appropriate enough name for a place where hollyhocks sing and dishes wash themselves, or where lightning strikes a man and implants in his brain the entire history of a lost baseball league. But Gideon knows that Onamata is really the name of Drifting Away's murdered wife and means "traveling woman" (101). Onamata proves to be an angry, vengeful form of both the mother and the land, one whose spirit is not only represented in the town but incarnated in all the women of Gideon's experience, who prove to be travelers too, abandoners. Readers hear in the word also *onomatopoeia,* word magic, the name that is what it says, calling further attention to the feminine form of space in the novel.

In 1978, the novel's present, the field is an image of fallen nature, all "brambles and scrub growth" (127), but in 1908, "in the beginning," it is an image of perfection and, like the traditional paradise, is situated on a hilltop plateau. When Gideon and his friend Stan arrive in 1908, they have traveled not only seventy years, a human lifetime, but farther still, to strong time, sacred time. Stan says, "Even in the dark I can tell the field's perfect" (132). In its unfallen state the mental form of the primeval motherland is the field, nature made artifact, cultured, controlled. Still, this kind of excellence is, Stan says, "too perfect." He fears that playing here would spoil one for playing on ordinary fields: "You'd never feel quite the same way about playing anywhere else" (145), a comment with ominous significance for Gideon.

The origin of this sacred space lies in "time immemorial," but long ago in his shaman's rite Drifting Away recognized it in the form of a baseball field lying mandala-like beneath him (177–78). That was when he looked down from the top of the world, the "center of the sky," encircled by the four "grandfathers," each a divinity representative of a quadrant of space – "black for west, yellow for south, white for north, red for east" (180) – at Mother Earth imaged in the field below, the squared circle. "Baseball is as close to the circle of perfection," Drifting Away says, "as white men are allowed to approach" (177–78).

Standing by the field is mother church, the Twelve-Hour Church of Time Immemorial, which appropriately serves as both dining hall and funeral home, nourisher of the living and receiver of the dead. By the church stands an ironic tree of life and death, which is really a tree of Mother Nature, whose branches are, Drifting Away says, "the arms of Mother Earth" (219). It forms in its multiple trunks its own "small forest . . . a labyrinth" (220), invoking the complex symbolism of the labyrinth, with its notions of feminine space. This strong time and sacred space are cut off, bounded by the county line, as can be seen by the fact that the rain that will last forty days and nights and culminate in the flood that destroys Big Inning falls only in Johnson County (212). In the midst of the forty-day game the members of the Twelve-Hour Church sense that "something of great significance is about to happen," that "the very air is charged with the Spirit" (204). The sinister aspect of feminine space is revealed in the graveyard nearby, a garden dominated by the image of Onamata, Drifting Away's murdered wife, as the Black Angel of Death, a concrete image of rage and malevolent intent sprouted from her grave and standing as a funerary monument until late in the epic game. All these spaces – the field, the church with its labyrinthine tree, the graveyard, and the town itself, Big Inning – are in and of the body of Onamata, primeval space, primordial mother.

The season of Gideon's journey to the beginning, and to the motherland, is high summer (July 4 to the middle of August), when both the hero and the year are still youthful, if no longer young. In *Ironweed,* however, Francis Phelan's journey begins, according to the old Celtic calendar, on the eve of Samain ("end of summer"), the holiest, most dreadful of temporal boundaries, when all the doors between seasons and realms, summer and winter, this world and the otherworld, stand open and the dead crowd in on the living, "the unruly night when grace is always in short supply, and the old and the new dead walk abroad in this land" (29). Samain eve corresponds to Halloween in the Christian calendar, All Hallows Eve. Francis, at fifty-eight, also stands at the doorway of winter, and he encounters the details of mother geography in their winter aspects.

The first of these details is the graveyard where Kathryn Phelan, crone aspect of feminine space, "twitches nervously" as her son approaches. Francis's mother is an uncanny eater, fashioning in her grave crosses from the roots of dandelions and other weeds and consuming them "with an insatiable revulsion" (1–2). Like her, her "garden" is sinister, its blossoms "faded cloth flowers" and "dead gladiolas, still vaguely yellow in their

brown stage of death" (4). The mother's insatiable hunger is the ravenous appetite of the Great Mother, the "great maw" (with a pun on "ma")
for whom the dead are "stacked like cordwood, packaged cookies" (14).
In life, from her youth, Francis's mother has always represented feminine
nature in her negative, devouring phase. Even as she conceives Francis,
she lies on the "wedding bed like a corpse"; like Paglia's nature, she
"writh[es] with the life of newly conceived death": "Francis watched this
primal pool of his own soulish body squirm into burgeoning matter, saw
it change and grow with the speed of light until it was the size of an infant, saw it then yanked roughly out of the maternal cavern by his father,
who straightened him, slapped him into being"(99). The unmitigated
ugliness of this mother archetype is balanced in Francis's late childhood
by his mother's alter ego, her "near-namesake" and next-door neighbor,
the beautiful and seductive Katrina Daugherty. If Kathryn is the death
aspect of the woman, Katrina is exuberant, if voracious, life. In Katrina's
yard grows an emblem of that life, a tree with miraculous vitality, against
which Kathryn directs her energy, trying to kill the tree with salt because
it has been dropping leaves and pods in the Phelans' yard. It nevertheless flourishes, becoming "a giant thing in the world" (100–101). From its
branches Francis, pruning the tree, has been tempted by Katrina walking naked as Eve in the prelapsarian garden. Katrina, along with her garden and vital tree, seems to be the "good mother," nature disguised, appearing to be all that Kathryn is not – warm, loving, and nurturing. Later
Katrina's tree, this same emblematic tree of life/death, will appear transplanted and transformed into an apple tree that grows in the garden of
Francis's wife, Annie, at the home from which he has been absent for
twenty-two years: he "looked out the window. . . out at the collie dog and
the apple tree that grew in this yard but offered shade and blossoms and
fruit to two other yards adjoining, out at the flower beds and the trim grass
and the white wire fence that enclosed it all. So nice" (159). Annie and
her garden are analogues of Katrina and her garden; both represent feminine space, Mother Nature in her life-giving and nurturing phase. Kathryn and her graveyard and the family yard are associated with death. Their
apparently opposite character is illusory, however, as Francis will learn.

It is Annie's garden that the dead transform into a ballpark, the garden scene of Francis's youthful triumphs. Francis looks out an upstairs
window to find the shades that have been haunting him building bleachers (172) and filing silently into them (176). Francis says that they have
been released from the old trunk in the attic that has held the scent of the

reconstituted past and the "untouchable artifacts" of Francis's self and of the baseball career, long over, in which that self was realized. Just as the baseball relics have taken on religious associations, so the ballpark in the garden is transformed again, this time into a church, and the fans become worshipers: "It was a garden of acolytes setting fire to the very air, and then, while Francis watched, the acolytes erupted in song, but a song without sense, a chant to which Francis listened carefully but could make out not a word. . . . It was clear to Francis as he watched this performance . . . that it was happening in an arena of his existence over which he had less control than he first imagined" (180–81). Among these acolytes is the runt (a version of the baseball dwarf), "who knew he didn't belong in this picture," fitting a candle into the hole Francis has bit in the back of his neck. Francis recognizes the runt, and then the hymn as the Dies Irae (Day of Wrath), a hymn for the dead, and he grows fearful (181). Francis, however, has become situated in space: graveyard, childhood garden, Annie's garden, ballpark, church – all are condensed, distilled, collapsed, and disguised to form one space, the motherland. Like Gideon Clarke's, Francis's journey is a retreat, a going back in space and time.[1]

MOTHER, MISTRESS, SISTER, BRIDE

Both Gideon Clarke and Francis Phelan suffer from emotional wounds inflicted by the women in their lives. Moreover, in each case the women, although separate and several in profane space, are representatives of a single woman, crafted through the cultural impositions of language and psychological need, a being of radically dual nature whom Joseph Campbell calls "The Lady of the House of Sleep," a Freudian idea of the imaginative form of the feminine, the mother, the garden. Campbell says of her that "she is the paragon of all paragons of beauty, the reply to all desire, the bliss-bestowing goal of every hero's earthly and unearthly quest. She is mother, sister, mistress, bride. Whatever in the world has lured, whatever has seemed to promise joy, has been premonitory of her existence – in the deep of sleep, if not in the cities and forests of the world. For she is the incarnation of the promise of perfection; the soul's assurance that, at the conclusion of its exile in a world of organized inadequacies, the bliss that once was known will be known again." This is the image of the "good mother," young, beautiful, and comforting, who sleeps, as Campbell says, "in timelessness." She is the Marvellean garden, the perfect field, Katrina's yard with its miraculous tree, and the world when self and world are one. The imagination knows, however (and suppresses the knowledge), that beneath the beauty is the primordial ugliness of nature, the "bad mother," she who devours, denies, or abandons. As bad mother she is "absent [and] unattainable," as well as "desired but forbidden" (*Hero* 110–11). For both Gideon and Francis, the "dream of the promise of perfection" is shaped (and warped) in the unconscious by memories of a monstrous, unloving mother who, like Troy Maxson's mother, is an abandoner, physically or emotionally.

Gideon's mother (the ironically named Darlin' Maudie) leaves him when he is six, taking with her to Chicago his sister, Enola Gay, and his cat. She is thus the first "traveling woman" in his life, and her loss is the most emotionally crippling, exerting the greatest influence on his future relationships. This small, freckled, black-haired, flat-nosed, gap-toothed woman (of whom Enola Gay is a replica [53]) is the one he continues, unaware, to seek.

Gideon's mother has remote origins and numerous incarnations, however, for the pathological pattern is always already there in the inherited language of family, having existed from (the) Big Inning. It existed in Matthew Clarke's generation, influencing his choice of Darlin' Maudie. We learn, for example, that Matthew's sister, Nancy Rae, was also a traveling woman, leaving home at fourteen and last seen hitchhiking toward Chicago (25). The theme of abandonment is played again when Matthew's parents abandon him in early manhood. Thus it is that in Matthew's own House of Sleep there already lies the dangerous, desirable traveling woman. Matthew discovers her only when he "dream[s] his wife," his "ideal woman, conjuring her up from the scarlet blackness beneath his lids" (7–8).

This pursued dream materializes as the enigmatic carnival stripper destined to become wife of Matthew and mother of Gideon. Before he finds her, however, Matthew receives advice from a perhaps truer version of this same woman, a fat, splay-footed, flat-nosed, albino Gypsy fortune-teller in Chicago (revealed as yet another mother by the fact that Gideon, Maudie's son, is a near albino). This emissary of destiny appears from nowhere, directs Matthew back home to Iowa, and disappears (13). Matthew returns and finds Maudie. He falls in love with her and is simultaneously struck by lightning, receiving into his brain the entire history of the Iowa Baseball Confederacy. The league and the woman, story and nature disguised, unrecognized, language and destiny, share the same psychological space. They are one, equally beguiling and inextricably entangled each with the other. When Matthew Clarke is killed by a line drive, the history is "transplanted" to Gideon's brain intact (50), sending him off to continue his father's quest, for the woman and the league are already there, shadowy, inarticulate forms in Gideon's unconscious. So deep is the image of the long-lost mother that when he first sees Sunny, his future wife and replica of Maudie, Gideon falls in love instantly (74). Sunny turns out to be another traveling woman, repeatedly leaving him unannounced and returning without explanation, but it is only after she leaves him for the first time that Gideon realizes the basis of her appeal: "As if I were stepping out of a fog bank, I realized that I was married to a woman as like my mother as it was possible to be. *I want a girl, just like the girl that married dear old Dad.* . . . Shades of Oedipus, his father struck down by a staff on the road to Thebes" (81).

With this recognition Gideon begins to understand how fully his life is determined by forces of which he has been wholly unaware: "Chasing a dream, a dream no one else can see or understand, like running after a butterfly across an endless meadow, is extremely difficult. Now I could see that my father and I shared not only the dream of the Iowa Baseball Confederacy but something else as well, something he must have passed to me through his genes: a fatal fascination for transient women" (82). The fatal fascination Gideon suffers is a universal flaw, for the forms of woman in time are necessarily transient and therefore abandoning and sinister. Gideon here finds his obsession with the mother image to be genetic, a matter of DNA, as instinctual and ancient as humankind, but his first impulse is also a version of the truth: his Lady of the House of Sleep takes her form from an ancient mother archetype. Shades of Oedipus indeed.

Nevertheless, although Gideon's compulsive behavior toward Sunny can be explained by looking to his father's generation, and Matthew's behavior, in turn, by looking to models in his own family, the matter does not stop there. Deeper layers of the past have flaked off and been breathed in, these layers constituting a kind of cultural unconscious where the archetypes abide. Sunny is a woman who comes and goes, impossible to hold ("like smoke," she says), but there is a prototype and namesake in the history of Johnson County – in Big Inning, before it became Onamata, or "traveling woman" – in the person of "Sunny" Foth, who, like Maudie, Enola Gay, and Sunny Clarke, is small and dark with freckles (103). In 1907 (in the beginning) Sunny Foth shot her father, who had molested her, and then, like Sunny Clarke, "vanished like smoke" (109). Earlier still Sunny Foth's mother, another traveling woman, had abandoned her family and left for Chicago (103), the mythic destination of all transient women and origin of the visiting team for the epic game.

There is about all these women aspects of unadorned nature, the bad mother, irresistible and desirable despite danger and abandonment. When Gideon makes his journey back to Big Inning, however, arriving on July 4, he immediately meets and falls in love with Sunny's double, Sarah Swan. Sarah seems to be the paragon of all paragons of virtue of which Campbell speaks, lacking the aspects of the bad mother that the other women manifest. As Gideon will tell himself, whereas his mother, sister, and wife are "all dark spirits," "Sarah is light" (222). What Gideon does not comprehend and apparently will never learn is the necessarily dual aspect of the object of desire, even though this truth will present itself to him in the fact that Onamata, the original traveling woman, "is in all of them" (222), reincarnated in fragments.

In his quest for home, for psychological wholeness and reunion with the lost beloved, Gideon seeks what Joseph Campbell calls "the mystical marriage with the queen goddess of the world," a marriage that represents in one respect "the hero's total mastery of life; for the woman is life." The woman is also death, however, "the mother-destroyer, his inevitable bride" (*Hero* 120–21). Gideon experiences a vague apprehension of that double nature, but he is oblivious to its implications. For instance, at the end of the first day's play, when he says that all day he has seen "the face of a young woman, not exactly Sarah, not exactly Sunny," he turns his mind away from the truth of her. This composite image appearing on the first day of play is repeated metaphorically on the last, when Gideon watches Drifting Away, his double, walk off the field with Onamata in her form as the Black Angel: "The Angel's wings enfolded him and the two of them continued down the line, a statue and a myth halfway to being reunited" (291). This is a truer, more sinister image than Gideon knows, at once self-image and self-deception. For Gideon, the image is romantically satisfying. But is he correct? What he sees is the mortal, although heroic, man in the embrace of the eternal feminine – the Black Angel of Death, his mother, bride, garden, grave. Moreover, Gideon sees the man walking with her off the field, out of the gap, emerging from sacred space into ordinary time and space. Both mythmaker and protagonist pretend that all is well.

Onamata is mother (motherland and nature), however, she who spews forth and devours again, the archetypal Lady of the House of Sleep, infinitely desirable and horrifying. Appearing in this latter-day myth, she is an archetypal signifier, a shard of ancient myth, perhaps even of the Ur-myth, a piece that proves useful – nay, indispensable – to the *bricoleur,* a piece suitable for foundation or keystone. The new structure in which she finds a function turns out to be a narrative of triumph, telling how the protagonist came to terms with the mother-mistress-sister-bride; how she was raped, caged, and slaughtered; how the wild, unknown other became tame, known, encompassed. Critics, who are *bricoleurs* too, participate in the plot – story, space, conspiracy. Onamata is one woman and all women. The violence done her by "the white man" (i.e., by the Western imagination) and her relegation in the novel to a metaphoric existence are by no means anomalous. Even so, the *image* of the Black Angel and Drifting Away has its own message, one emerging from the textual unconscious and contradicting Gideon's narration. Looking straight at the image makes Drifting Away's plight clear. In her death aspect and funerary form, the mother has him enfolded in her wings. He is as good as dead.

Francis Phelan, too, is confronted and mystified by this same figure, and like Gideon he sees her true form without recognizing its implications. Toward the novel's end Francis, drunk in a flophouse, experiences an apparition of the feminine: "In the corner of the room Francis saw three long-skirted women who became four who became three and then four again. Their faces were familiar but he could call none of them by name. Their ages changed when their number changed: now twenty, now sixty, now thirty, now fifty, never childish, never aged" (195–96). Gradually, however, he begins to recognize faces – thousands of women all reduced to a trio plus one, the Fates of Greek myth and the universal mother understood as part of his own life's story: "The faces of all the women Francis had ever known changed with kaleidoscopic swiftness from one to the other to the other on the three female figures in the far corner. The trio sat on straight-backed chairs, witnesses to the whole fabric of Francis's life. His mother was crocheting a Home Sweet Home sampler while Katrina measured off a bolt of new cloth and Helen snipped the ragged threads. Then they all became Annie" (202).

Critics have tended to find in this vision a positive message, a reaction encouraged by the plot. David Black believes that as mother and lovers, here seen as the Moirai, become one woman, Annie, the "Great Goddess," they "merge into one life-giving, love-offering force"; he writes, "Woman manifests the power that moves Francis to heroic action" (184). Similarly, Peter P. Clarke finds that Annie "assumes the role of the Great Earth Mother 'through whom resurrection and new life may be attained'"

(175). Clarke concludes from his analysis of mythic elements in Francis Phelan's story that "the mythological background of *Ironweed* is a rich kaleidoscope of shifting images which elevate and ennoble the people and action of the novel," claiming that the avenging Furies in Francis's life undergo a transformation similar to that depicted in Aeschylus's *Oresteia*; they become, he says, the Eumenides, the Kindly Ones (175).

Mythographers know that Aeschylus too was a *bricoleur,* however. His mythology contained old archetypes, the rubble he found at hand; he fashioned from that wreckage his own system. Indeed, *The Eumenides* illustrates the figurative re-creation of reality by a master metaphor maker, an author who presided over the changing of the gods. The ancient Furies, whom Aeschylus transforms, originally avenged not "the death of a close family member," as Clarke asserts, but specifically matricide; Aeschylus uses them to make new mythic structures that assert the rights of the father over those of the mother and show therefore that Orestes is justified in killing his mother. Clearly the old pre-Greek Mother and her black-shirt guard of Furies have been plotted against, storied into a new mythic system wherein the mother may be killed with impunity, her Furies having been rendered no longer horrifying, maddening, and unappeasable but *kindly!*

Kennedy's plot attempts this same feat. Certainly Francis, like Orestes, entertains homicidal impulses toward his mother. When he encounters Kathryn's grave he thinks that what he should do is "shovel open the grave, crawl down in there, and strangle her bones" (16). Such filial hatred is ignored, however, as a chorus of critics participates in the plot by announcing the transformation of feminine horror into kindness. Even granting that the structure of the plot invites this reading, it is crucial to see that the textual unconscious has another message, one carried along in the figures, the rhetorical strategies, and the images. We have reason to believe that just as Gideon Clarke and Drifting Away are left in ironic and ambiguous circumstances, so is Francis Phelan.

Consider, for example, the novel's depiction of woman as devourer and its recurring images of teeth – both intriguing matters in view of the fact that Francis is nearly always hungry and is almost toothless. I have already remarked that even in her grave Kathryn is an eater; moreover, she is associated with the "great maw," who swallows the dead as if they were cookies. For all her beguiling beauty, Katrina, Kathryn's double, has "large, irregular teeth" (105). She, too, is a devourer, one who, she says, is aptly depicted as a "caged woman ripping apart the body of a living rabbit with her teeth": "Enough, says her keeper, you should not spend all you receive in one day, and he pulls the rabbit from her, letting some of its intestines dangle from her teeth. She remains hungry, with only a taste of what might nourish her." The image is stark and telling, defining the relationship between this "Venus" and Francis, her "Adonis," to whom she makes the sinister declaration, "Oh, little Francis, my rabbit, you must not fear me. I shall not rip you to pieces and let your sweet intestines dangle from my teeth" (109). Katrina says that the caged woman with a rabbit in her teeth "is the true and awful image of this life" (110), an image of relations between the sexes, woman and man, mother and son, that runs like a leitmotif through the novel. This caged, ravenous woman is nature red in tooth and claw, a Blakean horror of bondage and retaliation. Katrina rounds out her self-portrait by calling herself "an innocent monster," a "seductress of children, this caged animal with blood and intestines in her teeth" (111). Moreover, dandelions ("lion teeth") are associated with the dead but eternally living mother as both Kathryn and Katrina: Kathryn weaves crosses from their roots and eats them; Katrina's grave grows "wild with dandelions," a "freakish natural effusion" (111–12). They are, respectively, root and blossom of tooth-flowers, eaters. Clara, irate, hideously seductive on her chamber pot, is also a "monster" who has "most of her teeth" (78). Helen, eternally "pregnant," fat with a killing child-tumor, who sings "My Man" in a bar called "The Guilded Cage" (56), a transform of Katrina's cage, is all of these. She will not eat, however, except in a figurative, sexual sense in Finny's car (89), an act that identifies the great maw with both mouth and vagina of the mother. Peg, Francis's daughter, is of this ilk also, a woman blessed with "the most gorgeous teeth in North America" (183).

This cannibal mother figure is the Universal Mother of whom Annie is the final apparition, an ambiguous figure with false teeth (155). The toothed mouth/vagina of the devourer is a doorway, as in ancient temples, to a "primal location," "a location that evokes in [Francis] not only the memory of years but decades and even more, the memory of epochs, æons, so that he is sure that no matter where he might have sat with a woman and felt this way, whether it was in some ancient cave or some bogside shanty, or on a North Albany lumber pile, he and she would both know that there was something in each of them that had to stop being one and become two . . . when what they are saying has nothing to do with time's forevers but everything to do with the simultaneous recognition of the eternal twain" (156–57). To become one with her satisfies the Freudian tenet in *Beyond the Pleasure Principle* of instinctual desire for restoration of an earlier state, the condition gained by passage through that templar orifice, the great maw, to that primal location of womb and tomb. 'Tis a consummation/consumption devoutly to be wished – and dreaded, with fear and anger directed toward the being so ambiguous, so disfigured and disfiguring.

MATRICIDE!

Whate'er is Born of Mortal Birth,
Must be consumed within the Earth
To rise from Generation free;
Then what have I to do with thee? . . .
Thou Mother of my Mortal part
—William Blake, "To Tirzah"

As I already hinted, another Freud might well have directed his attention to the *Oresteia,* a key narrative as regards the male's relationship with the mother and companion piece to the Oedipus narratives. Here the son does not desire the mother but murders her. The tale reveals an archetypal pathology in the son-mother relationship, one that condones violence against the mother as sanctioned by the male-born (i.e., motherless) goddess Athena. Once mythically privileged, such violence is reenacted not only against the mother per se but also against her emissaries and representatives, against all women with the possible exception of the Virgin – Athena, who converts the Furies to the Kindly Ones, and Mary, her Christian counterpart. As I remarked, baseball's mythology contains bricolage and transformed archetypes from this tale, too; "plotting" against the mother, it disguises its motives and intentions, to be sure, but nevertheless reveals them in a high female mortality rate and a proliferation of violent acts against women. We are led to conclude that mother love and mother hate are mythemic in this body of tales and that the mythic work of bridging the gap between them requires all the tropological arts of displacement and condensation. Despite the mythic work, when all has been said, an unresolved tension remains, a hallmark of this body of myths.

Onamata, primeval mother, is the first matricide in *The Iowa Baseball Confederacy,* and as in the case of the murdered Clytemnestra, the avenging Furies rise from her corpse to pursue, harass, and madden generation after generation of her killer sons, each of whom reenacts the primal crime and suffers the consequences. The Furies, scattered from the murdered mother, in effect inhabit all women. To regain the beloved good mother, the plot reveals, it is necessary to kill again and again. As a result, a pattern of figurative matricide emerges and accelerates as the epic game and the forty-day rain end, when Drifting Away and the Black Angel of Death leave the field together. Now Gideon and Stan are again strangers in the past, where Sarah (Onamata's, Maudie's, and Sunny's representative) is struck and killed by a car. Within a few hours Gideon and Stan will have made their way back to the weed-infested world of 1978 and profane time, where Sunny too is struck and killed by a truck on the highway where she seems to be hitchhiking to Chicago. No body is found; she disappears "like smoke." Shortly Gideon will learn that while he was away Darlin' Maudie and Enola Gay have perished in a fire.

At this point almost all the women in Gideon's life are dead. The narrative has given form to the violent impulse toward the mother by killing off the women while the protagonist and his author stand helplessly by. At this point all but one of the incarnations of Onamata have released the furious fragments of the primal mother's spirit. There remains only Missy, who suffers from Down's syndrome, an eternal child, at once surrogate sister and mother, entangled instead of (or along with) Maudie in Gideon's earliest awareness of love: "One of my first memories, perhaps my very first, is of Missy staring down into my crib, cooing to me in a voice of universal love" (39). It is this mindless and simplest figure of love at the deepest level of the child-mind that the plot will murder last.

SHE WHO WAITS

As the novel closes Gideon and Missy are headed down a dusty road toward Gideon's home, dancing in a sort of exuberant delight. Suddenly Gideon notices that they have almost run into an Indian and his wife who have materialized ahead of them. It seems that the giant Indian and the Black Angel have walked all the way from Big Inning. Gideon looks into the eyes of the man and recognizes Drifting Away. "You made it," Gideon says. "Are you happy?" And then, "Haven't I seen you play baseball?" The Indian replies, "I only pinch-hit one time." "I saw you," Gideon says (309). Drifting Away offers what seems to Gideon a veiled invitation into the past: "Maybe I'll see you at the ballfield in Onamata," he says; then he stares at Missy and adds, "After," implying that any meeting and subsequent time travel must wait until Missy too is eliminated. Gideon immediately thinks of reunion with Sarah. He decides to take the *Baseball*

Encyclopedia with him this time, "A passport": "I take Missy's hand, so happy I think I might explode with joy. We look at our lengthy shadows on the road and realize that the magic has not deserted us after all. My shadow, lank, puppet-jointed, bears the headdress and profile of the classic Indian from the five-dollar gold piece" (309–10).

Does Gideon know at last that he and Drifting Away are one? He has Drifting Away's shadow, but he is "puppet-jointed," still being moved. He rejoices that the magic has not deserted Johnson County; to his mind Big Inning is there, not far away, and its gate is through an abandoned ball field. He has only to wait, bury Missy, and start out again on the long, long journey. Is there cause for optimism? Is he destined to master life and achieve the sacred marriage with the Lady of the House of Sleep? Will he live happily ever after sometime before the world changed? Will his mother-furies be transformed into the Kindly Ones?

Even with our willing suspension of disbelief, on finishing Gideon's tale we do well to be skeptical about all this. Gideon has not changed much. Joe Boyd, recall, matures in the course of his time travels. He loses his overriding passion for baseball, for one thing, and learns to appreciate his home and his life outside the ballpark. Gideon, however, is still obsessed with baseball and with the elusive woman who, he knows, is dead in 1908. Moreover, both Sarah (197) and Drifting Away (246) tell Gideon that he cannot live in the past, and so we must doubt any happy ending even as Gideon experiences his moment of unadulterated joy. We must doubt as well that Gideon can return to a past in which the primordial crime has not been committed, where Onamata as woman is not the embodiment of sexuality and death, and where Drifting Away is not condemned to labor for centuries to expiate his own part in the death so as to redeem a thing so sinister yet so compelling. We suspect, instead, that Gideon is bent on a course that will send him into the past and return him to the present, again and again, forever bereaved of "mother, sister, mistress, bride," ignorant and alone. Gideon abides in the dimensions of myth, wandering in inner space and psychological time, and as Eliot said, "If all time is eternally present / All time is unredeemable." From time immemorial, from the baseball vision of Drifting Away, from the murder of Onamata, and from the lightning bolt that fills Matthew's head with history of the Iowa Baseball Confederacy to the line drive that kills him and transplants that history to his son's brain, to Gideon's final vision of himself as puppet-jointed, with the headdress and profile of the classic Indian, Gideon's story is, as he says of a man fatally struck by lightning, "so biblical. So prophetic. So funny" (45).

And yet, if we step back for a wider view, we may find that the humor disguises something else. In this journey to the temple of art, to the timeless, sacred realms of beginnings, the protagonist has gained little wisdom, and readers have gained little hope for his subsequent felicity. The pathology he inhabits is too ancient, carried along in the genes and the language, in its mythic bricolage and archetypes, mystical lint that clings and will not be shaken loose. Kinsella leaves Gideon, full of joy and plans, dancing down a country road with an idiot, headed home, a near home and a far home. The dusty road is every road; Gideon, every traveler; and his companion, a universal haunt.

This image diverts attention from the fact that the novel plots against the mother by systematically slaughtering her emissaries, carriers of sexuality and death, most of whom are, like Clytemnestra, violent and abusive. From the rape and slaughter of Onamata to the incest against Sunny Foth and her violent retribution, the burning of Darlin' Maudie (an abandoning, sexually promiscuous mother) and Enola Gay (an urban terrorist), the vehicular homicides of Sarah and Sunny, and even the much-anticipated death of Missy (all that dancing should make a congenitally weak heart fail), the real mythos strives unsuccessfully to bridge the gaps between male and female, love and hate, life and death, plotting in the process a return to the beginning, "to cure the work of time."

SHE WHO SURVIVES THE PLOT

Ironweed presents a similar plot, similar mythemic elements, and a similarly unsuccessful attempt to bridge the gap between mythemes. Here, implicitly, is passionate filial love coexisting with equally intense hate. The plot displaces the object of both love and hate so as to realize the conflicting, unspeakable impulses. Francis Phelan has not killed the mother, although he wishes he could strangle her (still "alive") in her grave, but as do elements in *The Iowa Baseball Confederacy,* his story, his plot, kills her and her representatives with impunity. We do not know the cause of Kathryn Phelan's death, but we do know that Francis is glad that she is dead, would kill her again if he could, and imagines that, whereas his father must surely be in heaven, "his mother would be in purgatory, probably for goddamn ever. She wasn't evil enough for hell, shrew of shrews that she was, denier of life" (90). Francis's desire that his mother experience the purgatorial agony forever overtly expresses his hatred. He feels love, too, however, and that love, along with a fair amount of revulsion, is displaced first to Kathryn's "namesake," Katrina, and then to Helen through the image of fire, an ambiguous representation of both sexual passion and hatred. Katrina perishes in a fire, purgatorial flames given physical reality: "Smoke, not fire, killed her, just as the ashes and not the flames of her sensuality had finally smothered her desire" (111). She then is internalized "in the deepest center of the flames, smiling at him with all the lewd beauty of her dreams" (116). Helen, too, is of the character of fire: "Love, you are an unstoppable fire. You burn me, love. I am singed, blackened. Love, I am ashes" (97). Love burns, blackens, kills. Some of the hatred Francis feels for Kathryn is replicated in his relationship with Helen, whom he abuses: at one point he grabs her throat and screams "into her eyes" (83); he later threatens, "I'll black [your eyes] for you. . . . Straighten up or I'm gonna kill you" (84). Francis does not kill Helen, but his narrative does – she dies from the tumor that makes her appear pregnant. In each case the woman is associated with sexuality, fire, love, violence, hatred, and death. Most suggestive of all is the storied end of the prostitute Sandra, dead in the street not of fire but of ice and chewed by dogs (Jezebel's fate), the eater eaten.

We may well wonder at the mythic work performed by mother murder. Orestes kills Clytemnestra and Aegisthus and in so doing avenges his father's murder and gains his patrimony, the throne of Mycenae. In *The Odyssey* Telemachus, for whom Orestes was held up as a model of behavior, does not kill Penelope, for she remains faithful to Odysseus through the long years of his absence, but he does kill other women (household slaves and sexual partners of Odysseus – mother analogues) who have formed liaisons with the suitors. Always the woman who survives is one like Sarah in *The Iowa Baseball Confederacy,* or Annie in *Ironweed,* or Penelope in *The Odyssey,* one who is strong, beautiful, and sensual yet absolutely incapable of forming a relationship with a second man (satisfying, for example, Francis's desire for "a love of his own . . . a love he would never have to share with any man, or boy" [116]); one who waits heroically through nineteen years, or twenty-two years, or for who knows how long for Missy to die; one who waits, as it seems, in eternity, for one man to return home. She who survives the "plot" is that paragon of whom Campbell speaks, the "reply to all desire, the bliss-bestowing goal of every hero's earthly and unearthly quest." She is, in short, a persistent, often-transformed, ancient archetype, a signifying artifact, a fiction emerging from the depths whose form is dictated by the shape of desire, the woman who never was, the enfolding, nurturing, protecting garden of delights. In Francis Phelan's phrase, she is "so nice."

I [Apollo] come . . . to be tried with [Orestes], for I too
Must answer for the murder of his mother.
—Aeschylus, The Eumenides, *114*

In Aeschylus's revisionary mythmaking the primacy of the father over the mother is asserted and upheld in a landmark court decision: the first murder trial. Athena, who passes final judgment, accepts Apollo's argument that the "mother is not a parent"; she is merely the field that receives "the seed which the true parent, the father, / Commits to her as to a stranger" (117). Kinship relations are thus stated in terms that reverse the Oedipal message. The son does not hate and kill the father; he loves him, is loyal to him, and avenges his death. The son does not love and desire the mother, a woman to whom he is not *really* related, but he murders her.

In both stories, however, the father ends up dead – plotted against – and we must conclude that the father's death, obviously of crucial psychological significance, is accompanied by a wrenching ambivalence. It is therefore of interest that in the works under consideration both Gideon Clarke and Francis Phelan not only witness their fathers' deaths but, through sins of omission, help to bring them about. They then live with legacies resulting from the deaths for the rest of their lives. Gideon Clarke watches the fatal line drive come toward his father without a move to prevent its striking him. Gideon says that he believes his father moved his head forward "and allowed the ball to strike him"; "I swear I saw the ball reflected in his pupil" (46). What Gideon does not say is that if he had time to notice these things, then he had time to throw out a hand to deflect the ball. Gideon's legacy is passed immediately, as his brain fills up with his father's knowledge of the Iowa Baseball Confederacy, a bequest that will determine his behavior from then on.

Francis Phelan, too, watches his father die. Francis weeps "out of control" on the day his father is buried, for "he had been there when the train knocked Michael fifty feet in a fatal arc; and the memory tortured him" (15). When he is struck, Michael is walking backward toward Francis, who has brought his father's lunch to the train yard.[2] The text is silent about the fact that Francis has diverted his father's attention and then has uttered no warning cry. Like Gideon Clarke, Francis receives a legacy at the moment of Michael's death, a sort of lifetime pass on every freight train leaving town. The overt message in both texts is of filial love for a father and deep bereavement for his death. Moreover, whereas each son mourns his father's death, neither much regrets his mother's passing. But there are those other messages about both parents. Despite the hatred, the mother continues to be the unrecognized object of her son's quest; similarly, despite the grief, the father, the "true parent," is killed. Tales of both kinship relations are marked by an unconscious, disrupting discourse whose meanings are by no means obvious. I return in chapter 11 to a closer analysis of the textual unconscious in the father-son narratives of baseball's mythology.

"WELL, I'M HOME"

The dimensions of the field of play exert powerful narrative influences on the mythology. The journey home is a journey counterclockwise, back in time, back to the mother (suitably disguised), regressive to the beginning, to strong time, to an earlier condition, with the intention of curing the effects of time. Home is feminine space, ambiguously womb and tomb, garden, field, and graveyard. Hence going back is heroic work; Francis approaches his home limping like Oedipus, and he thinks, "Everything [is] easier than coming home": "But then he came home. He is home now, isn't he? And if he is, the question on the table is: Why is he?" Francis does not know why he travels this most difficult road, but he senses that an unconscious and utterly irresistible force has compelled his return: "Might as well ask the summer birds why they go all the way south and then come back north to the same old place," he tells Annie. Francis's nonanswer to his own question speaks its own unconscious message. Home, for all its dangers, is the destination of all journeys; his own earlier metaphor of running the bases as the image of his life of flight has acknowledged all along his inevitable, determined return. Annie's reply has sinister implications, suggesting a knowledge somehow inappropriate to or surprising in this paragon of all paragons: "Something must've caught you" (160). In the reader's mind flashes the image of Katrina, the caged woman, with the caught rabbit in her teeth. Annie is in a sense caged in the home to which Francis returns, just as Helen was figuratively caged in her self-narrative, epitomized by her singing of "My Man" in the bar called The Guilded Cage. Each woman may be glimpsed, like Katrina, with the rabbit-Francis in her teeth. Both the metaphor of the birds' instinctual migratory circling and the image of the caged woman with the rabbit in her teeth suggest a terrible and necessary symbiosis in man-woman relationships, relationships whose analogues are of predation and consumption. Home is both shelter and cage; once there, one can be fed or eaten. Both possibilities are present in a largely indeterminate play of signs.

As Gideon Clarke's story ends he is heading back to 1908, heading, he believes, to Sarah, the spitting image of his mother, going home. We can only speculate about his future. As Francis Phelan's story ends, he has indeed already come home – to Annie, representative of all women, to Annie's garden, which is Eve's garden, to Annie's attic, which has room for the trunk containing "his reconstituted past" and a cot. From the attic window he watches a neighbor releasing his pigeons, again evoking the notion of unconscious compulsion in coming home, which is also a return to one's cage: "They flew in a big circle and got themselves all worked up, and then old Jake, he'd give 'em the whistle and they'd come back to the cages. Damnedest thing" (226). Do they return to the home-cage because they must? Do they come for food, safety, and "mothering"? Annie clearly mothers Francis. She asks, "What can I make you for lunch?" She asks Francis whether he likes Jell-O, which is suitable fare for the toothless, the very old or the very young. Annie protects Francis from whatever dangers lurk outside the "sanctuary" of the "holy Phelan eaves" (225). As I already suggested, however, the figure of Annie is equivocal. On the one hand she is the paragon, the beloved of whom Campbell speaks, the "good mother." On the other hand she is the keeper of the cage to which Francis is compelled to return. She is nurturing, but potentially devouring. What is the meaning of those false teeth? "What can I make [of] you for lunch?"

Francis looks forward to the time when his cot can be moved to his grandson's room, a "mighty nice little room" (227). It is not the master bedroom, not Annie's room, but a child's room, suitable for occupation by the son in the mother's house. It is "nice," like Annie's garden-ball-park-temple. It may even have hanging on one of its walls a sampler saying "Home Sweet Home," the work of his mother's own hands. What is the human analogue of the whistle calling the pigeons back to their cage? Why do the summer birds come back home, to "the same old place"?

Francis's own summation acknowledges the mysterious ambiguity in the heroic journey home, to the sanctuary/cage to be protected/killed and fed/eaten: "Damnedest thing." The textual unconscious, encoded in image, metaphor, and significant silence, whispers a poignant human message, a message evolving, carried along in the stream of language from time immemorial, one that the mythology of baseball attempts to manage, whose contradictions it attempts to reconcile – a worthy, if seemingly impossible, task. In chapter 11 I return in more detail to the mythology's struggle to reconcile the contradictions of man-woman relationships, especially those of mother and son.

7

THE BALL PARK IS AN ARTIFACT,

MANICURED, SAFE, "SCENE IN AN EASTER EGG,"

AND THE ORDER OF THE BALL GAME,

THE FIRM STRUCTURE WITH THE MYSTERY

OF ACCIDENTS ALWAYS CONTAINED,

NOT THE WILD FIELD WE WANDER IN.

Gail Mazur, "Baseball"

THE CLERGY FILES FROM THE DUGOUT

TO THE MAKESHIFT COMMUNION RAILS

THAT LINE THE INFIELD GRASS.

William Heyen, "The Stadium"

HE IS A LESSON IN THEOLOGY,

MY NEIGHBOR, A FAN OF THE CUBS. . . .

I HAVE HEARD HIM

SUMMER EVENINGS AFTER WORK, EVANGELICAL

IN THE GARDEN.

Larry Moffi, "Comparative Theology"

AT PLAY ON THE FIELDS OF THE GODS

BASEBALL, CONVERSION, AND CRISIS ART

The complex relationships among myth, religion, and literature (or more broadly, the arts or culture) and their evolution through time are a Gordian knot. If we understand religion to inhere in its forms of expression, primarily its texts, and literature (including traditional myth as it has come down to us) broadly to mean "texts," then myth, religion, and literature are overlapping domains. In fact, *myth* and *religion* are often treated as synonymous terms.[1] If we insist that ritual be a part of religion, however, then only those systems or texts currently accompanied by ritual acts of believers could be considered religions. A text may therefore begin as a religious text and evolve into myth. The Homeric Hymn to Demeter, for example, was presumably at one time religious, accompanied by ritual; now, of course, it is not, having become myth.

The relations may be viewed differently, however, with myth rather than religion seen as originary and religion and literature representing two alternative forms. Tzvetan Todorov, discussing the evolution of Northrop Frye's criticism, finds that he moved after a while to a recognition that the affinity between religion and literature exists "not because the latter arises from the former or should replace it, but because both are varieties of mythology, adapted to different societies." The function of both religion and literature is to provide "an imaginative vision of the human situation" (Todorov 102). But there is a problem here as well, for one would have to say that within a single society the imaginative visions of the human situation may take all three forms – religion, literature, and myth – and that if "a myth is a narrative that discloses a sacred world," as Hatab says, and if mythicity inheres equally in modern and ancient texts, as Gould shows, then we may have to abandon our attempts to rectify the boundaries separating the three realms. Indeed, it might be more productive to speak not of boundaries but of common ground and to assert that religions, myths, and literary texts meet in the gap and find common expression in the art emerging from that space. Of all three we can say that when they are most engaged, such expression is not just art or artifact but "crisis art."

Crisis art is born in a linguistic, archetypal, intertextual world, employing all the symbolic and figurative force of language I have thus far considered. Its function, however, is not to express "an imaginative vision of the human situation" (although it may do that too) but rather to permit one to shape, control, and hence to live with or beyond absolute, zero-degree terror. The crisis art expressed as myth/religion is born in the peculiar construction of the human brain, as well as in the mysteries of the human psyche, manifesting the species-specific human propensity for psychic self-defense in forms of religious experience – the meeting of the sacred or uncanny, including visual and auditory visitations, sudden, inexplicable conversions, quid-pro-quo acts of propitiation and expiation, and other types of ritual behavior and narrative shapings. Such experiences are enacted as ritual or drama and narrated as myth or fiction.

All rationalist discourses announcing the present or imminent demise of religious practices and beliefs in the arrival of a secular, scientific age underestimate this psychological predisposition.[2] When Lacan declared that the gods belong in the psychological depths, the "field of the real" (*FCC* 45), the realm from which analysis is barred, the elusive "not nothing," he acknowledged the innateness in human beings of the religious impulse and the tendency toward religious experiences. Such impulses and experiences are borne out by the evidence of history and prehistory, of texts and artifacts, all of which reveal unequivocally that humans are now and always have been religious. Although many wish to claim that religion is a response to ignorance, one properly "outgrown" in a scientific age, humans are religious because they are not and never have been ignorant of ultimate facts. Because they know of human mortality, of the irreconcilable opposition of life and death, they marshal against such knowledge their psychological defenses and predispositions, all their linguistic acumen. They create religions, they undergo religious experiences, and they record them in texts and other art forms. We live in the scientific age, but we encounter the uncanny, the *Unheimliche;* we know, but nevertheless (and therefore) we believe.

Baseball provides a milieu, a symbol system, and a space for religious experiences of all sorts, including the life-altering experience of conversion. In *Ironweed* Francis Phelan, a notably secular, cynical man, takes a rationalist view of his experiences with the uncanny. He believes that he can understand the visitations of the shades as psychological projections, his own creations, and therefore things subject to his control; that is, he knows. Then there comes a moment when he realizes that this is not the case, that the ghosts have a mind- and life-altering reality that he is helpless to resist; that is, he believes. The crucial moment of conversion occurs as Francis watches the spooky backyard baseball fans become "a garden of acolytes" who erupt in a wordless, senseless outpouring of dread, "an antisyllabic lyric," sounding like birds and frogs: "It was clear to Francis as he watched this performance . . . that it was happening in an arena of his existence over which he had less control than he first imagined when Aldo Campione [one of the shades] boarded the bus" (180). The "signals from this time lock" are "ominous"; that is, they are of the character of omens, prophetic signs, messages from another, sacred realm, from the Other, whose peculiar prophet is "the runt," the dwarf "who [knows] he doesn't belong" and through the acknowledgment of whom Francis recognizes "the chant of the acolytes at last as the 'Dies Irae,'" the Day of Wrath, eliciting in Francis a spiritual fear, an "illumination" in the fiery garden that leads to his conversion (180–81).

Francis's terror and conversion within the venue of garden/ballpark/

church are representative of the tragic underside of the mythic/religious experience, an aspect Joseph Campbell sees as central. He says that mythology consists of "a rendition of forms through which the formless Form of forms can be known"; comparative mythology is "a study of the deceptive attributes of being through which the human mind, in various eras and areas of its domain, has been united with the secret cause in tragic terror, and with the human sufferer . . . in tragic pity" (*Primitive Mythology* 55). *Pity* and *terror* are Aristotle's terms to describe the passions inspired and purged by tragedy. Campbell's claim is that they are likewise the primary emotions aroused and purged by those sacred texts (oral or written) that preceded the emergence of tragedy as a genre in Athens in the fifth century B.C.E., as well as those arising spontaneously among other peoples in other times and places. Pity is the outward-directed sorrow for another; terror is self-contained and self-referential. Our neighbor suffers and dies, and we feel pity; for our own suffering and inevitable death we feel terror. The tragic vision, in this view, is at the center of all mythic/religious thought.

The tragic vision of myth/religion can be conveyed and ameliorated only through art, Campbell's "rendition of forms," these forms being constructed from internalized archetypes, from the ruins at hand. Francis Phelan's vision is realized through transformations of ancient archetypes. It is a bricolage of failed and crumbling systems (ancient myth, baseball, Catholicism), structures of meaning, all metaphorically equivalent, that constitute a store of psychological defenses. The vision itself is an artifact taking form in response to Francis's recognition of extreme jeopardy. It emerges within the open space, the temple, of art – for Francis, this garden/ballpark/church. The vision and the narration of that vision are both forms of what I have called crisis art. That crisis lies behind the emergence of art was the insight of Friedrich Nietzsche in his intriguing analysis of Greek drama, *The Birth of Tragedy*. Here is Campbell discussing this point:

> Friedrich Nietzsche, in *The Birth of Tragedy* (1871), wrote of the paralyzing spiritual catastrophe known to mystics as illumination: that glimpse into the ground of being that transforms the spectacle of this world into a display of unsubstantial appearances. India's "veil of Maya," the Buddha's "all life is sorrowful," and Shakespeare's "to be or not to be" are expressions of the insight of this moment; so also, the existentialist "nausea." But how should anyone struck with such a

sense of the senselessness of any form of action in this field of deluding forms be ever recalled to an affirmation of life in this world? Nietzsche's reply is, by art! (*The Sacrifice* 60)

More specifically, Nietzsche claims that "in this supreme jeopardy of the will, art, that sorceress expert in healing, approaches him; only she can turn his fits of nausea into imaginations with which it is possible to live" (Nietzsche 52).

What both Neitzsche and Campbell have in mind is the human-crafted thing raised as a barrier or screen against the fundamental religious recognition of metaphysical horror. The first such art forms are myth and religion. Tragedy is a later, highly evolved art form, yet one with "purely religious origins" (Nietzsche 47).[3] Nietzsche says, "It was to be able to live that the Greeks, out of a profound need, brought forth their gods" (cited in Campbell, *The Sacrifice* 69). Analyzing the gods created out of human need, Nietzsche found two principal types: Dionysos, through whom one experiences "rapture in the violence of that will in nature that pours through time like a torrent, annihilating even while generating the ephemera of what we take to be reality"; and Apollo, through whom one experiences "delight in the beauty of the forms even as they pass – as though to plead, 'if this be a dream, then let me dream!' " These two types result, respectively, in the arts and religions of "impulse" and "measure" (Campbell, *The Sacrifice* 60). The two, representing opposite conditions of the human soul, combine in tragedy, the imaginatively triumphant art form crafted in response to the tragic vision or illumination (Nietzsche 19).

Nietzsche's claim as to the Greeks may be expanded to all humanity: "It is to be able to live that we, out of a profound need, bring forth our gods." In his lectures published as *The Varieties of Religious Experience*, psychologist William James says, "The ancient saying that the first maker of the Gods was fear receives voluminous corroboration from every age of religious history" (74). The need arising from illumination, that blinding glance into the heart of light and its accompanying spiritual nausea, is an aporia, an emptiness that human creativity fills with "gods." This trait explains the seriousness we find in religion and its emphasis on pity and terror. Francis Phelan confirms his own terror, illumination, and conversion as originally Dionysian in a final act of expiation: "Francis walked to the doorway of the freight car and threw the empty whiskey bottle at the moon, an outshoot fading away into the rising sun. The bottle and the moon made music like a soulful banjo when they moved through the heavens, divine harmonies that impelled Francis to leap off the train and seek sanctuary under the holy Phelan eaves" (225). Francis's Dionysian ecstasies, represented in the combined music (art) of whiskey bottle and moon (drunkenness and lunacy), yield to, or perhaps merge with, the clarity and serenity of Apollo, fading away "into the rising sun," Apollo's emblem, the heart of light. It is the artifact, the music, that permits him to live. His conversion complete, Francis heads home at last.

William James likewise argues for the centrality of the tragic in the religious experience, seeing it as the ground bass in the comic score of the human condition, which is why religion is above all *solemn:* " 'religion' . . . signifies always a *serious* state of mind" (41). The religious consciousness often has a "complex sacrificial constitution, in which a higher happiness holds a lower unhappiness in check":

> In the Louvre there is a picture, by Guido Reni, of St. Michael with his foot on Satan's neck. The richness of the picture is in large part due to the fiend's figure being there. The richness of its allegorical meaning also is due to his being there – that is, the world is all the richer for having a devil in it, *so long as we keep our foot upon his neck.* In the religious consciousness, that is just the position in which the fiend, the negative or tragic principle, is found; and for that very reason the religious consciousness is so rich from the emotional point of view. (52)

James calls the fiend "the negative or tragic principle." Characterized in Campbell's terms, he is one of the forms in which "the formless Form of forms" can be known, "one of those deceptive attributes of being" that masks a universal, underlying principle of human life, the face of terror glimpsed in illumination. His ultimate home is the Lacanian field of the real; his essential character, the not nothing. In art he of necessity takes his form from the linguistically accessible archetypal signifiers. One of the forms in which that terror is made visible is Francis Phelan's runt with a votive candle stuck in a hole bitten in his neck. He, like the fiend with a foot on his neck, is one of the forms assumed by the "negative or tragic principle" in the world's crisis art.[4]

Although by its nature the fiendish "secret cause" in tragic terror *is* secret (unconscious, belonging to the field of the real, that realm, as Lacan says, to which approach is barred), and therefore by definition unknowable, we can deduce two of its essentials, death and isolation. Whereas consciousness of mortality, of the ephemeral inconsequentiality of all things, may be primary, spiritual loneliness is nevertheless a significant part of illumination, for the catastrophic spiritual event commonly leaves the individual in a deep and often terrifying metaphysical solitude. Francis's garden illumination, with its chorus of shades, shows him both faces of the fiend. Thus, the awareness of death and the experience of isolation together constitute the core of the fiend's persona.

The reasons for this constitution are not difficult to find. They are (like Gideon Clarke's fascination for transient women) "carried in the genes." As to the first, an aspect of human biology links us with the rest of the animal kingdom and dictates that each individual subject to sexual reproduction will die; another aspect inheres in a peculiarly human characteristic, our awkward triune brain, with a "mind" that inhabits it, partly consciously and partly unconsciously.[5] This latter circumstance establishes that the conscious person is naturally (e.g., of physical necessity) alienated both from his or her unconscious aspect, that demonic Lacanian pit from which the shades emerge, a vast and ancient realm of motives, compulsions, and ideas of whose existence one is unaware but that nevertheless makes itself felt, and from the gap between them that religion/myth – crisis art – attempts to fill.[6] The unconscious, of which Dionysos is often seen as the embodiment, may be the source not only of the spiritual catastrophe known as illumination but also of the art/religion by which one survives the experience. Nietzsche's notion is that consciousness and the unconscious are unequal partners in the imaginative life of the individual, that the "Apollonian consciousness" is "but a thin veil hiding from [one] the whole Dionysiac realm" (28). This psychic lopsidedness produces within the individual an instability, a potential agon of unreconciled, even warring, entities. At any moment, when the thin veil shifts in the wind, a conscious David may be called on to confront an unconscious Goliath. Something like this condition is what James calls the divided self, the likely subject of sudden conversion. All this points to isolation at the center of the human condition and means, John Donne's claim notwithstanding, that each conscious person is an island surrounded by an oceanic unconsciousness, across whose reaches lie other islands, unknowable like ourselves, and other seas.

The analysis that follows, then, focuses on these two aspects of the fiend – death and isolation – and the means by which baseball's myths take up the age-old task of art, the sorceress expert in healing, of confronting him and keeping a foot on his neck.

BASEBALL, DEATH, AND THE DEVIL

Is there a baseball devil?
—W. P. Kinsella, Shoeless Joe *162*

If our foreknowledge of death distinguishes us from other animals, an awareness gained in early childhood and accompanying us like a shadow throughout our entire lives, the common reaction to this sinister knowledge is, as I said, to craft a defense, to make artifacts against oblivion – words spoken of gods, designs for sacred dances or dramas, and scripts, acts, and stories performed and spoken to account for and counteract the pity- and terror-producing fact. William Butler Yeats has in mind such defensive artifacts when, in "Sailing to Byzantium," he writes of the desire to be gathered "into the artifice of eternity." There he will take "such a form as Grecian goldsmiths make," removing himself from the final peril through art.

Like the forms of Grecian goldsmiths, baseball is an artifact, a crafted thing, a game of youth, clement weather, and summer. Its rituals and myths might seem unlikely to hold intimate commerce with themes of death and dying, but that is not the case, for like other myth systems, baseball is obsessed with the negative or tragic element, and like the Reni painting, it is all the richer for having a devil in it, even though its treatment of the topic is not always reverent or even straight-faced. Indeed, humor itself – an aspect perhaps of James's higher happiness or Nietzsche's Apollonian consciousness – may be charged with the task of holding a lower unhappiness (the Dionysian terror) in check; humor, equally with metaphysical joy, may help us keep our foot on the neck of the fiend. *Ironweed,* for all its high seriousness, ambiguity, and terror, is in balance a comic novel.

As I demonstrated in the last chapter, baseball has an array of means for defeating time, and to defeat time is to avoid death. The progress of the game, however, provides ample opportunity for ritual death in a variety of forms. The batter-as-hero faces perils: if he's out, he's dead, and so an out of any kind (a strikeout, a "twin killing," a sacrifice, being caught stealing, etc.) will do him in, although a beanball may do the job in a less allegorical sense. Fielders, too, have their scrapes with disaster: line drives, collisions with teammates or base runners, and dangerous pitfalls and barriers that may or may not be signaled by warning tracks. A relief pitcher may "kill a rally," and a timely pinch hit may "keep the game alive." Our language for these events reveals their symbolic value: these are matters of life and death. The rhythms of the game, inning by inning, imitate cycles of life and death, as does the game as a whole. One team wins (lives), the other loses (dies), and as at Valhalla, the resurrected heroes defeat this death by returning to the battle the next day or the next season.

As the scene of ritual enactment, the field is like other hallowed grounds: the ritual space of primitive celebration, called the "dancing ground" (Young 93–123); the dedicated space of cathedral or temple where rites are performed; or even the consecrated space of burial grounds where services performed for the dead are often intended to ensure the continuing life of the deceased in this or another world. It remains for baseball's mythographers to make the analogies apparent. For instance, as the epigraph from Gail Mazur's "Baseball" suggests, such places are structures wherein predictable (i.e., ritualistic) action occurs and where "the mystery of accidents [is] always contained," as it most certainly is not within the profane world, the "wild field we wander in." And as in Heyen's "The Stadium," there may come a moment when we recognize that the ballpark is indeed a place of worship, where those charged with conducting holy ritual file "from the dugout / to the makeshift communion rails / that line the infield grass." As mentioned, W. P. Kinsella frequently associates the ball field with consecrated space. In *Shoeless Joe* his protagonist, Ray Kinsella, breaks into the Minnesota Twins' park at night, telling his companions, "There's something both eerie and holy about [an empty ballpark]" and "A ballpark at night is more like a church than a church" (160). In *The Iowa Baseball Confederacy* the close proximity of the Twelve-Hour Church and the ballpark at Big Inning, along with the intimate relations between activities on the field and in the church, renders the two sites merely two manifestations of the same holy ground. In a Kinsella short story, "The Last Pennant before Armageddon" (in *The Thrill of the Grass*), Wrigley Field gains sacred significance as scene of the prelude to the last battle and the end of the world. The sacrosanct nature of the field is acknowledged by Jackie Kapp, protagonist of Eric Rolfe Greenberg's *The Celebrant,* in his refusal to set foot on it: "It's a player's place, not mine. I never earned my way, and I'd feel it cheating to steal onto the field" (152).

Such examples make it clear that any action occurring on such hallowed ground will represent significant facts, truths at the edge or even beyond the reach of language. Each event will point beyond itself to the universal, human event, "the Form of forms." Life confronts death in the re-creation of an ancient ritual of stick and stone, bat and ball. We understand that the pitcher's real business is to kill the batter. (Robert Coover's protagonist, Henry Waugh, uses the strikeout sign, a *K* in a circle, to indicate deaths in his baseball league.) But the pitcher is fair game, too, for the batter's real business is to kill him by "hitting him." In baseball narratives there is often a rather fearful symmetry in the deaths of players. For example, in *The Iowa Baseball Confederacy* the two team mascots, Little Walter for the Cubs and Gideon Clarke for the All-Stars, are struck by beanballs; Little Walter is actually killed, and Gideon is rendered unconscious and laid out for dead. In Coover's *Universal Baseball Association* the symmetry is between pitchers: Damon Rutherford is struck by a beanball and killed; Jock Casey, who threw the beanball, is then fatally struck by a line drive. The two events are subsequently collapsed into a single ritual sacrifice. In *The Iowa Baseball Confederacy* the right fielder is struck by lightning ("God's instrument"), translated to heaven before the eyes of players and spectators, and subsequently replaced by the "Black Angel of Death," a funerary monument. In *The Natural* Bump Bailey plays his part by "bumping" the outfield wall with such force that he is killed, to be replaced by Roy Hobbs, his successor and double.

Bump Bailey's semisuicide is not anomalous, for running through the texts is what may be called a suicide motif. In *The Iowa Baseball Confederacy* a strange character named Sigmund Foth, "a man not known to be a fan," blows himself up behind second base, and two of the All-Stars wander from the field to throw themselves into the swollen river. In *The Celebrant* rowdy fans tumble from the grandstand roof to their deaths, and the protagonist's brother commits suicide by driving his car off Coogan's Bluff; it shatters and burns "against the black walls of the Polo Grounds" (264). All in all, the self-caused death is frequent enough to lend eerie echoes to the expression "suicide squeeze." As these images of death accumulate on the game's green expanse, the carnage rivals that of a battlefield in an ironic yet natural qualification of the paradisiacal garden.

I discussed the garden, battlefield, and feminine functions of the field in chapter 5, but the subject of death emphasizes that baseball's sacred space is also graveyard. Historically, burial grounds have been considered holy, and as consecrated ground they were unavailable for the spiritually outcast. Unbaptized children and suicides, for example, have traditionally been refused burial in Christian cemeteries. Ancient Egyptians considered the graveyard, as the dwelling place of ancestors, to be the holiest of sites. The dead are often thought to "live" in such places, to remain accessible through rituals for the dead, or to find there a gateway into another mode of existence.

The baseball field, too, also functions as graveyard; it is not uncommon for this dying place to become a burial ground, taking into itself those who have played and died on it. For instance, most of the many pieces of Sigmund Foth embedded in the field at Big Inning are simply left there or worked in so that the field will be ready for the weekend game (Kinsella, *Iowa Baseball Confederacy* 104). In *Shoeless Joe* Eddie Scissons, "the world's oldest living Chicago Cub," is buried at his own request in a brand-new Cubs uniform in left field. The image of the ancient man buried in the field is echoed in "Mystery Baseball," where "Deep under second base lives an old man, / bearded, said to be / a hundred" (Philip Dacey, in Johnson 18–19). Both old men are in some ways ghosts, spirits of past players and plays who stir and walk in the place where memory and park meet. In the case of Eddie Scissons's funeral, a contingent of pallbearers is drawn from the ghostly team that plays on the field, so the whole affair presents an image of death on death, death and a deeper order of death. In Malamud's *The Natural* Roy Hobbs buries his broken bat, "Wonderboy," in left field, where he has played. The bat, broken in Roy's next-to-last at-bat, is a metaphor for Roy himself. As he buries it, Roy wishes that "it would take root and become a tree" (183). I have already mentioned the graveyard statue, "The Black Angel," that moves from the cemetery to the ball field at Big Inning – an apt emblem of the nature of the space.

Where there are violent deaths, suicides, graves, and funerary statues, it is unsurprising to find spirits, spooks, and other supernatural beings. God "hunkers" in the dugout in Gary Gilder's "Speaking in Tongues" (in Johnson 39); the grandfathers, gods of the four quadrants of the cosmos, appear in the stands dressed in Salvation Army uniforms to play hymns during the seemingly endless game in *The Iowa Baseball Confederacy*. Satan uses the vehicle of baseball to stage a comeback, revising Milton's myth (Philip Wedge, "Satan Vows to Make a Comeback," in Johnson 117). Mr. Applegate from the eternal infernal, a sinister enough Yankees fan, tinkers with the pennant race in *The Year the Yankees Lost the Pennant*. The teams in Philip Dacey's "Mystery Baseball" field an invisible tenth man who taps players on their shoulders or whispers "dark rumors" in their ears (in Johnson 18–19). Francis Phelan's shades construct a ball field and stay to worship there. Roy Hobbs strikes out and sees the form of the dead Bump Bailey "glow red on the wall" where he suffered his fatal collision (Malamud, *The Natural* 214).

The ultimate example of the park-as-graveyard is found in Ray Kinsella's ballpark (which he calls a "giant work of art" [Kinsella, *Shoeless Joe* 261], reminding us of Nietzsche's claim), a park that has been carved from his cornfield. Here is a strangely populous graveyard haunted by benign and comic versions of the sinister tenth man or the glowing, malicious ghost of Bump Bailey. Within the confines of the field – this artifact – ghostly, youthful, vigorous players luxuriate, revitalized; a mood of restrained joy prevails like that which Virgil depicts on the Elysian Fields. The players' ontological status is ambiguous, however. They do not enjoy full life (like Rider Haggard's She, they age and die with stunning swiftness, as the example of Moonlight Graham shows), yet they seem to avoid full death. There are even two orders of half-life on the field, the solid-seeming home team and the translucent phantoms "that might have been outlined and cut from fog" (*Shoeless Joe* 197) against whom they play. Players enter and depart through a makeshift, "very ordinary" door that looks like the mere "shape of a door" sawed in the fence. Even Ray does not know (and does not ask) what orders of being, what worlds, lie beyond. The space of this field, like that in "Mystery Baseball," is skewed, warped out of shape, abutting on uncanny realms from the mere contemplation of which Ray's imagination recoils:

> I try not to wonder what is beyond that gate, to speculate on what kind of limbo my ballplayers lay in. Do they smell of mothballs, like dolls packed away in an old woman's trunk for fifty years? Are they stored on shelves? Is there a warehouse full of ancient baseball players packed away in bales, brittle and dry, faces full of eggshell cracks? Or do they merely move on to another ballpark, another town? . . . Or do my players go back to a phantom hotel, change clothes, and head out to shadowy restaurants, bars, and nightclubs? (260)

The players say only that outside the park they sleep, wait, and dream (221). The field is a green center from which otherworldly dimensions stretch out as far as the mind is willing to go, and possible forms of being assail the imagination. The field itself is not only a place where players enjoy a semi-existence; it is itself of the nature of transition, of "in-between," a composite space where this world and other worlds overlap, where the living, the dead, and the dying meet and play, like Annie Phelan's garden become both ballpark and church filled with ghostly acolytes.

All these examples of the graveyard aspect of baseball fields lead to the conclusion that baseball and its texts, despite our contrary expectations, invite the fiend to the park. This fact then leads to a necessary question: what do they signify, those deaths, those burials, that commerce with the sacred and the spooky? Answering this question requires another excursion into ancient texts.

RITUAL SACRIFICE: LIFE FROM DEATH

I have shown that accidents are held in check in baseball's plot, that the acts and events therein are rule governed and therefore purposeful. There is a name for purposeful death occurring on holy ground in the context of ritual: sacrifice, perhaps the oldest of all sacred rituals[7] and an age-old form of crisis art. Therefore, to understand baseball's insistence on representing death and dying, it will be useful to turn our attention to the nature and functions of ritual sacrifice.

The first thing to recognize about sacrifice is that it is paradoxical. The sacrificial death is performed as a means of fostering life, the force that flows through the natural world (its plants and animals), the human community, and in its metaphysical form, the human soul. Each individual sacrifice is understood as being what Campbell calls a "local representation" of an originary event involving the death of an immortal being "at the beginning" (*The Sacrifice* 37). Examples of dying deities include the Babylonian Tiamat and Kingu, the dying and reviving god Dumuzi, the Egyptian Osiris, the Greek Dionysos and Persephone, the Phrygian Attis, the Norse Ymir, and the Aztec Tlateutli. Some of these are primordial giants whose bodies are used to construct the earth (Tiamat, Ymir, and Tlateutli); others are ritually slain, often as consort/child of the Great Mother, to ensure the continued life of nature or the individual soul (Dumuzi, Osiris, Attis, Adonis, Dionysos, Persephone, and Jesus). The dying god sometimes is taken underground and sometimes is buried in the fields; alternatively he or she may be dismembered and either eaten (Dionysos)[8] or scattered (Osiris). Sometimes the god is consumed symbolically (Jesus).

Addressing the case of the primordial being slain to construct the earth, Campbell offers as paradigmatic the myth of Tlateutli, the originary Aztec immortal. At the beginning this goddess was dismembered, her parts formed into the earth, and she was commanded to bring forth plants and animals, whereupon she developed an insatiable craving for human hearts, requiring countless human sacrifices. It was said that "she would not be quiet until [human hearts] were brought to her. Nor would she bear fruit until she had been drenched with human blood" (*The Sacrifice* 37). Inasmuch as she exacts a terrible quid pro quo, the death of the divine being constitutes both a *giving* and a *taking*. This death, as first death, becomes a model for the individual, the devotee, whose death is rendered meaningful as mimetic of that first death, as partial reparation for it, and as transcendentally identical with it. Campbell explains that two complementary themes are present in the myth of Tlateutli: "One is of death as the generator of life; the other, of self-offering as the way to self-validation. In the symbolism of the sacrifice both are comprehended" (37). Behind this paradoxical approach to keeping a foot on the neck of the fiend is the practical recognition that "life lives on life" (37), alongside some metaphysical sleight of hand whereby, for the mortal individual, death can be made a doorway to life, felicity, reunion, and return to one's proper home. Given such ideas it is not hard to see how sacrifice might become a consummation devoutly wished for among the faithful. Although there are examples of slaves and captives sacrificed in such rites, it was often the case that the slaughter of only the best, the bravest, or the most aristocratic (e.g., the king, the consort/child of the goddess through a human surrogate, or the most skillful athlete)[9] could accomplish the difficult work of the sacrifice, that is, of the artful defeat of death through death.

There is an ironic triumph in these means of managing death. Through ritual and myth, they give humans a measure of control over the ultimately uncontrollable. In the face of the recognition that life lives on life, that death is inevitable as well as terrifying, the ritual deaths yield to the inevitable while removing the element of accident and imposing a sense of purpose on their occurrence. An accompanying myth explains that death, the ultimate horror, is really cause for celebration, the means of achieving life, a theme implicit in Saint Paul's remarks on the death of Jesus: "O death, where is thy sting? O grave, where is thy victory?" (1 Cor. 15:55). In *The Iowa Baseball Confederacy* the original sacrifice of Onamata and the subsequent deaths of those several women in whom her spirit had established residence reveal the reciprocal pattern depicted in the rituals for the goddess Tlateutli. However conceptually gruesome the rite, significance is created and assigned: there is a sense in all these many deaths that the grave is not victorious.

The deaths in baseball's texts often have this sacrificial character. Each is necessary, purposeful, and meaningful; the narratives reveal each to be life enhancing and life restoring, that is, its own opposite. Bruce Pearson's story is of this type: his self-validating death generates life. His death is necessary (he is "doomeded"); it has purpose and significance as revealed in Henry's text (it provides the coherence and spirit required by the team); and it fosters the renewal of both the individual players and the collective life of the team. Red Traphagen advises Henry on the making of his text, saying, "It must be more about Pearson being doomeded," because otherwise, some people will think it is "about baseball or some such stupidity"; he insists, "Stick to Pearson, Pearson. You must write about dying, saying 'Keep death in your mind'" (243–44). Henry knows that baseball is not stupid ("It is a game loved by millions in 4 countries"), and he knows with his artist's sensibility that, although Bruce's death can redeem the team, only the game – its plot in both senses – can redeem Bruce.

Osiris, whose life-restoring death was celebrated in Egypt and elsewhere for over three thousand years (Clark 98), provides the mythic archetype for one of the more bizarre of baseball's sacrifices. The tale, told in *The Iowa Baseball Confederacy* by Marylyle Baron, is that of Sigmund Foth, whose self-sacrifice is an originary event occurring in Big Inning in 1906–7, before the epic, world-changing game in 1908. Sigmund, a mysterious stranger who settles in Big Inning, has a German accent and a German first name, one that calls to mind not only ancient Germanic heroes but also the father of psychoanalysis. He has a non-German last name, however, and looks exotic, fox faced and dark skinned. He is maybe Spanish or Italian, speculates Marylyle, but readers suspect that the exotic element is Native American. His eyes give off light "like jewels way down in a bag" (103), a characteristic he shares with shaman-trickster figures like Loki in Norse myth, for example, or closer to home, Drifting Away, whose eyes also reflect and give off light (176).

Sigmund leads a thoroughly disreputable life in Big Inning. He steals from his neighbors, brutalizes his wife and children, and sexually abuses his daughter. His son leaves home after a brawl with Sigmund, and a year later Irma Foth, his wife (one of the many traveling women of the novel), runs off with a salesman headed for Chicago. Surprisingly, Sigmund grieves inconsolably over his wife's leaving, and not long afterward he drapes dynamite over himself "like armor," goes to the baseball field (Drifting Away's particular space), and blows himself up. As a result, "They didn't find enough of Sigmund Foth to bury" (104). The few pieces they do find are buried in the Lutheran graveyard; the rest is left in the field.

Sigmund's response to Irma's leaving may be unexpected and extreme, but her response to his suicide is at first even more inexplicable. She returns to town and begins a passionate public mourning for her dead husband as she searches for the fragments: "She went around like a diviner, only instead of a forked stick she used her fingers. . . . She'd walk a few steps, her right-hand fingers splayed and stiff, pointin' at the ground. Then she'd stop, sort of frozen like a bird dog, and that Amish boy would start digging. . . . And when he got something dug up, why she'd sift the soil until she found what she was lookin' for, and she'd stuff it into a canvas sack, the kind the mail used to travel in" (107). When she has finished retrieving Foth's body parts, the field looks "as though it ha[s] been shelled." Marylyle adds as an ironic afterthought, "lucky it was fall and the season was over." The sacks containing the body parts are full of life; they chitter like squirrels. Irma returns to the Foths' farm with the sacks, "and the next Sunday Irma and [a reformed – in both senses of the word] Sigmund Foth [come] to the Lutheran Church" (107–8). Sigmund's story has a final dramatic moment when his daughter, full of hatred toward her abusive father, shoots Sigmund on the church steps: "The body of Sigmund Foth then changes form, turns from a body into a stack of canvas mail sacks, each one of them bumping and chittering like something wants out real bad" (109). Sigmund is buried again and his old gravemarker revised: "Sigmund Foth, 1864–1906–1907" (109). Sigmund's story is, as they say, hideously funny. When told in a realistic setting, many aspects of the tale are fantastic, to say the least, but the kernel of the plot is older than history. It is a story of love, death, inconsolable grief, and resurrection. It is, as mentioned, the transformed story of Osiris, Egyptian vegetation (and later universal) god.

Osiris, who embodies the life force of vegetation and therefore of the human community, is killed and dismembered by his brother Seth (another form of the fiend), and the parts are scattered in the fields. Like Irma Foth, Isis, sister and wife of Osiris, "found the fragments of his body . . . and proceeded to put them together, mourning him all the while" (Clark 109). The mourning is loud, ritualized, and public. Once reassembled in mummy form, Osiris enjoys restored power and can, from his position in the underworld, renew the natural world of vegetation in its yearly cycles. One primitive manifestation of Osiris was as a mummy in a linen bag stuffed with grain, a detail that recalls Sigmund in the mail sacks. Clark comments that "if this was watered, the corn sprouted through the meshes of the bag so that the god was seen to grow" (118). We are not told whether Irma used this method. Especially crucial to both tales is the sacrifice of the embodiment of life (divine and human), whose death is, through the reassembly of the dismembered parts and restoration to life, shown to be not death at all but life. This is the paradox and the miracle of the art form called sacrifice, which is stressed in one of the hymns to Osiris: "Osiris! you went away, but you have returned, / you fell asleep, but you have awakened, / you died, but you live again" (quoted in Clark 113). Sigmund, too, died and lived again, and died again. As Osiris is universalized over time, the artifact or text of the god's passion, death, and revival provides a paradigm for containing the death aspect of the fiend: "Osiris was not only the fertility demon turned universal god; he was also the prototype of every soul who hoped to conquer death" (Clark 134).

Transformations of ancient sacrificial archetypes, Sigmund and Irma – back in the beginning – play out a tragicomic version of the drama of death that generates life. Sigmund in the mail sacks, the life power strong in the gobbets of flesh, is the ironic image of Osiris in a bag, waiting to live again and thus to restore life at large. The baseball field, the little world of the epic game, is the field that receives the fragments of Sigmund's body, its green perfection in some sense having been fostered by the sacrifice, as was the vegetation in Egypt by Osiris's death and resurrection. The tale of Osiris is crisis art, a means of managing death and affirming life. Sigmund's tale, a comic, degenerate evocation of the sacrificial archetype, simultaneously requires and defies interpretation. Certainly some of the old meanings and effects are present in Sigmund's tale, and a kind of sinister sacrality inheres in Sigmund's death, life, and death, but the tale is as equivocal as it is evocative. Modern forms of the sacred have rendered the story as ambiguous, as funny, and as uncanny as Sigmund's chittering mailbags and his stuttering grave marker.

My exploration of death in baseball literature has revealed ancient mythic motifs, transformed or deformed archetypes, operating just beneath the surface. The deaths are significant and controlled; they occur within sacred or uncanny time and space and at times perform an astonishing deconstruction through the art of myth and ritual: this apparent death is in fact its opposite, a celebration of life, the defeat of death. This is the situation – in James's phrase – wherein the "complex sacrificial constitution" of the religious consciousness operates and "a higher happiness holds a lower unhappiness in check." Like the Reni painting, baseball's texts are the richer for having a devil in them; also like the painting they usually (but not always) depict the fiend in his death aspect with a foot firmly on his neck. The other aspect of the fiend that I identified – isolation – is complex in both perception and representation, matters to which I now turn.

ISOLATION AND THE ENCHANTED PLACE OF ART

*Since in the world of time every man lives but one life, it is in himself that he must
search for the secret of the garden.*
—Loren Eiseley, cited in Campbell, Creative Mythology 624

*We must pass through solitude and difficulty, isolation and silence, in order to reach
forth to the enchanted place where we can dance our clumsy dance and sing our
sorrowful song.*
—Pablo Neruda, "Toward a Splendid City"

The experience of the "paralyzing spiritual catastrophe known to mystics as *illumination*" of which Nietzsche speaks is not universal. James distinguishes between the healthy minded, "who need to be born only once," and the sick souls, "who must be twice-born in order to be happy" (155). The twice-born are those who undergo the experience known as sudden conversion (a form of Nietzsche's illumination), and James suggests that they become candidates for conversion because they are divided. They sense an inner conflict, a warring of wills, a terrible insufficiency in the recognition not only that, although they wish to live forever, they are tainted with mortality and the stink of death but also, and even more devastating, that they exist in a solitude so absolute that to live they must, as Nietzsche put it, bring forth gods and, as James would add, connect with them. James cites John Bunyan's report of his own spiritual catastrophe to illustrate this sort of psychological division. In his autobiography Bunyan portrays himself as a man at war with himself. He senses a sinfulness, a lack, in the world and himself and feels that evil warring with his immortal soul. He concludes that to settle the inner battle he must "pass a sentence of death upon everything that can properly be called a thing of this life." "This life" means life in the world, as distinct from "the world to come." The things of this world include not only pleasures and Bunyan's wife and children but also temptations, sin, and death. The effect of his illumination is to resolve the inner conflict in favor of life, or immortality in the world to come, and against life in the world. Thus in Bunyan's case the means of resolution involve bringing forth for himself gods ("God through Christ"), with whom he makes connection and who resolve the conflict by validating spiritual life and devaluing temporal life. It is a painfully won resolution, involving removing himself from all contact with wife and children and all the affairs and processes of life, but in the end it is his only means of ending the metaphysical isolation of self from self (James 175).

The illumination or sudden conversion is likely to involve ecstasy, standing outside oneself and hearing as from a separate source the winds that blow from the unconscious. This pneuma may be experienced as a vision or voice of compelling authority, as in Saint Paul's conversion, and often involves not only self-surrender but an absolute change of personality, mind, and heart. Saint Paul, known as Saul of Tarsus, underwent his illumination on the road to Damascus, to which he was traveling for the purpose of persecuting Jesus' followers. His experience involved both visual and auditory elements, a blinding light from heaven and the voice of Jesus commanding him to proceed to Damascus and await further instructions. There his blindness was healed and this most vehement of Christian opponents began to preach in the synagogues that Jesus "is the Son of God" (Acts 9:1–20).[10] The point to be made here is that illumination or conversion is, as Nietzsche says, devastating, producing profound changes of self and behavior, requiring "art" to enable one to return to an affirmation of life in the world. Indeed, when illumination bursts into consciousness, it may come in the form of art.

Baseball's literature provides examples of conversion wherein the art that enables one to live takes its form from the nature of the game. Two such illuminations, symmetrical and complementary, occur in Kinsella's *Shoeless Joe*. Indeed, the novel begins with the first of these, that of Ray Kinsella, who undergoes his spiritual catastrophe while sitting on his verandah at twilight. Like Saint Paul's, Ray's experience involves both vision and audition. He hears not Jesus but the "scratchy Middle American" voice of a ballpark announcer, appropriate accents for what he calls "the great god Baseball" (4, 6). In the world of baseball the announcer, like God in Genesis, speaks events into being. What he says is "official." Ray is the only one who hears the voice booming across the twilight, saying, "If you build it, he will come" (3). The voice is accompanied by a vision: "I instantly envisioned the finished product I was being asked to conceive. I could see the dark, squarish speakers, like ancient sailors' hats, attached to aluminum-painted light standards that glowed down into a baseball field, my present position being directly behind home plate" (3). Unlike Saint Paul, Ray – a post-Freudian, post-Jamesian man – suspects that the source of his conversion from farmer to prophet of the game is within him, erupting from the unconscious, without warning, at the moment of illumination: "Was it really a voice I heard? Or was it perhaps something inside me making a statement that I did not hear with my ears but with my heart? Why should I want to follow this command? But as I ask, I already know the answer. I count the loves of my life: Annie, Karin, Iowa, Baseball. The great god Baseball" (6).

For all his suspicion that the voice has an interior source, it is no less compelling than that heard by Saint Paul or Moses. Like Saint Paul's, Ray's illumination involves not only radical change (he says that a "cosmic jigsaw puzzle" has "altered [his] life" [192]) but risk. And both Saint Paul and Ray respond to spiritual catastrophe by art, by bringing forth gods. Saint Paul creates a religion; Ray creates what seems to be a ballpark but turns out also to be a religion. At one point Ray's uninitiated and disbelieving brother asks, "Is this some kind of religion?" and Ray responds, "It might be" (199). As J. D. Salinger, one of Ray's converts, implies, people will come to the ballpark like pilgrims to a shrine: "They'll watch the game, and it will be as if they have knelt in front of a faith healer, or dipped themselves in magic waters where a saint once rose like a serpent and cast benedictions to the winds like peach petals" (252).

The second illumination in the novel is that of Eddie Scissons. It involves a clear case of ecstasy, of standing beside or outside oneself. It is a shattering, even maddening experience in the Nietzschean mode of paralyzing spiritual catastrophe. Eddie, an ancient man who has lied for years about having pitched three seasons for the Chicago Cubs (1908–10), and therefore being the oldest living Chicago Cub, has the ego-shattering experience of sitting in the left-field bleachers and watching himself as a young man, Kid Scissons, pitch for the Cubs on Ray's phantom field and gain in the process an "infinite ERA." When Kid Scissons is relieved, he "walks off the field, head bowed," and "slumps onto the bench in the dugout"; simultaneously, the ancient Eddie Scissons "sinks slowly to his bleacher seat, looking devastated" (226). The slumping of Kid and the sinking of Eddie are a single gesture of the divided self, a gesture of defeat and unendurable knowledge. Eddie's illumination has forced him to look beyond the veil of Apollonian consciousness into the heart of light; as a result his personality disintegrates and reforms around the experience.

Perhaps he has seen that Kid and Eddie are indeed both ephemera, bubbles of foam on the sea of becoming and, as such, absolutely inconsequential. Whatever the exact nature of his vision, Eddie's next act is predictable. It is, like Saint Paul's, almost a stereotypical response to vision. Having been given a sense of mission, or commission, he must necessarily express and confront it through art, speech, text, or linguistic act. Saint Paul translated his vision into language as he addressed the crowds in the synagogues; Eddie translates his vision for those, living and dead,

assembled in the ballpark. Specifically, Eddie Scissons reveals his knowledge of identity with Kid Scissons by putting on the clothing of his other
self, a Cubs uniform, which is also his burial clothing. Over this he wears
a long pale-gray overcoat, his own type of prophet's garb, and he returns
to the bleachers to offer his own version of Moses on Sinai or Jesus speaking the Sermon on the Mount. Ray remarks, as he and others look up at
Eddie from the left-field grass, that Eddie is "wild and windblown, looking for all the world like an Old Testament prophet on the side of a mountain." The opening words of Eddie's sermon are both "revealed" and
revealing: "I take the word of baseball and begin to talk it. I begin to speak
it. I begin to live it. The word is baseball" (227). Although Eddie's "con-
gregation" is uneasy, he continues, "his voice filled with evangelical fervor." Ray's "god Baseball" has found his prophet; he has laid his hand
on Eddie's mouth, and Eddie cannot choose but speak.[11] New Testament
echoes in "the word" connect the game with the Word, or Logos, Jesus
as depicted in the Gospel of John: "The word of baseball is spirit and it
is life" (229). More emphatically, the word heals: "The word will set captives free. The word will open the eyes of the blind. The word will raise
the dead" (229). This is, of course, what he desires, to be healed of his
division and live forever, for Eddie, in his profound need, has brought
forth his rather Dionysian god on this, the last day of his life. He will be
buried in the vestments of his creed by long-dead ball players acting as
pallbearers, "deep in left field, where the grass is most lush . . . , the col-
or dark and luminous as ripe limes" (198).

Ray's experience of illumination and Eddie's are not only complementary but also mysteriously symbiotic. They are of the same persuasion.
Ray's vision might not have occurred had he not bought the farm from
Eddie; Eddie's vision could not have occurred without Ray's park. There
is a necessity in the relationship and the experiences that bespeaks a
"plan" – whether we call it "cosmic jigsaw puzzle" (as Ray does), predes-
tination, fate, or something else. Although Eddie is dead, Ray's religion
will grow and prosper. His first convert, J. D. Salinger, will be also the first
martyr, undergoing a saintly rapture as one "chosen" to pass through the
center-field gate to whatever mysteries or wonders, whatever modes of
being, whatever deaths or lives, lie beyond.

8

ANY "HABITUAL AND REGULATED ADMIRATION," SAYS PROFESSOR
J. R. SEELEY, "IS WORTHY TO BE CALLED A RELIGION." William James,
Varieties of Religious Experience 76

YES, I WILL BE THY PRIEST, AND BUILD A FANE
IN SOME UNTRODDEN REGION OF MY MIND.
John Keats, "Ode to Psyche"

YOU WERE MADE FOR ONE ANOTHER, MATHEWSON AND YOU. . . .
YOU THINK HE'S A KIND OF GOD, AND I SUSPECT THAT HE SHARES YOUR
BELIEF. Eric Rolfe Greenberg, *The Celebrant* 178

ECSTASY AND ART IN
ERIC ROLFE GREENBERG'S
THE CELEBRANT

 The Celebrant is an extraordinary exploration of fan psychology belonging to the literary tradition of the confession. The novel
presents confessions of a fan, as he calls himself (61), the word *fan* revealing its religious affiliation, for it derives from the word *fanatic,* one who
keeps a fane, a temple or church; *fanatic* has come to designate one who
is possessed by irrational zeal, usually religious or political. The word
Christy Mathewson applies to the narrator is *celebrant,* another word from
the religious lexicon, meaning one who performs or participates in a religious ceremony or rite. Jackie Kapp, the narrator, is one of the best stud-

ies of fan psychology in the form of hero worship since Joseph Conrad's Marlow, the narrator of *Heart of Darkness*. Indeed, the relationship between Marlow and Kurtz is in some ways similar to that between Jackie and Christy Mathewson in *The Celebrant*. Both Kurtz and Mathewson capture the imaginations of the men who tell their stories, men who see them as extraordinary, heroic, godlike. In each case the story told is self-revelatory, depicting the encounter with the Lacanian shades and with apparitions and echoes from the field of the real, where the gods belong. Each is a tale of wisdom won at incalculable cost. In Jackie Kapp's case the narrative reveals the devastations of spiritual catastrophe, the Nietzschean defense of bringing forth gods, and the production of crisis art.

Jackie Kapp's relationship with Mathewson can be usefully compared to that between Eddie Scissons and Kid Scissons, for the similarities of the situations highlight their differences as well. Recall that Eddie sits in the stands and watches a young and athletic version of himself pitch for the Cubs, fail miserably, and retire to the bench in shame and defeat, emotions shared by both Kid and Eddie, for Eddie acknowledges that the two are one and that neither is consequential. His acknowledgment of identity may be seen in his stint of madness as he puts on the uniform of the young pitcher, vestments in which not only to deliver the oration – artifact of his illumination – but also to be buried. Eddie's response is to bring forth the Dionysian divine, wild, windblown, and passionate.

Jackie Kapp, too, sits in the stands and watches a young and athletic version of himself pitch for the Giants, but Christy Mathewson does not fail; rather, he succeeds extraordinarily and leaves the field in triumph. After a brief period of mystical identity with Mathewson, Jackie *consciously* acknowledges their vast differences, seen especially in Mathewson's excellence and his own inadequacy. Like Eddie, Jackie turns to art as a means of expressing his experience, but he chooses an Apollonian mode: craft rather than sermon, patterned beauty rather than rapture, although the Dionysian element is present, too. Another difference is crucial. Eddie's illumination is achieved in anticipation of death and is one of connectedness. Jackie's illumination occurs when he is young (although he feels old), and he will live with the effects of it for the rest of his life. The result is a reverent outpouring of devotion, at once joyous and melancholy, arising from the artist's reaction to the uncommon beauty he both perceives and creates, detached from his conscious ego, its connection to himself denied. Like Bunyan, Jackie will be called on to make sacrifices for his god.

To understand the impact of these events, it is useful to review some facts of Jackie Kapp's character and life leading up to the moment of his illumination. From the beginning his narrative voice is that of a thoughtful, tactful, reserved, and even diffident man who relates the account of his own fanatic attachment to the legendary Giants pitcher, Christy Mathewson, an attachment conceived in 1901 and continuing to 1925, the year of Mathewson's death, and even beyond.

The son of a Jewish immigrant growing up in New York in the waning years of the nineteenth century, Jackie learns both English and baseball on the city streets and becomes a "neighborhood celebrity" (12) as a skillful pitcher with an unhittable curve. When, at the age of seventeen, he is offered a professional contract with the Altoona Club of the New York–Pennsylvania League, his parents will not hear of it (13). Not only are professional athletes held in low esteem, but "all the pressure of a family's traditions, hopes, and plans" descends on Jackie to join the family jewelry business and to do his filial duty by educating the next younger son (14). Forced to choose between family and baseball, Jackie chooses family. As it turns out, however, he has not altogether banished Jackie the pitcher, his emotional identity; he has merely hidden him away in his unconscious interior, a position in which he will assume the lineaments of a god and from which he will one day reemerge with the devastating impact of illumination. In the meantime, Jackie the artist evolves as he discovers a "flair for design" and gradually assumes the task of designing the family line of jewelry. He continues for a while to play baseball as an amateur until his pitching arm fails and "the dream of Altoona and the big leagues" fades, apparently forever. He follows the fortunes of the New York Giants.

Eli, Jackie's older and best-loved brother, is a salesperson for the family business. On his sales trips he often entertains clients at local big-league ballparks. When Jackie joins Eli on one of his trips, they take customers to the ballpark in St. Louis to watch the visiting New York Giants play the local club. Christy Mathewson pitches a no-hitter for the Giants, the occasion of Jackie's illumination. While watching Mathewson pitch, Jackie undergoes a mystic identification with the pitcher that unites the banished and submerged pitcher, the emotional identity, with the drudge in the family business, the conscious identity, through the sensibility of the emerging artist, the lover of beauty. Inevitably, from this moment, beauty, life, and connection will assume for Jackie the form of Christy Mathewson and his feats; Jackie's response to illumination will be art in celebration of Christy Mathewson, hero, other self, and god.

The moment of Jackie's illumination comes in the last inning of the no-hit game, during the description of which Jackie details for his companions Mathewson's strengths and virtues. As Mathewson prepares to pitch the bottom of the ninth inning, on a sweltering July day, Jackie sees that he is "as fresh as when he had begun" (26) and as "young as an April morning" (20). Jackie says, "All question left me. This was Mathewson's place and moment; my whole being was with him" (26). One of the clients mutters, "So young!" and Jackie, actually a year younger than Mathewson, thinks, "And I was old": "My youth had ended on a ragged lot by the Hudson when the curve ball had beaten my arm and my spirit – no, when I'd folded the contract into a drawer and reported for work at Uncle Sid's shop. I was on the road, yes, but as an old man, hawking samples in old men's hotels, learning how I might bet to keep old men happy. I watched Mathewson, and he became my youth" (26). For a while the identification becomes absolute – far closer than that of Eddie and Kid Scissons, even though it could be said that Kid is likewise Eddie's youth. Indeed, Jackie himself pitches the last half-inning: "I waste a pitch high, ball one. I take Warner's toss, wrap the ball in my glove hand . . ." (27). When there are two outs, Jackie hears as from another, distant man "a lone incomprehensible cry from the grandstand." This can only be the cry of Jackie the spectator heard on the field by Jackie the pitcher, the collapse and reunion of the divided self made audible. Yet the cry is "incomprehensible," and it will remain so through the years of Jackie's devotion. He continues with the task at hand: "I turn, I bend, I look for Warner's sign" (27). The last out is made, the no-hitter in hand, and "the crowd's hoarse voice rises in the heat, the Giant bench empties, the fielders race to the mound, and the team leaps to touch and embrace – Mathewson" (27). The division, momentarily healed, is reestablished in the conscious mind. Jackie has started to say "the team leaps to touch and embrace *me*," but he stops himself at the last moment, regains a sort of equilibrium, and substitutes *Mathewson*, reassuming the distance he will seek to maintain (at least at the conscious level) through the course of his long devotion to the remarkable Mathewson.

That same evening Jackie finds himself on the train that the team is taking to Chicago. He stands outside the team car, watching Mathewson as his teammates serenade him; he sees that the pitcher is bigger, more intelligent, and more handsome than anyone else in the car: he was "by far the largest man in the car and, in that company of athletes, the most perfectly formed. His face was made of straight lines: a strong jaw, high cheekbones, a direct nose, a level brow. His eyes were intelligent and alert. His skin was deeply tanned" (29)

To his conscious mind the projected excellence is wholly other now. Jackie seems to have no recognition, or even the memory of recognition, of the brief period of ecstatic identity: "I watched him through my own mirrored image in the glass and sensed an immense distance from him. He was everything I was not. I couldn't approach him; what might I say? . . . There was a gulf between us that I felt I must not cross. I had nothing to offer him" (29). Jackie is now aware only of the immense distance, the gulf, that separates them, of his own inconsequence and the other man's rare beauty. Jackie's sight of both faces at once – Mathewson's viewed through his own reflected image – presents him (if he could understand it) a version of the experience in the ballpark. He sees through himself, looking beyond his own face to an image of aesthetic perfection, unaware of its source.

As I noted, Eddie Scissons's art is Dionysian, wild, windblown, and unrestrained, whereas Jackie's is of a calmer Apollonian sort, which takes delight in the beauty of forms. But it too is crisis art, and in it – as in Attic tragedy – Apollo is joined with Dionysos, the serene with the mad. The passion that generates this art is not the weaker for being shaped and restrained. What it lacks in impulse and rapture it supplies in abundance – love, joy, melancholy, endurance. Predictably, Jackie's crisis art emerges immediately after his double vision – in the park and on the train – and his recognition of the gulf, the abyss, between himself and Mathewson, the other's divinity and his own isolation and insignificance: "I turned and walked back to my compartment . . . and began a sketch. I had in mind a commemorative of the no-hit game, a ring. I drew a square center stone set diagonally in the geometry of the playing field and bordered it with four diamond baguettes. I set it on a shank of gold and on the base I drew words for engraving: *St. Louis / July 15, 1901*" (29).

Like the double image he has just seen, the sketch of the ring is revealing in ways of which Jackie is unaware. He says that the ring is commemorative of the game, but it is more than that. Jackie has reproduced the mandala of the field, that image at once of cosmos and soul, which when crafted into a ring he will present to Mathewson. Diamonds mark the bases and home plate of the larger diamond. Jackie thinks that the center gemstone – a ruby – represents Mathewson (as it does), but again, it signifies more. It represents above all the moment and place of reunion of the divided self, for symbolically the jewels connote "hidden treasures of knowledge and truth"; the cut and polished gem "signifies the soul" (Cooper 89–90). The ring itself is "equated with the personality, and to bestow a ring is to transfer power, to plight a troth, to join personalities" (Cooper 138). From the recesses of his mind Jackie has produced in a code he cannot read the secret of his own spiritual catastrophe; unaware, he has plighted his troth.

There is a way to understand more specifically what has happened to Jackie. William James asks, "Is there, under all the discrepancies of the creeds, a common nucleus to which they bear their testimony unanimously?" He finds that there is such a common nucleus "in which religions all appear to meet." It consists of two parts: "1. An uneasiness; and 2. Its solution": "1. The uneasiness, reduced to its simplest terms, is a sense that there is *something wrong about us* as we naturally stand. 2. The solution is a sense that *we are saved from the wrongness* by making proper connection with the higher powers" (454). For Jackie there is clearly the sense of something wrong about himself, a something that rises to the fore when he watches Mathewson; his salvation from the wrongness occurs in the brief moment of connection, of identity, with Mathewson. What makes Jackie's conversion (and clearly it is a religious conversion, as I will show) so complex is that although an unconscious connection has been made, his conscious mind retreats from it and insists on an immense distance between himself and Mathewson. The proper distance for worship is, according to Jackie, "from afar" (42).

When Jackie is trying to convince Eli to make the ring he has designed, Eli asks, "Can you give me a reason why we should?" (37). Jackie replies that he wants to make the ring because Mathewson is "marvelous," and a bit later he adds, "a miracle"; "I have to let him know that I know" (37), he says. When Eli asks, "With this ring?" – a phrase that echoes a traditional marriage ceremony – Jackie says merely, "Yes" (37). Not understanding, but seeing how important it is to Jackie, Eli agrees to have the ring made, and he even delivers it himself, Jackie being unwilling to cross that gulf. It is the first of seven rings that Jackie will design and have delivered to Mathewson over the years, each representative of a triumphant moment in the athlete's career and yet each, too, both reiteration of the spiritual crisis and profession of faith.

Over the years the relationship between Jackie Kapp and Christy Mathewson is punctuated by three meetings; it evolves pathologically for both worshiper and god; and it ends tragically in a series of events coincident with the debacle of the Black Sox Scandal of 1919. During the interval of eighteen years Mathewson goes mad, and Jackie, not only "fa-natic" but under the influence of Mathewson's delusions, sacrifices his brother Eli on the altar of his faith. By virtue of the distance on which Jackie insists, he fails to recognize the effect that his offerings have on the object of his devotion. Readers, nevertheless, perceive the incipience of Mathewson's later madness in his reaction to the first offering. Mathewson sends a note of appreciation, saying that Jackie's artistry, in its field, "certainly surpasses my own in mine" (38), a figurative reflection of the connection Jackie has forged through pitching, and making Mathewson's "artistry" a metaphor for Jackie's "pitching." If Mathewson is sincere, should we suspect that both devotion and need flow back from "god" to man? Eli reports that Mathewson "appeared *fascinated* that his achievement had moved a spectator to create such a souvenir. He neither declined the ring nor offered to pay for it." Jackie thinks that this shows the pitcher "accepted it in the spirit of its giving" (39; emphasis added). Recognizing the profound, largely unconscious motives for the gift, we may hear something disquieting in these words, as indeed we should.

The first two meetings serve to intensify Jackie's sense of Mathewson's superhuman excellence. The initial meeting occurs when McGraw, the Giants' volatile manager, leads Eli and a reluctant Jackie unannounced into Mathewson's apartment. When Mathewson appears he has just come from the shower: "Mathewson emerged from an interior hall. He was naked, save for a white towel draped about his shoulders; his hair was wet, and droplets of water gleamed on his pearl-pink skin. Momentarily surprised at seeing the two of us with McGraw, he drew his muscles taut, and his whole body rippled with power, water sparkling in the rays of the sun" (71). Jackie, the artist and devotee, is obviously stunned by the sight. Noticing this, McGraw asks, "You never saw such a body, did you?" Although Jackie does not respond, he thinks, "Not of flesh . . . ; once, in marble" (71). His reference is to a display of Greek statuary he saw on a visit to the Brooklyn Museum, of which he had at the time commented, "I especially admired the athletes, gods in marble" (39). To Jackie, Mathewson seems to be the image of the divine and the embodiment of the beautiful. Although implicit from the first in Jackie's giving of rings and his reactions to both Mathewson's person and his feats, a now more explicit, albeit subtle, theme of eroticism enters the complex picture of religious emotions, an eroticism common enough in the annals of religious fervor (as in the ecstasies of Saint Teresa and Saint Bernard, for example). At this meeting, too, Mathewson manifests a surprising gratitude for

Jackie's tributes, indicating a corresponding need on the part of the hero and a growing reciprocity in the relationship. The purpose of the visit is to discuss Jackie's design for a championship ring (for which Mathewson has been the inspiration), and during the visit Mathewson praises the design, accepts it unconditionally, and requests that Jackie autograph the sketch for him (67). He tells Jackie, "I think your work is extraordinary," to which Jackie replies, "So is yours." This exchange elicits "an impolite noise" from McGraw, who, like Eli, is mystified by the relationship. "I can't explain," Eli says to Jackie, "this thing you've got over Matty" (71). Mathewson's response is similarly inexplicable, and not only to McGraw and Eli but to Jackie himself.

When Mathewson's letter in response to Jackie's third offering arrives, it is elaborate in its praise: "Once again I am honored to receive a model of your artistry. With luck I may yet claim the city's largest private collection of your work" (82). Jackie himself can understand neither Mathewson's pleasure in the gifts nor his eager acceptance of an invitation from Jackie's father-in-law to have dinner with him and Jackie: "I couldn't fathom Mathewson's eagerness for my company. Perhaps he was merely polite, perhaps unduly impressed with my craft; perhaps he had from Eli some impression of my feeling for him and wanted to examine with his own eyes this strange specimen of idolator" (83). Jackie's concerns here are almost exclusively self-referential. It does not occur to him, nor could it occur to him, that Mathewson, like himself, is a man in need.

During this second meeting, the dinner at Mr. Sonnheim's club, Jackie, overcome with shyness in the presence of Mathewson, remains for the most part a silent observer. After listening to a philosophical discussion of the primitive origins and meaning of baseball, Jackie hears Mathewson's views on gambling and, by implication, on the activities of Eli, an inveterate gambler: "I cannot see any dignity in [the gamblers'] occupation," Mathewson says, "and I fear their influence" (88). This comment has ominous overtones, in view of the scandals looming years in the future, one involving players on the club Mathewson will later manage (Cincinnati) and the other being the disastrous Black Sox affair. Jackie also learns the astonishing fact that his first offering has, in effect, saved Mathewson's career. Not only has it "restored the moment" of triumph and given it "an enduring character," it has also strengthened Mathewson's resolve to stay in the game, now grown somewhat meaningless: "After my last turn of the season, when I'd won and it hardly mattered that I'd won, when I was giving some considerable thought to whether I'd play again the following year, out of nowhere came this marvelous piece of work. It made the moment real again, and I never wear it but that I feel it anew" (89). Out of nowhere comes this marvelous piece of work; the career continues, and the tragic course is set for both Mathewson and Jackie.

Fourteen years pass before the two men talk for the third and final time, with only an occasional letter or handshake between them. During that interval the family jewelry business flourishes as a result of its affiliation with Mathewson, initiated through Jackie's offerings; Eli's habitual gambling accelerates, becoming addictive, and he is excluded in disgrace from the family firm; Jackie has a son (named Matthias, but known, of course, as "Matty") and a daughter who dies in the flu epidemic of 1917. During all this Jackie remains close to Eli, supportive and loyal through the crises caused by his gambling. Mathewson leaves pitching on the fifteenth anniversary of his no-hit game in St. Louis to manage the Cincinnati club. He soon resigns in dishonor, as he feels, when members of the team are accused of gambling. "In contrition" he joins the army and, in the cleanup of Europe after the Great War, is exposed to poison gas (by his own intention, as we learn later). He then returns, his health ruined, in a black mood of depression and despair.

In 1912, during this interval, Jackie has an interesting meeting with Mathewson's friend Hugh Fullerton, a journalist. Fullerton gives Jackie important information whose implications Jackie is as yet unable to appreciate. Jackie learns that Mathewson has given Fullerton the impression that he and Jackie are "very close"; Jackie denies this, mentioning only that he has commemorated Mathewson's achievements. Fullerton replies, "He showed me the rings you've done for him, yes, but he also said that you'd seen him pitch every important game of his career, that he has a gift from you on the fifteenth of July every year, that you followed him on the road, that you were . . . what were his words?" Jackie does not correct what, so far as readers can know, is a grossly exaggerated statement of his devotion (he does, after all, have a job and family, and he has not mentioned the annual gifts) but instead asks, "His greatest fan?" Fullerton replies, "Nothing so mundane as that. No, it had a special connotation, something . . . the celebrant of his works. That's what it was" (195).

By giving this religious name to Jackie, Mathewson has revealed an exalted self-image that can exist only in response to, and in symbiotic relationship with, that of his worshiper. Fullerton senses some of these implications as he goes on to develop his theory of the demands made on heroes by their fans and of the reciprocal demands made on fans by heroes. Celebrants, he says, "expect the superhuman," and "expectation becomes demand": "The world makes you a god and hates you for being human, and if you plead for understanding it hates you all the more. Heroes are never forgiven their success, still less their failure" (196). Jackie denies emphatically that he has made such demands: "Not me. Never me." Fullerton ignores the disclaimer, asserting a parasitic relationship between celebrants (among whom he includes himself) and the "demigods we create and celebrate": "We're the worms that eat at the bodies of the great" (196), a grim enough picture of holy communion. But heroes also make their demands. Fullerton says that as Mathewson's "high priest," his "celebrant-in-chief," Jackie must "equal in fashioned stone anything he may do on the field" (196). For this reason the celebrant may actually hope that the hero fails, so as to avoid producing the necessary tribute.

Toward the end of his analysis Fullerton says, "I suspect that your work is infused with the wish that you were he," and further, that inside every sportswriter and fan is a "frustrated athlete" (197). There is some insight here too, but he has not quite hit the mark. Jackie's response to the no-hitter, eleven years earlier, indicates that his case is more complex than that of ordinary fans. In the emotional interior where Jackie the pitcher (Fullerton's "frustrated athlete") lives, and from which the artist's visions emerge, the connection has been made. Jackie does not wish he were Mathewson; he is Mathewson. This identity is still unconscious.

At the time of the last meeting between Jackie and Mathewson, it is 1919, Cincinnati and the Chicago White Sox have just played the fourth game of the World Series, and Cincinnati, the underdog, leads three games to one. Mathewson sits with Fullerton in the pressbox and marks questionable plays on Fullerton's scorebook until the fifth inning, when he leaves the game. Jackie is in Chicago because Eli has wagered all he has (his stock in the family business, amounting to $40,000) on the White Sox to win the series and then has heard the rumors of a fix. To avoid financial ruin, he asks Jackie to "lay off" enough to get him even, although Jackie is not a bettor, having in his life made only a single bet – a quarter, which he lost. Out of love and loyalty to Eli, but in great anxiety, Jackie ventures into the world of high-stakes gamblers and finds takers for thirty-five of the forty thousand. He is to put up the cash at midnight, but before he can do that, there is the game, a talk with Fullerton, and a visit to Mathewson, who, Fullerton says, is dying and desperate.

On Jackie's arrival at Mathewson's hotel room, a friendly conversation ensues until Mathewson learns why Jackie is in Chicago. He confirms what Jackie already knows about the fix and then, in effect, dares Jackie to leave and to act on that knowledge: "If that's the sole reason you've come here, you may go now to exchange your notes and rescue your brother" (260–61). Jackie cannot leave, and Mathewson knows it. Now Mathewson begins to grow agitated, and his earlier propensity to see himself as godlike emerges as a full-blown delusion. He soon lapses into a kind of Scissonsesque oration; Mathewson, however, speaks not as a prophet but as a god, and not of salvation but of damnation. Like Eddie Scissons, he is mad, and his words reveal the nature and extent of his aberration. He tells Jackie, "It isn't Eli who stands on the precipice. . . . It's you, you, who sways there. It's you that risks damnation. Do you see that?" (261).

Behind the aberration are the rings, always the rings. Mathewson counts them, the milestones in his career, the visible sign of his divinity, reviewing it all for Jackie and in the process beginning to speak of himself as Christ, betrayed, suffering, dying, and rising: "I'd walked among those men on the field, I was as they were yet far better than they could ever be. I'd achieved the perfection you celebrated in stone. Then followed doubt, failure, and finally betrayal; then followed my death, for it was death, in the explosion and pain. And then I rose from that death, I walked among the people as of old, and finally, finally, I came to sit in judgment of those I'd walked among, to root out their sin and damn them for it" (262). An angry god, he will damn the guilty "for eternity"; he will drive the money-changers "from the temple" (262). In his isolation and pain Mathewson challenges Jackie to remain faithful: "They diced for His robe while He suffered on the cross. Will you do that, while I lay dying? No, you will not. No matter what may follow you will not do that. Not you, . . . not you" (263). Mathewson is right. Jackie will not betray Mathewson. He cannot betray him.

Jackie returns to his own hotel and scrawls a fatal note for the Chicago gamblers: "All bets off" (263). On the train back to New York, in a strange repetition of his earlier response to Mathewson, when he designed the first ring, Jackie produces more crisis art. This time, though, his imagination reacts to the evening's events by casting out Dionysian images; instead of producing a soul image in the form of the serene, shining, geometrical baseball field and pitcher in stone, he fills a sketchpad with "fantastical drawings on themes of death and resurrection" (264), the themes

Mathewson has appropriated to himself and, by implication, to his celebrant. He devises plans to support the now destitute Eli.

Even though Jackie gives Eli the money he had planned to bet so that Eli can pay off the New York gamblers, Eli knows the implications of Jackie's choice. Consequently, Eli makes other plans. He buys a new car and drives it full throttle onto Coogan's Bluff: "It hardly slowed as it jounced over the thin grass and solid rock; it sailed high into the air over the cliff and described a full somersault before it hit the jagged cliffside and tumbled over and over and over again until it came to rest, shattered and burning, against the black walls of the Polo Grounds" (264). Eli is a baseball park suicide, and Jackie's description of the act might have been transcribed from his sketchpad, a fantastical image of death, if not resurrection, taking form in the world.

Mathewson takes seven more years to die. When he does, Jackie receives from his executor the autographed drawing given to Mathewson in 1904 and a note explaining that the rings have been buried with him. Jackie weeps for the man who has now become legend. As he says, "the legends abide" (268). The novel ends with Jackie's meditation on another pitcher, "The Only Nolan," and another fan, but he returns, as always, to Mathewson:

A boy watched [The Only Nolan] pitch that [shutout] game and was inspired by it. I do not know where the inspiration led him or what it finally cost him in family and fortune, but I met him as a man one evening, and we talked baseball. . . . The greatest pitcher he ever saw was The Only Nolan. The greatest I ever saw was Christy Mathewson, on a terribly hot day in St. Louis, young as an April morning in that sweltering July, the perfect pitcher. It was my happiness to celebrate that perfection; in his age and suffering he would accept that vision of my youth, entwine it with his own hard faith, and end in madness. Eli, Eli!" (269)

"Eli, Eli!" is a cry of anguish for a dead brother sacrificed to a noble but insane god, and we understand this meaning first. Behind this, however, is another, older cry, that of the dying Christ: "*Eli, Eli, lama sabachthani,*" translated as "My God, my God, why hast thou forsaken me?" (Matt. 27:46). It is this older echo, ambiguous and despairing, that we hear next, an echo not only of the man who is God but, ironically, of the god who is man, in his last extremity harboring messianic delusions, accepting, as Jackie observes, the vision of his celebrant. That celebrant now, in his turn, echoes the terror of the mad man-god and of the god-man (Christy and Christ), and earlier still, of King David, who begins the twenty-second psalm with, "My God, my God, why hast thou forsaken me?" As the cry reverberates through texts and times, the words take on a tragic universality, expressing in brief the terror of the isolated soul, the divided self. "Eli, Eli!" – Jackie's words encapsulate his hard-won wisdom, a conscious understanding at last of the import of his own spiritual catastrophe, that old illumination through which he has made connection and which he has re-presented in a lifetime of crisis art.

9

DURING MY FIRST YEAR AT OREGON STATE I WROTE "THE NATURAL,"
BEGUN BEFORE LEAVING NEW YORK CITY. BASEBALL HAD INTERESTED ME,
ESPECIALLY ITS COMIC ASPECTS, BUT I WASN'T ABLE TO WRITE ABOUT THE
GAME UNTIL I TRANSFORMED THE GAME INTO MYTH, VIA JESSIE WESTON'S
PERCIVAL LEGEND WITH AN ASSIST BY T. S. ELIOT'S "WASTE LAND." . . . THE
MYTH ENRICHED THE BASEBALL LORE AS FEATS OF MAGIC TRANSFORMED
THE GAME. Bernard Malamud, "Reflections of a Writer" 16

WE ARE STILL MERE NATURALS, NO BETTER THAN FOOLS AND
MADMEN. Anonymous sermon (1680), cited in the *Oxford English
Dictionary*, s.v. "natural"

BERNARD MALAMUD'S *THE NATURAL* IN THE WASTELAND

In the epigraph Bernard Malamud announces both his
enterprise – mythmaking – and his method – bricolage. The novel,
Malamud's myth, is crafted of mythic rubble from the Western past, with
transformed and deformed archetypes whose chains of association constitute an uncanny semantic field, ambiguous even to the point of absurdity. Both novel and method are figured in the ominous, tilted, darkened tower from which the Judge surveys the world of the players, an
architectural relic standing as a transformation of the Tower of Babel
and reflecting its complexities. The scene over which this Lacanian ser-

pent is raised on its putrescent rod is Knights Field, an artistic gap at whose infernal opening the shades of a textual past gather and speak their messages in a confusing cacophony of themes, tropes, and dialects, all of which are incomprehensible to the protagonist whose destiny is the subject of their babble. The author thus invites his readers into an echo chamber of explicit mythicity and intertextuality.

Soon after its publication critics of *The Natural* began to explore Malamud's mythic orientation. First among these is Leslie Fiedler, whose Freudian exegesis discusses allusions to the Grail legends explored by Jessie Weston in her *From Ritual to Romance,* and others have followed his lead. So central is the reading of *The Natural* against Weston's discussion of Percival, the Fisher King, and fertility ritual that it is almost obligatory in critical analyses of the novel. In interviews Malamud frequently validates such readings (see, e.g., Lasher's *Conversations with Bernard Malamud*). Earl Wasserman's Jungian reading of the novel's Arthurian and fertility motifs is perhaps best known.[1] He says of Jessie Weston, Sir James George Frazer, and T. S. Eliot that they "have transformed the significance of Arthurian myth for the modern mind, and their anthropological and psychological interpretation now almost necessarily invests the myth" (440), an intertextual claim whose implications he does not examine.

A common but, I believe, mistaken assumption in these discussions is the continuity of the heroic tradition and the close analogy of either chivalry or fertility rituals to Malamud's baseball. The Jungian notion of archetype as an innate, psychological given may blind critics to crucial textual facts, and it is in such cases that Eric Gould's redefinition of the notion becomes indispensable. The archetype as a linguistic entity (rather than a mental one) obeys the laws of language, not the principles of "human nature." The point is that as language evolves, changes, and develops new or ironic signification, so does the archetype. As I have shown, in approaching myth the critic is faced with the relationship between Paul Ricoeur's "sedimentation," the pull of tradition (the impulse to repetition of a story form, genre, character type, or entrenched ideology), and "innovation" (the impulse to deviance, contradiction, irony, or antinarrative) ("Life in Quest" 24–25). Gould's archetypes (but not Jung's) freely participate in the contest between sedimentation and innovation, producing in the process equivocal and ironic complexities.

The common critical bias in discussions of *The Natural* has been on the side of sedimentation, with an almost complete disregard of innovation. Richard Kearney argues that both author and critic address this interplay between sedimentation and innovation: "By creatively reinterpreting the myths of the past, narrative can release new and hitherto concealed possibilities of understanding one's history. And by critically scrutinizing the past it can wrest tradition away from the conformism that is always threatening to overpower it. To properly attend to this dual capacity of narrative is, therefore, to resist the facile habit of establishing a dogmatic opposition between the 'eternal verities' of tradition, on the one hand, and the free inventiveness of critical imagination on the other" (66). Kearney's point is that a myth is not exhausted by one or even many narrative reinterpretations, a claim in accord with Gould's insight that mythic archetypes, beginning as signifieds, become themselves signifiers and hence become subject to endless transformation. Further, as Kearney points out, any contemporary retelling or reinterpretation may "disclose uncompleted and disrupted narratives which open up unprecedented possibilities of understanding" (66).

The situation is further complicated and meanings are multiplied exponentially when, as in the case of *The Natural,* not one but many archetypes, myths, or shards of myths go into the construction of the new narrative. As mentioned, without exception Malamud's critics have paid attention to tradition or sedimentation and ignored innovation, yet it is in the interplay of sedimentation and innovation that meaning arises. The implied comparison of Roy Hobbs to the hero of romance, for example, is not so interesting as the fact that for Roy, the mythic past returns as an alien world, mysterious and even sinister, a world in which, in his ignorance and confusion, he is compelled by a post-Freudian fate and awkwardly makes his way toward a peculiarly modern form of tragedy. The dramatic irony produced by the discrepancy between the reader's knowledge and the protagonist's ignorance approaches the order of irony of *Oedipus Rex.* Given this situation, the critic should recognize the tension and outright enmity between the novel and its pre-texts, its mythic shards. Ignoring the jostling and contradictions of mythic signifiers and their intertextuality[2] leads critics to readings that are facile, off the mark, or simply wrong. To demonstrate the inadequacy of such "mythic" readings as the novel has received, it is useful first to identify the landmarks of Malamud's intertextual geography and describe the particular character of each, so as to be in a position to judge the contributions, singly and collectively, of the mythic materials, as well as contradictions, ambiguities, and equivocations that result within the mythic scene of the novel.

Such an examination reveals that in the novel innovation overwhelms sedimentation, producing an entirely new myth from the bricolage of the material lying at hand, a myth in which talent is neither supported by grace nor directed by destiny but rather is the companion of ignorance; where the protagonist's (natural) excellence is counterbalanced by his "naturalness" (his folly and madness); where a seemingly cosmic promise of success is at odds with the grim inevitability of defeat; where intense desire to live forever runs head on into *natural* limit, posed like a brick wall in the hero's path. The novel's pre-texts in effect open up a temporal expanse through which the protagonist wanders, an exile, the signifying trope of whose life is that of erring in both its senses, of errantry, wandering, and of errancy, error.

In the epigraph Malamud mentions two pre-texts, but when we turn to Weston's *From Ritual to Romance* and Eliot's "The Waste Land," we cannot stop there, for both of them are themselves pastiches. Weston's "Percival legend" is actually a collection and analysis of Grail legends by various medieval authors, their accounts based on yet older tales and characters reaching into Celtic myth. Weston's premise is that the medieval versions are Christianized transformations of pagan ritual and myth, structures intended to ensure the well-being of the people and their lands, whose roots reach into prehistory. Eliot's poem takes its title from a theme of the Grail legends, that of the Fisher King, whose land is rendered lifeless by the infirmity of the king himself. In a note to that work, Eliot, like Malamud, acknowledges yet misrepresents the influence of Jessie Weston: "Not only the title, but the plan and a good deal of the incidental symbolism of the poem were suggested by . . . Weston's book on the Grail legend: *From Ritual to Romance.*" Influential on an aspect of that incidental symbolism is Weston's identifying certain key images from Grail legends – the lance or staves, the cup or Grail, the sword, and the dish – with the major suits of the tarot deck. Curiously, however, critics have ignored the tarot deck as a pre-text of *The Natural,* although both Weston and Eliot pay significant attention to it. Eliot has, selectively and idiosyncratically, incorporated tarot symbolism into his poem. Eliot continues, "Indeed, so deeply am I indebted, Miss Weston's book will elucidate the difficulties of the poem much better than my notes can do" (50). The matter does not stop there, however, for both Weston and Eliot are inspired in their writing by Sir James George Frazer's *The Golden Bough,* a work of comparative anthropology exploring ancient European fertility rituals, their remnants in literature, and their continued presence in festivals of the late nineteenth century.[3] The following paragraphs offer explanations of key elements in Weston's, Frazer's, and Eliot's works as they constitute pre-texts for Malamud's novel. The first section on Percival and the Grail quest, along with the section on Roy Hobbs as knight errant, involves covering old critical ground, yet my description focuses on details that prove most useful in my attempt to assess the character and actions of Roy Hobbs, the novel's protagonist. The discussions of tarot symbolism, the King of the Wood, and "The Waste Land" address matters on which, for the most part, others have remained silent.

FROM RITUAL TO ROMANCE

PERCIVAL AND THE QUEST FOR THE HOLY GRAIL.

Percival (also Perceval, Parzival, Peredur, and Pryderi) is perhaps the best known of the Grail questers, and he is distinguished from the others in several ways. Most interesting is that he "comes from outside the circle of Arthur's knights"; he is "the supreme outsider" (Cavendish, *Arthur and the Grail* 154). The son of a dead knight, Percival is raised in rustic isolation by his mother, who fears for his life should he follow in his father's footsteps. Percival discovers the chivalric way of life only when several knights in full panoply wander into his remote woodland. The young man is so struck by the knights that he immediately leaves home to seek knighthood for himself. A second distinctive feature seen in the Percival legends is stressed in the *Perceval*. According to Weston, this is "the insistence upon the sickness and disability" of the ruler of the Grail castle and the surrounding lands, a ruler known as the Fisher King, whose disability has "reacted disastrously upon his kingdom, either depriving it of vegetation, or exposing it to the ravages of war" (19–20). Weston finds that the aim of the Grail quest in all versions is to benefit both the king and the land (21). Percival, then, the precursor of Roy Hobbs, is characterized by his ignorance, his alien origins and outsider status, his natural aptitude for knighthood, and his potential role of redeemer of or successor to the Fisher King and thus of restorer of fertility.[4]

THE GRAIL QUEST AND TAROT SYMBOLISM

As mentioned, Weston finds that the major symbols of the Grail ritual correspond to those of the four major suits of the tarot pack: staves, cups, dishes, and swords. Each suit includes the King (representing the self or spirit), the Queen (or soul), the Knight (the focusing of energies/selfhood), and the Page (the body) (Cavendish, *Man, Myth, and Magic,* s.v. "tarot"). In addition, there are twenty-two trumps, or honors cards. Each of these represents, according to most commentators, a stage in the spiritual progress of the individual, a journey toward self-realization and wisdom, or as Campbell puts it, a journey through the fear of death to "the knowledge of that mystery which, in theological terms, would be known as the Image of God within us" (*Tarot Revelations* 25). Most and perhaps all of these honors are of interest in *The Natural,* and two are of crucial significance: the Fool (one of the old meanings of *natural*) and the Tower (the structure dominating the scene of Knights Field). Roy's suit is staves, and potentially the king is his card (*Roy* means "king"; for a while he is the "King of Klouters").

SIR JAMES GEORGE FRAZER AND THE "KING OF THE WOOD"

Weston saw behind the Christianized tales of Grail questers more ancient seasonal rituals of the sort Frazer explores in *The Golden Bough.* Frazer takes his title from the bough required to be won and carried by the hero who would replace the aging King of the Wood.[5] The hero sought the post of priest-king, guardian of the sacred tree and grove. As successor to the old king he was "at once a priest and a murderer." His ordeal, however, really only began when he killed the old king and succeeded him, for inevitably one day someone would come to kill him too, and he had to be constantly on guard, as Frazer explains: "For such was the rule of the sanctuary: a candidate for the priesthood could succeed to office only by slaying the incumbent priest in single combat, and could himself retain office only until he was in turn slain by a stronger or a craftier. Moreover . . . he could fling his challenge only if he had first succeeded in plucking a golden bough from the tree which the priest was guarding" (3). The title of the murderer-priest was "King of the Wood," a post held, as Frazer comments, by "precarious tenure," for "surely no crowned head ever lay uneasier or was visited by more evil dreams. For year in year out, in summer and winter, he had to keep his lonely watch, and whenever he snatched a troubled slumber it was at the peril of his life" (4).

This man, the priest-murderer-king and guardian of the sacred tree, was also a magician, and further, he was identified with the life force of the tree he guarded. His function was, through his strength and virility, to exert a homeopathic magic on his people and land, making them fertile and healthy. A part of his duty thus involved participating in sacred marriage rites with the moon goddess (whom Robert Graves calls "The White Goddess") under her local name – Diana in the Grove at Nemi – through her priestess surrogate. He derived his power not by right of birth but by natural right, that is, by virtue of his ability to seize the sacred bough and defeat his predecessor, thus exhibiting a greater power. The assassination of the aging king and his replacement by the youthful successor imitated the progress of seasons, the succession of winter by spring, and thus, through a process of homeopathic magic, ensured the return of light and life. The golden bough, Frazer argues, was mistletoe, which grew in the sacred oaks and was thought to be born of lightning, the powerful weapon of the gods. When plucked and carried by the challenger, it was thought to embody the soul of the old king, who was himself understood as the oak spirit and whose life was, in effect, destroyed in the breaking of the bough.[6]

T. S. ELIOT'S "THE WASTE LAND"

As to the "assist by T. S. Eliot's 'Waste Land,'" I have already remarked that Eliot, like Malamud, was influenced by Weston and Frazer, but Eliot exhibits as well the reductive and despairing imprint of Freudian myth, a paradoxical system of belief whose chief characteristic is disbelief, for it is profoundly skeptical of human motives and virtues, its devotees paralyzed by self-consciousness. Eliot's poem depicts the terror of living in a post-Freudian wasteland, amid the rubble of failed systems of meaning and belief, where "you know only / A heap of broken images, where the sun beats, / And the dead tree gives no shelter, . . . / And the dry stone no sound of water." This is a modern, urban version of the land ruled by the impotent Fisher King, wounded in the genitals, or by a weakening, aging King of the Wood. It is a place where the reader will see "fear in a handful of dust" (ll. 22–30). Eliot's method is to create an interwoven texture of "broken images," a poem like a rag rug constructed of scraps of Western literature and religion to form a pattern of despair, relieved, some argue, by hope buttressed by sacred mythic rubble or bricolage: "These fragments I have shored against my ruins" (l. 431).

Eliot's speaker is the wounded Fisher King himself. London is his Waste Land, spiritually arid and morally bankrupt, and its citizens are dead people in a dead land. This Fisher King is tormented by a terrible Freudian understanding of himself and humankind and is isolated in his despair. His land is littered by "broken images," remnants of outmoded systems, of outworn certitudes and meanings. He awaits without expectation the arrival of a hero who might heal him and restore the life of his kingdom. At the end of the poem the sacred, which is never actually present, merely approaches in the voice of thunder, like Blanchot's sacred, a nonabsent absence standing a few feet away. In Revelation, in his vision of last days, John of Patmos was warned not to write "what the seven thunders have said" (Rev. 10:4); Eliot audaciously closes his poem with the words of the thunder announcing perhaps the coming of rain to the barren wastes: "Datta. Dayadhvam. Damyata" ("Give. Sympathize. Control"), followed by "Shantih shantih shantih," meaning, Eliot says, "The Peace which passeth understanding" (55).

These summaries will come back into the discussion as I attempt to sort out the intricacies and mysteries of Roy Hobbs's life and world. In a way, Malamud's Roy Hobbs might have been the hero required by Eliot's Fisher King, but he will fail, not because (like Eliot's speaker) he knows too much but because he knows too little. Readers know that he inhabits the Freudian wastes, but he does not know this. And although he is a naturally gifted stranger in a strange land whose redemption seems to lie within his power, he is, unfortunately, a "natural," a fool and a madman, a distant relative of Don Quixote, abjectly ignorant of himself and the task he undertakes.

To find our way through the archetypal and intertextual labyrinth of the novel, it is useful to consider separately the influence of Malamud's pre-texts before attempting to make some general assessment of Roy Hobbs and his mythic enterprise.

ROY HOBBS, KNIGHT ERRANT

Like Percival of the Grail legends, Roy Hobbs is a rustic, ignorant of the world and its ways. He does not know, for example, how to order a meal in a dining car (8), and he is terrified at the thought of being alone in Chicago (27). Yet just as Percival has a natural genius for knighthood, Roy has a natural genius for baseball; each is called from his isolated home, destined to wander and to err. Percival is a knight errant; Roy Hobbs is a New York Knight errant. If we knew the image that haunted Percival, we might envision him riding in icy armor through endless forests, seeking shelter and food. We do know the image that haunts Roy; it is of "the train that never stopped." When, after fifteen years of aimless wandering, he finally arrives in the New York Knights' dugout, he tells himself that "now it was time to ease up," "to sit still and be quiet," but "the inside of him was still streaming through towns and cities, across forests and fields, over long years" (33). Neither Percival nor Roy can stop; neither has a home to which he can return. Percival's father dies before his son is born, and his mother dies of grief on his leaving home; Roy's father is dead, as is the grandmother who raised him for seven years, and his mother is an enigma of whom Roy says merely that she was "a whore" (143). Only in his dreams does the train stop, setting "him down in a field somewhere in the country" (46). The sound of a train can make him go "freezing cold" (121); illness and death assume the image of the train (148). In the final moments of his story, in his misery and defeat, Roy hears the train again: "He felt the insides of him beginning to take off (chug chug choo choo)" (185).

Roy's wandering brings him to the land of an ironic Fisher King. As is often remarked, the field of Pop Fisher is a wasteland. It has suffered from drought, "a blasted dry season," and, Pop says, "no rains at all. The grass is worn scabby in the outfield, and the infield is cracking" – a condition duplicated in the soul of the manager: "My heart feels as dry as dirt." The drinking fountain in the dugout yields only "warm, rusty water." Like the Fisher King, Pop also suffers a persistent malady, not tragically debilitating but "unnatural" and embarrassingly trivial – athlete's foot on the hands (32). The absence of water has ruined the land, and the contagion has spread to the people, the team and fans, who are an assembly of bunglers, misfits, and grotesques. As Roy watches the team, he is dismayed, but he wants also to laugh: "They were a nutty bunch to begin with, but when they were losing they were impossible. It was like some kind of sickness" (55). They require charms against catastrophe (55–56). The fans "in the patched and peeling stands" are not much different. The stadium "often resembled a zoo full of oddballs, including gamblers, bums, drunks, and some ugly crackpots" (56).

Death is thematic here. Roy arrives on Memorial Day, a day to honor the warrior dead, but Pop says that it is "not for the soldiers" (32). He coaches what he calls a "dead-to-the-neck ball team" (31). At thirty-four rookie Roy Hobbs is "starting with one foot in the grave" (34). The team has suffered a series of casualties: one man has been beaned and paralyzed, and another has "stepped on a bat, rolled down the dugout steps" and "snapped his spine in two places." As the equipment manager, Dizzy, tells Roy, "We sure been enjoying an unlucky season" (34). Before Roy takes a regular position in left field, Bump Baily, his predecessor, hits the wall going for a fly, breaks his skull, and dies (66–67).

All in all, these diminished correlatives, the wasteland (the ball field and stadium), the society (players and fans), and the Fisher King (Pop Fisher), are in dire need of a hero to restore life and prosperity, to accomplish what Weston describes as "the freeing of the waters" (25) that will cure the drought and restore life and fertility. Roy Hobbs is potentially that hero. After keeping Roy on the bench for three weeks, Pop Fisher, angry at Bump Baily for his inept fielding, sends Roy in to pinch-hit for the first time on June 21, the summer solstice, telling him, "knock the cover off of it." As the ball comes toward him Roy swings "from the toes," and with the crack of the bat "a few drops of rain spattered to the ground" (58–59). The cover has indeed been knocked off the ball, and what at first seemed a game-winning home run is ruled "a ground rules double"; Roy is returned to second with the game tied. The game is then suspended because a torrential rain arrives, and "by the time Roy got in from second he was wading in water ankle deep" (59). He has apparently magically, miraculously, freed the waters, but the ironic effects of the suspended game will make all the difference.

This is Roy's first game as a Knight, and the team's, the land's, and the manager's redemption appears to have begun. It rains for three days, greening the field (62), and the weather in general moderates, becoming "better, more temperate, with just enough rain to keep the grass a bright green and yet not pile up future double headers" (69–70). In three weeks the team achieves "a coordination of fielding, hitting and pitching" (68) and begins its climb out of the cellar. Pop Fisher's "hands healed and so did his heart" (70). A "new breed" of fans arrives "to cheer the boys on" (69).

That this prosperity is tied to Roy's presence and achievements is evident in the effects on all concerned when he goes into a slump. The Knights begin dropping in the standings; Pop's hand ailment returns (103); the team resumes its old inept play and magical practices to ward off evil; and the grotesque element of the crowd reasserts itself (106). When Roy comes out of his slump, however, the team, the fans, and the manager come with him. A phenomenal winning streak takes the team to first place.

Roy's prototype, Percival, like other Grail questers, assumes the hero's role and task: to heal the king, restore the land, and in one version, to defeat the enemy of the Fisher King (Weston 17). Percival fails because he does not ask crucial questions concerning the Grail and whom it serves. We may attribute such reticence to the quester's ignorance and the bad advice he has received, as some narrators assert, but the unasked questions may also be understood to reflect an unreadiness or inability to progress intellectually and spiritually toward self-realization. Roy also fails, despite opportunities, to ask the pertinent questions or to explore the "higher" meanings of his life and ambitions. For example, at the very outset of his journey at age nineteen, Harriet Bird asks Roy, "Isn't there something over and above earthly things – some more glorious meaning to one's life and activities?" Roy, utterly mystified, asks, "In baseball?" She replies simply, "Yes." In his ignorance and inexperience, Roy can only rack his brain (22–23). The tales of both heroes break off abruptly, but in some versions of the Grail story we are shown the aftermath of the hero's failure: "The Fisher King is very sorrowful, for he has fallen into a doleful sickness. This sickness has come upon him through one whom he welcomed as a guest, to whom the Holy Grail appeared, and because he did not ask whom it served, all the lands were stirred up to war" (Weston 16). The Fisher King, ill beyond remedy, will die. "There is no cure of the king or restoration of the land," Weston comments; "the specific task of the Grail hero is never accomplished" (17). At the end of Roy's tale we feel that Pop Fisher, like his prototype, cannot survive this defeat. His enemies, too, will prevail; his "land" will fall into fatal contention, "battles, conflicts, and his knights will perish" (Weston 18).

The Grail, about which the hero fails to ask, is said at times to contain the blood of Christ and at others, the mass wafer, a type of "Food of Life" served ritually at "Mystic Meals" and intended to ensure immortality. The womb image of a hollow vessel containing the sacred food in association with a weapon as phallus (usually a lance, but at times a sword) (Weston 158–59) expresses in gustatory and sexual metaphors the Grail's spiritual significance. Roy's "eating disorder" and his sexual desire for Memo Paris, both of which are pathological, misdirected, and insatiable, may seem to stem from his failure to understand the more glorious purpose of which Harriet speaks. He may thus attempt to satisfy his hunger with physical food served on ordinary dishes and with sexual union with Memo, when what he requires is spiritual sustenance carried in a holy vessel by a mysterious maiden. What is in doubt is the availability of such sustenance, that higher something (for which even Harriet cannot find words) in Roy's world, a matter never in doubt for the medieval knights to whom sacred vessels and weapons appeared ("the Holy Grail and the lance with angry blood welling from its point"). Percival may have failed to ask the pertinent question, but for Roy there may well be no pertinent question. If there is, and it is discovered and asked, the modern reply might well prove unthinkable or unbearable.

ROY HOBBS, KING OF THE WOOD

Roy Hobbs's name is magic in the way of ancient names, which were thought not merely to reveal but to determine character.[7] *Roy* means "king"; *Hobbs* is a form of *hob*, a "wood sprite or elf," itself a form of *Robert* or *Robin*. Hence *Roy Hobbs* is a transform of *Rob Roy*, the name of a legendary Scottish plunderer, and a loose translation of *Robin Hood*, the name of an outlaw leader of Sherwood Forest, a thief, and an outsider. Baumbach similarly translates the name as "king rustic" (26). Roy's name dictates that he become "king" of the wood in which he has been born and reared (like Percival) and of which he has recurring memories, usually of himself as a child with a dog alone in a deep woods (36, 86, 94, 98, 161).

According to Frazer, however, to become King of the Wood one must first capture the golden bough growing on the sacred oak guarded by the incumbent king. Frazer makes the case that mistletoe – the Druids' "all-healer" – is that golden bough, a plant parasitic on the oak, hanging between earth and sky, its magic enhanced if it is not allowed to touch the earth. Indeed, it was believed to have "fallen from the sky, a gift of the divinity" (Frazer 591) and thus to embody divine power. A favorite time to gather mistletoe would have been Midsummer Day, the summer solstice (592), the day of Roy's first at-bat.

Enriching the mythology of the golden bough is the notion that the bough contains the life or soul of the oak and hence of the deity or priest-king, the man who both embodies in human form the sacred tree and remains identical with it (Frazer 594–95). The mistletoe's remaining green (young) in winter, when the oak itself is leafless and apparently dead, may well be the basis for the belief that the life of the oak is in the golden bough, as is the life of the king (604). Frazer summarizes these parallels as follows:

> The priest of the Arician grove – the King of the Wood – personified the tree on which grew the Golden Bough. Hence if that tree was the oak, the King of the Wood must have been a personification of the oak-

spirit. It is, therefore, easy to understand why, before he could be slain, it was necessary to break the Golden Bough. As an oak-spirit, his life or death was in the mistletoe on the oak, and so long as the mistletoe remained intact, he . . . could not die. To slay him, therefore, it was necessary to break the mistletoe, and probably . . . to throw it at him. (605)

The idea that the king's soul or life is in the mistletoe is an example of a motif called the "external soul." Frazer cites numerous examples of the hero or magician who remains invulnerable (and therefore immortal) because his life powers are vested in an object inaccessible to his enemies. Only by learning the nature of the object and its location can an opponent kill the hero, who dies when the object containing his soul is broken, burned, or otherwise destroyed (603–7).

One more association completes the symbolism of the golden bough, the idea that it embodies the celestial fire of the divinity, the sun's fire or lightning. Chief Indo-European gods had names derived from the verb "to shine" and were identified with the light and power of the sun (Zeus, Jupiter, Tyr, and Tiwaz are deities of this ilk). The god's weapon frequently was identified as the lightning bolt, which he hurled like a spear from heaven to earth. Frazer speculates that the ancients saw significance in the fact that the oak tree, the sacred tree, host of the mistletoe, is struck by lightning far more often than other forest trees of Europe, perhaps on the order of sixty to one (607). It thus was both elevated above other trees but also vulnerable. In *The Natural* Pop Fisher knows this and warns Bump Baily against pride: "As for you Bump Baily, high and mighty though you are, some day you'll pay for your sassifras. Remember that lightning cuts down the tallest tree" (40). Frazer speculates that observing the vulnerability of the oak to lightning strikes, people might well have supposed that "the great sky-god whom they worshipped and whose awful voice they heard in the roll of thunder, loved the oak above all the trees of the wood and often descended into it from the murky cloud in a flash of lightning, leaving a token of his presence or of his passage in the riven and blackened trunk and the blasted foliage. Such trees would thenceforth be encircled by a nimbus of glory as the visible seats of the thundering sky-god" (607). The King of the Wood, then, "personated in flesh and blood" the great sky-god "who had kindly come down from heaven in the lightning flash to dwell among men in the mistletoe . . . the Golden Bough – growing on the sacred oak." Therein lies the purpose of the priest-king's constant vigilance, to guard "with drawn sword the mystic bough which contained the god's life and his own" (609).

In *The Natural* Malamud merges the mythology of oak and mistletoe, or golden bough, into a single object that is both oak and thunder blossom, god and man. It is, of course, the marvelous, animate, half-human bat Wonderboy. Roy tells Pop Fisher and Red that he took the wood for the bat "a long time ago" from a "tree near the river where [he] lived" that was "split by lightning" (51). He does not say that it was an oak, but we surmise as much, for at the very outset of the novel Roy has a vision of his boyhood expressed in symbol, "seen" from the train window: "There flowed along this bone-white farmhouse with sagging skeletal porch, alone in untold miles of moonlight, and before it this white-faced, long-boned boy whipped with train-whistle yowl a glowing ball to someone hidden under a dark oak, who shot it back without thought, and the kid once more wound and returned" (3). The lost home is seen in the images of the bone-white farmhouse and skeletal porch, the corpse of a home alone in untold miles of moonlight. The someone hidden beneath the dark oak is the old king, whom Harriet Bird (with an allusion to Freud's *Totem and Taboo*) would call the "primitive papa" (21), spirit of the oak. This tree must be the one riven by lightning, the celestial fire, which has left a token of the god's presence or passage, a supernatural power in the tree that Roy harvests as he cuts out the wood for the bat, the golden bough. This helps to explain the sense one has that Wonderboy (the name Roy brands on the bat) is alive. "Wonderboy" is, in fact, an alias of Roy, the youth who made it, and represents that boy's external soul. Its wood is white (51), but it shines golden in the sun (67). If we have any doubts, Wonderboy's birth from lightning is apparent in Roy's first at-bat as a Knight. Roy connects with the ball, and the sound produced is that of thunder: "a noise like a twenty-one gun salute cracked the sky." The "straining, ripping sound" announces, like thunder, a miraculous rain (59).

The bat being Roy's external soul, he remains invulnerable so long as the bat is intact; he "dies" when the bat is destroyed. With the bat Roy seems for the most part invincible; without it he is impotent. Roy knows this and takes special care of the bat, keeping it in a bassoon case, oiling it with sweet oil, and boning it so that it will not chip (51). During Roy's slump Pop Fisher wants him to use another bat, but Roy is afraid to do so: "He felt he didn't stand a Chinaman's chance without his own club. And if he once abandoned Wonderboy there was no telling what would happen to him. Probably it would finish his career for keeps, because never since he had made the bat had he swung at a ball with any other" (111). (Roy's speculation is, of course, prophetic.) Bump Baily, whom Roy "murders" and replaces, also seems to recognize that the bat is the locus of Roy's "life," for his first attack against Roy is actually an attack on Wonderboy, which he plans to cut in two with a hacksaw. When Roy discovers what Bump intends, Bump stands with the bat in his hands, having momentarily taken possession of the golden bough, but Roy seizes it and twists it from Bump's grasp. Bump also recognizes the sexual implications of the golden bough, because he calls Roy "wonderboy" with reference to Roy's almost inadvertent sexual encounter with Memo Paris (49). Bat and phallus are again identified when, during his slump, Roy swings and misses, and Wonderboy "resemble[s] a sagging baloney" (113), the phallic significance tied to the king's role in homeopathically promoting fertility.[8]

All this reveals that Wonderboy is indeed a transformation of the golden bough that the young Roy seized, taking as his own the divine spirit and fire. If Frazer is correct, however, the bough when seized also contains the life of the old King of the Wood. Possession of the bough makes Roy a claimant to the throne, but he must be more. He must also be a contender, because according to ancient law he must kill the king if he is to become king. There are three confrontations in the novel that enact just this sort of crucial and final combat. Early in the novel is the contest between the young Roy Hobbs and Walter "the Whammer" Wambold; later there is the contest between Roy, now a thirty-four-year-old rookie, and Bump Baily; and at last there is the crucial meeting of the now decrepit Roy and the phenomenal rookie pitcher Herman Youngberry. In each confrontation both contestants risk everything.

On the surface only ten dollars are at stake in the contest between Roy and the Whammer. Sam Simpson, Roy's alcoholic mentor and father surrogate, issues the challenge: "I got ten dollars that says he can strike you out with three pitched balls, Wambold" (16). At this time a thirty-three-year-old veteran, the league-leading hitter, and a three-time winner of the Most Valuable Player award, the Whammer is clearly "king." Roy is a nineteen-year-old nobody on his way to a tryout. The Whammer accepts the challenge only because Harriet Bird, a "snappy goddess," looks on, and as she says, she loves "contests of skill" (16). At risk, therefore, is not just the money but each contestant's "life" and, it is implied, the favors of the "goddess." Sam, who was a catcher during his professional years, wears a washboard chest protector and catches the three pitches. The last strikes such a blow that he dies later that night. The Whammer, the batter, dies a baseball death by striking out, but more than that, it is implied that he is now finished. As the third pitch approaches, the ball is a flame (a bit of that celestial fire which Roy owns) that the Whammer wants to crush "into a universe of sparks," but he misses, hears a gong, and understands that he is, "in the truest sense of it, out." He leaves defeated, "an old man" (20), and disappears from the world of the novel.[9] Roy, the pitcher in this contest, is the winner, the new King of the Wood, but it is a Pyrrhic victory, for within a day or two Harriet Bird, whose favors he has won, will shoot him and "kill" Roy the pitcher, who is the third casualty in the affair.

Harriet Bird is the only one who recognizes the crucial nature of the contest. After it is over she says that it was an "inspiring sight." Seeing with a mythic, post-Freudian eye the reenactment of an ancient drama, she says it was reminiscent of "David jawboning the Goliath-Whammer, or was it Sir Percy lancing Sir Maldemer, or the first son (with a rock in his paw) ranged against the primitive papa?" (21). It is all these, but in particular it is the Freudian son-father battle reflected in the ritual of the golden bough and in all battles for succession to power and privilege. Roy thus "kills" two fathers in the contest.

The second contest for the kingship occurs fifteen years later. Roy, now a left fielder, joins the New York Knights as a rookie, a challenge to Bump Baily. Roy has the eerie feeling at first (when he has only heard Bump's voice, "strong, rawboned") that Bump is the Whammer. Baumbach notices too that the voice is also that of Roy's father ("familiar from his boyhood") (27). Bump is built like the Whammer, and he is also the league's leading hitter (40). Now the contest involves Wonderboy, as well as the "sun field" (left field, a position both men will claim), the batting title, and as before, a mysterious woman who passes from the "father" to the "first son." Her name now is Memo Paris, of whom I will say more presently. But beyond all this, each man's life is at stake. Bump tries to destroy Roy through the external soul in the bat, and although Roy does not actually kill Bump (who dies when he runs into the wall), people know that Bump would not have been hustling after the difficult fly if not for Roy's challenge. Pop Fisher takes pains to reassure Roy that Bump's death is not Roy's fault, but he subconsciously knows the truth and feels "uneasy" (66).

The third contest between king and challenger occurs in Roy's last at-bat. Wonderboy, the locus of his external soul, has been broken in the previous at-bat, and for the first time Roy uses another, ordinary, nonmagical bat. Roy's last plate appearance produces not one but two challengers – one who fails, and one who succeeds. The Knights are one run down, with the tying run on third, and two outs in the bottom of the ninth. The stage is thus set for the traditional baseball climax, and as at the end of *The Year the Yankees Lost the Pennant,* everything rides on this last game, last inning, and last out. It is now Roy's place and moment, circumstances under which the hero-redeemer may exert superhuman talent and effort on the side of virtue and life so as to achieve a glorious victory. When Pop Fisher sends Roy to the plate, he says, "Go on in," and adds the significant instruction, "Keep us alive" (179). Although the time is ripe, Roy's fire and light are failing: "the blank-faced crowd was almost hidden by the darkness crouching in the stands. Home plate lay under a deepening dusty shadow but Roy saw things with more light than he ever had before. A hit, tying up the game, would cure what ailed him. Only a homer, with himself scoring the winning run, would truly redeem him" (179). Facing him, the pitcher Vogelman, who has been soundly beaten before by Roy, sees the batter's "burning eyes" and thinks that he stands in "like a goddamn gorilla" and that "he ain't human." Vogelman's manager sees Roy differently: "He looks old and beat up" (180), but Vogelman is intimidated and issues three balls. As he prepares to deliver the fourth pitch, he suffers impaired vision: "Gazing at the plate, he found his eyes were misty and he couldn't read the catcher's sign. He looked again and saw Roy, in full armor, mounted on a black charger. Vogelman stared hard, his arms held high so as not to balk. Yes, there he was coming at him with a long lance as thick as a young tree. He rubbed his arm across his eyes and keeled over in a dead faint" (180). To Vogelman, Roy still has the look of the hero, but the golden bough has been broken; the hero is already dead. Vogelman, however, does not see with the hero's eye; he fails to unseat the old king.

It is time for a new challenger. The rookie relief pitcher Herman Youngberry takes the mound with a three-ball count, a situation that, as several critics have noticed, places him in exactly that of the young Roy Hobbs when he faced the Whammer all those years before. Like the "glowing ball" thrown by the boy Roy, and the fiery orb pitched by Roy to the Whammer, Youngberry's pitch is of the nature of fire; it "lit its own path." He strikes out Roy, the "King of Klouters," on three pitched balls, and Roy goes down "with a roar": "Bump Baily's form glowed red on the wall. There was a wail in the wind. He feared the mob would swarm all over him, tear him apart, and strew his polluted remains over the field, but they had vanished" (182).

The golden bough having been broken, it was only a matter of time before the old King of the Wood would fall. Roy knows he is dead, and he expects the mythic fate of Osiris, to have his remains strewn in the field. Roy's symbolic acknowledgment of this death comes later, after the field has grown dark, when he drags the pieces of Wonderboy into the sun field, where he has played. There he digs a "grave in the dry earth," buries his soul, the bat broken so smoothly that it almost looks whole, seems indeed to have "willed its own brokenness," tying it together, "wishing it would take root and become a tree" (183). In the image one can see the sacred oak rising from the grave – Roy and Wonderboy, the king and the golden bough, infused with divine fire, reborn.

THE KING'S CONSORT

Each of the three contests "kills" the league-leading batter in his turn, the Whammer, Bump Baily, and finally Roy, and associated with each of these contests is a woman. Harriet Bird watches the confrontation between the Whammer and Roy and as a result of Roy's victory switches her interest from the former to the latter. Memo Paris, Bump Baily's girlfriend, is passed to Roy by Bump while Bump is alive, and she apparently turns her attention to Roy after Bump's death. Iris Lemon watches Roy's last game but leaves in an ambulance before the last at-bat because Roy has hit her in the face with a foul ball intended for Otto Zipp.

Within the mythic dimensions of Roy's world, however, the three women are one woman, just as all the men are, in succession, one king.[10] Both the men and the women are fungible, replacing each other in the service of a single, overriding plot in which the role is crucial but the players are exchangeable. To ensure the life of the people and land, the King of the Wood, as the human embodiment of the sky-god, had his sexual obligation to his fated bride, the moon goddess, or in Frazer's terms, "the Queen of Heaven": "For she too loved the solitude of the woods and lonely hills, and sailing overhead on clear nights in the likeness of the silver moon she looked down with pleasure on her own fair image reflected on the calm, burnished surface of the lake, Diana's Mirror" (609). As in Eliot's "The Waste Land," however, sexual relations in Roy's world lack the simple, ritual character depicted in the myths. To be bridegroom to this transformed, twentieth-century goddess archetype is not for the reticent or the faint-hearted, for she is a complex, changeable, desirable, and terrible mistress, suffering her own sexual hangups, what might in Harriet's case be called a fatal obsession, seen in her carrying the phallic symbol of the gun and using it to destroy the "best" athletes she can find, or in Memo's case suffering from a strange ailment of her breast. Even in her ancient form the moon goddess is multifaceted, with three revolving aspects reflected in her waxing, full, and waning phases. She is maiden, mother (or nymph), and crone, mysteriously several and yet one: youth, maturity, and age; life and death; womb and tomb; beautiful and repulsive; and compelling alike in her beauty and her horror.[11]

As king, Roy is "chosen" by the goddess (65), as he recognizes from time to time, and his life is one of compulsory service to her. Harriet chooses Roy after he has defeated the Whammer; Memo "chooses" Roy, thinking he is Bump, when she steals into Bump's hotel room in the night; Iris chooses Roy because he is a hero, and she "hate[s] to see a hero fail" (119). Roy is helpless to evade this office, and he tells Iris that he leads a determined life, that "his fate, somehow, had always been the same (on a train going nowhere) – defeat in sight of his goal." Iris asks, "always with a woman?" and Roy responds, "I sure met some honeys in my time. They burned me good." When Iris wonders why Roy picks that type, he says, "It's like I say – they picked me," and Roy admits that he cannot say no to "that type" (121).

The name of the most compelling of Roy's three women, Memo Paris, hints at the true nature of this archetypal woman. *Memo* is a short form of *memorandum,* "let it be remembered" or "remember." *Paris* is the name of the Trojan prince Zeus selects to award the golden apple to the fairest of three goddesses, the contestants being Athena, Aphrodite, and Hera, the three forms of the goddess associated here with virginity, sexual desire, and marriage, respectively. Paris awards the apple to Aphrodite, angering Athena and Hera but receiving as his bride Aphrodite's human representative, the fatally beautiful Helen of Troy, and with her trouble beyond imagining. Hence this form of the goddess comes to Roy with a warning hidden in her name: "Remember Paris."

Unconsciously, at least, Roy recognizes that the three women are one, for at moments between sleep and waking, in dream or delirium, he makes the connection. For example, on his first night in the team's hotel, Roy is in bed, and the bed is moving like a train, taking him "into a place where he did not want to go" (46), "a roaring locomotive, . . . screaming into the night." He sees himself, fifteen years earlier, with the bassoon case containing Wonderboy, approaching Harriet's door for the fatal tryst between "crazy Harriet (less and more than human) with the pistol, and him, cut down in the very flower of his youth, lying in a red pool of his own blood" (46). As he quiets down, a second image replaces the first, that of an Iris-like woman in a "field somewhere in the country." Finally, almost asleep, Roy sees a door that "seemed to open in his mind," through which steps Memo – "this naked, redheaded lovely" (46). Thus Harriet yields to Iris, and Iris to Memo, the three revealing to Roy the complexity of the Woman, his bride. Roy's unconscious conveys a similar message to him when he lies ill and delirious in a maternity hospital. He first looks into "glaring" lights that hurt his eyes, and then he sees that "Iris' sad head topped Memo's dancing body, with Memo's vice versa upon the shimmying rest of Iris, a confused fusion that dizzied him" (149).

To complicate matters, the women from Roy's childhood – his mother and grandmother (for whom his feelings are almost pathologically ambivalent) – become identified through image and epithet with Harriet, Memo, and Iris, who in turn are identified with one another. The Freudian-Lacanian implication is that the determinism from which Roy suffers – his being "chosen" – is self-generated, a fate emerging from the depths of his own psyche. For example, during Roy's puzzling conversation with Harriet, he notices that her eyes are sad, and he feels "a curious tenderness for her, a little as if she might be his mother (That bird.) and tried very hard to come up with the answer she wanted – something you said about LIFE" (23). Later, when Memo asks Roy what his mother was like, he says, "a whore" (143), and his final recognition of Memo is that she, too, is "like a whore" (184). Roy was cared for by his grandmother, who is associated with food. When Memo urges Roy to eat, he says that she sounds like his grandmother (143). When thirty-three-year-old Iris admits that she is a grandmother, however, Roy is terrified of getting "serious with her," for "it could only lead to one thing – him being a grandfather" (128).

Malamud stresses the identity of the three women through means of color symbolism. Harriet Bird ("battle bird," with her black feathered hat, evocative of the Nordic raven-maidens, the Valkyries, "Choosers of the Slain")[12] has black hair, wears black, and either carries a white rose (7) or stands beside a vase of white roses (28). Memo Paris has red hair and wears black, and the first time that Roy sees her, Iris Lemon has black hair and wears red with a white rose pinned to it (110). Before he meets Iris, Roy considers this difference. Memo, "flaming above and dark below" is irresistible, but "what if the red were black and ditto the other way?" In this case he is indifferent: "He could take her or leave her" (65). When Roy visits the fortune-teller Lola during his batting slump, she tells him only that he will "soon meet and fall in love with a darkhaired lady"; she can tell him nothing more, for "the future has closed down." Roy responds, "The trouble with what you said is that I am already in love with a swell-looking redhead" (105). It is clear that Roy is dazzled by appearances, by an accident of hair and dress color, and he cannot see beyond such superficial distinctions, at least not consciously. Roy does fall in love with the dark-haired lady, Iris, but it is the last thing he does before he swings Wonderboy for the last time, when the bat, in a splendid crash of thunder and blinding flash of lightning, splits itself in two lengthwise and lies on the ground, "one half pointing to first, the other to third" (176). It is no wonder that Lola can see nothing beyond Roy's falling in love. Wonderboy "dies" in almost the next instant, and with it Roy's external soul; enter Herman ("her man") Youngberry to deliver the coup de grace: *Le roi est mort, vive le roi!*

Like the recurring colors, themes of violence, blood, and roses mark Roy's relationship with Woman. One of Roy's early memories is of his mother drowning his black tomcat (an animal associated with the lunar Diana [Cooper 30]) in a bathtub full of scalding water: "The cat fought to get out, but she shrilly beat it back and . . . gave it no mercy." The mother's blood stains the water (171). Harriet Bird's hotel room in Chicago has a view of an "endless dark lake" (the bathwater grown immense). She stands there wearing a "gossamer thing" (spider webs), black-widowish. As Roy shuts the door behind him, she reaches into "the hat box which lay open next to a vase of white roses." She fits a "black feathered hat" with "a thick veil" of mourning on her head and, ceremonially attired, asks the ritual question, "Roy, will you be the best there ever was in the game?" When he says, "That's right," she shoots him with a silver bullet (Diana's metal) and, "making muted noises of triumph and despair," dances "around the stricken hero" (28). Harriet's reasons for shooting Roy are mysterious, but fifteen years later Memo too shoots Roy, grazing his shoulder, and we know her reason: "You filthy scum, I hate your guts and always have since the day you murdered Bump" (185). Memo has called herself "a dead man's girl" (70), and the attack on Roy, as well as her conspiracy with the Judge, has about it an element of revenge. In a way Harriet, too, has been a "dead man's girl," having aligned herself at first with the Whammer, the man whom Roy has "buried" (24). We are led to conclude that the archetypal woman and the hero's relationship to her have indeed changed; something has gone awry with the pre-scribed sacred marriage, for the King of the Wood's nuptials with the moon goddess in Roy's mythic universe are dangerous business, trans-acted with a stern, violent, unforgiving bride, the widow and avenger of the slain predecessors, a Freudian revision of the old ritual that substi-tutes father for old king, "bad mother" for the moon goddess, and Oedi-pal son for the hero. Thus Roy has difficulty in consummating the "mar-riage": the bride Harriet shoots him when he comes to her bed; Memo Paris, it is hinted, evades the promised consummation by poisoning Roy (148); Iris does finally welcome the hero, but only after he has undergone a sort of death (like the black tomcat) in that dark, endless lake (124).

Of the three women, only Iris is not violent; instead, she is the victim of Roy's violence. As mentioned, he lays her low with a foul ball intended for Otto Zipp, and the last impressions Roy has of Iris are of blood and roses, a taste and smell of crucial significance in Roy's unconscious and replicat-ing the blood and roses of the Harriet episode, powerful determiners of Roy's response: "Bending over, he kissed her mouth and tasted blood. He kissed her breasts, they smelled of roses. He kissed her hard belly, wild with love for her and the child" (175). Given the disaster of Roy's last at-bat, we assume that Iris and the unborn child have moved irretrievably into the past from which, Roy concludes, he has learned nothing (185). "He coulda been a king," a faceless, nameless woman pronounces.

This is the lesson, it seems, that Harriet, Iris, and even Memo have tried to teach him. Harriet has asked, "Isn't there something over and above earthly things – some more glorious meaning to one's life and ac-tivities?" (22). In a long discussion with Iris Roy says, "My goddamn life didn't turn out like I wanted it to." "Whose does?" Iris replies. A bit lat-er Roy says, "I had a lot to give to this game." "Life?" asks Iris, and Roy responds, "Baseball" (120). Roy can see no glorious meaning in his life; he has no sense that for him baseball is life, mythically understood, that life is baseball, and that he should have a lot to give to both. His victories are won "naturally." He is afraid to die. His obsession with breaking records grows out of his terror of aging and death: "You sorta never die" if you break records. Iris asks, "Are you afraid of death?" Roy, who does not understand, replies, "Now what has that got to do with it?" (121). Iris comforts even as she questions Roy, seeks him when he makes a suicidal dive to the bottom of the lake, and makes love with him on the shore in the moonlight. On the way home, frightened herself, she seeks comfort from Roy, but he has none to give. Her last question to him is "When will you grow up, Roy?" (171). Earlier Memo, in her way, questions Roy about his motives. When he tells her that he knows he has "the stuff" and "will get there," she asks, "Get where?" He answers, "Where I am going. Where I will be the champ and have what goes with it." Roy does not know what being the best there ever was or being the champ means; he does not know what goes with it. Memo does not answer Roy but draws back from him (92). This conversation, like that with Iris, occurs by moonlight (the element of the goddess) and beside water, Diana's Mirror, but here the mirror is dark, like Memo; there is a sign nearby reading "DANGER. POLLUTED WATER" (90).

"He coulda been a king." Roy has a genius for baseball, a miraculous golden bough for a bat, and a burning desire to be the best (without knowing what that means). He has defeated the old kings and become, like them, "King of Klouters" (127). Indeed, he could have been a king, but he had trouble with the Queen of Heaven, with the goddess, "snappy" or not, through a modern neurosis created by Freud. That trouble defeats him – that and time, the silver bullet in his gut, the special gift of his bride. Within and beyond this trouble born of ignorance is the problem of living as a modern man with and within the "terrifyingly ancient" past, among its plots and meanings, without the vaguest notion of what is expected of him. "I never did learn anything out of my past life, now I have to suffer again" (185). One of the notions of Greek tragedy was that the suffering of the tragic protagonist led to wisdom. That was its solace. What Roy endures is suffering that leads only to greater ignorance. This brings us to the last of Roy's personae, that of the "natural" or fool.

ROY HOBBS, NATURAL

Jessie Weston went no further than to identify major objects of the Grail ceremony with the four suits of the tarot and to suggest that the Grail legends provide a glimpse of a remote, secret religious society whose doctrines were both revealed and concealed in the legends' images and events. Critics writing on Malamud have explored this symbolism no further than to identify Wonderboy as lance and Harriet's hat as cup, both sexual images. Nevertheless, both Eliot and Malamud incorporated images as well from the tarot trump cards, both freely interpreting and adapting the tarot symbol system as suited their needs. Malamud's novel invokes the symbolism of tarot as one of its largely pictorial languages, or systems, of signification. Because the symbolism is pervasive and a full treatment of it would require more space than can be allotted here, I want to focus attention on two trumps, the Fool and the Tower, for these inform my reading of a major theme (wisdom through suffering) and the major agon (the moral struggle against evil). Along the way I suggest the directions that a complete analysis might take.

THE FOOL

The Fool, Cavendish says, is regarded by many as "the most important and most profoundly mysterious card in the pack" (*Tarot* 59). Certainly Malamud has recognized its centrality in Roy Hobbs's existence by naming his novel, and hence his protagonist, *The Natural,* long a synonym for *fool,* "one naturally deficient in intellect; a half-witted person," according to the *Oxford English Dictionary.*[13] As the epigraph suggests, however, both fools and naturals have long been considered mad: "We are still mere naturals, no better than fools and madmen." Characterized by both folly and madness, the natural or fool is, on the one hand, emblematic of the human condition. He is Everyman, each person who journeys through life ignorant of who one is, where one is going, and why. On the other hand, the natural is unique, his madness indicating in earlier times that he is linked with the divine, in the "grip of a god or spirit" (Cavendish, *Tarot* 59), hence "touched," spiritually naïve, unfallen, yet appearing insane to those in the fallen world. Roy Hobbs embodies this paradox of naturalness. He is both common (Everyman) and yet unique (divinely touched, as evidenced by Wonderboy, but also subject to modern forms of madness, e.g., insatiable hungers, compulsions, and neuroses).

Unlike the other twenty-one trumps in the tarot deck, the Fool is unnumbered (it is usually assigned zero as its numerical designation). Without a definitive place in the sequence of twenty-two, it is "wild," like the modern joker into which it evolved, hence capable of replacing any other card or assuming the role of any other. Cavendish describes the various depictions of the Fool: "The Fool is generally a man in jester's motley with cap and bells. He has a bundle slung over his shoulder on a stick and carries a staff. He is walking along an open country, and in some packs is about to walk over a cliff because he is not looking where he is going. A peculiar animal, which may or may not be a dog, is following him closely and is either jumping up at him or biting his leg. He is sometimes shown chasing a butterfly which flutters in front of him, leading him over the cliff. In Oswald Wirth's design there is a fallen obelisk in the background and a crocodile lurks in the abyss, waiting to seize the Fool when he falls into it" (*Tarot* 59). Not surprisingly, the Fool has been linked to new beginnings, human and seasonal. He is the child or youth destined to overthrow the old order or replace the decrepit king; he is the springtime of renewed life, succeeding the dead of winter, motifs that return us to the legends of both the Grail and the golden bough. The Fool as child has been linked explicitly with Wagner's *Parsifal,* the "native simpleton of Arthurian legends" (Cavendish, *Tarot* 66), and hence (by way of Weston's study) with Roy Hobbs.

In the novel recurrent images identify Roy with the Fool as child or native simpleton. The first of these is an image directly from the tarot card of the boy Roy (often with a staff) accompanied by his dog, a pair who roam always through the forests of Roy Hobbs's mind. When Roy has at last, at the age of thirty-four, been issued his first major league uniform, when he has, therefore, arrived at the end of a long journey, he sits in the locker room, with its "tomblike quiet," feeling inexplicably depressed: "[Roy] was [here], all right, yet in all his imagining of how it would be when he finally hit the majors, he had not expected to feel so down in the dumps. It was different than walking out, jumping back on a train, and going wherever people went when they were running out on something. Maybe for a long rest in one of those towns he had lived in as a kid. Like the place where he had that shaggy mutt that used to scamper through the woods, drawing him after it to the deepest, stillest part" (36).

Another time Roy and Memo are driving toward the ocean on their first date, and Roy feels a sense of contentment, the "cutting down [of] the inside motion . . . which got him nowhere." The momentary serenity leads Roy to a meditation on his own driving ambitions and evokes again the image of boy and dog: "He remembered how satisfied he had been as a youngster, and that with the little he had had – a dog, a stick, an aloneness he loved . . . , and he wished he could have lived longer in his boyhood. This was an old thought with him" (89). Roy clearly wants to return to that boy; failing that, however, the boy returns to him. A bit later Memo drives with the lights off on a moonlit dirt road. Roy has concluded that he is tired of Memo (she is "too complicated"), but at the same time he "desire[s] her more than ever." In this condition of extreme ambivalence, he finds himself "wishing he could go back somewhere, go home, *whenever* that was" (emphasis added). Roy's longing is for a *time,* a past time "back there," home not as a place but as a spiritual condition: "As he was thinking this, he looked up and saw in the moonlight a boy coming out of the woods, followed by his dog. Squinting through the windshield, he was unable to tell if the kid was an illusion thrown forth by the trees or someone really alive. After fifteen seconds he was still there" (94).

The moon disappears as Memo races the car through the darkness, and in terror that they will hit the boy, Roy reaches over and switches on the lights: "As the road flared up, Memo screamed and tugged at the wheel. He felt a thud and his heart sickened. It was a full minute before he realized they hadn't stopped" (94). Roy insists that they have hit "somebody." Memo says "it was just something in the road," but Roy has heard somebody groan. "That," says Memo, "was yourself" (94). Somebody – the boy with a stick and a dog or the Fool – has come from whenever home is/was and stepped by moonlight into the path of a runaway car; somebody has groaned. The somebody who has been hit and the somebody who has groaned are one. Later Roy returns to look for these woods and this boy. When Roy and Memo return to the hotel, Pop, who has waited up all night, expresses fears for Roy, worrying that he will die. Roy reassures him, ironically and more truthfully than he knows, saying, "Nothing is going to kill me before my time. I am the type that will die a *natural* death" (emphasis added). Nevertheless, Pop reminds Roy of his age and advises him to "be wise and avoid any trouble." Roy naturally cannot be wise, and he denies his mature age: "I am young in my mind" (96).

Nevertheless, the child that he and Memo did (and did not) kill haunts Roy's imagination as he returns to his room. Roy is running down the corridor, pursued by Max Mercy, the journalist who "mercilessly" seeks the truth of Roy's past, when Roy finds himself running not in the corridor but in the woods, where the "moon bursts forth and the woods glow": "Out of it appeared this boy and his dog, and Roy in his heart whispered him a confidential message: watch out when you cross the road, kid, but he had spoken too late, for the boy lay brokenboned and bleeding in a puddle of light, with no one to care for him or whisper a benediction upon his lost youth" (98). For a while longer tormenting himself over the possibility that the car had struck the boy, Roy finally concludes that Memo "must've been right," "for it did not appear there ever was any kid in those woods, except in his mind" (98). Something, however, has been damaged. Roy has one good game after this incident and then goes into a batting slump of season-threatening proportions.

A few weeks later Roy is at the depths of his slump. The team has arrived for games in Chicago, and a distraught man stops Roy to ask him to save his boy, a fan of Roy's, "hurt in an accident playin' in the street."

The child is dying, "not fightin' much." The father pleads with Roy to hit a homer for the boy and thereby to save him. Although skeptical of his chances, Roy promises to "do the best [he] can" (109–10). Under Iris's magical influence Roy does hit a homer and later surrealistically imagines that "everybody knew it was Roy alone who had saved the boy's life" (114). Which boy? The boy on the country road? The boy on the Chicago street? Roy the man young in his mind? Roy who will die a natural death? All these images coalesce in the persistent image of the Fool, the young man with a dog and a stick who does not watch where he is going.

Whereas the boy with his dog roaming the forests of Roy's mind is an image of the Fool as representative of Roy's inner nature, his self or soul, two other "persons," one positive and one negative, represent Roy the natural in the world of baseball. The first is Wonderboy, a wooden icon of the inner boy, of which I have already remarked that it represents Roy's external soul. It is the staff that the Fool carries with him in all his depictions, as Roy always carries the bat. It also suggests the emblem of Roy's major suit, staves, also known as batons, clubs, or lances. On the design of the suit is the inscription *virtus ardua,* meaning "excellence, strength, or virtue difficult of attainment," in whose equivocations one might indeed find Roy's motto.

The negative representative of Roy the Fool is found in the small, nasty person of Otto Zipp, self-appointed critic and "fan." Otto Zipp's name gives him away: Ought O Zipp, or 0, 0, 0, a triple announcement of the numerical sign of the Fool. As a dwarf Otto represents Roy the child, as well as Roy's spiritual smallness; in his nastiness he represents Roy's self-hatred and doubt, his folly and ignorance, his status as an outsider. Roy inherits Otto Zipp, as he does Memo Paris, from Bump Baily. A fan of Bump, Otto is one of the grotesques in the "patched and peeling stands" when Roy arrives. Otto defends Bump from his detractors by honking a horn and shouting curses through a loudspeaker at those who razz Bump for lack of effort. Bump rewards Otto's devotion with a kiss on the forehead each day as he takes his position in left field, so Otto objects more loudly than anyone else the first time Roy pinch-hits for Bump. After Bump's accident, however, Otto offers Roy the chance to acknowledge him as brother, kindred Fool, and self by presenting his forehead for the ritual kiss, "but Roy passed without looking at him" (62), an error prompted by ignorance.

Otto disappears from the stands as, with the advent of Roy, a "new day dawned on Knights Field" (69) and returns only when Roy goes into his slump: "Otto Zipp had reappeared like a bad dream with his loud voice and pesky tooter venomously hooting Roy into oblivion" (106). Otto serves here as an instrument of self-criticism. He disappears again during the pennant race, when the team can hardly lose, only to return like an evil omen for Roy's and the team's final game, shouting from time to time, "Throw him to the hawks" (166). As the "fixed" game progresses and with Roy doing his best to live up to his bargain with the Judge, Roy directs all his rage and self-hatred toward this loudest and foulest of critics, who sits like Roy's conscience, watching him from short left field. Once, when Roy's gaze falls on Otto's "surly face," he feels "suddenly anguished" at his own treachery, but he directs his passion toward this other Fool, fouling three balls in his direction, the last of which bounces off Otto's skull and strikes Iris who, once again, is standing for Roy. Otto has a "dark lump on his noodle" (176), and the golden bough not only has touched the earth but has been left lying in the mud. On Roy's next swing Wonderboy dies with a towering, thunder-and-lightning producing foul. Otto and Wonderboy – two representatives of Roy the Fool – have been dispatched, and as he predicted, Roy dies a "natural" death. Otto remains to the end, presenting Roy one last dreadful image of himself as Fool. Roy strikes out, ending the game, the season, and his own baseball "life," the other fans vanish, and only Otto remains to enact a taunting parody of the heroic deed: "O. Zipp climbed down out of his seat. He waddled to the plate, picked up the bat and took a vicious cut at something. He must've connected, because his dumpy bow legs went like pistons around the bases. Thundering down from third he slid into the plate and called himself safe" (182). The narrative does not say whether Roy at this moment acknowledges his kinship with Otto, the Fool.

THE TOWER

One of the most sinister and mysterious aspects of the novel's scene is the dark tower that looms over the field, menacing players, coaches, manager, and fans. The man who rules the club from that vantage point is the Judge (with a capital letter, an epithet for God). In his name, Goodwill Banner, lies evidence of both his character and his tower, for both are transformations of archetypes implicated in the fall of mythic systems: the "Judge" Jahweh who confused the language of humanity and the general theme of failed language and language pressed into the service of confusion, ambiguity, deceit, and fraud. The Judge in his deceitful aspect is a flag (a banner, the pennant, goal of Roy's quest) announcing goodwill; in his true nature he is a banner (an interdictor) of goodwill. The ambiguous name is just right for this prince of frauds, a sophist and formidable opponent for a natural, a mythically illiterate man who when asked if he has ever read Homer can think only of "four bases and not a book" (21).

Indeed, the Tower card of the tarot deck is most frequently understood as representing the Tower of Babel, whose builders wanted to construct a tower that would reach into heaven – the ruined tower standing for frustrated ambition, language used as an instrument of power, and the terrible failure of human language to promote community, felicity, cooperation, and connection. The French title of the Tower card is *La Maison Dieu*, "House of God," which is very close to the biblical *Babel*, which in Babylonian meant "gate of God." The tower depicted on the card is being struck by lightning, and the top of it has broken loose and is falling. Two human figures also are falling, as in depictions of the Tower of Babel. Cavendish points out that Wirth, a designer of tarot decks, called the card *Le Feu du Ciel*, "Fire from Heaven" (*Tarot* 123), hence lightning, whose implications I have already examined. Here its supernatural power is demonic, a parody of that which blossoms as the golden bough.

The Judge's tower is "curious" and rises "on a slight tilt above the main entrance of the ball park" (69). Its curious nature, its slant, and indeed its mere presence are all disquieting. When Roy ascends the stairs to ask for a raise, the steps are "slippery," and the office is "half dark." On the wall is a "shellacked half of a stuffed shark" and a framed "motto piece": "Be it ever so humble, there is no place like home," "Nihil nisi bonum [Nothing but the good]," "All is not gold that glitters," and "The dog is turned to his vomit again" (72). The floor of the office is slanted, too, as are the meanings of the Judge's mottoes. None by itself is unambiguous, but their inclusion within a single frame makes them comment ironically on one another. There certainly is no place like this home, the residence of the human shark whose image hangs beside the mottoes on the wall, for in its ostentatious humility the Judge's home is the place of the dog's return, its vomit creating a noisesome ambience in which the exalted Latin moral – "nothing but the good" – sounds hollow, just as the Judge's pious platitudes echo ironically in the moral darkness that is his element. Pop Fisher has warned Roy before his visit to the Judge that when "triple talk is invented . . . he will own the copyright" (73). In the course of negotiations Roy does hear his share of triple talk and the confusion of tongues. The Judge is fond of biblical forms and speaks in parable (the parable of the marvelous cow); proverb ("The love of money is the root of all evil" [74]), moral advice ("Emphasis upon money will pervert your values"), and philosophical speculation (the discourse on the "unity of darkness" [75]). The Judge plans a disquisition on this last subject, to be titled "On the Harmony of Darkness; Can Evil Exist in Harmony?" Roy responds, "All I know about the dark is that you can't see in it" (75). Although Roy does not have the moral sophistication to recognize evil, it can and does exist in darkness, for that is the Judge's element. In this unequal linguistic duel, confusion prevails. Roy (who has gone seeking a raise from $3,000 to $45,000) ends up not only without a raise (the Judge believes in a strict interpretation of the language of contracts) but owing the Judge for a uniform Bump Baily ruined. As his parting bit of advice, the Judge, remaining true to form by saying one thing and meaning another, offers, "Resist all evil." Roy is left to make his way down the slippery stairs in the "pitch black" (77).

In an intriguing reversal of these negotiations, the Judge visits Roy in his hospital room to convince Roy to take a bribe and throw the last game. His theme now is that evil can come from good intentions, and good from evil intentions (160–61). For a while almost convinced by the Judge's arguments, wherein good is made evil and evil good, Roy manages to escape the rhetorical trap by recalling an incident in his childhood, that of a "natural." It concerns a time when the dog had become lost in the woods and Roy, unwilling to leave the dog alone in the woods at night, went in after him. The boy became lost as well, and the "payoff of it was that the mutt found him and led him out of the woods. That was good out of good" (161). Nevertheless, Roy has learned from the Judge, and in the ensuing negotiations he does to the Judge what the Judge did to him earlier; he has learned something about ironic moral discourse as well, for as the Judge leaves, Roy, having accepted the proposition to throw the game, quotes an old saying, "Woe unto him who calls evil good and good evil" (163), evoking the Judge's ironically appropriated "*Honi soi qui mal y pense*" ("evil to him who evil thinks"), the motto of the Order of the Garter. It is by no means cause for celebration that Roy is now figuratively at home in the Tower, with the Tower's residents and the Tower's language.

The foregoing examples demonstrate the presence of tarot symbolism in the novel, but they cannot convey how pervasive it is. Clearly the subject deserves fuller treatment than I can offer here. For instance, after Eddie the porter finds a pair of "bewitched" dice, Roy uses them to throw snake eyes three times in a row. Afraid of the dice and wanting no "outside assistance in games of chance" (6–7), Eddie throws them away when

the train stops. Simultaneously, however, Harriet Bird, sinister and beguiling, steps onto the train. Her tarot number must be two – the Female
Pope, whose celestial sign is the moon, the enigmatic Woman embodied
three times in Roy's career, a career under the influence of this symbol of
the "vanity and emptiness of all worldly ambitions" (Cavendish, *Tarot*
101). Roy's Wheel of Fortune is figured in the Ferris wheel, stopped (as
is his career) like a giant clock; his goddess Fortuna takes the guise of
Harriet Bird. Indeed, the signs of the tarot pack confront Roy at every
turn, their coded enigmas serving to confuse, rather than to instruct, the
protagonist.

ROY HOBBS IN THE WASTE LAND OF INTERTEXTUALITY

The foregoing analyses make it clear that Roy's fictive world is radically intertextual, crowded with archetypes, and the question then arises
as to what function or functions are performed by the incorporated mythological and legendary texts, images, and figures. What meanings are
conveyed by these transformed archetypes? In 1975 Malamud said that
he saw the mythological pre-texts as a "system of metaphor. It enriches
the vision without resorting to montage" (in Lasher 61). But *montage* is
exactly the word to describe Eliot's poem (which has provided the assist),
a thing composed of broken images – quotations, allusions, figures,
themes, snippets – drawn from here and there throughout the history of
Western texts. It is even in some ways an appropriate term for Weston's
and Frazer's studies. Malamud's statement, therefore, seems to be a bit
of authorial misdirection or irony in which the truth lies hidden and where
system and *montage* rub against each other to produce sparks. The work
in question, *The Natural,* is rich and equivocal, a fact Malamud himself
underscored: "This guy gets up with his baseball bat and all at once he
is, through the ages, a knight – somewhat battered – with a lance; not to
mention a guy with a blackjack, or someone attempting murder with a
flower" (in Lasher 61). Rich indeed – montage, pastiche, hodgepodge:
bat, lance, blackjack, flower; athlete, knight, thug, murderer! Clearly
Malamud knew about texts, intertextuality, and transformations.

As mentioned, however, critics have been slow to appreciate both the
richness and the resulting transformations wrought by montage and the
journey of texts through the ages. Focusing on sedimentation rather than
innovation, they have seen a stability in the encompassed texts that permits them to travel intact from medieval Europe to twentieth-century

America, from a context of chivalry to one of baseball. The significance and stability of the old romances, their conventions, and their beliefs are, they say, mirrored in something called "the human condition," and so, according to this view, the ancient text is archetypal (in the Jungian sense of innate, universal, and changeless, bearing a pattern equally appropriate for Arthurian knight and New York Knight). Daniel Walden, following Leslie Fiedler, puts this proposition succinctly: "Malamud has, in *The Natural,* found, not imposed, an archetype in the life we presently live; in his book, the modern instance and the remembered myth are equally felt, equally realized, and equally appropriate to our predicament" (153). Robert C. Lidston dismisses the oddness of "mixing Arthuriana and baseball" by resort to the claim that both are by nature legendary and therefore relevant to the "human condition" (75). This assumption leads to a perception of sameness, continuity, and universality among heroes and across time. Arguing in this vein Lidston concludes that Roy Hobbs is like Tennyson's Percivale and that Percivale's lessons are Roy's. He says, "For Roy's story Malamud has drawn on the legendary dimension of our national game and once again demonstrated the power of myth to reveal inner struggles which transcend times and customs" (80).

As I have argued, however, neither texts nor archetypes are stable or univocal, so the matter of intertextuality is a complex one. Malamud's novel is full of ghosts of earlier texts and myth systems. When these are called together for service in a twentieth-century novel, they cannot bring their original contexts (the world in which they operated as living myths), and so they do not bring their original pattern, order, and meaning. On the contrary, like demons entering a house on the skirts of a new bride, they bring equivocation, disorientation, enigma, the *Unheimliche.*

The mythic dimensions of Roy Hobbs's world are created by echo, allusion, suggestion, parody, and image, which are the hallmarks of a postmodern scene. The novel's mode is irony, its theme is terror, and Roy Hobbs is unmistakably a twentieth-century man. When I consider the plight of Roy Hobbs, I am reminded of a short story by D. H. Lawrence called "The Woman Who Rode Away," a troubling tale of a woman in quest of she knows not what who rides out of one mythic world (that of a desiccated Judeo-Christianity) and into a more ancient, yet living, belief system where she becomes a human sacrifice to gods she does not know and for purposes she cannot imagine. Both Lawrence's heroine and Malamud's Roy Hobbs confront ancient sacrality as aliens, ignorant outsiders, compelled to serve unknown forces for unknown reasons. In each case the ancient, as it appears in the postmodern scene, is uncanny yet required, like Eliot's "broken images," obscure archaeological shards used to shore up one's ruins, whose messages in the collocation of the modern text may yet prove significant or merciful, charged with grace.

In its own context living myth perhaps offers its devotees the intact image, the comforts of system and "truth." It assigns meaning, orders chaos, and gives significance not only to society's organization and endeavors but to the individual and his or her life. We assume that the medieval knight knew why he wandered, why he fought, and why he died. If asked, he could have spoken, perhaps, of higher meaning in his life and activities. The challenger knew what was at stake and why as he faced the old King of the Wood. These imported myths, however, do not provide for Roy Hobbs, a man seeking significance in baseball, the only myth system he knows. He wants to walk down the street and have people say, "There goes Roy Hobbs, the best there ever was in the game" (26); he wants to live forever through records. But the broken images, the ghosts of kings, priests, knights, and goddesses – the archaeology revealed in the novel's textual digs – these, like Harriet, Iris, and Memo, keep insisting to Roy that this game called baseball is figurative, a haunted garden situated, perhaps inadvertently, on an old ritual ground or graveyard. As I have shown, Roy claims to have "a lot to give to this game," yet when Iris asks, "Life?" Roy does not make the connection. Malamud has this figural existence of the game in mind when he says that he transformed the game into myth: "The myth enriched the baseball lore as feats of magic transformed the game" ("Reflections of a Writer" 16).

Roy cannot see the "figures" on the field and in the game, not because he is stupid but because, as a twentieth-century man, he is mythically impoverished, ignorant, wandering a spiritual wasteland. The imported texts are exotic, out of context. He cannot step into the world that created them and that they in turn helped to create. In a poem related thematically to "The Waste Land," T. S. Eliot describes the condition Roy exemplifies, in which men, "seeds upon the wind," struggle "in torment towards GOD," "blindly and vainly, . . . crying for life beyond life, for ecstasy not of the flesh." Roy Hobbs is such a seed, a man crying for life, for ecstasy not of the flesh. Roy's eating disorder is traceable to this motive, as he attempts to satisfy spiritual hunger with material food, like those who, Eliot says, come at last "to the withered ancient look of a child that has died of starvation" ("Choruses from 'The Rock'" VII).

Malamud's imported texts consist not only of the medieval and more ancient materials but also of Eliot's "The Waste Land," which is woven into the novel's web of intertextuality and contributes its own stark vision. Anyone who has studied "The Waste Land" should, therefore, beware any unequivocal or too comfortable reading of Malamud's text, even if the novel were less bleak than it is. The poem and the novel are alike in their archetypes, their pre-texts, alike in their montage structuring, their bricolage, and alike in their incorporation of modern Freudian myth. In short, both epitomize literary postmodernism, described by Mark C. Taylor as "historically allusive": "Through the use of irony, parody, pastiche, and citation, postmodern artists attempt to draw attention to the historical dimensions of experience *in a way that accentuates the contrasts and heightens the tension between past and present.* . . . Such strategies 'combine the memory of things long past with the drama of innovation' [Ricoeur's 'sedimentation and innovation']. This turn to the past is of more than historical interest. Historical images harbor vestiges of a yet more distant past – a past which [has been described] as 'terrifyingly ancient'" (emphasis added). The invocation of the terrifyingly ancient past, the radical past, is a fiendishly clever maneuver for the wasteland artist: "This radical past that is never present but is always on the verge of arriving marks and remarks the approach of the sacred" – not the presence of the sacred but only its approach, the imminent arrival of the "eternal now" always deferred. It is in this characteristic, Taylor says, that one is able to "glimpse the inscription of the sacred in postmodern art" (5); an uncanny sacred, one might add, not necessarily reassuring in its drawing near, for the frequent response to it is madness or terror. It is exactly here, in the understanding of the sacred, that Eliot's and Malamud's postmodern texts are in outright contention with their pre-texts. The difference can be seen, for example, in the figure of lightning, an image that travels through Frazer, Weston, and Eliot to Malamud, an image present only in its aftereffects in another postmodern work that Mark C. Taylor sees as paradigmatic, a massive sculpture by the French sculptors Anne and Patrick Poirier entitled *Paysage foudroyé* (Thunderstruck landscape).

Taylor discusses this sculpture as an example of postmodernism in which the approach of the radical past, and with it the approach of the sacred, may be discerned. Taylor cites the artists' own description of their enterprise as an attempt through "errings across architectures, ruins, and gardens . . . to understand the relations of archeology and mythology with our mental universe" (Taylor 7). This is in some ways an apt description of Roy Hobbs's task. The thunderstruck landscape produced by the

Poiriers is devastated, barren, and broken, presented as the aftereffect of the battle between the Olympians and the Titans, in which Zeus (Jupiter) prevails because of his superior weapon, lightning. It is, not surprisingly, reminiscent of Eliot's poem, seeming to be a visual image of "The Waste Land," and more than this, an apt metaphor for Malamud's fictional world. In it one can see the past laid bare, in ruins, as in an archaeological dig, evocative, disturbing, mysterious. It is an attempt, as the Poiriers state, "to penetrate . . . 'poetic' spaces contained in a region of our being that is accessible only with great difficulty" (cited in Taylor 7), a region of the linguistic unconscious. This similarity helps to account for some critics' descriptions of Malamud's scene as evocative of psychological space, as does Baumbach when he calls it "fluid and magical – the landscape of a dream" (27) or Pifer when she says that it constitutes a "territory of art" existing somewhere between "the world of fact and that of dream" (139).

As a result, readers of the novel, like its protagonist, wander the gap, these poetic spaces, seeking some significance in the ruins of the mythic landscapes, the novel's intertextual geography, some place of rest, some comfort. The imported texts speak differently in the new context, however; far from being stable, permanently relevant to the human condition, now they seem uncanny, their messages equivocal. An allegory may demonstrate the process of metamorphosis the pre-text undergoes. Suppose a man attends church on Sunday morning and sees on the altar a bouquet of white roses, which he associates with the minister's sermon on the purity and love of Christ. The roses are set outside after the service, and a madam from a local house of ill repute takes them home to adorn the foyer of her establishment. The man drops by, sees the roses (text) in the new setting, and is surprised and confused. Is their significance intact? What tensions now exist between the old (con)text and the new? When the man returns to church the following Sunday and sees the "same" roses on the altar, has their meaning changed? Does the concept of love associated with the roses in church carry over to the whorehouse, or is it ironically altered by love's associations in the new setting?

Like the rose-salvaging madam, the intertextual artist places the broken images of abandoned metaphysics from (arche)textual digs for display in the modern setting. They do not travel any better than the roses. A common critical theme is that Roy Hobbs is guilty of moral failure and Freudian crimes of immaturity, infantilism, attachment to the mother, and so forth. But the question of moral freedom – the ability at each crossroads to make a choice, for good or ill, based on rational or ethical principles, for the effects of which choice one is wholly responsible – is always defined by recourse to the cultural context – the mythology – in which it is raised. Take the example of Oedipus, whose myth enters *The Natural* via Freudian psychology. Having learned from the oracle that he is destined to murder his father and marry his mother, Oedipus chooses not to return home. What he does not know, of course, is that home is not Corinth, as he believes, but Thebes, toward which, having made his ethical choice, he travels, directed by fate, to fulfill the very destiny he seeks to avoid. Within his myth system he commits no fault, and so he is not condemned for moral failure or infantile attachment to his mother. When such Oedipal themes as father murder, mother marriage, and fate arrive in Roy Hobbs's story, however, the whole mythic context has changed. In this world Iris can ask Roy the question Jocasta would not and could not have considered: "When will you grow up?" Now critics can speak knowledgeably of flaws like infantilism and compulsive behavior; they can condemn Roy's agon as moral failure. Freudian compulsion and unconscious motives may be analogous to fate, but these more personal, less grand directors of human lives are, unlike the Fates, unable in most critics' views to excuse error. Like the vase of white roses in the house of prostitution, Oedipus's "text" in Roy Hobbs's world is equivocal, ambiguous.

The old texts arrive as invited but "uncanny" guests, bringing their battered metaphysical baggage and prepared for a permanent stay. In one of the best essays I know on the topic of intertextuality, "The Critic as Host," J. Hillis Miller develops a theory of intertextuality and its equivocal effects based on the mutual and shifting relations between earlier and later texts as parasites and hosts and as guests and hosts. He speculates about the function of the older texts, whether as guests or parasites, in the new. The later text, whether poem, novel, sculpture, or criticism, is of necessity equivocal (rather than univocal), whatever its claims, because in encompassing earlier texts the new one permits meanings to proliferate beyond the power of any single text to control, and the temporal journey, as the example of the roses suggests, is a two-way street. Does the later text "reprogram" the earlier text "to make it utter its own message," or "could it be the other way around?" Miller continues: "Could it be that metaphysics, the obvious or univocal meaning, is the parasitical virus which has for millennia been passed from generation to generation in Western culture in its languages and in the privileged texts of those languages? Does metaphysics enter the language-learning apparatus of each new baby born into that culture and shape the apparatus after its own patterns? The difference might be that this apparatus, unlike the host cell for a virus, does not have its own pre-existing inbuilt genetic code" (147).[14] The apparatus to which Miller refers is what I have called the archetype as signifier. Is the later text, in this case *The Natural,* like the host cell for the pre-texts as virus, a host on which a textual parasite feeds? More bewildering, is the later text a parasite on the older text? A guest? Are the older and newer texts friends or enemies? Do they maintain a symbiotic relationship? Miller finds the relationships to be equivocal, as are all relations of language. The new work "both needs the old texts and must destroy them." It is "both parasitical on them, feeding ungraciously on their substance, and at the same time is the sinister host which unmans them by inviting them into its home" (149).

Nothing remains unambiguous in these complex and unstable relationships, yet those very ambiguities permit a variety of univocal readings. For example, in one view the chivalric legends and older myth systems bring heroic models and metaphysics into the realm of baseball and the geography of the novel, which grow to encompass them. Hence Harriet Bird is seen as accurate in her assessment of the confrontations that result – "David jawboning Goliath-Whammer," "Sir Percy lancing Sir Maldemer, or the first son (with a rock in his paw) ranged against the primitive papa" (21). Her catalog includes Roy Hobbs with the old, the ancient, and the "terrifyingly ancient" – chivalric, biblical, and Freudian archetypes. By this reading, Roy Hobbs's stature and endeavors take size and significance from the presence of the guest texts, and a critic would be correct in seeing Roy Hobbs as a universal hero, which is the position taken by Earl Wasserman, who asserts that the mythic pre-texts "by which man once measured the moral power of his humanness" provide an opportunity by which "Roy's baseball career may slip the bonds of time and place and unfold as the everlastingly crucial story of man," revealing itself as "symbolic of man's psychological and moral situation" (440). Daniel Walden, following Wasserman, similarly analyzes the case: "What is behind the scenes, however, is 'a novel that coherently organized the rites of baseball and many of its memorable historic episodes into the epic inherent in baseball as a measure of man, as it once was inherent in Homeric battles or chivalric tournaments or the Arthurian quest for the Grail.' [Wasserman] . . . Malamud pictured Roy as the eternal quester who adjusted his character to his goal. Jessie Weston, among others, made available the significance of the Arthurian myth. . . . For Roy . . . the journey to the 'secret of the sources of Life' is begun" (154).

Such critics find no irony in the juxtaposition of situations, no tension among texts, no struggle, no alarm. Nonetheless, a closer look at the language of Harriet's interpretation calls into question not only its truth value but the concept of heroism as imaged in martial careers and militant metaphors. Her word choice is strange: "jawboning" is at once colloquial (in the sense of *talking* someone into compliance), comical, and inaccurate, both more intimately violent and primitive than need be. Samson is the biblical hero with a jawbone, not David, who uses a sling and stones. "Goliath-Whammer" is funny, not imposing. "Sir Percy," a diminutive of Percival, along with "lancing" rings of skepticism, too colloquial for the high seriousness of chivalry. Finally, Harriet's image of the "first son" (and all that the term implies of the tradition of primogeniture) is positively animalian. One cannot avoid the image of a snarling, drooling, prehuman primate with a rock – a baseball? – in its "paw" at the end of a too-long arm. Moreover, the alliterative jingle in "primitive papa" clearly undermines the paternal dignity of a Laius berating Oedipus, a Kronos attacked by the lightning bolts of rebellious son Zeus, or a King David facing ambitious son Absalom. Harriet knows Freud, so she cannot know Percival.

Like the roses in the whorehouse, these heroes in the novel have undergone a change of significance in their new context. They are, to say the least (and perhaps the most), equivocal. Indeed, they call into question not only the hero's motives but the possibility of heroism. If Roy Hobbs had possessed more sophistication, more insight into himself and his intertextual universe, he might well have answered Harriet with the words of one of Eliot's twentieth-century men, J. Alfred Prufrock: "I am not Prince Hamlet, nor was meant to be." Yet even that reply would be ironic, for Freudian reasons: both Hamlet and Roy, like Oedipus, suffer problems with their fathers and mothers. Would the disclaimer indicate repression and denial? Nevertheless, the old texts, which are powerful vehicles of human imagining, will have their say. In *The Natural*, as I have suggested, the abundance of pre-texts produces cacophony, confusion, equivocation, and ambiguity. Together these pre-texts constitute their own Tower of Babel, and like the Judge's mottoes, they jar against one another, negate, qualify, or comment ironically on one another. Roy does not know and cannot discover, among the figures and broken images of his textual world, who he is, where he is going, or why. Which elements speak of genuine value? Which, if any, point the way to spiritual health and joy? Readers can and do ignore the intertextual complexity and impose moral lessons on the tale. Wasserman, reading the work through Jungian symbolism, assigns blame in psychological terms. Roy's failure is infantilism, he says, born of struggles with the bad mother that prevent his growing up: "Because Roy's failure to be the hero is his failure to accept the mature father role, it is properly a boy who ends the novel, begging hopefully in disillusionment, 'Say it ain't true, Roy.' . . . For in the boy is each new American generation hopefully pleading that those on whom it depends will grow mature through the difficult love that renders the life of the human community the self-sacrificing and yet self-gaining purpose of their vital resources" (459). Walden echoes this accusation, writing that Roy's "fatal flaw was his inability to surmount his infantile yearnings" (155). Alternatively, critics can fault Roy for the failing Harriet intimated: he "placed the setting of baseball records over more spiritual values" (Lidston 80).

Some readers, however, those grown too intimate with this lonely, ignorant outsider, this natural, and the ruins of old metaphysics that constitute his space, hesitate to condemn him. It might be said that to fault Roy for failing to gain moral, spiritual, or psychological wisdom is a bit like condemning Eliza Doolittle for not learning aristocratic English in the streets of London. Refined English is not to be found in Eliza's world, nor wisdom in Roy's. And, one suspects, just as Eliza could not recognize cultured speech if she heard it, neither could Roy recognize wisdom. For neither character is it (to use an intertextual pun) in the cards.

A dominant figure in Eliot's "The Waste Land" is Madame Sosostris, "famous clairvoyante" and "wisest woman in Europe." "Clear seer," fortune-teller, reader of tarot cards, and caster of horoscopes, she has a "bad cold," and with it, one assumes, runny eyes and impaired vision. Tiresias, another wisdom figure, whom Eliot borrowed from the Greeks, is reduced in modern London to the status of voyeur, a "peeper" rather than a seer. Lola, the fortune-teller in *The Natural,* is similarly handicapped: she is near-sighted. All three figures are apt emblems for the pre-texts that inhabit the linguistic space of the poem or novel. They are changed, ill, degenerate, and squint-eyed. The old metaphysics, vital in other times, other places, coexists ironically in the modern scene with the modern myths of baseball, of Freudian or Jungian psychology, or, some might add, of poststructuralism.

Malamud's thunderstruck landscape shows the effects of lightning, his master trope, as both devastating and creative. Received from a precursor text, "The Waste Land," reverberating from an ancient wood, a vision of last days, a fallen tower where linguistic complexity was said to originate, the novel encompasses an intricate web of implications whose total effect is found not in the old myths or in a close analogy between old and new but in the new thing: the bricolage emerging from this pastiche, in this context, for this protagonist who finds in that texture not meaning, not wisdom, certainly not solace and community, not, alas, home, but the *Unheimliche,* relentless equivocation, despair, error, and errantry, the signifying trope, as I said, of Roy Hobbs's life.

The effects of intertextuality also complicate Robert Coover's *The Universal Baseball Association,* to which I turn my attention next, for Coover's novel invites into the text as guest, parasite, and host some of the most powerful pre-texts of Western civilization.

10

MEANWHILE THE MIND, FROM PLEASURE LESS,

WITHDRAWS INTO ITS HAPPINESS:

THE MIND, THAT OCEAN WHERE EACH KIND

DOES STRAIGHT ITS OWN RESEMBLANCE FIND;

YET IT CREATES, TRANSCENDING THESE,

FAR OTHER WORLDS, AND OTHER SEAS,

ANNIHILATING ALL THAT'S MADE

TO A GREEN THOUGHT IN A GREEN SHADE.

Andrew Marvell, "The Garden"

DO I DARE

DISTURB THE UNIVERSE?

T. S. Eliot, "The Love Song of J. Alfred Prufrock"

PLAYING GOD, PLAYING MAN

J. HENRY WAUGH IN THE HOUSE

OF JOY

Robert Coover's *The Universal Baseball Association, Inc., J. Henry Waugh, Prop.* (hereinafter *The UBA*) is the story of a middle-aged accountant who has invented a one-person, tabletop baseball game into which he pours his creative energies, his love, and his keen sense of play and in which he finds fellowship and family, delight, and despair. By day he keeps books for the firm of Dunkelmann, Zauber & Zifferblatt ("darkman" ["mystery"], "magic," and "clockface" ["time"]); by night he "works" as "auditor," proprietor, and "prop" – support and property – of the Universal Baseball Association. The novel consists of seven chapters corresponding to seven consecutive days, followed by an eighth chapter occurring after a hiatus of one hundred league years, a structure suggested by the first chapter of Genesis and the last book of the New Testament, that is, creation and apocalypse. The world of the novel is ruled by a "personal god" who oversees the activities of a population whose lives are governed by the roll of dice, the natural laws of this universe.

COOVER AND THE METACREATIVE ENTERPRISE

The usual way into Coover's work generally, and *The UBA* in particular, is through the door of metafiction,[1] a critical approach that finds that Henry is author, the Universal Baseball Association (hereinafter UBA) is his text, and the novel is "really" about writing fiction. "Metafiction," says Mas'ud Zavarzadeh, "is ultimately a narrational metatheorem whose subject matter is fictional systems themselves and the molds through which reality is patterned by narrative conventions." Metafiction is, in other words, a theory of fiction masquerading as fiction itself, self-conscious in its artificiality, or as Zavarzadeh says, "exult[ing] over its own fictitiousness" (39). Given this definition, metafiction as a critical concept distinguishes between fictional systems and reality, in a way that fails to capture the essence of the matter. We need a critical term for the creative enterprise that claims that there is no reality outside texts or (what amounts to the same thing) that if there is, we cannot know it. There are only narratives – sacred and profane texts, histories, stories, metaphors, parables, treatises, theories, scripts, and commentaries – that, taken together, constitute reality. I propose the term *metacreative* to designate such a philosophy of texts. When it is genuine, metacreative work is neither trivial nor remote from human concerns, for it is engaged not with the making of fictions but with the making of reality or realities. It is, in other words, the mythic enterprise.

The metacreationist's task is to confront the existing textual universe (what Northrop Frye calls "a mythology" [*Creation and Recreation* 7]), which is constructed of Gould's archetypal signifiers (linguistic, mythical debris or bricolage, plots, figures, images, and tropes, all arranged in a vast and intricate intertextual web) with a new narrative, his or her (re-)creation of the world, and in the process to disturb that universe. Why would anyone want to do such a thing? The answer involves the granting or seizing of power. This was William Blake's recognition: "I must

Create a System [universe], or be enslav'd by another Man's / I will not Reason and Compare: my business is to Create" (*Jerusalem* pl. 10, 120). Coover takes a similar stand when he speaks of the "human need for pattern, and language's propensity, willy-nilly, for supplying it," and of his own unwillingness to be made subject to the stories, the artifices, of others, however time-honored and however entrenched the reality they have produced. Coover says:

> Every effort to form a view of the world, every effort to speak of the world, involves a kind of fiction-making process. Memory is a kind of narrative, as is our perception of what the future is apt to bring us, our understanding of anything going on out in the world – even our scientific understanding of the world has to be reduced to a narrative of sorts in order to grasp it. . . . Men live by fictions. They have to. . . . We have to isolate [bits of input] and make reasonable stories out of them. All of them, though, are merely artifices – that is, they are always in some ways false, or at best incomplete. (in LeClair and McCaffery 68)

Although they are necessary for us to live, these stories can oppress (or "enslave") those who grant them authority, which explains Coover's resistance: "So if some stories start throwing their weight around, I like to undermine their authority a bit, work variations, call attention to their fictional natures" (in LeClair and McCaffery 68). He does not use the terms *sedimentation* and *innovation,* but it is clear that Coover has concepts similar to Ricoeur's in mind here. Also clear is Coover's intention to work on the innovative side of the equation. The point to be made concerning the new creation emerging from the metacreative endeavor is not so much that it exults in its own fictitiousness as that it insists on the fictional nature of *all* stories, with the corollary that reality is an artifice that, having been shaped by texts, is now given new form in the new text. The metacreative author's intertextual project, the direct or indirect confrontation of old texts, old archetypes, is central, for any attempt to recreate the world occurs necessarily within a world – the space, the tower – already constituted of texts. The new text calls attention to the older ones, echoing them, elaborating, contradicting, "work[ing] variations," and inviting them in. This is the intertextual gesture, generous and sinister at once.

Consequently, texts of all sorts may challenge existing accounts of reality; they need not be metafictions or metacreations, but they cannot help being intertextual. They may take the form of myth, sacred history, philosophy, theology, history, or science. To disturb the universe, however, it is necessary either to substitute a new authorized text (a new reality) for the existing version (e.g., a heliocentric for a geocentric theory of the universe) or, as Coover says, to resort to parody or irony, to undermine their authority by working variations and calling attention to their fictional natures. Parody and irony, Coover's chosen techniques, need not be projects of negation (although for some writers they are); they can equally offer opportunities for affirmation. One of the questions I will consider is whether *The UBA* affirms a new reality or merely denies an old one.

In the history of ideas the project of creating a system, disturbing the universe, or undermining the authority of stories that throw their weight around is evolutionary in its mildest form, often revolutionary, and at times positively cataclysmic, involving a thorough stripping away of the existing realities made of texts, what Northrop Frye calls our "cultural insulation that separates us from nature [nontextual reality]." That cultural insulation, he says, is "rather like . . . the window of a lit-up railway carriage at night": "Most of the time it is a mirror of our own concerns, including our concern about nature. As a mirror, it fills us with the sense that the world is something which exists primarily in reference to us: it was created for us; we are the centre of it and the whole point of its existence." Our stories, taken together, may give us a comfortable complacency, the notion that we have it all figured out, ordered, in control. But when a new text comes along to challenge existing accounts of the world, to disturb this comfortable universe, there may come a period of radical disorientation, a crack, an abyss opening in the universe of words, a moment when the mirror "turns into a real window" "through which we can see only the vision of an indifferent nature that got along for untold æons of time without us, seems to have produced us only by accident, and, if it were conscious, could only regret having done so. This vision propels us instantly into the opposite pole of paranoia, where we seem to be victims of a huge conspiracy, finding ourselves, through no will of our own, arbitrarily assigned to a dramatic role which we have been given no script to learn, in a state of what Heidegger calls 'thrownness'" (*Creation and Recreation* 6). "The humanly creative," says Frye, "is whatever profoundly disturbs our sense of 'the' creation" (11). In the end, however, as Coover observes, the human need for pattern is supplied by the language of the new text, or reasserted by the old, or neither quite succeeds in prevailing, in which case a debate ensues over which reality is really real (as the ongoing debate between creationists and evolutionists exemplifies). At such moments we gather our verbal comforters around us, for we will not and cannot gaze too long through the real window at the meaningless progress of indifferent nature.

One of the points to be made about *The UBA* is that Coover has masterfully re-created the first two steps in the sequence of reality reconstruction, first challenging the stories that throw their weight around by working variations and calling attention to their fictional nature, and second, in chapter 8, presenting the abyss, the gap between texts, the mirror become window, the world whose inhabitants find themselves victims of a huge conspiracy, in dramatic roles with no scripts, in a condition of thrownness. We shall have to decide whether in that gaping abyss a new dry land – an apocalyptic new earth and new heaven – is taking shape.

THE UBA AND ITS PRE-TEXTS

As I previously suggested, in his re-creative enterprise Coover has taken on some of the most imposing of all pre-texts. He has said that he structured his novel after the first biblical narrative of creation (Genesis 1:1–2:3), "seven chapters corresponding to the seven days of creation," and this, he says, "naturally implied an eighth, the apocalyptic day" (in Gado 149). Of this eighth day/chapter Coover says, "It's not a gloss on the text from which it borrows its design, in the sense of being a theologian's gloss; it's an outsider's gloss, an ironist's gloss" (in LeClair and McCaffery 73), in which claim we may recognize the (generous yet sinister) intertextual invitation. Appropriately enough, given this pre-text, Coover's protagonist is *J. Henry Waugh* (JHWH, an ironic transform of the Old Testament God Jahweh or, more commonly, Yahweh), and Coover's novel, like the creation (according to Bishop James Ussher's calculations),[2] begins on a Tuesday in mid-autumn (17).

Because the novel's structure (creation followed by apocalypse, with a one-hundred-year hiatus between chapters 7 and 8) corresponds to the first chapter of the Old Testament and the last book of the New Testament (Revelation, or the Apocalypse), by implication it covers as well everything between, all biblical texts and all of human time from creation to destruction. We thus are led to see the novel as an outsider's Bible, a revised sacred history. In his revision Coover exploits all the possibilities inherent in baseball, its plot in the sense both of ground or space and of game or story, returning to the beginning, to sacred time and space, in order to work variations on what may be called *the* archetypal plot of (creation of) creation and to re-create the world with his own account. If we miss this point, we miss much of the novel's richness, as well as its poignancy and power. In general, critics have missed the point, perhaps because the metafictional approach invites an understanding of the relation between texts as one of analogy. McCaffery is typical in finding the relationship between Henry and his UBA as *analogous to* that between Yahweh and his universe: "As the puns in the title of the book tell us, J. Henry Waugh (JHWH, the Jehovah of his world) is *a sort of deity* presiding over a universe made up of baseball players – in effect, he is the 'prop' upon which the universe rests because he has created this *imaginary* world and all the players in it" (42; emphasis added). Analogy claims only that Henry is to the UBA as Yahweh is to the universe, but as analogues, Henry and his UBA are easily devalued, placed at a distance from reality, from "real" human concerns and genuine religious, theological, philosophical, and historiographical issues. Henry's world is only imaginary; God's is real. Henry's world is "a machine for the production of a narrative" (Caldwell 164). The primacy of Henry's "imagined world is established as a result of conflict with the 'real' world" (Eisinger 156). This is a comic novel in which one experiences "the confusion of the realms of illusion and reality" (Shelton 79). Seen as analogue, Henry's world is illusory and reveals its creator's pathology; it is created "to fill his empty existence" (Shelton 80) or as a result of "the poverty of the protagonist's relations with other human beings" (Caldwell 163).

The situation changes entirely when we recognize in Henry and his UBA not analogues but the fusion of identity implied by metaphor, which is, as Eric Gould argues, the coin of myth and mythicity. Unlike analogy, metaphor claims that Henry *is* Yahweh; the UBA *is* his creation, the human world; and the players *are* human beings. The world of the UBA is neither more nor less imaginary than, for example, that depicted in the first chapter of Genesis, the one Milton creates in *Paradise Lost,* your world, or mine. All are narrative representations of the thing beyond the window. The abstract, unknown, and incomprehensible are reified through metaphor and narrative. For Coover, the first cause and nature are Henry and the UBA, respectively; for the Priestly writer of Genesis 1, they are Yahweh and his heaven and earth; for Milton, they are God and garden. Although Milton's text is that of the theologian, and Coover's that of the ironist and outsider, Coover's enterprise can be usefully compared with Milton's, for Milton, too, returned to Genesis (chapters 1–3) and subjected it to revision (or re-vision). Milton added much, including a prologue (the war in heaven and the fall of Satan), a villain (who remains for many readers more compelling, more "real," than the God from whom he rebels), and a reason for the creation absent from the Bible (it was, says Milton, to restore the population of heaven to its antebellum numbers), as well as detailed scenes and conversations to "assert Eternal Providence, / And justify the ways of God to men" (1:25–26). Although Milton's views were not entirely orthodox in his day, his creation has become, among speakers of English, nearly as authoritative as the biblical accounts.[3] Milton's world has become for many *the* world – reality. Coover's narration is more radically heterodox (not a "theologian's gloss"), but his motive is similar to Milton's and his enterprise certainly not less serious. Coover's vision and version are, as he says, those of the outsider, the ironist, the skeptic who tells the tale of origins to create the world as he knows it, to justify not the ways of God to men but the ways of men to God, the focus of the last chapter. The result is a narrative that is at once serious and joyful, terrifying and wonderfully funny.

IN THE BEGINNING

Coover's problems are in some ways the eternal problems facing those who create cosmologies and describe events "at the beginning" whose etiological significance lingers into the present. The biblical narrator begins unself-consciously, "In the beginning, God . . . "; Coover, like Milton, must choose another moment. Milton avoided the problems of the opening moment by pushing back the start of the story to cover events antecedent to the Creation in a time before God considered creating the world. Coover selects a time in the year LVI, when the world is, while humming along and evolving, perhaps beginning to run down. A generation or two of ball players have come and gone, and their history has been duly recorded by their maker, Henry. Henry, however, is aware of that moment in the past when he was faced with the "disadvantages" of the "abrupt beginning" in the year I; unlike the biblical narrator, Henry senses that this is "too arbitrary, too inexplicable" (45).

The problem of the inexplicable beginning is not confined to Henry's universe, and indeed, the reason for the Creation traditionally has been a matter for speculation and debate. The question is often phrased something like this: in his perfect inclusiveness, what did God need? What could he have wanted? One common explanation for the Creation depicts

God as an artist or author, full of spirit, inspiration, abundance, and plenitude, all requiring expression in matter. The mechanism of the Author-God's creation involves the infusion of spirit or mind (idea or word) into preexistent matter so as to give it order, shape, purpose, and life. The matter of nature, like the blank paper of an empty book, requires divine inscription, speaking, and authorship/authority to achieve order, "composition," to arrange itself into a cosmos. God speaks, and things come into being; God names, and things are: "God said, 'Let there be light,' and there was light" (Gen. 1:3); God speaks to matter, and it arranges itself as instructed: "And God said, 'Let the waters under the heaven be gathered together unto one place, and let the dry land appear.' And it was so" (Gen. 1:9). The universe is a book of God that he speaks into being. In Genesis 2 Adam, the man, reveals his godlike character by naming the animals. Name something and you make it what it is or what it can become. In *The UBA* Henry can perform the creative verbal act that brings his players into being, and he finds this power quite amazing: "Name a man and you make him what he is. Of course, he can develop. And in ways you don't expect. Or something can go wrong. Lot of nicknames invented as a result of Rookie-year surprises. But the basic stuff is already there. In the name. Or rather: in the naming" (48).

Clearly, this God-the-artist account of the reason for creation uses a metaphor based on human creativity and begs the question: God created because, like human beings, he is creative, because he could, because he spoke. Like humans, God is a text maker; he is the Supreme Author. An alternative explanation is to be found in the mystic tradition, represented by such men as Jacob Boehme and Emanuel Swedenborg. This line of speculation claims that the impulse of delight, joy, laughter, or sport both prompted and provided the mechanism for divine creation. God exists from eternity in a condition of joy; the universe itself comes into being as divine play or laughter, as Boehme explains: "Joy . . . was from eternity in the great mystery . . . as a spiritual melody and sport in itself. The creation is the same sport out of himself, viz. a platform or instrument of the Eternal Spirit, with which he melodises" (210). According to this view, creation is an outpouring of divine laughter; it is joy, song, play, sport. God is characterized by eternal delight, and his creation is a playful effusion of that delight into physical being.

J. Henry Waugh and his creation are equally compatible with both views. Henry is author, and the UBA is his text. Like the God of Genesis, he speaks things into being, makes players who they are by naming them, and, single in his creativity, speaks spontaneously, to no one. When Lou expresses concern, remarking, "You've been talking to yourself sort of lately sometimes," Henry replies, "I've been talking to myself all my life" (160). But he is also, like the God of the mystical tradition, characterized by feelings of delight, a jauntiness that from the players' perspective must have existed from eternity. He exhibits a strong impulse to play that manifests itself in creative sport, in games of all sorts – not only the UBA, his last and best world, but earlier, other games, other worlds, other texts: "He'd always played a lot of games: baseball, basketball, different card games, war and finance games, horseracing, football, and so on, all on paper of course" (44). Most interesting of his other sportive creations is a world like the one created by the God of Genesis, the world we know, a variation on Monopoly

> using twelve, sixteen, or twenty-four boards at once and an unlimited number of players, which opened up the possibility of wars run by industrial giants with investments on several boards at once, the buying off of whole governments, the emergence of international communications and utilities barons, strikes and rebellions by the slumdwellers between "Go" and "Jail," revolutionary subversion and sabotage with sympathetic ties across the board, the creation of international regulatory bodies by the established power cliques. . . . He even introduced health, sex, religious, and character variables. (44–45)

Just when we realize that this is a familiar world, the narrator comments that "it never caught on" (45). Henry thus creates another game (his tabletop baseball) and another world (the UBA). Henry, as bookkeeper, accountant, and auditor, is drawn to baseball as text: "Real baseball bored him"; what he likes are "the records, the statistics, the peculiar balances between individual and team, offense and defense, strategy and luck, accident and pattern, power and intelligence." Especially important to Coover's god as keeper of books is the fact that "no other activity in the world had so precise and comprehensive a history, so specific an ethic, and at the same time, strange as it seemed, so much ultimate mystery" (45).

The human population in a world where both divine creation and human life are conceived as games is properly designated as *Homo ludens* (playing man); its creator, *Deus ludens* (playing god). *Homo Ludens* is also the title of a book by J. Huizinga to which the novel makes reference in chapter 8, a matter to which I will return. Huizinga traces the origins of culture to play, an activity in which he finds mind's opposition to mechanism (nature's laws), the imposition of order on the random and absurd, and the intervention of will in the workings of nature. Play is from this perspective like myths and other stories, with their narrative order, their plots, and their ability to act as time shelters against the randomness and absurdity of cosmic progress: "Play only becomes possible, thinkable and understandable when an influx of *mind* breaks down the absolute determinism of the cosmos. The very existence of play continually confirms the supralogical nature of the human situation. Animals play, so they must be more than merely mechanical things. We play and know that we play, so we must be more than merely rational beings, for play is irrational" (3–4).

Whereas for Boehme – in a different context – play is foundational of divine creativity, for Huizinga it is the ground of human creativity, a way through or beyond the absolute determinism of the universe: "Now in myth and ritual the great instinctive forces of civilized life have their origin: law and order, commerce and profit, craft and art, poetry, wisdom and science. All are rooted in the primaeval soil of play" (5).[4] Coover exploits not only the mystic idea of divine joy and play but also Huizinga's vegetal claim by re-creating the emergence and flowering of culture (and its various aspects – religion, philosophy, social organization, politics, art, and as record of it all, history) from the soil – the playground – of the UBA. The dice, with their fifty-six combinations, the Stress Chart, the Chart of Extraordinary Occurrences, and the special strategy charts (20) provide the mechanics for this universe, its laws of nature, a kind of mechanistic three Fates. In addition, like the Old Testament God when he parts the Red Sea or causes the sun to stand still, Henry can influence, suspend, or manipulate his own laws to perform an occasional miracle, although like Zeus in *The Iliad,* he is reluctant to interfere even to save his "son."

Time, events, and the "precise and comprehensive" record of them (45) are central to Henry's game, the universe of the association, and to Henry's role as god/bookkeeper (Book keeper), an ancient idea of God given expression in the religious notion that God is intimately concerned with the behavior of human beings and keeps a precise and comprehensive book (a kind of balance sheet) on each person's acts, good or evil. Meaning emerges in this book, the past giving significance to present events and the present altering the understanding of the past. Henry's preoccupations are focused in this role as keeper of the book.

Henry uses an accounting term, *auditor,* to explain his relationship to the UBA. *Auditor,* of course, has the double meaning of accountant and listener, and Henry performs both functions. He tells Hettie that he keeps financial ledgers on each club covering all manner of financial dealings and contracts, but he also maintains "a running journalization of the activity, posting of it all into permanent record books," and, he says, "I help them with basic problems of burden distribution, remarshaling of assets, graphic fluctuations. Politics, too. Elections." Even more telling, however, he explains that there are "rewards and punishments to be meted out, life histories to be overseen." And there are people to kill: "People die, you know. . . . Usually, they die old, already long since retired, but they can die young, even as ballplayers. Or in accidents during the winter season" (27–28). In addition, as events shortly prove, they can be killed by a beanball or a line drive. Henry's divine role of auditor merges with that of Book keeper and, not surprisingly, historian. For Henry's creatures, baseball is life, and history is the record of games and seasons.

Coover's remarkable achievement in the novel is to manipulate the orientation of readers in such a way as to force them to reexperience Western religious history from the outsider's perspective. To do this Coover leads readers back to the beginning, induces them to identify with the creator, Henry, and then plunges them into the creation, as creatures in this world whose making they have witnessed. Readers thus move, in a sense, from playing God to playing man through the metaphor of the game. The change is from a position of knowledge and power (albeit precariously held) to one of abject ignorance and weakness, where readers are participants in a terrifyingly absurd affair in whose milieu both players and readers seek some meaning, some reason to go on.

The only biblical model I can think of for such a radical shift of perspective is found at the opening of the Book of Job, between chapters 2 and 3, where readers move from the God's-eye view to that of Job. For a while Job's ignorance and questioning are commensurate with those of Henry's players in chapter 8, but then, from the inaccessible skies, God speaks in the whirlwind, a God in whose manifest existence, if not in his message, Job takes comfort. Homer exploits the terrors and ironies implicit in such changes of scene (from Mount Olympos to the battlefield outside Troy) and provides a useful parallel, but again, Homer knows that Zeus exists, however limited and arbitrary he may be. Milton's narrative in *Paradise Lost* shifts from heaven to hell to paradise, but most readers agree that their greatest emotional response is generated among the fallen angels in hell, whose debate, carried forward in a tone of high seriousness, is too heroic, too knowledgeable, and too cognizant of the existence and power of God to serve as a prototype for the speculations and debate in Coover's chapter 8.

What distinguishes Coover's text from these other texts that shift perspective is that the latter posit the clearly continuing existence of the deity, however remote or fallible. By contrast, the great unresolvable mystery in *The UBA* is Henry's status. Players and readers alike cannot, at last, see beyond the hundred-watt sun to discover whether Henry exists. Has he survived the one hundred league years that have elapsed between chapters 7 and 8? If so, is he senile? Insane? Henry's absence from the novel and perhaps from the skies arching above the small world of the players prompts in readers regret, uneasiness, and even disorientation. The reasons for such readerly responses are to be found, curiously enough, in the high degree of realism in both Henry's world and that of the players.[5] Henry is primarily a person, funny, likable, fallible, and subject to the stresses and fears of modern life. He is a man who enjoys a pastrami sandwich and a beer, who fears his boss, who meets a friend in a coffee shop for breakfast, who takes home the neighborhood B-girl for a romp in the hay, and who, incidentally, creates a world. It is his humanity that causes readers to identify with Henry and to care about him. But the players, too, are realistically drawn, emerging from their tabletop world as fellow human beings. In what follows I first explore the narrative means by which in the first seven chapters the mythic and the realistic combine and Henry emerges simultaneously as God and man; then I look at the means by which the men of the UBA gradually take on character, consciousness, and autonomy; finally, I examine the means by which the remarkable balance of chapter 8 is achieved – the balance between absurdity and significance, between belief and disbelief, between the devastating and the funny, between terror and joy.

J. HENRY WAUGH, PLAYING GOD, PLAYING MAN

The biblical narrator stresses the element of order in God's making of the universe. Confronted with the dark, watery, primordial chaos, God must create order, and his first act begins that process by casting light into the darkness, a sourceless verbal light that comes into being with the speaking or the naming of it, dividing the light from the darkness and naming the day and night.[6] More order emerges on the second day with the separation of waters on either side of a firmament, the dome that God names "heaven." Further order is obtained on the third day by separating the dry land ("earth") from the waters ("seas") and commanding the earth to bring forth vegetation. Yahweh creates the orderly progress of time on the fourth day, in some ways further refining the work of the first day, by placing in the dome of heaven the sun, moon, and stars "to divide the day from the night" and "for signs and for seasons and for days, and years." On the fifth day God animates the air and the waters by speaking the birds and the fish into being; on the sixth day, he fills the earth itself with life, creating the land animals and, in the divine image, human beings to "have dominion over" the fish, the birds, and the land creatures. The creatures of the fifth and sixth days are blessed and infused with sexual energy, a form of (pro)creative impulse, and enjoined to "be fruitful and multiply." Where there was darkness, sterility, and chaos, now there is light, life, and order – divine artifact and first playground. The six days of creation are followed by a day of rest, establishing the seven-day rhythm of the week to punctuate the time of moon and sun.

Coover's protagonist, present only in the first seven chapters, creates a world in six days of play (Tuesday through Sunday), followed by a "blue season" of reflection, writing, and record keeping, each day/chapter punctuated unobtrusively by images corresponding to Yahweh's creation of that day. For example, the motif of chapter 1 is light, corresponding to Yahweh's creation of light on the first day. It is present in the person of Damon Rutherford, who brings "light and health" to the association (18), and in the myriad images of light that glitter in Henry's world. The following passage exemplifies the playing out of this motif and the creative force of Henry's vision of it:

> The night above was dark yet the streets were luminous; wet, they shimmered with what occasional light there was from street lamps, passing cars, phone booths, all-night neon signs. There was fog and his own breath was visible, yet nearby objects glittered with a heightened clarity. He smiled at the shiny newness of things springing up beside him on his night walk. At a distance, car head lamps were haloed and tail-lights burned fuzzily, yet the lit sign in a darkened window he was passing, "DIVINEFORM FOUNDATIONS: TWO-WAY STRETCH," shone fiercely, hard-edged and vivid as a vision. (18)

Lights and lamps glitter and shine everywhere. We may hear ironic echoes in such phrases as "shiny newness of things springing up" and "divineform foundations," and we may feel a sense of mystery or magic in a scene that takes its gleaming character from Henry's presence, his vision of it.

In chapter 2, corresponding to the making of the firmament, we read that "Henry walked today in a perfect vault of well-being, crystalline and impenetrable, and there was nothing the wrath of Zifferblatt could do to crack it" (35). The image of the firmament, dividing the waters from the waters, recurs as Henry walks in the rain: "The rain tumbled like gentle applause on his umbrella. Under it he walked, skirting the puddles, dry in the deluge, as though glassed in under a peaked black dome" (46). The creation of vegetation on the third day is parodied in the scene in the flower shop of "B. Valentine, Floriculturist and Modeler," a figure who makes "eternal" vegetation out of plastic (79–81). A theme of time and seasons runs through chapter 4, invoking the creation on the fourth day of the sun, moon, and stars. Here we see the swift or slow running of time, the obsession of Mr. Zifferblatt ("clockface") with time, and the temporal discrepancies between Henry's scene and that of his players: "It was autumn, but Henry felt plunged into the deepest of winters. But no, it was the middle of a baseball season, remember? Green fields and hot suns and shirtsleeved fanatics out on the bleaching boards" (129).

Chapter 5, which is dominated by the dinner with Lou at Mitch's Bar & Grill, is organized through images of fish and birds, the creations of the fifth day. Henry and Lou order duck for the main course and begin with seafood cocktails; pictures of fish and birds adorn the walls; from time to time Henry is frightened by a dark bird that flaps in his breast; a former UBA player is there, as a naval officer, with his hand under a sea-blue skirt; the waitress drops their drinks on the table like a clutch of eggs; Mitch walks like a penguin. All in all, the sexual energy involved in being fruitful and multiplying prevails. Chapter 6, corresponding to the sixth day and the creation of land animals and human beings, begins with "broken dreams about a zoo or a circus" (171); Henry dreams of a mule, tries to make a dirty joke about an ass, and feels "crude and stupid, like a beast" (172); Hettie, his night's companion, makes "an enormous bovine yawn" (173); Lou arrives to eat pizza and drink beer with Henry, leading to "animal satisfaction" (179); Lou gives a long account of a movie about bees, communicating with bees, and bees transformed into humans.

At this point, however, the progress of imagery and days breaks down, as the text moves rapidly forward through biblical primordial history to the flood in Genesis 6–9. Whereas God sends the great flood to destroy "all flesh," restoring the primordial waters, Henry's world is destroyed by a beer flood caused by Lou Engel. God saves a remnant from the flood; Henry rescues the sodden scoresheets. God puts his bow in the sky as a sign that he will not destroy the earth again; Henry, in an act of commitment to the UBA (which he has considered destroying), manipulates the dice to kill Jock Casey with a line drive and vomits a "red-and-golden rainbow arc of half-curded pizza over his association" (202). Chapter 7, corresponding to Yahweh's day of rest, marks the end of league year LVI and moves Henry into what he calls the "blue season," the "static part of the game" (205), a time of recording, summarizing, and planning.

Much of this borrowed, largely imagistic structure is subtle and easily missed. More clearly indicative of Henry's god status is the vertical orientation of the two worlds and the discrepancy in size. Henry has a God's-eye view of the small world of the league, as when Damon finishes his perfect game, and his teammates lift him to their shoulders: "From above, it look[s] like a great roiling whirlpool with Damon afloat in the vortex," a "wild world that ha[s] literally, for the moment, blown its top" (17). There is discrepancy between Henry's omniscience and the league members' limited awareness: "Barney Bancroft didn't know what Henry knew. He didn't know about the different charts. He didn't even know about aces and why it was the good ones often stayed good over the years. Of course he must have sensed it" (39).

Like God's time in Psalm 90, where a divine day is equivalent to a thousand years, Henry's time moves more slowly than that of the players, on the order of one of Henry's years to six league years. But Henry can speed up or slow down time in the world of perpetual daylight and summer where his players exist. He can even suspend time when he turns his attention elsewhere. As Henry returns from work the day after the perfect game, all is as he has left it, scorecard, final entries, dice still showing the final out: "In a sense it was still that moment, and if he wanted to savor it or if he got occupied with something else, it could go on being that moment for weeks. And then, when things got going again, would the players have any awareness of how time had stopped? No . . . but they might wonder how all the details of that moment had got so firmly etched in their minds" (52).

Their minds? The exact ontological status of the players remains ambiguous, as does the relationship between worlds. Henry's neighborhood has a bar named Pete's; the players frequent a bar named Jake's. Henry calls Pete Jake and wonders sometimes "if anybody ever walked into Jake's bar and called him Pete by mistake" (21). In the blue season following league year LVI, the players' barkeeper, Jake Bradley, "paraclete," dies, a victim of the "death rolls," but when Henry goes out, he wonders "where he could go now for a drink," wonders "where they'd hold the wake. At Jake's maybe, but not at Pete's" (216). Pete's bar in Henry's world is gone (and presumably Pete with it) with the passing of Jake Bradley, barkeeper in the players' world. In his own world Henry now spots a new place, the Circle Bar, and when he enters he finds behind the bar a newly retired UBA player, Helborn Melbourne Trench, and the boys all gathering for a grand opening (217). The Old Testament God could wander at will into the world of his own making, for a talk with Adam, a picnic with Abraham, or a wrestling match with Jacob. Henry, too, seems to abandon his position beyond the sun to commune with "the boys," but the boundaries are fuzzy and shifting.

All in all, through the first seven chapters Henry is so realistically presented that readers come to know and like him, to have a stake in his life and fate. He is a unique, comic figure, capable of great joy and grief, of fellowship and love. Although there is little hint of what is to come, at the end of chapter 7, with the gathering in the Circle Bar and Henry delighted to see "the whole goddamn whooping and hollering lot of them!" full of plans, a new song for Jake Bradley forming, an evening of drinking and sex stretching out before him, a theme of affirmation running through it all – just here Henry disappears from the novel, as if the victim of some death roll somewhere, and the reader is left in the world of the players. Like them, the reader is mystified and bereft, trying to make sense of the world without J. Henry Waugh, Prop.

THE READER AS PLAYER

Chapter 8 is the players' chapter, but now and then throughout the first seven chapters readers are moved down and away from Henry's perspective and into the world of the league, seeing persons and events through the consciousness of one of the managers or league officials. Readers usually experience such shifts without disorientation, for they accept the fiction that at such moments Henry, as puppet master, is moving his creatures, thinking and speaking for them. But there are hints here and there of a growing autonomy on the players' parts, a consciousness, of Henry's awareness of their questioning, resisting, or making demands on him. There is, in addition, one telling episode following Damon Rutherford's wake, a wild, drunken affair at Pete's or Jake's (Henry remembers the one at Jake's, but not the one at Pete's). The episode involves Sycamore Flynn, manager of the Knickerbockers, whose pitcher, Jock Casey, has beaned and killed Damon, and it has a nightmarish quality that draws the reader into the world of the players, anticipating events in chapter 8.

It is night, Flynn is alone, and he decides to walk from the train depot to the hotel, a route that takes him past Pioneer Park, where Damon died. Flynn passes under the shadow of the stadium, which is pitch black and sinister: "It bulked, unlit in the dark night, like a massive ruin, exuding a black odor of death and corruption – no, no, just that modest stink of sweat and garbage all old buildings had, and ball parks especially. It caused an unreasonable dread in him, a stupid dread; to purge it, he crossed over, touched it, felt the solid stone, just plain ordinary lifeless matter. A ball park. Like any other. The arched entranceways, he noticed, had no gates" (118–19). Flynn is a bit embarrassed that he has crossed the street to see whether the building is real. He even skins a knuckle on a wall as a "kind of self-punishment," but the readers, like Flynn, begin to feel uneasy. Until now the "real" image of Pioneer Park is of Henry's tabletop, spread with charts, scorecards, and dice. Flynn questions the reality of this hulking stone ruin smelling of death and skins a knuckle. At first readers too question its reality, but strangely, not the skinned knuckle, not Flynn's creeping terror, and their view of reality slips. Like Flynn, the readers are bothered by the gateless entrances, openings into an ill-defined somewhere through which one can slip unimpeded and unintended, psychological and physical black holes into a mini-universe of warped, curved, and squeezed time and space. Flynn returns to investigate: "It shouldn't be that black in there" (119). Gradually, half-afraid, Flynn is drawn into something "more like a tunnel than the entrance to a ball park," a labyrinthine blackness in which he becomes lost: "Don't think. Just lead to panic. Move, just move, hustle. . . . Going around in circles. Or maybe a spiral. What kind of a goddamn ball park was this anyway? Don't question it. Keep going. Seemed to be climbing now. . . . He was sweating . . . heart going too fast! He dropped his right hand to feel its beating and smacked up solid against a sudden right turn in the wall" (121). Eventually Flynn emerges from the maze to find himself in the visitors' dugout, looking out on a dark, shapeless, but no longer pitch-black field. He is fairly sure that he sees "them" there in the dugout: shapes of players ("goddamn spooky benchwarmers"), more shapes on the dark field, and the black tunnel behind him; he feels "the night wind. The lifeless field. His own heart which was going to fail, going to break, going to quit" (122)

During Flynn's ordeal readers suffer from double vision. The tabletop scene has metamorphosed, transformed itself. Like Yahweh's creation, another reality, another world, has emerged with the speaking of it, and the reader is privileged to watch as a world comes into being: "Flynn was near tears. Behind him, he realized, past Casey, past home plate, there was an exit. Maybe it was a way out, maybe it wasn't. But he'd never make it. . . . He couldn't even turn around. And besides, he wasn't sure what he'd find at home plate on the way. 'I quit,' he said" (123). In what shapeless darkness does Flynn wander? Is it like the dark, formless void before Yahweh's first speaking? Of what stone is the stadium built? What ontological facts can account for the skinned knuckle, the ghostly shapes, and the black spiral of space, the sheer uncanniness of the situation? What is needed is someone from above or beyond this horror to say, "let there be light," and someone does so: "But then the lights came on" (123).

Immediately readers are wrenched back into Henry's perspective, as, hung over and grieving the loss of his favorite, his "son," Henry stares "woozily down upon those three ones on his kitchen table [the fatal roll], trying to put all that scene back together again, get some order in this damn operation" (124). Nevertheless, Henry was elsewhere when Flynn, small, lost, and terrified "down there," wandered that lower world, questioning the nature of reality, while others, half-formed beings, waited, suspended in space and time.

THE UBA IN THE BALANCE

It is not surprising that Barney Bancroft, Old Philosopher, creature of an accountant God, would choose to title his league history "The UBA in the Balance." The word *balance* suggests balance sheets, assets and liabilities, of course, but it also suggests the fragility of this world that has hung in the balance. After Henry decides to save the league at the end of chapter 6 (his decision is announced with his "rainbow" covenant) and disappears at the end of chapter 7, a hundred league years elapse before readers find themselves once more in the small world of the players. Barney Bancroft's history has become the "authorized version."

The time is Damonsday CLVII. The scene, again, is Pioneer Park, that hulking stone ruin. Descendants of the players of league year LVI prepare to reenact the "Parable of the Duel," a secret initiatory rite for the new crop of rookies, during which (it is hinted) two (those playing Damon Rutherford and Jock Casey) will be sacrificed. A hundred-watt sun blazes in a cloudless sky over a field of green, a crowded stadium, and fans mad with excitement – all in a world where sects, factions, parties, creeds, and theories have proliferated as the population struggles to find or construct meaning and impose order in a world without apparent purpose. Sounding like Shakespeare's Macbeth, and coming to similar conclusions, Paul Trench meditates on the absurdity of his existence and this "game": "Beyond each game, he sees another, and yet another, in endless and hopeless succession. He hits a ground ball to third, is thrown out. Or he beats the throw. What difference, in the terror of eternity, does it make? He stares at the sky, beyond which is more sky, overwhelming in its enormity." Such speculations arise from despair, the notion that life is indeed a tale told by an idiot, signifying nothing; Paul Trench senses that he is "nothing at all": "So why does he even walk up there? Why does he swing? Why does he run? Why does he suffer when out and rejoice when safe? Why is it better to win than to lose? Each day: the dread. . . . He wants to quit – but what does he mean, 'quit'? The game? Life? Could you separate them?" (238). The meditation has an old, familiar tone; Paul's dread, a familiar feel.

Within the world of the players there are many approaches to the ontological problems Paul Trench faces. There are the believers – the pious ones – belonging to various sects, the Damonites, for example, or the Caseyites, "an heretical sect attempting to bring back the golden age of Patrick Monday, celebrate the mystery of Casey's uniqueness, his essential freedom, God active in man, and, as Cuss McCamish would say, all that shit" (222). But, as the attitude of McCamish demonstrates, there are also doubters, scoffers who claim that Rutherford and Casey are only "subhuman masks." These are men who exhibit "skepticism, doubt, fear" yet also "the ability to act, to participate": "Cute idea: old-fashioned humanism founded on abiding ignorance and despair, but who says man's condition is, eternally, dread and doubt? Funny how you can play that game so many ways" (223).

There are those who claim that Rutherford and Casey are "nothing more than another of the ancient myths of the sun, symbolized as a victim slaughtered by the monster or force of darkness. History: in the end, you can never prove a thing" (224). As the chapter unfolds we hear the pious, the pompous, the irreverent, the erudite, the flip, the frightened, the angry, and the confused. Taken whole, the chapter is terribly funny, a cacophony of voices and views with none privileged and none dismissed. Readers are forced to be a part of it, for although they know more than the players, they too struggle to make sense of it all. Readers do not know who is running the show; they do not know where Henry is or whether he exists, for he last appeared a hundred league years ago in the Circle Bar. To make matters worse, the players' world and concerns and ours are disquietingly congruent. We can easily recognize these voices and this situation. Players say the things we say, as in the following remark Raspberry Schultz echoes E. M. Forster's "What I Believe": "I don't know if there's really a record-keeper up there or not, Paunch. But even if there weren't, I think we'd have to play the game as though there were" (239). "Irreverent" Gringo Greene, on the other hand, accepts the absence of a record keeper, asserting that although he deserves "love, truth, beauty, meaning, and eternal life," he'll "settle for a fuckin' drink" (226).

Amid the passionate voices of belief or disbelief, engagement or disengagement, learned academicians make pronouncements. Professor Costen Migod "Cuss" McCamish, "Doctor of Nostology and Research Specialist in the Etiology of Homo Ludens," agrees with Schultz ("distinguished folklorist and foremost witness to the ontological revelations of the patterns of history") that you should not "make fun of things you don't understand" and, further, discloses that he has "come to the conclusion that God exists and he is a nut" (233). As doctor of nostology, Professor McCamish studies the senile stages of an organism or race of organisms (Henry and his world?); as research specialist in the etiology of *Homo ludens*, he seeks to know the origins, causes, or reasons for playing man (the population of Henry's world and our own). He shares with Schultz the retrospective view, seeking ontological revelations in the patterns of history; with Schultz, too, he shows an interest in "game theory" – "Occult Schultz" even plays "some device with dice" (234).

Nostology, nostalgia, origins, patterns – hopelessly ignorant, residents of a world without purpose or order, they do the only thing they can do: they order the chaos through play. Huizinga stresses this "positive feature" of play: "It creates order, *is* order."

> Into an imperfect world and into the confusion of life [play] brings a temporary, a limited perfection. . . . The profound affinity between play and order is perhaps the reason why . . . play seems to lie to such

a large extent in the field of aesthetics. Play has a tendency to be beautiful. The words we use to denote the elements of play belong for the most part to aesthetics, terms with which we try to describe the effects of beauty: tension, poise, balance, contrast, variation, solution, resolution, etc. Play casts a spell over us; it is "enchanting," "captivating." It is invested with the noblest qualities we are capable of perceiving in things: rhythm and harmony. (10)

Tension, poise, balance, contrast, variation – Huizinga's terms describe the effects of Coover's chapter 8. The chapter is itself a form of play whose subject is play. In it the game of baseball is a culture in which people play other games, including religion, politics, folklore, history, and life. Moreover, recall that Henry's reason for returning to baseball, via the UBA, as *the* game of games is almost a paraphrase of Huizinga's remarks: Henry is drawn to baseball for its order (its records and statistics), its beauty ("the peculiar balances"), and for its enchantment (its "ultimate mystery") (45).

Balance, the key term in Barney Bancroft's league history, is crucial to play, art, and life, which are three realms of significance converging in the UBA. Coover underscores the relation between game and life in his comments on the use of games in his fiction: "We live in a skeptical age in which games are increasingly important. When life has no ontological meaning, it becomes a kind of game itself. Thus it's a metaphor for a perception of the way the world works, and also something that almost everybody's doing – if not on the playing fields, then in politics or business or education. . . . And formal games reflect on the hidden games, more so in an age without a Final Arbiter" (in LeClair and McCaffery 72). Coover might be describing the situation in his chapter 8, yet Professor McCamish has concluded that God exists not as Final Arbiter but as nut. Some critics have concluded from this pronouncement and the general situation of the players, their views and strategies and their sinister ritual, that Henry has gone mad and still plays at dice with his universe. This conclusion, however, is possible only if one insists that Henry and his world are real and that the players and their world are imaginary. The novel will not let us sustain this position, and neither will Coover, who refuses any comment on the status and role of Henry in the last chapter (LeClair and McCaffery 73).

"God exists and he is a nut." *Nut* can mean someone eccentric, but it does not usually refer to a lunatic. It can equally describe someone playful, not serious. More interesting, *nut* is a term for someone or something difficult to know or understand, a tough nut to crack. "I don't believe in just making fun of things you don't understand," says Shultz, and Mc-Camish agrees, "God exists and he is a nut" – a playful, difficult enigma. *Homo ludens,* his creatures, made in this god's image, will continue to play.

As the novel ends, the game, with its killing ritual, is about to get under way, and after the collage of belief and disbelief, fear and laughter, certitude and doubt, a single mood prevails: joy. The last scene involves Hardy Ingram, playing the ritual role of pitcher Damon Rutherford (the man doomed to receive the killing blow from the beanball), and Paul Trench, his battery mate, whose meditation on the absurdity of life I examined previously. Paul goes to the mound and tries to speak, but he cannot. He might have said, "It's terrible," or "It's all there is," but he can find no words. Hardy-Damon seems to see Paul-Royce's despair, to recognize his fear of the "blackening sun," the "burning green grass, and the eyes, and the crumbling," and he says, "Hey, wait, buddy! you *love* this game, don't you?" "Don't be afraid," he says. "It's not a trial. . . . It's not even a lesson. It's just what it is." Then he smiles and "lights up the whole goddamn world." In the end there is the game, which cannot be separated from life. There is laughter, courage, and a willingness to play, a resurgent joy as "the black clouds break up, and the dew springs again to the green grass," and the baseball shines "hard and white and alive in the sun" (242).

There is celebration here, certainly – celebration of a new day, a new game, and a new season. Nevertheless, the novel and the chapter are haunted by the word *balance.* "The UBA in the Balance" describes not only poise but peril. The baseball shines "hard and white and alive in the sun": "It is beautiful, that ball" (242), but it is also sinister, for it is a killing ball. A hundred years before, at the event now being reenacted, this "same" ball was "brand-spanking new and glowing white in the sunlight" (67), and it struck and killed Damon Rutherford, the man whose smile lights the world. In all this play of light is a precarious balance: on the one side, an eternal sun that gives one hundred watts of light, a blackening sun, a burning sun; on the other, Damon's smile, an ephemeral flare that lights the world, restores the dew to the grass, and chases the clouds. The novel ends in *this* brief, startling, joyous light.

The powerful pre-texts have been invited in, called to labor beneath a sun that has shone since the beginning, 4004 B.C.E., the year I, and continues to this moment to shine, with one hundred watts of brilliance, on this little world, this playground, Pioneer Park, a garden full of light and life and yet exuding at times "a black odor of death and corruption." Readers are left, like the UBA, in a precarious balance, in this disturbed and re-created universe. The new mythological world has been constructed from the shattered remains of older ones, old archetypal stuff, bricolage. The mythic shards carry into the new construct an uncanniness, battered, much-traveled semantic baggage, and equivocation spoken within the temple, the precinct of art, the sprawling, crumbling, often remodeled house of language – the death-smelling architecture of a home called Pioneer Park.

BLESS ME, EVEN ME ALSO, O MY FATHER. Gen. 27:38

I WILL NOT LET YOU GO, UNLESS YOU BLESS ME. Gen. 32:26

THOU ART MY BELOVED SON; WITH THEE I AM WELL PLEASED. Mark 1:11

I AND THE FATHER ARE ONE. John 10:30

POP SAID, "I COULD OF PLAYED BALL IN THAT PARK," AND I SAID, "POP I WILL PLAY THERE SOMETIME AND IT WILL BE THE SAME THING." Mark Harris, *The Southpaw* 49–50

"CATCH IT, DAD," I SCREAMED.
    I MET DIMAGGIO A FEW YEARS AGO ON A SMALL PLAYING FIELD AT THE PRESIDIO OF SAN FRANCISCO. MY SON, WEARING DIMAGGIO'S OLD NUMBER 5 ON HIS LITTLE LEAGUE JERSEY, ACCOMPANIED ME, EXACTLY ONE GENERATION AFTER MY FATHER CAUGHT THAT BALL. DIMAGGIO GAVE HIM A POINTER OR TWO ON BATTING AND THEN SIGNED A BALL FOR HIM. ONE GENERATION PASSETH AWAY, AND ANOTHER GENERATION COMETH: BUT THE EARTH ABIDETH FOREVER. Stephen Jay Gould, "The Streak of Streaks" 8

BASEBALL IS FATHERS AND SONS PLAYING CATCH, LAZY AND MURDEROUS, WILD AND CONTROLLED, THE PROFOUND ARCHAIC SONG OF BIRTH, GROWTH, AGE, AND DEATH. THIS DIAMOND ENCLOSES WHAT WE ARE. Donald Hall, *Fathers Playing Catch with Sons* 30

FATHERS AND SONS, BLESSINGS, AND BASEBALL'S MYTH OF ATONEMENT

I have said, with Lévi-Strauss and others, that much of the work of myth is unconscious, that a myth is a linguistic artifact whose function is to create a space for the meeting, confrontation, and attempted reconciliation of binary opposites, of whose exact nature both myth-maker and audience are likely unaware. The language itself – each word, each phrase – echoes into the caverns of the past (personal and collective) with ancient, archetypal meaning and feeling and with Freudian-Lacanian insistence on the exploration of a few crucial subjects: the body, kinship relations, birth, life, and death. A few key narratives, archetypal plots, images, acts, and figures recur, according to Freud, because they meet the tests of effectiveness, familiarity, and universality (discussed in chapter 1); these are linguistic structures of persistent utility, albeit of evolving, equivocal character. A mythology is a collection of narratives that reveal their consanguinity through their situation in time and space; their common language; their assumptions, images, themes, and mythemes; and their manner of proceeding with their work. This is not to say that all myths in a mythology will carry similar meanings, explicit or implicit, conscious or unconscious. As noted, each tale added to the body will be a composite of the traditional and the inventive. The more inventive the tale, the greater the transformation or deformation of the archetypes.

If there is a compelling preoccupation central to baseball's mythology, it may well be found in the realm of kinship relations, and specifically in the father-son relation. The opposites it seeks to reconcile rest in the conflicting emotions of love and hate and the conflicting acts of competition and cooperation, along with such corollary matters as youth and age, power and weakness, the growing and the dying, and failure and success. Baseball's focus on the father-son relationship is intriguing given psychologists' growing recognition of the importance of this relationship to men's mental health and happiness. Psychologists now recognize, for example, the particular importance of a father's approving his son's life and career, and thus validating them, by giving his blessing to his son. Baseball's mythology has long recognized such matters and has drawn repeatedly on certain enduring archetypes and key narratives in which to perform its mythic work. In working out the ambivalent emotions associated with kinship relations, baseball's sons stand in the shadow of both Oedipus, who loved his mother and killed his father, and Orestes, who killed his mother and loved his father. The presence in the mythology of these intertwined archetypes results in an intriguing complexity.

Two stages in a boy's childhood especially require the loving presence and approval of his father, the pre-Oedipal period (the first three or four years) and the close of adolescence, the transition to adulthood. In the early period, part of which is preverbal and imagistic, the son develops powerful feelings of love and hero worship for the father, a being perceived as bigger than life whose strength promises protection from reengulfment by the mother. This early "dyadic" relationship with the father persists, even as the child enters the "triadic" phase of Oedipal attachment to the mother, with accompanying feelings of competition, fear, and even hatred of the father. At neither stage is the relationship with either parent a matter simply of love or hate, comfort or fear, attraction or repulsion; rather, it is a complex coexistence of conflicting attitudes and emotions.[1] Although receiving little theoretical attention, the second crucial moment in the father-son relationship, at the entry (delayed or not) into adulthood, has, according to psychologist Peter Blos, special impact on the subsequent emotional health of the son: "At the termination of adolescence a new stage in the life of the growing son appears, when the father's affirmation of the manhood attained by his son, conveyed in what we might call the father's blessings of the youth's impatient appropriation of adult prerogatives and entitlements, reaches a critical urgency" (11). Stable, productive adulthood depends on the resolutions reached with the father at this moment, on the father's blessing that not only affirms the son's future life but also resonates in the remote, inarticulate, emotion-charged past – the earliest dyadic and triadic phases of the son's ego formation – and permits emergence of the adult model, known as the ego ideal. Blos explains:

> The adult ego ideal is an agency of autonomous aspiration; as such it is guarded as a cherished and beloved personality attribute whose archaic origin lies in father attachment, father idealization, or briefly the isogender ("negative") complex. . . .
>
> The restraining and punishing father is also the rescuer of the son from being taken over by infantile delusions; this so-called rescuer is the early personification of the reality principle who makes growing into manhood an attainable expectancy, evoking loving gratitude which, as I see it, is to become immortalized in the adult ego ideal. (38–39)

What has been called the father's blessing is a modern version of an ancient idea, a form of word magic through which the power-invested, idealized, and beloved father opens the doors of adulthood to the son, offering his approval, permitting the emergence of the adult ego ideal, and rendering filial success at least likely. Lacking this blessing, the man will be somehow stalled in his psychic development, with damage to all his relationships and enterprises.

Themes surrounding this crucial relationship with the father, the son's quest for atonement, blessing, and the psychic rewards that ensue, are endlessly repeated in baseball's mythology. As Donald Hall puts it, "Baseball is fathers and sons" (30). Its narratives tirelessly represent the relationship crucial to the psychic well-being of every man and, in so doing, disclose and attempt to resolve matters of essential, enduring, poignant human concern. At the same time baseball's mythology works its own peculiar variations and reaches its own solutions to this most complex of human relationships.

This focus helps to explain the curious facts mentioned in the introduction relating to mothers and their representatives. The parade of maternal maladepts presented in the literature serves an important function in the mythological enterprise of father-son atonement. The three works under particular attention in this chapter – Mark Harris's *The Southpaw*, David Small's *Almost Famous*, and David James Duncan's *The Brothers K* – reveal the mythic agenda of much of baseball literature, which is, by accident or design, to obtain the father's blessing, to become *at one* with him, and in the process, to depict and yet avoid the psychic dangers embodied in the mother.

MOTHERS AND SONS: SEPARATION

Concerning my mother I can tell you practically nothing, for she died when I was 2.
—Mark Harris, The Southpaw 17

"You'd better leave, Ward," said the kid. "You're upsetting mother."
"There's nothing wrong with her that a kick in the ass wouldn't cure."
—David Small, Almost Famous 16

I let [Mama] go, even tried to smile at her. And she smiled back – insanely – and raked her fingernails across my face. I grabbed her again, begged her to calm down. But she was crazy now, biting, kicking, throwing her skull back against mine. . . . I wished to hell I was smarter, or better at baseball.
—David James Duncan, The Brothers K 368–69

In contrast to the fathers, the mothers presented in baseball's mythology are an unattractive, abusive, cruel, unnatural, mad, and sexually flawed gang of grotesques. Roy Hobbs's mother is typical, a woman who "didn't love anybody" (Malamud, *The Natural* 144), who removed herself from Roy's life when he was seven, a woman whom he remembers in his crucial last game as having drowned a black tomcat in a tub of scalding bathwater (171). When Memo Paris asks Roy, "What was [your mother] like?" his response is terse and pointed: "A whore. She spoiled my old man's life. He was a good guy but died young" (143). The situation

Roy sums up regarding his parents is in some ways paradigmatic. The "good guy" father, who dies young, is contrasted with the bad mother, who often lives on and endures as a sort of psychological lesion in the mind of the son. In *The Iowa Baseball Confederacy* Gideon Clarke's mother is likewise unloving. She abandons Gideon when he is six, taking his cat with her.[2] Troy Maxson's mother abandons him when he is eight, promising to return for him but failing to do so. Henry Wiggen's mother – of whom we know "practically nothing" – dies (and thus abandons him) when Henry is two. The motherless son is left to be raised by the father, who is in most cases a "good guy." (The apparent exception, Troy Maxson's father, is nevertheless both responsible and present, unlike his mother, and earns a measure of grudging respect for these qualities.) In other words, what the abandoning mother leaves behind is the father-son dyadic relationship, a relationship most usually forged through and enacted in baseball.

If the mother does not abandon the son physically, she often does so emotionally, not only denying love but retreating into madness, religious fanaticism, or compulsive behavior typically associated with some form of sexual pathology. In such cases physical or verbal violence between mother and son is likely to ensue. Kathryn Phelan, for example, is not a whore like Mrs. Hobbs but goes to the other extreme: she is a "virginal mother" who suffers from "spiritually induced terror" of sexuality and, as Francis sees it, has been "dead all her life" (Kennedy 98–99); she is a "denier of life" for herself and others, especially Francis's father and himself. As a result Francis nurses a festering anger toward her so intense that it is not laid to rest when she is. As mentioned, even when dead Kathryn is an object of such conscious hatred that Francis wants to crawl down into her grave and "strangle her bones" (16). That there are other, unconscious attitudes only makes the situation more poignantly ambiguous and constitutes another mythic task.

Francis Phelan's violent impulse against his mother is only one of numerous examples of a recurring mytheme, one that contrasts the son's struggle for atonement with the father and his need to exclude the mother, to separate himself from her. The conflicting emotions of desire and fear, love and hate, which invest the son's relations with both parents, tend to become polarized through the language and symbols of the game, directing positive emotions toward the father and investing him with all positive attributes while directing negative emotions toward the mother, the embodiment of all negative attributes. On such polarization, one might argue, rests the possibility of achieving psychic wholeness and direction for the adult life.

The simplest means of handling the situation is narrative murder, the solution of *The Southpaw*. Henry Wiggen's mother is summarily removed from the narrative when Henry is two, still in the pre-Oedipal phase. He is a son left in the happy circumstances inhering in the dyadic father-son relationship, with the father an object of unambivalent love, even hero worship. Alternatively, the mother can be eliminated without regret and with a kind of vengeful and demeaning satisfaction, as is the mother of Wally Shaw, Ward Sullivan's uncanny double in *Almost Famous*. Young Wally returns from school one day when he is eight to find his mother unregrettably dead, "outright dead," "casually dead," having "died from boredom" while snapping beans – beans that the family have for dinner that same night (65).

If the mothers survive what may be seen as a mythic impulse to eliminate them, however, they are depicted as a malevolent, neurotic, or psychotic gaggle, appropriate recipients of the fear, hatred, and violent impulses of baseball's sons. Consider the narrative brutalizing of Laura Chance, mother of Kincaid Chance, narrator of *The Brothers K*. Laura is a woman who, the tale insists, gets no more than she deserves. Laura's fanatic, unbending, unloving treatment of her children has led one son to call her a "stupid fucking bitch" and another to pick her up bodily in a bear hug: "Mama in a frenzy was trying to break my hold. But I'd been wrestling with Irwin for two decades. 'Stop Struggling,' I said. And when she didn't, I just lifted her in the air and squeezed a little. 'Hoooof!' she went, and the wind and fight went out of her" (367). The minute she gets a chance Laura rakes her son's face with her fingernails and suffers another "hug": "Hoooof!" "Hoooof!" "Hoooof!" (368). A bit later Kincaid describes the effects of the free-for-all on his mother: "She just stood there. Her blouse had my blood on it, and was ripped at the shoulder. The lipstick Ellen G. White said never to wear was smeared down onto her chin. I'd squeezed her so hard there was snot stopping one nostril" (369).

The archvillain of the tale is clearly Laura Chance, an embodied, disruptive force, a bad mother, a sometimes mad religious fanatic, who, alone or in conjunction with her minister, Elder Babcock, manages to damage her husband's baseball career (she is his "number one flaw" [253]), his life, and the lives of her children. She is prone to abandoning her family either emotionally or physically, and after a while Kincaid, the narrator, comes to prefer her absence to her presence: "Mama's absences were a relief to me, her returns a mild disappointment, and unlike Peter, I had no great curiosity about the motivations of either. I felt at times that she loved me. I also felt, almost constantly, that she disliked me. And I was satisfied to reciprocate. It damaged us. But that's the way it was" (247).

The "parts" of Laura Chance, the blood, the smeared lipstick, and the snot – these are details in a portrait whose overall effect is contemptible rather than pitiable. They are physical signs of a pathological nature, of a moral and psychological ugliness that pervades the lives of her family, threatening to maim or destroy them all. This tendency to linger over emblematic details of physical ugliness, to present the *significant* parts, has the effect of reducing what might be a person, a mother, to a scattering of psychological warts. In the *Iowa Baseball Confederacy* Gideon's insistence on inventorying Darlin' Maudie's homely features is similar. In *Almost Famous* Sarah Sullivan, an object not merely of filial dislike but of outright hatred, is likewise depicted as the sum of repulsive details. As he addresses his mother, Ward Sullivan speaks not to a woman but to a "hank of frizzy hair and sunglasses peering at him from above the pink quilt" (17). To Ward his mother is a "feeb" whose "natural rhythm of violence punctuated by periods of depression was caused by . . . bad wiring" (40). She has a "freaky side"; she "hate[s] life," saying, "It's so bitter. It's such a joke" (259). Like Kincaid Chance, Ward Sullivan uses physical means to control his mother when she is in a frenzy. At one point Ward and his brother "half-carr[y], half-drag her, kicking and struggling, back into the bedroom," where they hold her down while a doctor administers an injection, a sort of knockout punch (276–77).

Madness, violence (suicidal or murderous) between mother and son, physical control of the mother by the son, abandonment of the son by the mother, outright enmity and even hatred on both sides – these characterize baseball's mother-son relationship. To complicate matters, the mothers, as despicable a parade of harpies as ever haunted a mythology, pollute all male-female relationships. Their attributes are generalized to all women, their representatives embodying every psychological danger, in and out of the game (e.g., they cause batting slumps, eating disorders, reclusive withdrawal, and compulsive behaviors), posing every threat to joy and life (especially life as baseball), and speaking every prediction of doom. This flawed primary relationship produces what appears as a pervasive misogyny in baseball's myths. Ward Sullivan's double, Wally Shaw (a man whose initials Ward shares and whose name Ward uses when he arranges for his girlfriend's abortion [202]), makes the danger explicit:

"Women and baseball [do not] mix"; in other words, baseball as masculine life excludes women by every narrative means available. Ward speculates, "Was it that men and women didn't mix, that they were always certain to be in subtle opposition to the basic needs of the other? Was it the law of cosmic disharmony that Shaw had put his finger on?" (123). This law of cosmic disharmony ranges women (especially mothers) on one side and men (especially sons and fathers and the game of baseball) on the other. Mothers, and with them all women, are to be excluded from baseball and from the lives of men as part of the "American way." Ward considers this truth as he prepares to move from the minors to the majors: "He was young and he was an American man. He had been brought up to think that if you had anything important to do you did it alone or with a few select male friends. . . . He wanted to think about nothing but baseball." He nevertheless has become entangled with another crazy woman (Bluette Fingers), a woman in eerie ways just like his mother, Sarah Sullivan: "He was getting mad. She's making a big deal out of this, he thought. She's trying to force me to choose between her and baseball. By God, he thought, if she pushes me I know what my choice will be" (130). Blue does push him – by attempting suicide. Ward is coerced into agreeing to take her with him to the majors, although he secretly plans to sneak out without her. He drinks too much at his farewell party, and driving home through the rain he sees in the headlights his double, the ghostly, rain-drenched figure of Wally Shaw, swerves to avoid him, and crashes into a bridge. Ward's career is over. He, like Shaw, was almost famous, his life a "travesty of expectation transformed into miserable failure" (65). More important, he kills Blue in a sort of narrative realization of the violent impulse inspired by the mother. And then, crippled and without options, Ward goes home, which is an asylum where, helpless as a baby, he lives a nightmarish perversion of the Oedipal drama.

At one point in the sustained irony of his life, Oedipus confesses to Jocasta that, although the man he believes to have been his father has died of natural causes and, therefore, that part of the prophecy has been averted, still there is the other part of the prophecy to fear. Jocasta, in one of the most ironic speeches in mythic history, answers:

> Fear? What has a man to do with fear?
> Chance rules our lives, and the future is all unknown.
> Best live as best we may, from day to day.
> Nor need this mother-marrying frighten you;

Many a man has dreamt as much. Such things
Must be forgotten, if life is to be endured. (ll. 842–48)

Perhaps no love is more beset by fear, horror, and psychological danger than mother love. No relationship is so susceptible to ambivalence as
the son seeks to grow up, to distance himself from this beguiling, repulsive figure who haunts his unconscious. Constructing a bitter parody of
the mother-son relationship and of the psychological journey away from
home and mother, Philip Roth combines many of the motifs that run
through baseball's narratives in a horrifying and terribly funny episode
from *The Great American Novel* concerning a young player known as
"Nickname," the second baseman for a "homeless" ball team who suffers
from homesickness, or mother-longing. To cure the malady an older player takes Nickname to what at first appears to be a house of prostitution.
Readers are uneasy from the outset, however, because the password to
enter the house is the phrase "I'm home, Mom." According to an old
sailor and former shortstop, the street on which the house is found is
unique in all the world "for fixin' what ails you." The house itself, like
others on the block, is white with green shutters "and a water sprinkler
turning on the well-kept lawn"; there is a tricycle overturned on the porch.
Nickname is worried: "'Hey,' whispered Nickname, 'some *kid* lives here.'"
His guide, Johnny Baal, also known as Big John, replies, "Kee-rect. And
his name is you." On the speaking of the password, the door swings open
"just as doors do when magic words are spoken in fairy tales." Standing
inside is a personification of the mother image buried in the personal or
national unconscious, a pretty young woman in a blue apron with yellow
flowers holding a baby. She welcomes the young man, saying, "My little
Nickname's home!" (151). Oedipus has returned to Thebes.

This "mom" is, as she will later uncharacteristically complain, a woman (an image) who cannot age; she is "The Eternal Mom" (156). She administers patient, loving, uncomplaining care to those who pay the price
for her services, which include bathing, feeding (pablum and applesauce),
storytelling, singing lullabies, and other duties on which she elaborates:
"Cleaning the mess out of the diaper of just about everybody and anybody
who has fifteen bucks in his pocket and is out looking for a good time.
Oh, there are nights when I've got applesauce running out of my ears,
nights when they practically drown me in the tub – and I haven't even
talked about the throwin' up. Oh, there's nothing that's out-and-out dis-
gusting, that they don't do it" (156). For all his homesickness, Nickname

wants out; for all her Eternal Momness, "Mom" would rather be a grand-mother or working in a war plant. The drama, ancient and unsatisfacto-ry, is performed in the psychological theater where the mother image is forged and in which mother-son relationships are enacted, a theater from which, it seems, few escape. Roth extricates Nickname (also called *niño,* "baby") and his father surrogate, "Big John," from the scene under cov-er of a raid by the vice squad: "The van for the 'mothers' was over an hour in arriving; it grew cold out in the street, and though the abuse from the policewoman grew more and more vile, the 'mothers' never once com-plained" (160).

In a stroke of genius Roth permits the internalized good mother to complain about her working conditions. He reveals the genuinely terri-fying relationship of sonship (terrifying both to the mother and to the adult son), and he satirizes the Freudian romance, with its Oedipal tri-ad, by making the "father" the son's guide into the pleasures of the moth-er's house. (At the same time, he permits the "father" to complain about the price: Big John asks, "You know what you can get for four bucks down by the lake?" [158].) Finally, Roth reveals the analogies, in the world and in the mind, between motherhood and prostitution and the relatively high price of mothering.[3]

When we ask why baseball's mythology is so hard on mothers, why it makes them ugly, why it depicts them as whores, feebs, fishwives, religious fanatics, sexually depraved or pathologically inhibited abandoners, de-niers of life, and all-around spoilers, we might simply assume that a per-vasive misogyny drives the narratives. But it is not that, or not exactly that, or not only that. Nor is it, as Wally Shaw has it, some law of cosmic dis-harmony. Finding the answer leads us away from surface facts and plots to the gap, the mythic unconscious where the real work goes forward. As I already suggested, we can say as a preliminary answer that a central concern of baseball's myths is to reconcile fathers and sons, to rescue from the abyss of time the abiding love born in the earliest phases of childhood, later submerged or subverted but like "The Eternal Mom" always there in the mind's and heart's beginnings, perhaps salvageable, almost certainly necessary to sustain the son and permit him to prosper emotionally in adulthood. The myths supply models of reconciliation, plots and possi-bilities, and psychic satisfactions within the space of art.

The attempted reconciliation and the journey to beginnings it entails appear to be baseball's central myth, the endlessly repeated tale of a de-scent into the abyss of time and, sometimes, the journey back. The object of the quest is part feeling and part relationship, a beloved father-hero and a blessing. The journey, like an archaeological dig, reaches the oldest layer only by disturbing the more recent levels. The dyadic first layer lies beneath the triadic – Orestes and Agamemnon before and beyond Oedipus, Laius, and Jocasta. Mother attachment, father rejection, and all the psychological drama of the Oedipal phase must be removed to find the mind's deepest layer. In a sense the mother must be dislodged or even sacrificed to find the father, the hero and template for the son's adult ego ideal, and most important, to recover the relatively unambiguous, guiltless masculine love that existed there at the beginning. That recovery is facilitated both by a mythic renunciation of the mother (rendering her an unfit object of affection or attachment, hence the dead, absent, violent, pathologically flawed mother) and by a mythic annunciation of oneness of father and son and the establishment of a connection between the father-son relationship and baseball, from whose pristine confines women are barred: baseball and women do not mix. Baseball provides the scene, the behaviors, and the language for discovery, reconciliation, and growth.

FATHERS AND SONS: BLESSING AND ATONEMENT

There he is. Papa. There is my father.
—*David James Duncan,* The Brothers K *4*

Look at him, come to his high hour,
leaning his body toward the pitch
with every sinew, bone and cell alive –
my father was exceedingly rich.
—*William D. Barney, "A Post Card out of Panama"*

As they left the park . . . he realized his son has taken his hand. He felt an uplift of his spirit. On the open trolley he put his arm around the boy's shoulders.
—*E. L. Doctorow,* Ragtime *196*

Sons' memories of fathers surely are sacred.
—*Pete Rose and Roger Kahn,* Pete Rose: My Story *43*

Baseball's myths present a stunning contrast in their depiction of mothers and fathers. What was your mother like? A whore, a feeb, a fishwife. What was your father like? "He was a good guy but died young" – Roy Hobbs's answer might have been spoken by other protagonists of baseball literature: Gideon Clarke, Ray Kinsella, Ward Sullivan, Francis Phelan, and Kincaid Chance, to name a few. One motif that stands out in the narratives is that of filial devotion revealed in the sons' detailed early memories of a close, loving relationship with the father. No similar relationship with the mother is ever mentioned. Henry Wiggen, the most confident, complacent, and successful of baseball's protagonists, has no mother, has endured no Oedipal strife, and has enjoyed a life-long dyadic relationship with his father. There is no bitterness in his family relationships, and his earliest memories are of his father, of their easy companionship, and of baseball. Hero worship is apparent in Henry's "autobiography": "The earliest thing I remember was Sundays in summer, going out in the morning with Pop to look at the sky" (Harris, *The Southpaw* 19). The narrative is replete with descriptions of Pop's uniform, bits of Pop's baseball wisdom, Pop's prowess as a pitcher, and Henry's own unmitigated hero worship. Henry says, for instance, "I always carried Pop's glove, and I was proud to do it. . . . It had that leathery oily smell which is 1 of the best smells I know" (19), or "I would sit high in the seat when we went rolling in town so as everybody could see me with Pop" (20), and concerning Pop's pitching, "it was beautiful and amazing, and it made you proud" (21).

Ward Sullivan remembers himself as a prodigy of three, sitting on his father's lap and reading to him (Small 22). Gordon Sullivan, the father, is a kind, self-sacrificing man married to a crazy, unloving wife: "Gordon Sullivan was going to be one of those people who took care of everything, so to speak, while other people drank and screwed and jumped off window ledges. One of the nice rewards, it seemed, was this little reading kid on his lap, twice a week" (29). Gordon is without doubt a good guy. Essentially wifeless, he finds the little reading kid to be a reward, a source of joy. Thus, while Ward Sullivan suffers abuse and neglect from his mother, he enjoys a close, dyadic relationship with his father, who approves what he is and does, and with his grandfather, Ward Rideout, for whom he is named, another almost-famous major leaguer who teaches Ward Sullivan baseball.

Kincaid Chance, one of a number of baseball's sons who are inept at the game but who find that it centers their memories of and relationships with their fathers, likewise reports an earliest memory of sitting on – or rather lying across – his father's lap: "Papa is in his easy chair, reading the Sunday sports page. I am lying across his lap. . . . The lap is one thing: a ground, a region, an earth. My head rests on one wide, cushioned arm of the chair, my feet on the other. The rest of me rests on Papa. The newspaper blocks his face from view, but the vast pages vibrate in time to his pulse, and the ballplayer in the photo looks serious. I ask no questions. I stay quiet. I feel his slow, even breathing" (Duncan 3). The father is, for the child, a solid thing, a comfortable and safe ground of being, a universe taken in through all the senses of sight, sound, smell, and touch. For this son, there is no contest between the religious-fanatic mother and the base-ball-playing-and-obsessed father. To escape the mother and experience the freedom and delight of father-son companionship approaches the miraculous: "When I consider the odds against me watching baseball on Sabbath (100 to 1?), going fishing on Sabbath (1,000 to 1?), and doing both alone with Papa . . . (1,000,000 to 1?), I feel as if my life has left the world of odds-making and entered the world of Miracles" (16).

The hero worship explicit in such remembered scenes becomes mut-ed as the son grows, maturing into steady devotion and advocacy of the father, and culminating in the reception of a bitter, hard-won blessing and traumatic atonement. The exception, of course, is Henry Wiggen, whose psychic development proceeds without grief or anger and whose adult ego ideal, modeled on Pop, emerges without a hitch. Pop does not smoke or drink; neither does Henry. Pop is a big eater; so is Henry. Pop was a south-paw wise in the ways of the game; so is Henry. Pop is a good guy; so is Henry. The unstinting blessing of Pop falls on all that Henry does. It is the local, paternal equivalent of the universal blessing of Ecclesiastes: "Go eat your bread with enjoyment, and drink your wine with a merry heart; for God has already approved what you do" (9:7). Henry cannot there-fore fail in his relationships or his enterprises. For Ward Sullivan and Kincaid Chance, however, the situation is more complex; the price of blessing and atonement is high, namely, renunciation of the mother and death of the father.

As *Almost Famous* opens Gordon Sullivan is in the hospital, dying of cancer. Sarah Sullivan refuses to visit him; weak, self-centered, and, it is suggested, *voluntarily* demented, she demands the attention of the entire family. Ward, crippled from his accident, has become stalled in his psychic development (living an even more nightmarish version of Nickname's stay in the home of "The Eternal Mom"), working in a peanut-butter factory by day and playing dice baseball by night, obsessed with maintaining in pris-tine condition the Cadillac given him by the Red Sox on his signing with them years before. In his closet hangs his mended and stained baseball uniform, damaged in his career-ending accident, a symbol for Ward him-self, scarred, unsatisfactorily mended, reclusive, and useless.

Like the biblical patriarch, Gordon Sullivan blesses his sons in anticipation of his death, determining the course of their lives through his
words. Gordon's blessing is in the form of a holographic will on which
he elaborates to Ward from his hospital bed. In a Jacob-and-Esau reversal Gordon gives control of his estate to the younger brother, Gordie, thus
conferring on him the blessing of the first-born, the place of the father.
Ward, like Esau, is given little, along with the harsh blessing of exile: "I've
left you $20,000. Not much, is it? But it's enough to get you out of that
peanut butter factory. And out of the house. You don't belong here in
Pennsylvania – none of us do, for that matter. But you especially. So you
take that money and go somewhere else and make a fresh start. Go back
to Maine, maybe. But you ought to go somewhere because hanging
around here is killing you. I know you think you lost your chance when
the ball playing came to an end. But that was a long time ago. It's time to
forget and move on" (50). The old notion about blessings was that the
words spoken are efficacious, that they are powerful instruments to accomplish what is spoken. Once spoken, the words cannot be recalled. The
force of the blessing was the father's – a sort of law, a pre-Lacanian "Name
of the Father" – to determine, for good or ill, the future course of his sons'
lives. Gordon Sullivan acknowledges this power: "You think I've sold you
short. But I haven't. I've given you a break. But I know this: regardless
of what you feel, *you'll do what I say*" (51; emphasis added). In effect
Gordon has said to his son, his "ballplayer, [his] three-year-old reading
baby," you are an exile; you will leave home (house, mother, Pennsylvania) and go home, to the real, true home (Maine). There Ward must start
again, begin a life free from the curse of memory: "It's time to forget and
move on."

In these matters Ward has, in effect, no more choice than Jacob or Esau
had. He has a blessing whose wisdom he does not at first understand, one
that brings him grief but that he is powerless to avert. Gordon does more
than speak the blessing, however; he sets Ward's destiny in motion by
asking Ward to take him for a drive, a last journey that will lead back to
Maine, "home" (379), the archaic home, the first home of the fathers.
Along the way the dying Gordon tells Ward to "talk baseball" (381), and
Gordon dies just as they near the river that flows past the real home, the
place from which Gordon and Ward have been so long exiled. Ward has
achieved atonement with his father; he will live the life his father determined and blessed. He has escaped Sarah, her sinister home, and his own
nearly endless childhood. With his father's blessing he emerges for the

first time into genuine adulthood. It is only now that he can acknowledge and enact a new role, no longer son but father.

He will settle in Maine, build a house, and summon to his new home both Terry, the woman he did not want to marry, and little Gordon, the son he tried to abort. As he holds the baby for the first time, he finds him beautiful, the "most beautiful, profoundly peaceful creature" he has ever seen (412). This moment evokes Gordon Sullivan's holding Ward on his lap all those years ago. The generations circle around from Ward, the grandfather, to Gordon Sullivan, to Ward Sullivan, formerly son and now father of little Gordon. In Ward's holding little Gordon is an image of the father-son dyad, of unconditional, masculine love and approval. As the novel closes the family is playing ball in a meadow. Grandmother, mother Sarah (free for a while from the sanitarium), and Terry (perhaps future wife) are ranged on the porch like Francis Phelan's fates, a "gallery." Ward is at bat. He yells toward the porch, "Hey, Terry. . . . Is the kid watching?"

Gordon Sullivan's blessing in anticipation of his death is archetypal. He is blessing, determining, and conspiring with the son concerning his life. But for the intervention of Harriet Bird, Sam Simpson, Roy Hobbs's surrogate father, would have similarly blessed and determined Roy's life and enterprises. As he lies dying on a train headed for Chicago, Sam gives Roy his billfold – his money, even his identity – and his blessing: "Go on kiddo, you got to. See Clarence Mulligan tomorrow and say I sent you – they are expecting you. Give them everything you have got on the ball – that'll make me happy." When Roy starts to protest, Sam adds, "You got to" and "Do like I say," to which Roy can only reply, "Yes, Sam" (Malamud, *The Natural* 26). Like Ward Sullivan, Roy has received his "father's" dying blessing. He knows what he must do; he has no choice. That it will take Roy sixteen years to perform Sam's instruction is indicative not only of the power of the intervening female but of the blessing itself. It will not be denied.

Similarly, in *Shoeless Joe* Ray Kinsella's father, John, is behind the compulsive behavior Ray performs in the course of his journey into madness and illumination. The Voice is that of the "Father." The man for whom the field is prepared is double, both John Kinsella's hero (i.e., the father's "ego ideal") and John Kinsella himself. Ray is helpless to ignore the command he receives, which is at once blessing and shaping the course of his life. Ray's psychological attachment to Shoeless Joe and even the tour of ball fields Ray makes on his way to find J. D. Salinger have been determined by John Kinsella's dying words, his blessing. From his deathbed

John Kinsella tells "the story of the Black Sox Scandal for the last time," and like Gordon Sullivan, he issues a command: "You must go. . . . I've been in all the major league parks. I want you to do it too" (15). Ray nods in agreement. It will take many years for Ray to fulfill the terms, implicit and explicit, of his father's blessing, but fulfill them he must; his psychological well-being depends on it. If it requires a voice conjured from the depths of the unconscious to reiterate the blessing and set the enterprise in motion, so be it.

A still more extreme version of the blessing occurs in *The Iowa Baseball Confederacy*. Matthew Clarke, killed by a line drive, has no time for a conventional blessing, so he shapes his son's future by a "brain transplant," a literal atonement. Gideon speaks of the event: "I was never able to conceive what [my father] suffered, until, upon his death, when I was sixteen, I received his legacy, which was not money, or property, or jewels (though I was not financially bereft), but what I can only liken to a brain transplant. For upon my father's passing I inherited not only *all* the information he alone had been a party to, but also his obsession to prove to the world that what he knew was right and true. . . . I will pursue the elusive dream of the Iowa Baseball Confederacy" (Kinsella, *Iowa Baseball Confederacy* 4). Ray's father has issued a terrible blessing; Ray and his father are one.

The pattern repeats itself in all these cases and others. There is a blessing, a speaking by the father, in anticipation of death or at death that exerts irresistible influence on the son, determining his behavior as he struggles with adult life. In some respects the narratives are a reiteration of the working out of the father's blessing. In *The Brothers K* Hugh Chance, the father, blesses his children through example and parable, both recalled (respoken, remembered) at his wake. Hugh Chance, a pitcher, has spent his life struggling with ill chance. Around the dinner table each night he repeats a simple blessing: "Give us grateful hearts, our Father." When he dies young, as the fathers do, the children ritually speak of him. Freddy remembers a "hitting tip" that is really an instruction for living: "He said there are two ways for a hitter to get the pitch he wants. The simplest way is not to want *any* pitch in particular. But the best way, he said – which sounds almost the same, but is really very different – is to want the very pitch you're gonna get. Including the one you can handle. But also the one that's gonna strike you out looking. And even the one that's maybe gonna bounce off your head" (621–22). To want whatever comes, whether its effect is beneficial or disastrous, is, in the broadest sense, to have a grateful heart. Peter, speaking for all the sons, makes the connection in his memorial address to his dead father: "Give us grateful hearts . . . our Father. . . . And make us ever mindful of the needs of others. Through Christ, Papa's and Mama's Lord, amen. And through love for each other, amen. And through our sufferings, if that's what it takes, and our romances, our good housekeeping and our ballplaying, our friendships and our enemyships. Whatever works best, our Father" (623). This elaboration of Hugh's dinner-table blessing is spoken not to the divinity but to the father, formalizing the blessing whose effects will descend to the children. Kincaid Chance affirms and accepts the harsh legacy, this blessing of suffering and gratitude, by saying, "Amen."

The father's death is a leitmotif that runs through the mythology of baseball, often in its reiteration providing a period of dyadic closeness for father and son and a closure of the son's sonship. As the young father dies the mother is typically absent; the father, the son, and the game momentarily constitute the world, the game encapsulating the love and deflecting the pain of death and impending separation. Ray and John Kinsella, who is sleepless with pain, listen to a broadcast of a baseball game and tell baseball stories. On their journey "home" Ward and Gordon Sullivan think and talk baseball to keep at bay the knowledge of impending death. Irwin, Hugh Chance's son, alone is permitted to attend to his father's needs in the last few weeks of his life. He sits speechless nearby as Hugh reads the box scores. Gideon Clarke witnesses the line drive approach and strike Matthew, who is engaged at the moment in marking his scorecard. Roy Hobbs leans close for a brief private exchange with Sam Simpson and receives the blessing of baseball.

As the father dies, the son, often through the "blessing," is compelled either to take up the father's work, work at which the father has labored but in the performance of which he has fallen short, or to take on the task of redeeming the father through the telling of his story. For alongside the motif of early death is another: baseball fathers are consigned to the bush and minor leagues of life. Pop Wiggen, Ward Sullivan's grandfather, John Kinsella, Roy Hobbs's father, Hugh Chance – all are might-have-beens in the game of baseball and the game of life. Sam Simpson drank himself out of the majors in three short seasons and spent the rest of his life looking for a "son" to perform the work at which he had failed. Matthew Clarke, not a player but a baseball historian, bequeaths the task of writing the history of the Iowa Baseball Confederacy to his son, work realized as the narrative itself that "proves" the validity of Matthew's life's work. In the case of John Kinsella, the working out of his blessing on his son creates the situation in which he may himself be resurrected and redeemed, given his chance, unrealized in life, to perform and succeed at his work of catching in the major leagues. His sons, too, are given another chance at rapproachment. The smile John bestows on his sons is their smile: "I don't hear his reply, which is spoken in a gentle voice and accompanied by another smile, Richard's smile, my smile" (Kinsella, *Shoeless Joe* 254). Henry Wiggen becomes as much like his father as possible in order to pitch in the major leagues, work his father might have done but for the adverse circumstances of his life: "Pop said, 'I could of played ball in that park,' and I said, 'Pop I will play there sometime and it will be the same thing'" (Harris, *The Southpaw* 49–50).

When, as occasionally happens, the son fails to receive the father's blessing, the result is psychologically debilitating, in effect denying the son his adulthood. In *The Seventh Babe* Jerome Charyn presents a protagonist named Cedric Tannehill, the son of Marcus Tannehill, copper millionaire. The father insists on the son's following him into business, but Cedric wants only to play baseball. As a result the young man presents himself to training camp as Babe Ragland, orphan. The name *Babe* is significant (as is the fact that Cedric is also called "the kid," even at the age of seventy), for it labels the psychological age of the son denied his father's blessing and thus stalled in his journey into adulthood. He is usually called "Rags," a corruption of Ragland, a name that invokes his orphan persona. Hopelessly estranged from his father, Rags nevertheless experiences a spooky encounter with him one hot night in a park in St. Louis just before Rags is to marry Iva Cottonmouth. Rags hears someone calling "Cedric Tannehill," and after several wrong guesses about the identity of the caller, he recognizes his father. Rags is touchingly eager for his father's approval: "Pa, did Griffey get our schedule for you? How did you know the Sox were in St. Louis? I hit one off Urban Shocker this afternoon. The dope challenged me with his sinkerball. I got it with the sweet end of my bat" (129). The only response from Marcus Tannehill is to jab the sleeping dwarf (Rags's "mate") with his cane. Still eager, however, the Babe tries again: "Pa, I'm getting married! At the Old North Church. On Sunday. Did the Cottonmouths write to you? Pa, will you come?" (129–30). For answer Marcus merely limps away on his cane. He speaks no word, offers no approval, no blessing, not even an acknowledgment of his son's work and marriage plans. Scarborough, awakening, denies that the father has come to the park, saying, "It's hot, you're scared of getting married, and you dreamed it" (130), yet the meeting is eerily real and psychologically telling. About to enter the adult world of marriage, Rags is desperate for his father's blessing. Later he grieves when he learns that his father has died, yet through his will Marcus continues to withhold his blessing (229–30). Rags in his bereavement seeks help from a witch doctor to "raise" his father, but the raising is ironic, for it produces the ghost of Marylou Cottonmouth, Medusa-haired terrible mother (-in-law), still vaguely seductive in swamp weeds and torn blouse, emblems of her suicide by drowning in the Fens of Boston (230–31).

Rags will never grow up, nor will his life and career flourish, except to the extent that he remains "ever young," still playing third base at the age of seventy, traveling forever, homeless, with his wife-brute-roomie, Iva, and a ragtag team of sockamayocks, "the rejects of a hundred tryout camps" (342) in an old Buick. Garland James, his old teammate, whom Rags lures away from a nursing home to play center field for the Giants, looks at Iva and wonders, "Shouldn't the girl have had some gray specks in her hair? She had to be seventy, or sixty-nine? Did you kick old age in the pants when you traveled with the Giants?" (343). Likewise Rags himself has failed to age: "The kid had to be seventy, or seventy-two. His back wasn't curled over. He didn't have wattles on his neck. His fingers were hooked and powerful" (342). There is about Rags and his companions an uncanny aura of magic heard in the "sirens" of the fire truck generator – women who serenade an old man, singing "Go with the Giants, go with the Giants" (345). There is about them the bittersweetness of changeless things, things out of time, in an old trunk. The effect of the withheld blessing follows the son forever.

RECONCILIATIONS AND RETURNS

Such are the complexity and ambiguity of kinship relations in the unconscious – and the parent-child relationship in particular – that the son's unabashed grief for the "good guy" father (who dies young and sends the son into his adult life with a blessing), while at one level perfectly genuine, tends to obscure the fact that baseball's myths, against all conscious, everyday logic and "rules of the game," typically use their narrative devices not only to praise but to bury the father. The myths often present a type of Jacob's wrestling match in which the son prevails, wresting from a defeated father a reluctant blessing. When Jacob's mysterious opponent and father persona, bested in the all-night struggle with Jacob, pleads,

"Let me go, for the day is breaking" – the day being representative of mundane, conscious acts and thoughts, along with suppression of the unconscious and its dream logic – Jacob, the son, answers, "I will not let you go, unless you bless me" (Gen. 32:26). The father persona in the wrestling match is paradoxically powerful (powerful in naming or language; he is Lacan's Name of the Father) and weak (capable of being defeated by the son's emerging strength/life). By the same rules the son is both weak (needing the father's naming and blessing, the linguistic send-off into life) and powerful (ascending in the spiral of generations). At this point the son is destined – at least in the unconscious – not only to survive but to surpass the father, to make it to the "bigs" in the game of life, whereas the father is consigned to the minor leagues, semipro or almost pro, almost famous, almost or only potentially successful, now failing in strength, failed in his endeavors, and dying. Roy Hobbs's father was an itinerant laborer who played semipro ball in the summers, which he spent with Roy. Pop Wiggen sacrificed his major league career to care for his motherless son, continuing to pitch semipro ball. Ward Sullivan's grandfather and Wally Shaw, his surrogate father (29, 121), are almost famous but do not make it to the major leagues because of family responsibilities and women problems; John Kinsella, Ray's father, likewise leaves a promising baseball career because of family responsibilities. Hugh Chance loses his opportunity when he mangles his thumb at his off-season job in a mill, a job taken to support his fanatic wife and growing family.

The father's failure is mythologically necessary, the fault of biology – family relations, sexual drives, and time – which frustrates plans and potential and spoils "the game," both of life and of baseball. In his ruthless pursuit of success Ward Sullivan recognizes such pitfalls: love, family, and emotional attachments are dangerous. Two generations earlier Althea Webster called Ward Rideout away from baseball and into work in the shipyard; Ward's mother, the mad Sarah Rideout, spoiled Gordon's life when he fell in love with her. Love, Ward finds, is not the real object of endeavor but "the consolation prize," "the thing people settled for when they didn't know what to make of their lives. But he knew where he was going. He was a ballplayer. This woman [Blue] wanted equal time. She acted like it was normal, natural, to drag around a whole lot of emotional baggage. She would have been amazed to learn he worried that maybe love would make him half a step slower, or dim his eye, or flaw his concentration" (Small 113). Twelve years later Ward is deep in the "statistical summary of the mythology" of his dice baseball game. The telephone rings, intruding into the numerical neatness of what is left for Ward of the game, and indeed of what has become his life. Ward knows it is Terry calling, to "rob him of this pleasure, [shatter] the eggshell moment" (164). Even though he is resentful and angry, when she invites him to her apartment, Ward feels "the old sleeping bat of biology [stir and flap] its wings," and when he tries to go back to the game, the mood has been broken; she has "ruined it" (167).

Baseball's sons, like other mythic heroes, are given impossible tasks: to gain the blessing of the beloved but feared, powerful but weakening, ultimately failed father, to surpass him, and to avoid the psychological dangers of both the beloved but feared woman to whom the father fell victim and all her various incarnations, who call with irresistible siren song, promising all but providing only grief and disappointment as they spoil life and ruin the game. While his story eventually leads Ward Sullivan out of his bitter resentment toward biology in general and women in particular, it does not negate the psychological truths the attitude expresses – the double bind of fathers and mothers (baseball and women), love and hate, mind and body, would and could.

The narrative burial of the father (an ingenious mythic strategy) emerges from just this double bind. To obtain the father's dying blessing is both to acknowledge the father's power, along with his right to exercise it, and at the same time, to deprive him of all power; it is to realize symbolically the eternal son's murderous, competitive impulse on an occasion that paradoxically but inevitably calls forth the profoundest experience and expression of filial devotion and grief. To become at one with the father is both to acknowledge the filial relationship and to take the father's identity as father, to be at once child and man, dwarf and giant. Roy Hobbs's failure to make the transition from childhood to adulthood is represented in his fevered dreams, where by turns he "waxe[s] to gigantic heights," becoming Roy Hobbs, man and hero, and "then abruptly [falls] miles to be a little Roy dwarf," child and outcast from the game (Malamud, *The Natural* 149).

Ward Sullivan cannot grow up until his father blesses him, prods him from his mother's house, and dies. Only then is Ward empowered to become a father himself, to establish his own home, to begin again, as Donald Hall puts it, "lazy and murderous . . . the profound archaic song of birth, growth, age, and death" (30). "Hey, Terry. . . . Is the kid watching?" Yes. The kid is always watching, the adult's internalized child who would build an ego ideal on the model of the beloved father, the murderous child devoted to the siren-mother, the beautiful son whose new eyes absorb an ancient image of father-giant-protector, a big man with a stick coming to bat in a meadow. One day, of necessity, this kid will bury and grieve over this man. And the account of the death may well find its way into a myth that will strive to reconcile the murderous impulse with the genuine grief.

Curiously, the myths often permit the mothers to survive the generational upheaval, a fact that undermines the overtly misogynistic fear and hatred with which they are approached and the brutalization and excoriation to which they are subjected. The narratives leave room for the possibility that somewhere in the world Mrs. Maxson and Mrs. Hobbs roam, perhaps still looking for their abandoned sons. Gideon Clarke's mother, Darlin' Maudie, blown to smithereens in Chicago, is nevertheless reincarnated in Gideon's own wife and perfected as Sarah in the past to which Gideon hopes to return. Ray Kinsella's mother (at a safe distance in a western state) is accessible by phone but cannot intrude between the members of the ghostly father-son dyad that exists on the phantom field of play. Kathryn Phelan, resurrected in Francis's unconscious, merges with and survives in the image of Annie, his wife. Laura Chance, separate but nearby, lives in a trailer on Irwin's farm. Even Sarah Sullivan, worst of them all, is let out of her madhouse and given at least temporary room in the "gallery," the porch of Ward's new home.

Somewhere, it seems, in the space of baseball – the game, the myth – is a white house with green shutters and a tricycle overturned on the porch, a father to verify the son's frightened recognition that some kid lives here, and inside, a pretty, ever-young woman in a blue apron. It is this space, this gap, to which symbolically a son returns to announce, probably reluctantly, "I'm home, Mom."

12

I NEVER LAUGH. I AM NO BUFFOON. I AM A DWARF AND NOTHING BUT A DWARF. . . .

THE WRINKLES MAKE ME LOOK VERY OLD. I AM NOT, BUT I HAVE HEARD TELL THAT WE DWARFS ARE DESCENDED FROM A RACE OLDER THAN THAT WHICH NOW POPULATES THE WORLD, AND THEREFORE WE ARE OLD AS SOON AS WE ARE BORN. I DO NOT KNOW IF THIS IS TRUE, BUT IN THAT CASE WE MUST BE THE ORIGINAL BEINGS. Pär Lagerkvist, *The Dwarf* 5–6

MUST HAVE BEEN DIFFERENT FOR POGO THOUGH. I MEAN HE KNEW ALL ALONG HE'D NEVER HAVE THE SIZE FOR IT. NO HOPE. John Sayles, *Pride of the Bimbos* 196

"EVERY INCH A MAN"
THE BASEBALL DWARF

This chapter title is taken from Philip Roth's *The Great American Novel*, naming a chapter that, it is claimed, "contain[s] as much as has ever been written anywhere on the subject of midgets in baseball" (189). I began this book by drawing attention to the recurrence of the dwarf in baseball's literature, a figure who often suffers violence on the field of play. It is appropriate that I return to that enigmatic figure and attempt to draw some conclusions about its mythicity and significance within this body of texts.

To be brief about it, my conclusion is that such narrative renderings are in no sense mimetic; the baseball dwarf has nothing to do with real people in the world, with adults who are smaller than average. Rather, he comes as a figure from the past, both personal and collective. His appearance is an invitation from the uncanny, the lost, the repressed, the primordial, the origin. First, he is a disguised image of the baseball protagonist, a Lacanian other from early childhood; a distorted form arising from the unconscious, rendered grotesque, the more misshapen as the more denied;[1] a figure who insists ludicrously on "playing the game," asserting his manhood, and having his say, despite all attempts to silence him; and, as a result, a figure plotted against in the mythology, becoming an object of narrative exclusion, violence, and death. Second, beyond representing this personal primordial, the baseball dwarf is a bit of bricolage, a signifier from antiquity cloaked with archetypal meanings and hence ambiguity, as the dwarfish presence evokes echoes and equivocations accumulated through countless appearances in literature, fairy tale, and myth, back through history into prehistory and to a time of not-altogether human evolution in the archaic forests of the world and the mind. Jerome Charyn's Scarborough is at one point seen as turning "into an ancient, sobbing five-year-old dwarf" (209), an image that captures a sense of both the personal and collective primordial. He is called "the brute," a term applied both to animals and to nonrational humans, as is his counterpart for the Yankees, Henry Watteau (113). A frequent epithet for the dwarf is "little monkey": John Sayles's Pogo Burns is called a "tough little monkey" (10), and both Denzel, a child and friend, and Dred, Pogo's sworn enemy, mistake Mr. Mumps, a chimpanzee dressed in human clothes, for Pogo (42, 235). There is a prehuman or protohuman aura about the archetypal dwarf, a sense that here is the human essence in its primordial shape, ancient, elemental, and knowing but also embarrassingly revealing, reflecting the image of oneself, unrecognized, glimpsed in a funhouse mirror. The word *dwarf* itself is an ancient word in the Germanic languages (of which English is one), its etymology as well as its first representative and archetypal role lost in time. Norse mythology claims that dwarfs emerged before other humans from maggots that grew in the carcass of Ymir, a primordial giant. Down the ages, through myth and literature, dwarfs assume many names and many forms – troll, midget, elf, pixy, gnome, runt, pee-wee, shrimp, fairy, and leprechaun. Under whatever name they appear, they are often tricksters, magicians, and wizards, guardians of secrets and treasures, denizens of dark woods and underground chambers. Occasionally helpful and benign, their aid must usually be coerced; often sinister, greedy, self-interested, mean-spirited, and ill-tem-pered, they give with spite and utter curses on the knowledge or gold they provide.

Both aspects – the personal and the archetypal, the archaic child and the primordial human – contribute to the character, action, and depiction of the baseball dwarf. At the same time the narrative treatment and fate of the dwarf, as the daylight reaction to this essential form of both indi-vidual and species, offer clues to the meanings, however disguised or re-pressed, insinuated by the textual unconscious.

At the personal level the figure is a relic from the first stages of psychic development (the pre-Oedipal and Oedipal stages),[2] when the uncon-scious is peopled with powerful, controlling adult-giants amid whom the child-dwarf wanders, a being in whose small body the immensity of self is confined, rendered impotent, often frustrated and ill-tempered, and given to tantrums, an object of ridicule to the giants among whom he lives. The diminutive size of the dwarf indicates his figurative age. At one point Charyn's Scarborough is seen as "terrorstruck," having "the look of a stunted child, lost in the middle of Fenway Park" (58). Height itself is the indicator by which children typically judge age; they assume that taller people are older than shorter people. Thurber's Pearl du Monville iron-ically denies the age-and-size correlation, calling everyone "Junior" and claiming to be one year older than each man he meets. Sayles's Pogo Burns, reduced to a thing, "burn[s] its low-pouched eyes straight into Bryce's crotch," Bryce being a six-foot, three-inch shoe salesman whom Pogo calls "Junior" (12). He refuses to buy shoes for himself from "any-one named Junior Booterie" (13). (In his personal role the dwarf is old, the first shape of self, in Wordsworth's phrase, "the father of the man"; in his archetypal role he is older still, unimaginably ancient.) In general the archaic psychological formation of the self as dwarf is indicated by the fact that the baseball dwarf is about the size of a child of two to four years: Kinsella's Little Walter is "a little over three feet tall" (*Iowa Baseball Con-federacy* 138); Thurber's Pearl du Monville is "only thirty-four, thirty-five inches high" (510); Roth's Bob Yamm is forty inches (189), and his O. K. Ockatur is three inches shorter (196); as noted previously, Pogo Burns is just a bit taller than the crotch of a man of six feet, three inches tall. The Oedipal child size of the dwarf reveals something both of his power and his danger as he wanders into the uncanny confines of the field of play. His power lies in the child's unrealized potential, the disruptive capabil-ity of his Oedipal impulses, and in the restorative function of beginnings;

the danger lies in his threat to adult status and the clear possibility of psychological regression or stalemate.

Baseball, however, is for giants. Its dimensions, frequently lauded as "perfect," are all wrong for dwarfs, seemingly designed especially to deny a place to such small beings. It permits "boys" to play, as long as they are the size of full-grown men with big bats; it tolerates only as freaks or clowns grown men who are the size of little boys with their little toy bats. When such figures from the unconscious find their way onto the field, into the gap of myth, the space of art, they may reveal their uncanny psychic and mythic origins in their manner of coming and going. In Thurber's "You Could Look It Up" the manager, Squawks Magrew, is drinking in a bar, feeling sorry for himself because of his team's inept play, when "up pops this Pearl du Monville outa nowheres" (510). (The dwarf's name is a loose pun on the French *m'envie*, "my desire.") It is as if, in his anger (which has caused him to start talking in a high voice, like a child) and need (and in his cups), the manager permits the release of the archaic self from his own unconscious. Magrew reaches out to touch du Monville "to satisfy hisself he [is] real" (511). At the end of his stint in the big leagues, the dwarf leaves as he has come; he "just vanishe[s] into the thin of air" (523). With the "disappearance of Pearl du Monville out back a second base," or with the exorcism of this psychological primitive, the "old zip come back" (524). To commemorate the psychological healing of the manager through the therapeutic appearance of the dwarf, Magrew's players have a pair of baby shoes bronzed, a souvenir of the uncanny coming and going of the child-dwarf. (The bronzed-baby-shoes image recurs in *Pride of the Bimbos,* where Dred, the "giant" who stalks Pogo Burns, plans to bring back the dwarf's shoes, bronzed with "the feet . . . still . . . in them," as proof to his associates that he has killed the dwarf [167].) Like the span of childhood, the dwarf's tenure in the game is brief; his coming and going are abrupt and often mysterious. Thurber's dwarf is in some ways typical, sharing his ability to appear and disappear with the dwarfs of fairy tale and myth, at once the helpful and hindering representative of the dark caves of the earth and the infernal realms of the unconscious.

A similar appearance occurs in *Ironweed.* At one point Francis Phelan becomes suddenly aware of a pattern of violence in his life, and he recalls a dwarf, "a runt" "too little to hit," with whom he had a violent confrontation, in which he bit a piece out of the back of the runt's neck (145). Then, at a crucial moment, just as Annie's garden has become ballpark and then church, the runt crazily reappears as a spook from the past, from an ancient "time lock," onto Francis's mental field of play: "And then, when he saw the runt (who knew he was being watched, who knew he didn't belong in this picture) putting the lighted end of the candle into the hole in the back of his neck, . . . he grew fearful" (181). Francis's fear is of a universal sort. The wound in the neck – "self-inflicted" – makes present and vivid the ancient fear of castration, highlighted by the acolyte's burning candle. Like Magrew, Francis has released a childish figure of himself, a herald whose message is coded in enigmatic images and acts. In Francis's unconscious the mutilated runt is associated with the acolytes' singing of the "Dies Irae," the "Day of Wrath," the anger of the Father, the gigantic and powerful source of both fear and grace. Francis next tries to remember the name of his first dog, unconsciously acknowledging the connection between the image of the curiously pious, masochistic runt, the real or imagined anger of the Father, and himself as child.

Another case of identity of protagonist and dwarf is seen in the relationship of Malamud's Roy Hobbs and Otto Zipp in *The Natural* (discussed in chap. 9). It is appropriate here, however, to notice that, like du Monville and *Ironweed's* runt, the dwarf Otto Zipp comes and goes in rhythm with Roy's shifting fortunes. He appears in the crowd as the embodiment of Roy Hobbs's ineptitude and failure, disappears when things go well for Roy, and reappears at Roy's final game, screaming curses from the stands. After Roy's baseball "death" Otto Zipp comes in to "pinch-hit" for Roy. In Roy's fevered dreams his unconscious acknowledges the identity of the two, as Roy grows "to gigantic heights then abruptly [falls] miles to be a little Roy dwarf (Hey, mister, you're stepping on my feet)" (175).

The archaic psychology of the dwarf, his Oedipal ineptitude, and his fear are underscored by the fact that while he is pressed into service as a pinch hitter, he is forbidden to swing the phallic bat, perhaps lest "Junior," as Robert Coover puts it, "explode one off his piece of lumber" (34) and disrupt the whole system. Magrew tells Pearl du Monville, "Just stand up there and hold that bat on your shoulder." Roth's Bob Yamm wears number 1/4 on his uniform and comes to the plate with his little bat and the severest of admonitions against swinging it. Frank Mazama, the manager, enforces the prohibition himself: "Every time he comes to bat, I am going to be perched up on the top of the grandstand with a high-powered rifle aimed at home plate. And if this little son of a buck so much as raises the bat off his shoulder, I'll plug him! Hear that, Pee Wee?" (190). Kinsella's Little Walter pinch-hits, coming to the plate not only with the understanding that he will not wield the bat (he could not anyway, for the bat is almost too heavy for him to lift [*Iowa Baseball Confederacy* 258]), but also with the understanding that he will let the opposing pitcher, who has vowed to kill him, throw at his head. The "impotent" dwarf, who cannot swing, takes the fatal beanball; like du Monville, Gideon Clarke's grotesque alter-ego is first summoned and then dispatched.

One sign of the dwarf's essential childlikeness is his tendency to be angry and violent. This figure from the unconscious emerges not only as an embarrassment but as one who bears an old grudge against "giants." In *Ironweed* Francis Phelan's runt hits him with an ax handle, splintering his leg bone. In *The Iowa Baseball Confederacy* Little Walter is unrelentingly ill-tempered. The dwarf rejects Grady's offer to help him with an equipment bag full of bats with "an unkind reference to Grady's size, intellect, and ancestry" (139). Otto Zipp in *The Natural* makes rude noises and shouts insults and curses at Roy from the stands. Roth's O. K. Ockatur, the epitome of baseball dwarfdom, has a "fierce hatred of all men taller than himself" (197), including his fellow dwarf Bob Yamm. Ockatur, a pitcher, faces Bob Yamm, who has been warned not to swing. Ockatur throws at Yamm's head; Yamm ignores the prohibition against swinging, starts to swing, and takes the ball in the face. The ball strikes Yamm between the eyes and blinds him, inflicting on him the punishment of Oedipus for the symbolically Oedipal crime of swinging the bat.

Baseball provides the scene, and its narratives the means, for conjuring from the past the image of the repressed, the ghost of the angry, ill-behaved, ill-tempered, grudge-bearing child. Once the dwarf is present in the game, the game's own means are used to exorcise the Lacanian shade. He is beaned, blinded, castrated, killed, and thrown from the game and the field where he knows he does not belong. The invocation and then elimination of this figure constitute a sort of psychic salvage mission, invoking the restorative or healing powers of the past and then ritually purging the dangerous, inappropriate, or out-grown feelings and responses.

All these connections of the baseball dwarf with the individual unconscious reinforce the wider implications of the archetype. As archetypal signifier the baseball dwarf evokes a cosmic time scale and more ancient associations, a reminder of the universal human condition of smallness, powerlessness, and moral fallibility, in contrast with the world-creating, world-ruling, and ultimately world-destroying divinities, encountered as giants. For example, Gideon Clarke, as dwarf, wrestles with his semidivine and immortal alter ego, Drifting Away, who is fifteen feet tall (Kinsella, *Iowa Baseball Confederacy* 165–66). Again, in Coover's *Universal Baseball Association* the discrepancy in size between J. Henry Waugh and the inhabitants of his tabletop world forces readers, as they watch over Henry's shoulder, to look down on the world of the players, to see their smallness and experience the irony of their religious and philosophical speculations couched in language somehow too big for them and therefore ludicrous.

Before his blinding Roth's Bob Yamm was to have written an autobiographical screenplay, "All Men Are Midgets," its title taken from Bob's ironically self-important resignation speech to the media. Bob Yamm and O. K. Ockatur, at the time teammates, have brawled in the dugout, a trivial occurrence over which Bob feels an exalted sense shame and disgrace. He concludes his speech with an appeal for "human solidarity and brotherhood under God, Our Maker": "I say 'Our' Maker . . . though as we all know there are those in this country who would still have us believe that He who made the full-grown did not make the midget also. Well, let me assure these skeptics, that ever since my own Hour of Crisis began in the Reaper dugout . . . I have heard His Voice, and it is not runty or pint-sized; let me assure the skeptics that He Who exorts, chastens, and comforts me is not less a God, nor is He any other God, than He Who made and judges the fully grown. On high, there is but one God Who made us all, and to Him, *all* men are midgets" (205). The Everyman-dwarf suggests the powerlessness and insignificance of the creature: Adam crafted of mud by the giant divine hands and set down, with dire warnings, in his small garden world, a world imaged innumerable times in the walled gardens known as ballparks.

At the same time, contradicting the image of impotence in the Everyman-dwarf image, there is the ancient ascription to dwarfs of arcane wisdom and magic powers. Dwarfs are said to have knowledge of spells; they know where the earth's treasures lie, and they make magic artifacts from them; they are speakers of curses, magicians, wizards, denizens of the secret places of the earth. Hence the dwarf may be associated with both weakness and power, and with both good and ill fortune. In *The Seventh Babe* the Yankees' dwarf is said to have "brought them two pennants in a row," but Scarborough "would only bring the Sox to perdition" (4). Otto Zipp's curses are clearly connected with Roy Hobbs's slumps and failures, yet Pearl du Monville's presence turns around a struggling team and restores it to pennant-winning form.

Two major baseball novels of the 1970s – Charyn's *The Seventh Babe* and Sayles's *Pride of the Bimbos* – offer evidence that the baseball dwarf, like other archetypal signifiers, is evolving, acquiring new dimensions and meanings, while at the same time retaining many of its traditional significations. In *The Seventh Babe* the dwarf Scarborough is moved from the periphery to a place near the center of the plot, with full development of character, to assume the classic American role of sidekick. In *Pride of the Bimbos* Pogo Burns, although "split" among several functions and roles, is unquestionably the work's protagonist. Both Scarborough and Pogo are players – although among the exiled and excluded – and both are plotted against, failing to survive their own narratives: Scarborough dies as a result a heart attack, and Pogo Burns kills himself. Both figures deserve a closer analysis because of what they suggest about the dwarf's increasing significance in the mythology. The primary issue is to determine what is suggested when the figure of primitive child–Ur-human assumes a central position in the narratives. One possible but not altogether encouraging answer is that this figure of the unconscious is growing more demanding, no longer a shade to be summoned and dismissed. The dwarf may be emerging as the essential and enduring form of the self, the ancient child, powerless, fragile, mortal, isolated, the small, tragicomical figure of fear and desire, a most unlikely hero.

DWARF AS SIDEKICK

Charyn's dwarf is one of the most complex developments of the archetype. The man with a single name, Scarborough (although he is also known as "Hump" and "the brute"), embodies the typical mystery, antiquity, and wisdom of the archetype. Although Babe Ragland guesses Scarborough's age at forty-five or fifty, the dwarf claims to be twenty-three at the novel's outset (27). But something other than mere chronological age is suggested when Rags makes Scarborough angry and accuses him of lying. Scarborough undergoes a transformation that reveals something of his "nature": "The furrows began to darken on Scarborough's head. He could have been eighty, looking at him. The sun poured into the room, *but his face was in some deep hollow that had nothing to do with Boston weather and Boston time*" (15; emphasis added). Scarborough is both aged and ageless. Both the personal and collective primordial are glimpsed in that deep hollow outside ordinary Boston time. Scarborough is not only small but misshapen. Formerly (he claims) a lumberjack, he is a hunchback, mascot, clown, and batboy to the Boston Red Sox; later he is magician, batboy, and first baseman for the Cincinnati Colored Giants; through it all he is roommate, adviser, and friend to Babe Ragland; and at last, he is the monster of Sackville Forest and demon, the most complex of shades emerging from the haunted basement of the protagonist's psychological house of mirrors.

"House of mirrors" in this context is the appropriate term, for each character in Babe's biological family – father, mother, self – is encountered over and over in the course of a narrative that spans fifty-plus years, taking Babe Ragland from a beanpole rookie of seventeen to an aged man, crippled but young, still the kid, and still playing third base at seventy. It is the story of a life passed in a diamond-shaped never-never land of lost boys. The characters will not hold still, however, either as to identity or as to role. The lost mother (dead when Babe is six) is encountered as both mother and bride in the Cottonmouth ladies, mother Marylou and daughter Iva, Babe's bride. It is difficult to tell which of these is older, either by appearance or by behavior. Through an Oedipal "Freudian error" of judgment, Babe ends up in bed with both of them at the same time (167). In a mirror image of this scene, however, Iva (bride-to-be and mirror image of her mother) had earlier ended up in bed with both Babe and Scarborough. Iva's act was "innocent" enough (78), but after Babe has taken her to her mother's bed, in retaliation she seduces Scarborough (and then the rest of the team), incurring the dwarf's deep sense of guilt. As wife of a "Babe" Iva is both bride and mother; of necessity she sleeps with Scarborough, the childish apparition and true form of Babe's self. After succumbing to Iva's blandishments, the dwarf attempts to hang himself in an Oedipal fit of self-loathing and is saved by Babe. Scarborough cries, a sound that "could have been an orphan wailing, or a lunatic" (179), the orphan being the adopted persona of Babe Ragland, who claims to have been raised, like Babe Ruth, in the "bad boys' home." When Scarborough, inseparable roommate and other self, dies, we are not led to believe that the Babe has buried an old haunt and moved on, for he looks up Iva, his own estranged wife, and asks her not to resume her role as wife but rather to be his roommate (311); she agrees and becomes "a different kind of brute" (315).

Scarborough is at the vortex of this whirl of identities and roles. In his size and habits he is the true identity of the never-mature Babe; the two are roommates, mates – that is, like two shoes, alike (at one point the Babe himself even temporarily becomes a hunchback [147]). Both are unlucky outcasts, fellow children with a passion for chocolate sundaes. And at one point, as previously mentioned, they share bed and bride: untold ambiguities and mysteries lurk in the image of the Babe and the dwarf on either side of Iva (schoolgirl, fiancee, and mirror image of her mother, Marylou) in the chaste bed of the roomies in the hotel of the "bachelor" team. In this crazy episode (73–79) everything is double and triple. The ambiguities of Oedipus, at once son and husband of Jocasta, and of Jocasta, both mother and wife of Oedipus, are in this trio of the Babe, Iva, and Scarborough given a sort of exponential complexity, for this is an Oedipal triangle with several twists. Babe, or the kid, as his name insists, is psychologically a child but physically a man. The girl-woman in his bed is his fiancee-bride but also a double for Marylou Cottonmough, the terrible mother. At the same time, she has been smuggled into the room as "Muggsy," orphan and Babe's teammate at reform school, in a way his double; nonetheless, in this guise she is referred to by the house detective as "runt," that is, a figure like Scarborough, in whose pajamas she sleeps. She is girl-boy, girl-woman, ballplayer-dwarf, and bride-mother, a dizzying whirl of personae. At a literal level Scarborough is psychologically mature, but he is physically child-sized. In his tropological function he is likewise complex, for as a trope for the individual, the figure of Scarborough presents the protagonist's ancient child-self escaped from the unconscious to take the twisted form of "Hump," brute, or batboy. At the same time, however, on a collective level, as representative of the species primordial, Scarborough goes beyond the figure of personal antiquity to mythic antiquity: he is the wise Ur-human, the father of the man, replicating and replicated in this strange trio of bedfellows.

Scarborough, as archetypal dwarf, has knowledge and abilities normal-sized people do not have: brutes "could peer into your dugout from behind their hump. Most brutes were blessed with freakish fields of vision. They could see around benches, and under a coach's shoes" (56). His affinity with mythical dwarfs and trolls also gives him something of their immortality. With this characteristic he finds his way at death to a primitive role, that of the ancient little man of the woods, a monster of the forest, a creature "small and rough" who "knocks you on your ass" (329). This figure is familiar, a most elemental archetypal signifier, but the Hump gives the signifier new implications, for after death Scarborough has returned to the woods (Sackville Forest) where he tried to hang himself after his "Oedipal crime" with "Miz Iva" (178), and when Babe encounters him in his eternal form, Scarborough is again hanging from a tree, a time-less image of guilt and expiation. Now, however, he is called "demon": "How did Scarborough get to be such a demon? Was it the kid's fault? Some curse that baseball had put on him? Was it better to bump people and hang from trees as the monster of Sackville Forest, or lie dead in the ground?" (331). To complicate matters, this uncanny little-old-man "Oe-dipus-Christ" of the dark forest has imported the game of baseball into the troll's ancestral home: "He was Scarborough, Scarborough, bump-ing with his body and holding baseball inside his head. He'd shove his brains out onto the road, taste the leather on his mitt. Who could stop him? Devils couldn't order him around. He'd have his first base in the woods. The hidden Giant, running, jumping, knocking into trees" (333). The ancient pastime of the "little men" is now merged with the play of the boys of summer, and the dwarf is paradoxically a "Giant" – a white dwarf who is a Cincinnati Colored Giant – in a remarkable, timeless space of art and mind illuminated by the dark light of his primordial forest home now refashioned as ballpark.

DWARF AS HERO

Despite his tropological roles and functions, Scarborough is richly drawn and eminently human, unlike Kennedy's runt and Malamud's Otto Zipp or Roth's ironically portrayed Bob Yamm. He is a loyal, responsi-ble man who suffers with and cares for Babe Ragland, a likable, funny man who would carry heavy luggage up eleven flights of stairs to earn a silver dollar for chocolate sundaes for himself and the kid. John Sayles's Pogo Burns is like Scarborough in his humanity and equally complex in his archetypal significations. Pogo is like an ancient but familiar psychologi-cal shadow cast between a father and a son. In his relationships with Denzel and Lewis Crawford, Pogo is a figure not only for the working out of themes central to the Oedipal question (father-son relationships and the father's blessing) but also for the exploration of the broad theme of manhood. He is so fully drawn and occupies so central a place in his narrative, however, that he must be considered the hero of his own life.

Pogo plays shortstop as "Big Bertha" for a traveling transvestite soft-ball team known as the Brooklyn Bimbos. He expects at any moment to be attacked by a giant black man named Dred. He enlists the aid of Den-zel Ray Crawford, son of his teammate Lewis Crawford, in watching for the attacker, and at the same time he acts as surrogate father and guide to the boy. Just as the players "reverse" their gender to play the game, so are the roles of dwarf and "kid" reversed. Here the dwarf plays shortstop (a pun on both his size and his tenure with the team) and the kid, Denzel, plays batboy: "Denzel Ray Crawford, nine years of age, a Texas League blooper no one really wanted responsibility for, veteran batboy of endless summers on the road, a boy too smart for his own good" (18). Denzel is a strange combination of figures like Malamud's Roy Hobbs and Harris's Henry Wiggen if we had met them as boys, in their dwarf phases. Denzel might describe his mother just as Roy Hobbs describes his own, as a whore. At the same time, like Henry Wiggen, he might say, "Of my mother I can tell you practically nothing." Like Roy Hobbs, Denzel is said to be "a natural" (195), and like both Roy Hobbs and Henry Wiggen, he is the son of a bush league baseball player, devoted to the game but failed in its execution. A typical baseball son, Denzel has been abandoned by his mother and raised by Lewis Crawford, a "good guy," the father who is not altogether sure that he is the boy's father.

Pogo stands between them. For Denzel, Pogo is both a reflection of the boy, a small misfit (Denzel can mimic Pogo's walk, gestures, and baseball act perfectly, and in fact takes over for Pogo after his suicide – Pogo's costume is "a perfect fit" [252] for Denzel), and the father that Lewis is not willing to be. For Lewis, Pogo is a teammate and the embodiment of a childish haunt, a psychological phase he is not ready to relinquish: when Pogo is buried in the funeral director's last child's coffin, Lewis worries "because finally there was no one left between him and the boy, and he didn't know how to handle it. Just didn't know" (258).

In and beyond both these roles, Pogo struggles with universal questions concerning manhood and his own identity as a man. What is manhood? How do you know whether you are a man? Does it have to do with your manner of dress or occupation? With your size, or age, or sexual prowess, or sense of responsibility, or courage? Does it have to do with your relationship with your father? With your father's approval? What do you do if you fail to measure up? Does it matter whether you are six feet, ten inches tall, like Dred, or small for your age, like Denzel, or of a size to be buried in a child's casket, like Pogo? Does it matter if someone calls you mister – like Mr. Mumps?

The manhood question is not Pogo's alone, although he is the person in whom the issues are focused. Manhood is in question for the entire team of "Bimbos." They are, after all, an odd assortment of failed baseball players, reduced to playing softball (a game appropriate for "girls' exercise class" [62]) in drag. After a game in full makeup, long-haired wigs, falsies, and women's clothes, bearing names like "Long Louise," "Pricilla Popfly," "Carlita del Croutcho," "Sally Buns," and "Big Bertha Burns," the team members are desperate to reassert their masculinity:

> The Bimbos' locker room was a locker room like others, the backslaps a little harder, the jokes a little raunchier, the curses gruffer and more elaborate. They had two hours of geek humor and wolf whistles, two hours of faggotry to scour from their hides. They washed their balls as if grooming a fine steed. . . . Denzel wondered at their balls from the corners of his eyes. Even Pogo, who like himself was short for his age, even Pogo was a man down there. He's a ballsy little guy, they would say of the midget from time to time. It was not so bad, thought Denzel, to be a little guy if you were a ballsy one. (19)

It is clear that the implications of femininity are a psychological soil that must be scoured away and that the first definition of manhood is based on "balls"; the person's size is implicated as an important second consideration. A full-grown man with balls is clearly a man, once he has washed away the scum of womanhood. A little guy with balls is not so bad. Denzel is just a little guy who hides "himself casually behind a washcloth" (19). Pogo occupies an ambiguous middle ground in this hierarchy, between the men and the boy. "Ballsy" is itself an ambiguous term, however, a metonym both for the fully grown male, manhood as maleness, and for a secondary characteristic of manhood, courage.

The mythology of ballsiness is written in the locker-room magazine hidden under a pile of wet towels, a publication that Pogo names "Wet Dream Magazine," with the "usual cover – women in their underwear chained to a dungeon wall, demon-eyed Nazi torturers" (87). The suggestion implicit in the title is that here is a glimpse into the dreamwork of the male psyche, its fears and desires, its never-ending attempts to deny "impotence," the archaic child, and to achieve full manhood. At different times both Pogo and Denzel read the magazine, looking for something. Pogo's dialogue with the magazine is only half-ironic; Denzel's is dead serious.

Pogo rejects the stories of the magazine as "nothing": "There was the Nazi story and a story on young girl hitchhikers luring men to their ruin and a phony detective thing . . . 'The Other Side of the Keyhole' by Steve Mann, Private Investigator," to which Pogo's reaction is "Private eye my ass" (87). The name of the "author" of the detective article, Steve *Mann,* focuses the manhood issue, for Pogo himself claims to have been a "private dick" (11), itself an ambiguous term, and he routinely entertains his teammates and Denzel with stories of his adventures (18).

Pogo's reading of the ads, however, the "meat of the magazine," the "con job in the con job" (18), reveals something of the depths of Pogo's longing, isolation, and self-hatred. The ads that catch his eye are those promising easy money, a fine physique, virility, or hair: "So I'm rich, slim and hairy. Bring on the broads" (90). Bring on the broads, indeed. Pogo notices ads for mail-order brides, foreign brides, and advice on "How to Pick Up Chicks" (not "ugly, fat or dumb girls," to which Pogo answers, "I'll take 'em. Not choosy. Give me your dumb, your fat, your ugly" [91]). Another ad assures the reader that beautiful girls want you to pick them up and offers to teach the reader their signals and "25 great opening lines." Pogo has an opening line: "Hiya beautiful, ever fuck a midget?" He continues, "Oh no. Rich and slim and hairy as I am, lonely and eager as they are, it's still a bad bet at five bucks" (91). He imagines his own letter in response to the ad: "'What if you give them the willies?' Pogo Burns, Shortstop" (92), with the emphasis on *short*. As they proceed, the ads appeal to the more and more desperate. "For Lonely Men Only" offers the solace of a latex lady "Designed for the ACTION-MINDED man" (93). Pogo rejects this alternative in favor of the "POGO BURNS METHOD" of "TOTAL MENTAL LOVEPLAY" and "JERKING OFF." Finally, on the last page is an ad Pogo does not have to read because he knows by heart: "Learn to be a PRIVATE DETECTIVE at home! Your key to an exciting, rewarding life. Be somebody, be a private eye" (94). Pogo knows this ad; he has fallen for it; he has been "somebody," a private dick. He characterizes this ad as "the biggest con job of them all" and reiterates the title he has given the magazine, "Wet Dream Magazine" (94). As indicators of manhood, sexuality and prestige (or worldly identity) are for Pogo ironic and utterly isolating, like wet dreams, like masturbation, all done under the scrutiny of the private eye. Professionally, socially, sexually – in all these realms he fails to measure up. He is a lonely man, in the language of the ad, a private dick.

The mythology of manhood presents a different face to nine-year-old Denzel, who finds the magazine hidden under towels, with its "ladies [not 'women'] in their underwear" and a "story about Nazis," but when Denzel reads the magazine it is not the same at all. Indeed, the two readings make it clear that the magazine is a sort of mirror wherein each reader finds himself, his fears and desires, and the promise of achieving that

which he lacks to be a man. Denzel is oblivious to the ads for sexual fulfillment, social success, and professional opportunity that catch Pogo's ironic attention; instead, he focuses on an ad for muscle building ("The Bull-
master Powerworker") which depicts a man "bulg[ing] all over with
muscles" protecting a girl standing behind him, and other ads promising that a person need "NEVER BE AFRAID AGAIN!" (118) or that
"even small, slight persons, using the Secret Techniques of the Ancient
Oriental Masters, can become a total self-defense Fighting Machine" –
"No Size or Muscle Needed" (119).

Denzel's dialogue with the ads reveals "heroic" tendencies, not only
his fear of enemies and wish for self-defense but chivalric pride, a desire
for dignity, and a strong need to protect others. Denzel's diminutive size
and helplessness are in part due to his age, but ominously he is declared
to be "small for his age." There is the unspoken probability that this child
is a dwarf, too, and that he suffers and will continue to suffer the same sorts
of humiliation and indignity as Pogo does, to be forced to live the life of
a psychological haunt, the ancient child, while hopelessly seeking valida-
tion in the world of men. For example, Denzel is excluded from a boys'
game of baseball because neither side wants to "get stuck with some little fairy" (50). Nevertheless, he exhibits a desire to protect others, as in
the scene where Denzel as a very small child "wrestles" with a rubber
snake outside the bedroom where his father and baby-sitter/surrogate
mother, Vaudie "Bouncy" Bovis, make love, "telling it he wouldn't let it
go inside to get them" (113), a scene with revisionary Edenic echoes. He
also attempts to protect Pogo against the giant who stalks him (3–5). But
both humiliation and chivalric intent are apparent in the events he thinks
about as he examines the ads in the magazine. He remembers a time when
some men started to follow Mrs. Bovis and himself on their way to the tent
where "Bouncy" does her exotic dance. The men made rude suggestions
and moved menacingly closer. Denzel, crying, attempted to ward them
off. They laughed at him. When they reached the tent and Denzel saw how
he looked crying, in shame he "put a towel over his head" (119–20). Denzel wants to protect his father, Pogo, and the other Bimbos from the "loud,
grating raucous laugh" from the stands: "Denzel wanted to punch the
lights out, to face each and every grin, to cram each voice down each
throat. He would never let anyone, anyone, laugh at him that way" (125).
In his head Denzel repeats the preformed reply to one of the ads: "Yes,
Honorable Master KUNG-FU, I wish to know the age-old Secrets of your
Ancient art. In return I promise to use deadly knowledge of KUNG-FU

for defense only and never to employ its Secrets toward evil ends. PLEASE RUSH" (125). That he chooses this reply is indicative of Denzel's heroic longings and his concept of manhood. It is filled with suggestions of honor, ancient warriors, and the eternal battle of good versus evil. To be a man is to be "ballsy," that is, courageous, honorable, dignified; not to let anyone laugh at you, as the men harassing Bouncy laughed at him and as the crowds in the stands laugh at his father and the rest of the Bimbos; and to be willing to defend the good against evil.

Ballsy apparently means different things to Pogo and Denzel; Denzel's definition is without the sexual implications. Pogo, however, has internalized Denzel's meanings and heroic longings as well, although they are now overlaid with a scum of cynicism. As the two talk in the laundromat, Pogo offers his insights on women in a misogynistic tirade, explaining that "you can't be nice to them," "you can't treat them fair" (144), and claiming that the trouble with women is that although they "think the world owes them more than they've been getting," they are "*not brave* enough to go out on their own and look for it, they expect some man to lay it at their feet." The reason: "Women got no balls" (146; emphasis added). Denzel immediately asks if that is why his mother abandoned him, and Pogo, backpeddling and clearly not wanting to hurt Denzel, moderates his stance and imagines several nonpersonal reasons why she might have left (147). Pogo's tirade on women cannot mask the fact that he too has acted in defense of a lady, and that is what has gotten him into trouble with Dred. Although Dred had treated the woman as Pogo has been advocating, Pogo explains that it was wrong in this case because "There's exceptions. Some of them are, uhm, special, and you treat them different" (148).

Pogo's story moves toward its tragic conclusion on the evening of Denzel's birthday celebration. Pogo's suicide at the end of the night's activities is clearly his despairing response to his failure of manhood. His elimination from the narrative is therefore not like that of Pearl du Monville's. There is little sense here that the appearance and dismissal of the dwarf have been restorative, that the ancient child has been called, faced, and thrown out of the game as a sign that the protagonist has matured beyond his inappropriate childish fears and desires, or that a helpful archetypal dwarf has come and fixed things and returned to his otherworldly scene. (The possible exception might be seen in Pogo's effect on Dred, who is Pogo's giant antagonist in one sense but perhaps a protagonist as well.) In most respects within the universe of his narrative, Pogo is just dead. The question asked in *The Seventh Babe*, "Was it better to bump people and hang from trees as the monster of Sackville Forest, or lie dead in the ground?" (Charyn 331), is here answered: better to bump and hang than lie in such terrible isolation, that ultimate deepening of the loneliness of the self from which Pogo, as Everyman, suffers; that is, better the *figural* existence of the dwarf than the literal, universal fate of flesh.

On his last night Pogo's fragile shell of manhood – dignity, courage, self-respect, and determination – cracks and falls away bit by bit. In the bar Pogo is unable to climb onto a barstool, although he tries repeatedly: "It was like he couldn't get any push from his legs" (222). Later, at the Venus de Milo Arms, when some of "the girls" have taken Pogo's clothes, he is desperate to find them but cannot climb the stairs to the second floor where he believes they are and where the women entertain men. Mama Moon says that she cannot imagine why he cannot climb the stairs, for "they're not at all steep." She makes graphic the scene of Pogo's humiliation as he stands naked at the bottom of the stairs in a whorehouse, wielding a gun: "The girls were all bunched at the top of the stairs giggling and so were a few of our ginnlemen visitors who had come out to investigate the disturbance. He did make quite a sight but all the attention seemed to upset him even more. He couldn't come up and he wouldn't let any of us down. His back was turned and it sounded like he was crying" (232). Pogo discovers his clothes outside the house of ill repute on the statue of Cupid (Eros) (for whom they are a "perfect fit"), an image suggesting the irrational forces of love and sexuality in the clothing of a dwarf.

Pogo ends his life alone, as he has lived, singing, drinking, and meditating in a stall in a public toilet in the trailer park. He sings in a deep voice that he trained as a boy: "At least he would sound like a man" (238). He thinks about his father, who had "too much pride to take orders from anybody. If there is such a thing as too much pride in a man" (239). At this point Pogo has no pride at all.

Pogo recalls a time when he was proud, when despite his size, he always tried to live in the real world, by which he means the world of ballsy men and manly endeavor: "Pogo went out on his own . . . always with an angle but always in the real world, a real job. Finally the private dick. Always reaching for what the real world had to offer, reaching for the top shelf. Pogo Burns was no circus clown like Warts Moynihan. Warts with his little wife, his little house, his little furniture like toys that kids play with, his little life in his little world. Make pretend. That wasn't living, it was Munchkinland. If something is too high for you, you climb it, you don't have a copy made to your size. You got to have some balls" (242).

But Pogo has learned earlier that evening that he can no longer climb: he could not climb onto a barstool, and later he could not climb the stairs in the Venus de Milo Arms. He remembers that he could not kill his father, who had pleaded for death: "If he had had any balls he would have killed the Old Man. He had never had any, never" (244). Pogo's review of his own life brings him at last to the conclusion that he had never had any balls and reveals to him that "there wasn't a decent life left for a man to reach for. There wasn't a decent death left for a man to face." His last admonition to himself is "Take your medicine, Pogo, like a big man" (245).

Mr. Mumps, the chimpanzee, is mistaken for Pogo; Pogo's clothes are a perfect fit for the statue of Cupid, as they are for Denzel (252), who is told, when Pogo disappears, "You got to be our midget." His father tells him, "Sometimes a man got to swallow his pride a little. There isn't any other way" (252). Swallowing one's pride and taking one's medicine seem similar. An ominous future opens up for Denzel as the notions of manhood, pride, dwarfdom, and humiliation converge. As he dons the dwarf's "Big Bertha" costume, Denzel fights back tears, "trying not to cry in front of all those men's faces that crowded around his in the mirror, trying to get through the initiation without ruining his mascara" (252). Afterward the men give him "manly pats on the butt for having done a good job and [call] him a ballsy little guy" (254), the very phrase they had earlier applied to Pogo, a fact that is not encouraging. Denzel enters the deep isolation of the dwarf. In a way he takes on Pogo's tragic identity and is left to face the problems of manhood alone. As Pogo is being buried Denzel is worried "because he didn't want to leave Pogo there in the ground and because Frostproof [the team's next stop] seemed like too long a ride to take alone" (258).

If Pogo fulfills the redemptive role so often played by the baseball dwarf, it is through his alter-ego, Mr. Mumps. Dred, blaming Pogo for his own failed manhood, his loss of prestige and pride, has stalked him throughout the novel with murderous intent. Dred approaches the trailer park where Pogo is holed up in the toilet just before Pogo's suicide. Dred has suffered a number of educational experiences, humiliations, and calamities on his way: he has been burned, bitten by a pig, preached to, and admonished; he is tired, half-shoeless, and has been run off the road by "a ghost-thing," an old black man with a wagonload of watermelons; he has even wet himself (236). At stake for Dred, as for Pogo and Denzel, are pride and manhood; killing Pogo, he believes, will restore both. In his miserable condition he is hiding in the woods by the trailer camp, sneaking up on Pogo. At that moment he sees a figure coming toward him with a "low silhouette" and a "rolling, bent-legged walk," a "midget walk" (235). Dred waits with his gun, tense and ready to fire. As the figure gets closer, however, Dred sees that it is "big-lipped and flat-nosed," that its arms hang to its knees, that it is "black and hairy" (235). It is Mr. Mumps, good-natured, friendly, and even "humane," who looks up at Dred "with liquid brown eyes" and "extend[s] its hand to shake." Dred says, "Fuck off, monkey!" but Mr. Mumps waits patiently with arm extended. Finally, Dred shifts the gun to his left hand and gives "the monkey's paw a quick embarrassed pump." On behalf of all the baseball dwarfs, whose surrogate he is, Mr. Mumps "smile[s] at him, two rows of big teeth and gums glowing electric blue in the faint moonlight, and pat[s] him on the knee" (236). Pogo's "double," a child-sized, dwarfish, Ur-human – indeed Dred's own primordial – has appeared and done his work. Dred's reaction is to find "something funny" in the situation and to achieve a rare, accurate glimpse of himself as "some crazy African crouching mustard yellow in a trailer-camp jungle, creeping in to murder some freak in woman's clothes and a baseball bat, some whiteman pygmy." The laugh that issues from Dred at this moment of insight builds up into "a hyena laugh, loud and high and on the very edge of hysteria" (237), and he returns to his car, still laughing, and shoots the watermelon sitting on its hood. Inside the toilet Pogo hears the laugh, "a cry from outside, a long crazy animal hoot," and "he answer[s] it" (242). The gestures of this moment – Mr. Mumps's handshake, smile, and pat, Dred's laughter, and Pogo's answer – create a link between past and present, primitive and civilized, Ur-human and human, child and man, the saved and the doomed, all accomplished in the meeting and merging of monkey, giant, and dwarf. It is a redeeming moment for Dred. The laughter sounds ironically in the toilet stall, however, where Pogo, taking his medicine "like a man," will shortly go the way of baseball dwarfs, carrying out the act of destruction from which Dred has turned back.

We are left at last with the image of Pogo-Denzel as Everyman in the world Bob Yamm described, where "all men are midgets." The foregrounding of the dwarf in *The Seventh Babe* and *Pride of the Bimbos,* and his trials and demise on the field or in the game, may indeed offer a truer view of the personae of the gap and its geography than is commonly acknowledged. The dwarf's myth is the story of the lost, abandoned, denied, disruptive past, of the self and the species, the immortal little man who shows up from time to time in the uncanny confines of the ballpark, who suffers a heart attack on first base, who hangs and bumps in Sackville Forest, who shape-shifts himself, transforming himself into child, chimp, or statue of Cupid, or who weeps, naked, alone, and utterly ridiculous at the bottom of a staircase in the "home" of Mama Moon, a little man whose manhood is in question, a tragicomic figure from the gap in whom all the human contradictions are vested and about whom the mythmakers cannot remain silent.

13

BASEBALL, BRICOLAGE, AND THE BEAUTIFUL

I have waited to the end to ask how one decides whether a myth or mythic narrative is good or bad. Is the standard of judgment an aesthetic one – for example, beauty – as it is for art in general? Is it truth, as it is for science and philosophy or intellectual inquiry in general? Perhaps the test of excellence is met by social or political relevance, increasingly the theme of some schools of criticism. The answers are elusive, which may explain why the question of better and worse is seldom raised explicitly in myth criticism (although an aesthetic screening may be implicit in the selection of works and the focus of attention).

Assuming, as I do, that myth is a linguistic artifact that performs human work in the search of meaning, the questions are what makes a good myth and, as a corollary, can a work be good myth and bad art.

To reiterate, baseball's mythology, like others, is a denizen of the gap, where art and language also play. It pays particular attention to language, its evocations and equivocations; it is bricolage, a new structure fashioned from the debris of shattered mythic worlds and other oddments lying at hand. Its syntax encompasses and attempts to reconcile significant contradictions: the profane and the sacred, love and hate, victory and defeat, youth and age, the present and the past, the timed and the timeless, the determinate and the indeterminate, the living and the dead. In its construction the mythmaker is attentive to the rhetorical intimations of the unconscious, the voices, savage or not, of the Lacanian shades. These voices may well be the essential "something of himself" by which, as the epigraph from Lévi-Strauss suggests, the *bricoleur* achieves his or her poetry. Although for such work baseball's mythmakers find what they need everywhere, they often as not discover both the mythic debris and the oddments within the game itself. They find mythic debris in the game's ancient archetypal signifiers (in the weathered stones of Eden's wall, for example, now pressed into use in its outfield fence, or in its base paths, the configuration of all journeys). The other oddments lying at hand are, as their name implies, various – a haunting image or memory, for example, an intertextual echo, an image from popular culture, or a historical allusion (or illusion). One of the richest sources of such oddments is the game's own record and its stories of individual players, games, and seasons.

On the one hand, then, a mythic structure made as bricolage is an artifact, a work of art, and as such must be judged by aesthetic standards – specifically the standard of beauty in which "truth" is implied. On the other hand, as myth it labors to reconcile life's contradictions, to provide significance, solace, and the "truths" that permit us to live. In this respect it must be judged by a mythic standard of excellence in which meaning or interpretation is primary. This doubleness suggests that when we try to assess the value of the work, we will find that there is an ambiguous space where literary criticism and mythic criticism confront the work with apparently different standards of excellence. Lévi-Strauss hints at this doubleness when he argues that in many ways mythological thought and scientific thought are similar. Their difference lies, he says, "in that the engineer [the scientist] is always trying to make his way out of and go beyond the constraints imposed by a particular state of civilization while the 'bricoleur' [the mythmaker] by inclination or necessity always remains within them." What this comes down to is that the scientist "works by means of concepts" and the mythmaker "by means of signs" (*The Savage Mind* 19–20). As I noted early in this study, however, following Derrida, Lévi-Strauss's engineer is probably itself an anthropologist's myth, a fact that would erase any clear line between them. Although mythical and scientific work may be similar, myth also shares characteristics with "pure" art in that it has an aesthetic dimension. "Art," Lévi-Strauss says, "lies half-way between scientific knowledge and mythical or magical thought. . . . The artist is both something of a scientist and of a 'bricoleur'" (22). Nonetheless, as Lévi-Strauss's own analysis also suggests, the mythmaker, the *bricoleur,* is both something of an artist and something of a scientist. For Lévi-Strauss, therefore, the doubleness of myth invites two tests of worth: beauty and truth, the concepts for which Matthew Arnold used the phrase "sweetness and light."

Another kind of doubleness is discovered when the question of the sacred or uncanny is raised. In its dealing in such matters, myth is seen to have links not only with ritual and religion but with literature. Our oldest myths – *The Epic of Gilgamesh,* the works of Homer, the Yahwist's biblical narratives – are both religious and literary texts. Nevertheless, Harold Bloom, in *The American Religion,* a work of what he calls "religious criticism," attempts to distinguish between his work as a literary critic and his work as a religious critic:

> Literary criticism . . . relies finally upon an irreducibly *aesthetic* dimension in plays, poems, and narratives. Analogously, religious criticism must seek for the irreducibly *spiritual* dimension in religious matters or phenomena of any kind. Aesthetic values, in my vision, transcend societal and political concerns, since such concerns increasingly are better served by bad art than by good. Spiritual values similarly transcend the claims of society and politics, which now also seem to benefit more from unimaginative than from imaginative beliefs. Literature and religion are not allied enterprises, except insofar as both are conceptual orphans, stumbling about in our cosmological emptiness that stretches between the unattainable poles of meaning and truth. (21)

The cosmological emptiness of which Bloom speaks is the geography of the gap, the realm of play, of strife, and of myth, the temple of art, all of which baseball, its scene, and its action represent. A literary work is, to put the matter in Bloom's term, either good art or bad art; religious texts or other phenomena are either imaginative or unimaginative, on the one hand, world-revealing or world-reshaping, and on the other, world-conforming. Bloom's distinction between the objects of literary and religious criticism as, respectively, aesthetic and spiritual values or dimensions (where "spiritual" is closely linked with "imaginative") is relevant to my enterprise, whose object of study is a body of literature (raising the aesthetic question) that constitutes a mythology (raising the imaginative question). Furthermore, Bloom's observation that societal and political concerns are increasingly better served by aesthetic or imaginative failures is a matter that I attend to later. Although Bloom uses the terms "religion-making imagination" and "myth-making imagination" interchangeably (97), his "religion" is narrower than "mythology" as I have defined it, being an aspect of myth specifically focused on what I have called the sacred or uncanny, the Lacanian "real." Taking Bloom's distinction into consideration, however, one might judge any individual work as being bad art (that is, it fails aesthetic tests) but good myth (that is, it manifests the mythmaking imagination and therefore shapes or contributes to the "realities" of the mythological world).[1]

Given these various kinds of doubleness, it should be clear that myths (in particular, baseball's myths) must meet a series of standards. First, as a science of signs a myth seeks truth and to some extent must be judged by the standard of truth, or perhaps by what we may call the standard of mythic truth; second, as crafted thing, or work of art, it must be judged by aesthetic standards; and finally, in its sacred, uncanny, "religious" dimension – insofar as it discloses a sacred world – it must be judged by spiritual or imaginative standards.

All these considerations come into play when we ask why some works strike us as beautiful and profound and others, in Stephen J. Gould's words, as silly and tendentious. The difference may be felt between the two versions of *The Natural* that I have examined. Those who have internalized the bleak vision of Malamud's novel may find not only a failure of truth but also an aesthetic and imaginative slackening in the filmmakers' revision (although the film's conclusion makes its own legitimate aesthetic claims). Nonetheless, seeming to verify Bloom's claim that political and societal interests are better served by the agreeable and the mundane than by the beautiful and imaginative, the filmmakers have produced a version with wider popular appeal than could have been possessed by one that attempted to convey the ironic integrity of the novel;

that is, the film version does not startle with its vision, stun with its beauty, or in any sense disturb our universe. For the most part it reiterates old assumptions, reassures, and serves rather than transcends the social and political interests of the "tribe."

In a literary context the aesthetic question is one that concerns Christian K. Messenger, who nevertheless links the aesthetic question with what we may call mythical concerns. He sees a tendency in recent baseball fiction to depend on "magic" and "history" to prop up otherwise weak narratives. He comments that "baseball fiction at present needs a less complacent use of magic and history, a stiffening against the national romance with baseball, without losing its memory and pleasure" (*Sport and the Spirit of Play* 383). Messenger's "magic," like Bloom's "religion," seems largely a synonym for the sacred or uncanny, and by this term Messenger means, I believe, not myth in the broader sense in which it is explored in this work but a kind of popular, easy, or fantastic (and in Bloom's sense "unimaginative") spirituality that an author may call gratuitously into a text. By "history" Messenger means events and figures from baseball's past, whose incorporation into a text may constitute a sort of predictable "re-cycling of baseball history and popular culture" (383) that, like magic (and often along with magic), is asked to carry aesthetic and imaginative burdens properly borne by character, plot, image, and most especially, force of language, the signs through which the *bricoleur* transmits some genuine human message, something of the self. Messenger finds a crucial difference, for example, between the appearance of shades in Kennedy's *Ironweed* and in Kinsella's *Shoeless Joe*. Francis Phelan's shades, Messenger says, "are haunting, not summoned as in Kinsella . . . to magic up baseball art" (384).

The difference Messenger has in mind is, I believe, akin to the distinction between imitating and stealing that T. S. Eliot makes in "Tradition and the Individual Talent": "Immature poets imitate; mature poets steal." Stealing, unlike imitation, permits a writer to make this or that bit of bricolage his or her own and to reimagine it, transforming it so thoroughly as to make it almost disappear into the new work, so integral has it become to that new structure. In Messenger's example Francis Phelan's shades are haunts of the homeland and house that rise of necessity on the traveler's return; they are both internally and externally necessary. Kinsella's "Black Sox" are summoned from baseball history and are depended on to bring their meanings with them. There is little interpretation or reinterpretation, little evidence that these signs convey something of the *bricoleur*'s self. What strikes me as genuinely mythic in Kinsella's *Shoeless Joe* is the disturbing yet necessary "meeting" of Eddie Scissons with his former self, Kid Scissons. This shade is real in the Lancanian sense, emerging self-willed from the realm of the gods. As was the case in the film version of *The Natural,* a popularizing impulse seems to have prompted the filmmakers to omit from *Field of Dreams* this terrible truth. To take another example, one cannot conceive of Coover's *Universal Baseball Association* without J. Henry Waugh (JHWH), a real uncanniness. He is protagonist, focus, and prime mover; he disappears into the work. There would be no plot without him. By contrast, the omission of Nancy Willard's Lord of the Universe would leave her novel (*Things Invisible to See*) largely intact. This figure, like Kinsella's ghostly baseball players, is depended on to import into the text some dependable significations; the originally startling imagining without a reimagining, an infusion of significance from the *bricoleur*'s self, degenerates into cliché, largely predictable and world-conforming. Without reinterpretation by the mythmaker, this figure seems to be there simply to "magic up" the work. Where Willard's novel does achieve aesthetic and imaginative excellence is in the depiction of those timeless, water-borne, wordless, paralyzing curses said to have infected Eve and all her descendants.

What Kennedy's shades, Coover's J. Henry Waugh, Kinsella's Kid Scissons, and Willard's curses have in common is what seems not only an aesthetic necessity but an imaginative remaking: they are stolen, not imitated; their metaphoric or figurative meanings have been so reworked, transformed, and equivocated as to make them disappear into the new structure, which is enriched rather than patched up by their presence.

In the remainder of this chapter I raise the issue of value or excellence in mythic texts specifically in conjunction with two aspects of baseball mythology's thematics. The first is the essential matter of mythic agon or contradiction, and the second concerns baseball's history as bricolage. In these two sections I address Messenger's concerns about the "complacent use of magic and history." Messenger's objection to such complacency in baseball fiction is surely legitimate. If it damages the fiction, does such complacency also damage baseball myth? Does the easy inclusion of magic and history affect the truth value of a tale, its aesthetics, or its spiritual or imaginative value? I believe that the answer in each case is yes. A closer analysis of these two elements may help to move us toward identifying a sound basis for myth criticism, not merely as a subset of literary criticism but in itself.

Religious doctrines and experiences alike share with poems a stance against dying, or to put this most simply, the category of the "religious" is set against death even as the "poetic" seeks a triumph over time. Criticism, as I conceive it, seeks the poetic in poetry, and should seek the religious in religion.
—Harold Bloom, The American Religion 36

The instincts that find no right and proper outlet in religion must come out in some other way. You don't believe in a God, so you begin to believe that man is a god. You don't believe in Heaven, so you begin to believe in a heaven on earth. In other words, you get romanticism. . . . Romanticism then, and this is the best definition I can give of it, is spilt religion.
—T. E. Hulme, "Romanticism and Classicism" 768

All religion is spilled poetry, bad and good.
—Harold Bloom, The American Religion 80

The first epigraph to this section claims that the task of criticism is to seek the poetic in poetry and the religious in religion. The second and third epigraphs, however, suggest the ambiguous relationship between literature (poetry) and religion, the kind of doubleness that one finds in myth. Keeping in mind the composite nature of baseball's texts as a body of literature that constitutes a mythology and thus at times discloses a sacred world, as well as the different scales of literary and mythic criticism identified by Bloom (the aesthetic and the imaginative) and the concerns Messenger expresses about the complacent "magicking up" of baseball fiction, I suggest that "good baseball myths" must be both aesthetically pleasing *and* imaginatively compelling. Given the linguisticality of myths (explored in chap. 1), I suggest that those myths that achieve this double excellence (meeting both aesthetic and imaginative tests) do so in the medium of the rhetoric of the gap, that is, in their resort to signs, rhetorical figures, and the intrusive tropological language of the unconscious, its metaphors, archetypal signifiers, and enigmatic images. Both genuine literary artist and genuine mythmaker exploit the language of the gap that stretches, as Bloom would say, "between the unattainable poles of meaning and truth" (*American Religion* 21); the second-order artist, like the unimaginative mythmaker, mistakes the received figures for truth, imagines that they speak for themselves, and denies the always essential function of interpretation or reinterpretation. Both superior literary artist and genuine mythmaker are metaphor makers and therefore world shapers.

There is a sense, as Bloom suggests, in which all vision, all creative making – whether in literature, myth, or religion – is metaphor (53). The second-order text takes its language ready-made, using old signifiers and dependable unequivocal figures, and either screens out or suppresses both the interpretative function of myth and the insinuations of the textual unconscious, presenting a derivative, predictable, and diluted but politically or socially correct message, its correctness essentially ensuring that it will be devoid of mythic contradictions.

What Bloom says of Emerson's model for American religious criticism appears relevant as well to the mythic literary work. That model, Bloom claims, is to be found in a "key sentence" from the "Divinity School Address": "The idioms of his [Jesus'] language and the figures of his rhetoric have usurped the place of his truth; and churches are not built on his principles, but on his tropes." Bloom comments: "Substitute Freud for Jesus as the antecedent for 'his' in this sentence and you receive a powerful insight into a minor but influential version of the American Religion, the Institutes for Psychoanalysis that forlornly dot our cities. The Freudian Fundamentalists (of the Ego Psychology sect) are as literal minded as the Southern Baptist Fundamentalists, and both groups believe that their sacred texts, the Standard Edition of Freud and the Holy Bible, somehow interpret themselves and are inerrant." Texts cannot speak for themselves, however, and especially rhetorical figures – metaphors, tropes, images – cannot speak for themselves; they demand interpretation or reimagination, a part of the self. Bloom goes on to comment that "Emerson knows that religion is imagined, and *always must be reimagined*" (*American Religion* 24; emphasis added).

Here, I believe, is a criterion for judging a work that is both literary and mythic. The superior work will speak in the language of surplus, of excess; it will seem to struggle with language, evoking in each trope, image, and word the siren song of the depths of which Blanchot speaks. It will record the rhetoric of the unconscious without always (or even often) knowing that it does so, implicitly acknowledging the complicity of language and desire. Literary myths, like myths in general, are stories of the gap, arenas for struggle and confrontation, for *significant* contradictions, the speakings against each other of irreconcilable opposites, of both conscious and unconscious language. Reni's painting of Saint Michael with his foot on the neck of the fiend can stand as a representative of this struggle. Here in pictorial language (in the science of signs) is a serious confrontation in which Saint Michael (and all that we might reimagine, reinterpret that he "means") seems, at least for the moment, to prevail; nevertheless, the painting shows us too that the fiend is not dead, nor will he ever be. Indeed, he seems even in his posture of defeat to be gathering strength for the next confrontation. Similarly, in *The Celebrant* Greenberg's image of Christy Mathewson in his coffin, buried with the devotional rings, reveals a series of significant and eternal contradictions: the timed and the timeless, decaying nature and indestructible art, the living god and the dead man, and all the ironies of belief and disbelief. Small's *Almost Famous* moves us from the sacred to the broader realm of myth; this work presents the father-son and mother-son relationships as mythic in this sense of agon, equivocation, and surplus. The point to which the narrative leads is like that portrayed in the Reni painting: a brief moment of stasis while the contenders get their second wind. Although Ward Sullivan may be seen as victorious in his own personal struggle for maturity and independence, nevertheless there are those suggestive and disturbing tableaux: Ward and little Gordon, Ward and mother Sarah, even Terry and son Gordon. Like the fiend in Reni's painting, Sarah, calm for a while and on leave from her madhouse, enriches the mythic scene not because she is subdued but because she is not defeated, not dead; her son's contradictory feelings of love and hate are not now reconciled, nor will they ever be. Nor will Ward's sense of his infant's astonishing beauty ensure his own survival in the new father-son drama about to unfold.

A genuine myth, which is marked by this sort of contention, may openly display its bricolage, its archetypal signifiers, as does Malamud's *The Natural*, or it may veil them, as in Small's *Almost Famous* or Harris's *Bang the Drum Slowly*, but whether they are overtly or covertly included, those fragments and oddments, those signifiers, will be touched by the mythmaker, reimagined and made to speak their equivocal old messages in a new setting, forced to constitute the structure and significance of the emerging myth. They will not, as in second-order narratives, appear simply to "magic up" their plots or to imply significance where there is none. Complacency, imitation, comfortable resolution – these are foreign to both the literary and imaginative excellence of myth, the artifact of the gap, and its evocative beauty.

BASEBALL'S HISTORICAL BRICOLAGE: BORROWED AND STOLEN

When it comes to the game every man has his own story.
—David Small, Almost Famous *38*

*But in order to make you understand, to give you my life, I must tell you a story –
and there are so many, and so many – stories of childhood, stories of school, love,
marriage, death, and so on; and none of them are true.*
—*Virginia Woolf*, The Waves *341*

*All of a sudden they are dead and you are glad you did not wreck their story for them
with the straight facts.*
—*Mark Harris*, Bang the Drum Slowly *196*

*He didn't doubt the guy's story, but he wondered what the exact difference was:
between the guy's life and the story of his life.*
—*Jay Neugeboren*, Sam's Legacy *174*

*When considering historical storytelling, the rhetoric of the fictive story offers a
useful model.*
—*J. H. Hexter, "The Rhetoric of History," in* Doing History *40*

*What we discover . . . is that the opposition – the simple opposition between myth-
ology and history which we are accustomed to make – is not at all a clear-cut one.*
—*Lévi-Strauss, "When Myth Becomes History" 40*

*Many modern historians hold that narrative discourse, far from being a neutral
medium for the representation of historical events and processes, is the very stuff
of a mythical view of reality.*
—*Hayden White*, The Content of the Form *ix*

The second aspect of the question of aesthetics and baseball's narratives identified by Messenger is what he calls writers' complacent recycling
of baseball history and popular culture. His term *recycling* is pertinent,
for it identifies a thoughtless inclusion of "stuff" with dependable meanings. As with the sacred and uncanny, in this matter too mythic excellence
will be a product not of recycling but of interpretation, reinterpretation,
and reimagining of the bricolage and other oddments (including the facts,
figures, and events of history) that go into a new myth. The same complacency that encourages some writers gratuitously to add magic to their
texts, Messenger observes, calls forth the unreflective appearance in their
texts – through magic or otherwise – of figures and events from baseball
history.

Baseball's texts, like its participants, are almost inevitably possessed
by the game's own past; that past is the ground against which any new
text, player, act, or achievement is figured, is defined, and has meaning.
Michael Seidel notices that those players who pursue Joe DiMaggio's

record hitting streak, despite their concentration and stamina, "are none-theless haunted by the fabled number 56 hovering somewhere in the middle distance" (207). This haunting of baseball's mythology by its own past is typical of myth, for from its beginnings myth has purported to be history or to rest on historical fact. Beyond this common mythic impulse to include, interpret, or become "history" is the fact that a significant portion of baseball's texts actually is history of various types – biographies, autobiographies, traditional histories of periods in the game's past, accounts of accomplishments (such as Seidel's *Streak*) or confrontations (such as James Reston Jr.'s *Collision at Home Plate*). I have chosen largely to exclude such historical texts from this study, but as I have read them I have often been struck by what seems to be a curious reflection between baseball's "realistic" and "imaginative" texts. One might say that as baseball's mythic narratives are pervaded by baseball history, so is baseball history pervaded by its myths. Examples of what I have in mind may be found in two Pete Rose biographies, one being the Reston book just mentioned and the other coauthored by Pete Rose and Roger Kahn, *Pete Rose: My Story*. One suggestive passage occurs in Reston's book at a point when he is describing the death of Pete Rose's father. Reston says, "Harry Rose, Pete's father and mentor, had died prematurely of a massive heart attack. He was fifty-seven years old. . . . When Pete Rose heard the news, he wept, and in the years to come, the mere mention of his father made Rose maudlin. He was, he liked to think, no more than his father made over and carried on, the fulfillment of a spirit, the realization of a potential, in the next generation" (181). Here Harry Rose appears as a real-life Mr. Hobbs, father of Roy, a good guy, a failed athlete, dying young. Here also is ascribed to Pete Rose the theme of father-son atonement, as well as the sentiments of Henry Wiggen, who assured his father that his own playing in the major league park would be "the same thing" as his father's playing there. The Rose-Kahn biography likewise includes the idea of father-son atonement, placing it in the emphatic last lines of the work, in the form of Pete Rose's announcement of identity with his father: "There's nothing really that special about me. . . . All I am is my own father, going on with my life in a different generation, and given more opportunity" (289). Reading such accounts, we may wonder to what extent one's life and thoughts are shaped by mythic art. What archetypal signifiers have trapped the real-life ball player or the real-life historian? I suggest that neither the fact that just these thoughts, from the billions available, are selected for inclusion in the Reston biography nor the fact that just these words are presented as Rose's "summary statement" in his own coau-thored biography is coincidental.

Reston's account then goes on to include an even more intriguing bit of history. It concerns Ty Cobb (a player whose record of 4,191 major league hits Pete Rose pursued and whose life and career apparently fas-cinated Rose) and Cobb's relationship with his own father: "Cobb's fa-ther had wanted his son to be a lawyer or a doctor, and thus, to pursue baseball was for Ty Cobb to violate his father's fondest hope. It was an essential disobedience that led to estrangement. 'My overwhelming need was to prove myself,' Cobb was to write. 'My father held me down, with-holding acceptance of me as the man I yearned to be'" (Reston 181). Cobb's situation exemplifies the father's withheld blessing, repeated in the situation of Marcus and Cedric Tannehill in *The Seventh Babe,* a damag-ing denial whose effects the son will experience his whole life. More of the myth follows: "If this produced the energy of anger, there was also am-bivalence. For Cobb's father had also [like Pete Rose's father] died early, turning him, like Harry Rose, into a spirit that hovered in the imagina-tion and goaded the son" (181). One cannot help but remember Cedric Tannehill's futile attempt, following his father's likewise untimely death, to call up his father's spirit. Did Harry Rose also withhold his blessing, his approval? Was nothing the son did ever to be good enough? Certain-ly these possibilities are hinted in the comparison.

And then, seemingly gratuitously, the historian adds a further bit of Cobb's biography: "Only three weeks before Ty Cobb entered the ma-jor leagues against his father's will, his mother shot him dead, as the pro-fessor ignominiously crawled through the window of the family house. Mrs. Cobb had mistaken her husband for a prowler. But then, she was having an affair with another man" (181). Here are both a significant in-clusion – seemingly irrelevant to Pete Rose's biography, but apparently necessary to be spoken –and a significant ellipsis. What is left unsaid between the statement that Mrs. Cobb had mistaken her husband for a prowler and the "fact" that she was having an affair? It seems that, even though Pete Rose's own mother is almost a nonentity, the terrible myth-ic mother is required in the story of the ball player, even if she has to be imported from another life. What was your mother like, Mr. Cobb? Mr. Rose? The answer might have been, like that of Roy Hobbs, "She spoiled my old man's life. He was a good guy but died young" (Malamud, *The Natural* 143). The eerie echoes continue. How would Pete Rose want to be remembered? Like Roy Hobbs, Rose wants people to say, There goes

Pete Rose, "the best switch-hitter that ever lived" (Reston 182). Clearly, history inspires and influences the shape and content of baseball's imaginative narratives; more telling, it is also becoming clear that imaginative narratives subtly affect the recording of subsequent histories and even the lives lived, the acts performed, and the hopes hoped.[2]

The barest facts of baseball's history, its dates and numbers, are not innocent of mythic implication, whether in imaginative or realistic texts. The year 1919, for example, echoes darkly in the muster of years, examined and reexamined in both history and fiction: as Buck Weaver in Stein's *Hoopla* says of the Black Sox scandal, "Mention 1919 and it's the first thing that pops up in their skulls";[3] October 7 is a day for dying – of the season, of Christy Mathewson, of Bruce Pearson; 56, 60, and 715 are not numbers only but mythic signifiers (when, in Coover's *Universal Baseball Association,* the number 56 begins to appear again and again, we do well to pay attention); and surely 1994, with its bleak late summer and early fall, will take its place in baseball's mythology, as will the triumph of 2131 in the late summer of 1995, to be explored, imagined, and reimagined. Michael Seidel acknowledges the nature of these numerical archetypes: "Famous numbers are part of baseball's mythology, and they seem to stand guard at the larger statistical treasure trove so essential to those who follow and love the sport" (207).

The question of the relationship between baseball's so-called realistic and imaginative texts (or history and fiction), as well as between realistic and fantastic or mythic fictional narratives, is raised with a suggestive frequency. In one sense such questions may reveal a suspicion, a dim recognition by all concerned, that baseball, its players, managers, fans, and writers have been "textualized," that in this field, at least, the boundaries between myth and reality are blurred or porous. Ostensibly, the question is about the relationship between the facts of the real-world record (names of players and their acts, dates, statistics, and so forth, or the realistic terms of players' lives) and the stories about those facts, inspired by those facts, or converging on the world of those facts. In another sense, however, the question raises the ancient issue, dating at least to the time of Plato, of the relationship between logos and mythos (described in the introduction), between the "true" and the "false." This distinction appears in Aristotle's speculations on the relationship between history and poetry, the relationship, in the words of Harris's Henry Wiggen, between "straight fact" and "story" (meaning "lie"). We want to make such a distinction; like Henry, we want to believe that we know the straight facts and can differentiate between these and stories.

The issue incorporates the related questions of objectivity and subjectivity, as well as the role of interpretation, the attempt to say not what happened but what it meant, which is the principal mythic function, its "intending-to-interpret" (Eric Gould 34). In the discussion of Reston's treatment of Pete Rose, I have already claimed a sort of symbiosis between the two orders of texts, but to make the case more compelling, I need to clarify what I mean by *history* in this context. I mean not the random, chaotic infinitude of events that happen within a particular period of past time or in a particular life (which can be called "historical facts") but the historian's account (what we call history), which is an attempt to render events intelligible or significant, to interpret.

In a now classic essay, "The Rhetoric of History" (1970), J. H. Hexter demonstrates certain principles of historiography by the example of the New York Giants' participation in the World Series in 1951, which is a historical fact. If the question "How did the New York Giants happen to play in the World Series in 1951?" is raised, one explanation is of the sort Hexter calls the "general-law type": "Whenever during the official National League season a National League team wins more games and loses fewer than any other team in the league [as did the Giants in 1951], it plays in the World Series" (in *Doing History* 30). Hexter observes that "from the point of view of the writer and reader of history, such an answer is patently unsatisfactory": "The reason is that in the context of the National League season of 1951, the appropriate response to the question, 'How did the Giants happen to play in the World Series of 1951?' is the historical *story* of how the Giants came to lead the National League at the end of the official season that year. A general-law explanation cannot tell that story; indeed, it cannot tell any story. It is not built to tell stories" (31). Hexter argues from this example that "general-law and narrative . . . are equally valid modes of explanation" and hence equally legitimate modes of historical discourse. Baseball's obsession with records provides data (perhaps more ample data than in any other field) for general-law explanations, but the completeness of the record presents countless questions, all of which are potential subjects of historical inquiry and storytelling. The validity of a given mode of explanation is to be assessed in the context of "what particular inquirers at particular moments seek to know" (31). Hexter clearly acknowledges the role of "inquirers" in the writing of history, their intentions and desires (what they "seek to know"), and we know that language is in complicity with desire. He sees such factors as influencing the choice between general-law or narrative explanations, but the principle influences as well the historian's basic decisions as to what, among a nearly infinite array of acts, events, numbers, dates, beliefs, intentions, and so forth, actually constitutes historical fact. Where in the homogeneous ticking of time are the key moments that call for "expansions of scale" (37)? Clearly events will to some extent determine such key moments (the Black Sox Scandal, for example) where historical storytelling seems required, but the nature and focus of that story will be determined by the historian, what he or she seeks to know and what he or she wishes to mean. Implicit in Hexter's analysis is the notion of a potentially infinite number of possible histories, although he wants to restrict the number by asserting that some expansions of scale (places where narratives are told) are "historiographically correct," whereas others are "incorrect" (37); having opened the door to human subjectivity, to the inquirer and his or her intentions and desires, however, it is difficult to close it against the "incorrect" expansion.

Even the phrase "seek to know" is problematic, for it implies that knowledge in some absolute sense may be found in the truth that the historian discovers and discloses, through either general-law or narrative explanation. Meaning or truth, however, the subject of knowledge, is not in things, acts, or events per se but in people and their language; in the field of history, that means in the historian's text. This was the position of Roland Barthes, whose "The Discourse of History" raises the issue in the context of a structuralist "second linguistics," a linguistics that would go beyond the boundaries of the sentence and into the realm of discourse. It is necessary to decide, he says, whether "it is indeed legitimate still to oppose fictive narrative to historical [narrative]." He asks rhetorically whether "the narration of past events, commonly subject in our culture, since the Greeks, to the sanction of historical 'science,' placed under the imperious warrant of the 'real,' justified by principles of 'rational' exposition . . . differ[s], in fact, by some specific feature, by an indubitable pertinence, from imaginary narration as we find it in the epic, the novel, the drama?" (127). Barthes's answer, developed in the course of his essay, is that historical narration does not differ from imaginary narration: "Thus, we close the paradoxical circle: narrative structure, elaborated in the crucible of fictions (through myths and early epics), becomes both sign and proof of reality." He announces, somewhat prematurely it seems, the imminent demise of narration in historical science, remarking, "historical narration is dying because the sign of History is henceforth not so much *the real as the intelligible*" (140). History is not the real (the straight fact) but the intelligible (the interpreted, the narrated story or "lie"). How is an account rendered intelligible?

In the tradition of Barthes, Lévi-Strauss, and others historiographer Hayden White has argued that there is a figurative or tropic element "in all discourse, whether of the realistic or more imaginative kind"; he believes that this element is "inexpungeable from discourse in the human sciences, however realistic they may aspire to be. Tropic is the shadow from which all realistic discourse tries to flee. This flight, however, is futile; for tropics is the process by which all discourse *constitutes* the objects which it pretends only to describe realistically and to analyze objectively" (*Tropics of Discourse* 1–2). In constituting the objects that it addresses, tropics actually determines "*what shall count as a fact* in the matters under consideration" (3). Unlike mythic narrative, historical narrative purports to need no narrator but merely to re-present past events that then speak for themselves, "tell themselves" (3), creating the illusion of unmediated contact with real events. Yet any narrative, whether realistic or imaginary, while maintaining the illusion of fullness, is "constructed on the basis of a set of events that might have been included but were left out" (10); they were left out of the realistic narrative (history) not because they were not real or did not happen but because they did not serve the intelligibility of the historian's plot and its continuity. White asks, "What kind of notion of reality authorizes construction of a narrative account of reality in which continuity rather than discontinuity governs the articulation of the discourse?" (10). Given such considerations, meaning consists of a "mixture of poetic and noetic levels of consciousness between which the discourse itself seeks to mediate in the interests of 'understanding'" (14). History thus appears to be, in Harold Bloom's phrase, "an orphan" like literature and religion, "stumbling about in the cosmological emptiness that stretches between the unattainable poles of meaning and truth" (*The American Religion* 21). Ty Cobb's mother's shooting of his father, a straight fact, appears in Pete Rose's story at the poetic level of intelligibility, as does the comparison of Ty Cobb's and Pete Rose's fathers. In part the truth and meaning of Pete Rose's life are made intelligible on a poetic level through the mythic function of interpretation.

The narratives of history, White argues, take the forms of "pre-generic plot-structures," or borrowing a term from Northrop Frye's literary criticism, "archetypal story-forms." (Levi-Strauss has in mind something similar but more sinister sounding, to which he refers as "fraudulent outlines" [*The Savage Mind* 261]). The historian's choice of plot structure is necessarily an interpretive act, constituting one of "at least two levels of interpretation in every historical work": "one in which the historian constitutes a story out of the chronicle of events and another in which, by a more fundamental narrative technique, he progressively identifies the kind of story he is telling – comedy, tragedy, romance, epic, or satire, as the case might be" (White, *Tropics of Discourse* 59). In providing the plot "the historian must draw upon a fund of culturally provided *mythoi* in order to constitute the facts as figuring a story of a particular kind," for "a given sequence of events [e.g., those associated with the French Revolution] can be emplotted in a number of different ways" (60–61), as romance or as tragedy, for example. The story of Roy Hobbs, as related in film and novel, demonstrates the techniques whereby the "same" story may be told as either a romance or a tragedy. White's emplotments are culturally transmitted ways of organizing experience. They are thus part of the Lacanian language into which we are born and by which we are trapped; they are internalized unconsciously. The historian's largely unconscious choice of a plot will, as mentioned, dictate to a greater or lesser extent the nature of the reality that is the subject of historical discourse – not only what will count as a fact but what data will, indeed must, disappear from the history, and of those facts included, just how they will be arranged and the sort of emphasis they will receive.[4] Matters of diction, style, and mood will likewise be implicated. That is, despite its links with straight facts, historical narrative, like a poem or a novel or a myth, is human-made, a crafted thing, a linguistic artifact, a product of the gap.

Mere random events in sequence have no meaning. Their meaning or intelligibility must be produced by a human interpreter who purports to find the meaning that he or she actually creates and assigns. White explains that the production of meaning is like a performance. This is so "because any given set of real events can be emplotted in a number of ways, can bear the weight of being told as any number of different kinds of stories. Since no given set or sequence of real events is intrinsically tragic, comic, farcical, and so on, but can be constructed as such only by the imposition of the structure of a given story type on the events, it is the choice of the story type and its imposition upon the events that endow them with meaning" (White, *Content of the Form* 44). White distinguishes between a "historical discourse that narrates" and one that "narrativizes," that is, one that "feigns to make the world speak itself . . . as a story" (2). White finds in historical narrative the same blindnesses, errors, and manipulations that Barthes finds in both myth and history. For Barthes, historical narratives are more or less "mythological," the less mythological texts overtly identifying their own methods and, as White says, "indicat[ing] the 'constituted,' rather than 'found,' nature of their referents" (*Content of the Form* 35–36).

From such considerations, myth and history – mythos and logos – are seen to be closer kin than they are usually thought to be. Both are linguistic, structures to which both conscious and unconscious elements contribute; both are forms of discourse in pursuit of meaning; both are screened through and reflect linguistic and cultural biases, as well as the determinations and desires of a human interpreter who assigns meaning to the stories told, purporting in the case of historical narrative to find rather than constitute that meaning.

We find ourselves once more in the ruined tower, the world of words, of narrative, whether realistic or imaginative. Within realistic narratives we find not only myth's mythoi, the emplotments, but also its insinuations, its unconscious rhetoric; within imaginative narratives we find the hard edges of historical fact. And so, to return to the problem of aesthetics and Messenger's reservation about the complacent, uninventive inclusion of history in baseball's narratives, we might also speak of the mythologizing of history, complacent or inventive. In either case we can see this question of history's place in baseball's texts as another version of the problem of "magicking up" a narrative. In the case of baseball's narratives, this complacent historicization means the easy inclusion of historical figures and facts that, through time and texts, have become archetypal signifiers in their own right. Uninterpreted, they purport to speak for themselves. What they say is predictable and, in Messenger's term, may be "ennervating" (*Sport and the Spirit of Play* 383). As in the case of magic, we can say that the genuine mythmaker steals and so transforms history as to make it disappear into the mythic structure and to utter new, strange, and perhaps truer messages. (Similarly, in "good" baseball history, mythological elements are stolen, masked as fact, and made to perform their narrative functions.) In its inclusion of baseball history, Greenberg's *The Celebrant* is the work of a genuine mythmaker. The included facts of dates, plays, persons, games, and teams, as well as the setting of the novel in the early years of this century, foster the illusion of historicity, but this is stolen history. The historical figure of Christy Mathewson is so transformed, reinterpreted, reimagined, and integrated into the myth of crisis art that he disappears into the structure and, as signifier, means what the new myth permits him to mean. By contrast, Barbara Gregorich in *She's on First* frequently invokes the name of Jackie Robinson as pop image and untransformed signifier, depending on the name to mean merely "first black man to play in the major leagues and suffer discrimination." As signifier, Jackie Robinson is intended, so it seems, to provide an analogue for and a depth of meaning to the otherwise two-dimensional protagonist, Linda Sunshine, first woman to play in the major leagues. Robinson is not stolen and reinterpreted; he is borrowed, complacently, to supply meaning to a Harlequin-romance sort of heroine in a narrative that, incidentally, has a baseball setting.

Shards of history – old "facts" – evolve into signifiers that can contribute to the beauty and truth of the new meaning structure into which they are transported, but the transportation of signifiers should change them, juxtapose them with new and even alien settings, characters, and events. When they speak in their new surroundings, they may sound ironic; they must sound equivocal. The complacent use of history in baseball narratives avoids the hard work of transformation, interpretation, and reimagining. Messenger points to E. L. Doctorow's *Ragtime* as an example of the "copying" of baseball history into fiction "in an inventive form" (*Sport and the Spirit of Play* 383), or one might say, in a reimagined form. Doctorow transports his baseball characters, especially John McGraw, horizontally through space rather than through time, a journey that nevertheless confronts the problem of time and play within sacred space. Messenger says of this scene that it concerns a character, J. P. Morgan, who "ponder[s] [his] relation to history and seek[s] an artistic or mystical release from it. . . . J. P. Morgan, seeking to flee his own era and be reincarnated, spends a discouragingly prosaic night in the Great Pyramid in Egypt. Upon his exit into the morning light, he sees running toward him, hand outstretched, 'a squat ugly man in pinstriped knee pants and a ribbed undershirt.' . . . It is John McGraw, manager of the New York Giants" (319). Messenger notices that Doctorow depicts the New York Giants, incongruously garbed in their baseball uniforms, swarming over the Sphinx "like vermin," an evocation of "scarabs (dung beetles), the Egyptian symbols of reincarnation which thus mock Morgan's quest" (319). Doctorow here clearly reimagines, transforms, and interprets these historical signifiers, McGraw and his players, transports them from one timeless realm, the Polo Grounds, to another, the Valley of the Kings, in a modern pastiche of signs and significations whose overall effect is both ironic and equivocal. The players as vermin are rendered obscene, yet as an image of dung beetles they are aids to reincarnation, evidence of which is what Morgan seeks. Morgan ironically cannot "read" the image as a version of the experience he seeks: "to feel in advance the eternal energies he would exemplify when he died and rose on the rays of the sun in order to be born again," even though he prides himself on being able to "make a distinction between false signs and true signs" (Doctorow 261–62). He expects to see ba birds, which he thinks would be a true sign of his impending rebirth, but instead sees ball player–scarabs, which he not only does not recognize as signs but from which he flees in distaste. Of course – and this is a crucial point – even if he did recognize the ball players as signs, the signs would not speak themselves but require interpretation, for any univocal interpretation is rendered virtually impossible by the mythic agon of clashing images, ambiguous symbols, and discrepancy between expectation and realization, all screened through an ironic and comic narrative voice.

Messenger identifies in conjunction with baseball's "Legend of the Fall" its "exiles and exclusions" and the production in baseball fiction of what he calls "counterhistory" ("Expansion Draft" 62–63), a concept closely akin to what I have called revisionary mythmaking. The impulse of counterhistory is to work within an imaginary circle drawn by "official history" but to give a voice to those whom exile and exclusion have effectively silenced. Messenger points to Philip Roth's *Great American Novel*, Jerome Charyn's *The Seventh Babe*, and Jay Neugeboren's *Sam's Legacy* as examples of counterhistory, the Charyn and Neugeboren works "contain[ing] by far the most imaginative studies of blacks, exiles, and baseball history" ("Expansion Draft" 63). As parts of baseball's mythology, such works incorporate the oddments of baseball history but in doing so reimagine, reinterpret, and transform that history, seeing it from the perspective of the exiled and excluded, from the vantage of what Messenger calls "shadow leagues," positioned "so far below the major leagues as to be invisible" (63). A curious effect of the view from below, however, is not to elevate or enlarge but to bring low and diminish. The outsider narrator must reveal in his or her counterhistory the untold truth or replace official stories ("history," "lies") with truth. Indeed, recurrent themes of baseball's mythology are the quest for truth, defense of the integrity of the record, elaboration of the record, and the suspect nature of general human history.

The need for counterhistory is itself ironic, for the game of baseball is inscribed in a code that aspires to full disclosure; its record purports, unlike those of mundane history, to be accurate, objective, and complete. Given this foundation the game's counterhistories present themselves not as mythos but instead as perfected logos, texts based, when it is dependable, on the record and inscribed in the unequivocal signs of mathematics – box scores, statistics, averages, dates, and records. Ward Sullivan, in *Almost Famous,* thinks of baseball's numerical records as "the statistical shorthand of mythology, the old beautiful summary of performance revealed in naked, unforgiving arithmetic" (164).

Coover's J. Henry Waugh keeps such a record for the Universal Baseball Association, what amounts to both a league history and a mythological "Book of Life," forty-six volumes containing accounts of games and plays, player biographies, write-ups of games, statistics, and so forth. These volumes, it is implied, are not a bit of ephemera whose inscriptions are subject to interpretation and revision but an enduring record of simple truth. The book is written in *permanent* black ink, free of error, omission, or the effects of time. This ideal history contrasts with the evolving equivocations of the world as recorded day to day in newspapers, which "[speak] blackly of bombs, births, wars, weddings, infiltrations, and social events." Profane history is at best suspect, as Henry tells Lou, anticipating the arguments of Roland Barthes and Hayden White: "You can take history or leave it, but if you take it you have to accept certain assumptions or ground rules about what's left in and what's left out." Perhaps the only dependable aspect of mundane history is numerical: "History. Amazing, how we love it. And did you ever stop to think that without numbers or measurements, there probably wouldn't be any history?" (49).

Baseball's literature often emphasizes this claim of truth, of full disclosure, and will tolerate nothing less. When the "official" record falls short of this objective, the text may take the form of a labor to set the record straight, to restore its pristine accuracy. Stein's Buck Weaver, one of baseball's exiles, sets out with this intent: "Maybe it's time some individual set down the actual truth for a change" (48). His own "corrected" history of the years 1912 to 1919 follows. Sometimes, ironically, mythically, the record ("historical truth") seems to be the real protagonist in baseball's imaginative texts. The attempt to set the record straight is the plot of Roth's counterhistory, his *Great American Novel.* Word Smith, Roth's aged narrator, labors to avenge the "colossal crime against the truth" that, "perpetrated by America's powers-that-be," tore from the "record book" the "chapter of our past" concerning a third major league, the Patriot League, which has been *"wilfully erased from the national memory"* (16). The missing chapter is a kind of national Lacanian ellipsis. The novel purports to be a record of the labor, never complete, to recover the lost chapter, a task at which the narrator continues to work even as the novel closes. Within his "embattled life," Smitty says, he "continues to survive on the strength of an impassioned belief" in art, "an art . . . not for its own sake, but for the sake of the record, an art that reclaims what is and was from those whose every word is a falsification and a betrayal of the truth" (381). In this funny reversal of the roles of fictional and historical storytelling, Smitty expresses a rather Aristotelian notion about the relation between art and history, the former's truth (logos) and the latter's falsehoods (mythos), hence the bridge of *fictional truth*. It is a notion that recognizes not only the myths of history but the truths of art.[5]

Neugeboren's counterhistory takes the form of Mason Tidewater's story of his life in the Negro Leagues, offering most graphically the view not only from outside but from below. He even writes from a small dirt room that will soon be his grave, a secret room beneath the basement in which he lives, under an apartment building in Brooklyn. From this vantage he offers a mythic agon entitled "My Life and Death . . . A Slave Narrative," in which is displayed the meeting of irreconcilable pairs: love and hate, black and white, submission and domination, homosexual and heterosexual love, freedom and slavery, life and death. Mason Tidewater is black but looks white. As white as he looks, however, he is known as the Black Babe. An extraordinarily talented pitcher and hitter, he develops an obsessive interest in and passion for Babe Ruth, who is white but looks black. (Ruth is often called "nigger" because of his features and deep tan.) Both men are subject to the labels "black" and "white," which, although shown to be meaningless when applied to the two men, nevertheless determine their lives. The label "white" determines Ruth's insider status, his wealth, power, and place in canonical history. The label "black" determines Tidewater's outsider status, his poverty, impotence, and obscurity. When the two men meet in off-season games, Tidewater dominates Ruth on the field, demonstrating his excellence and his right to a place in the game's history. On the field he absolutely neutralizes the potency of Ruth's famous bat. Tidewater says that he "had not wanted to allow him, on the field, a single victory" (309). Off the field, however, in a homosexual affair, Ruth absolutely dominates Tidewater, demonstrating the potency of the metaphorical bat and something of the power of "whiteness" over "blackness." Through it all their relationship is essentially sadomas-ochistic, with dominant and submissive role relations continually shift-ing. As Tidewater says, "His image was like a fire in my head, and I wished that fire to consume us both. I wanted, already, to be done with him, and yet I sensed that we had only begun, that, no matter how many times I proved myself his master on the playing field, I would, away from the play-ing field, forever submit myself to him" (309). Tidewater's submission is a form of voluntary slavery: "I did, with every act, sustain that slavery which was mine, and which, alas, I must have loved" (188).

Domination and submission, love and hate, meet in dubious battle in the mythic space of Tidewater's narrative. Likewise, white and black confront each other, but both *white* and *black*, like *mastery* and *submis-sion*, are shifting, ambiguous terms. At one point Tidewater reports that Ruth "liked taking me with him to nightclubs, and he could, in the way in which he showed me off – calling me 'the best white-black pitcher I ever faced' – be as cruel as, when we were alone, he could be kind" (313). The final confrontation between the two men is triggered by just this ambiguous white blackness, or black whiteness. Ruth, attempting to pro-voke Tidewater, says, "You're just a make-believe nigger anyway" (333). Tidewater strikes Ruth, knocking him out, and black teammate Brick Johnson takes up the charge: "Only you ain't just a make-believe nigger. . . . You just plain make-believe, from start to finish" (334). Ruth's and Johnson's accusations are too close to the truth, triggering Tidewater's violent reaction. Tidewater's fierce pride, along with both his self-hatred and his love-hatred for Ruth, are now deflected toward Johnson, and he chokes the life out of him.

Here is history – the historical person George Herman "Babe" Ruth – made metaphor in a mythic narrative that strives for intelligibility and meaning, the truth in and of that most complex of relationships between self and other, us and them, and in this case between black and white, in which self-love and self-hatred, insight and blindness, strive for rec-onciliation, for a kind of peace. There is no peace, but in the failure to achieve reconciliation, there is a kind of triumph, if only the sort of contingent triumph revealed in the Reni painting. In killing Johnson (another talented black pitcher) Tidewater metaphorically kills both Ruth and himself. He now is forced into an even deeper and life-long exile. Under a different name he wanders, homeless, from place to place and from job to job, playing by turns both black and white but exclud-ed alike from both black and white companionship: "I never played baseball again. I never saw my brothers or my mother or my sister again. I never saw any of the players from the Brooklyn Royal Dodgers again" (335). Nonetheless, the narrative is written and handed to a figurative son, a white son – Sam Berman –with a final understanding: "I find at the end what I did not expect to find when I started to set these thoughts down: . . . I regret nothing" (336).

Although nothing is regretted, still nothing is resolved. The message of the continuing irreconcilability of the mythic contradictions is carried, as it so often is, in images. The most telling images are two dolls, one Russian and the other a "pickanniny child" (250). Sam Berman, the protagonist outside Tidewater's story of his life and death, begins his tale with a meditation on the relationships among the generations, from grandfather to father to son: "He saw his grandfather as tallest of all, with Ben next, and himself last – like the painted wooden dolls he'd seen in souvenir shops (from Russia [the family's point of origin], he thought, or Poland), in which when you opened the largest one, there was one smaller, and when you opened the smaller one, there was one even smaller" (3). Sam sees himself as the smallest of all.

The "exquisite" pickanniny child is a crafted and beautiful thing, the work of an anonymous slave who, as it turns out, has hidden and died in the dirt room where Tidewater writes. The doll is his legacy, in a way, to Tidewater. Moreover, this doll, like the Russian doll, comes apart: "The boy's torso and head lifted, and inside it Sam saw another doll, identical to the first, only smaller" (250–51). Tidewater attempts to give this doll to Sam, but Sam recoils in terror. Tidewater says, "Don't be afraid. I'd like you to have it," but Sam *is* afraid and does not "want to hear anymore" (251).

Distilled in these two nested-doll images and Sam's refusal to accept Tidewater's gift are all the contradictions at strife in Tidewater's narrative. Here are two "babes," one white, one black, and their "sons," replicas of self, internalized, identical, and stretching down through the generations. As Sam's surrogate father, Tidewater makes the healing gesture, offers the gift of the black doll to the white man, offers relationship, reconciliation, and atonement. It is the moment, one might say, when Saint Michael stands triumphant with sword raised and his foot on the neck of the fiend. But the moment passes and its promise is suspended, as it seems, forever: Sam says, "Some other time, okay?" (251). Sam will never see Tidewater again. The suspended reconciliation of black and white, father and son, love and hate, age and youth, leaves these contradictions "in play" in the text, somewhere between the unattainable poles of meaning and truth – that is, in the gap.

GOOD MYTHS AND BAD

The excellence of myths lies in their performance of hard human work, the work of rendering the dizzying data of existence intelligible, of saying what persons, things, and events mean, of attempting to reconcile the absurdly opposite aspects of life so that we can carry on. *Bricoleurs* perform mythic work in a rhetorical mode – through signs, words, images, metaphors – to which both conscious intent and unconscious desire contribute their shares. The artifact constructed by the genuine mythmaker has something of his or her self in it. Its linguistic triumphs are hard won and briefly enjoyed. The body of works comprising the mythology of baseball mines both the bricolage of failed myth systems and the game itself and its past – its numbers and players, games and seasons – all now become archetypal signifiers, images, and metaphors and all requiring reimagining, interpretation, and reinterpretation. Baseball's compelling myths may open a space for the sacred and uncanny, a haunting not nothing arising from the mind's underworld and speaking its mysterious message in the rhetoric of the gap: an old black man-ghost driving a cart loaded with watermelons in the darkness of Dred's nearly completed quest (Sayles, *Pride of the Bimbos* 218); a "Bible man" who mysteriously dogs one's footsteps or an exquisite but terrifying carved doll that opens to reveal another, smaller doll (Neugeboren, *Sam's Legacy*); a dead child named Carol who haunts Sarah Sullivan and her house, whispering secrets about God and the connection of all things (Small, *Almost Famous*); the face of a dead teammate seen in the mirror where one's own face should be (Malamud, *The Natural* 126–27); a pack of hellhounds that race through a mad brother's ordinary day (Wilson, *Fences* 47); a paralyzing curse like a virus infecting the primordial waters and the river of time (Willard, *Things Invisible to See* 246); a moment of life-altering illumination (Kinsella, *Shoeless Joe* 189–90; Greenberg, *The Celebrant* 27); or a terrifying glimpse beyond a hundred-watt sun into an intense inane (Coover, *The Universal Baseball Association* 238).

Stephen J. Gould's concern with silly and tendentious baseball texts and those writers who "attempt to wrest profundity from the spectacle of grown men hitting a ball with a stick" is, I believe, directed at "bad myth,"

myth whose work has been too easy, what Messenger calls complacent. This is the imitative text where trope is granted authority and taken for truth, where truth has degenerated into cliché, and where the beautiful has subsided to the comfortable, the reassuring, or the pleasant. Bad myth is where play-strife is suspended and contradictions silenced; bad myth is a hodgepodge of borrowed remains, old signifiers and archetypes that are assumed to speak for themselves.

Gould concludes that the effort to find meaning in the game is silly because "baseball is profound all by itself" ("Creation Myths of Cooperstown" 26). Of course Gould is not entirely serious, for he also writes of Joe DiMaggio's fifty-six-game hitting streak that it "is both the greatest factual achievement in the history of baseball and a principal icon of American mythology" and that in extending the streak against all laws of probability, DiMaggio stepped out of science and into myth: "He sits on the shoulders of two bearers – mythology and science" ("The Streak of Streaks" 8). Gould concludes that "DiMaggio's hitting streak is the finest of legitimate legends because *it embodies the essence of the battle that truly defines our lives.* DiMaggio activated the greatest and most unattainable dream of all humanity, the hope and chimera of all sages and shamans: he cheated death, at least for a while" ("The Streak of Streaks" 12; emphasis added).

If no one, including Gould, had ever gazed at the game's green expanse, its geometrical design, its players and its action, as into the heart of meaning, if no one had ever felt constrained to record the insights of that gaze, Gould would not have been tempted to claim that baseball is profound all by itself. Gould, perhaps better than most, knows that meaning is in people and their language, not in things,[6] that without the meaning he himself, a true mythmaker, finds and assigns, no one could by means of the game "cheat death."[7] The game, the language of the game, its stories, and the echoing resonance of image and word in the mind, the playing and the speaking, the game and its archetypes and myths – all these things are irrevocably linked. And, yes, the mythology of the game, like other mythologies, does contain both the excellent and the ordinary, the profound and the silly.

This book, like me, has been haunted by the image of the ruined tower, and the writing of the book, I freely admit, has been labor both in and of the tower, the gap, the myth of myths. Believing, as I do, that we live inside the ruin and use its debris as we can to make sense of our lives, I find that my effort is one more bit of work by a *bricoleur* who used for the emerging structure the bits, the shards, the oddments that lay at hand. Yet the game remains more than any single pronouncement, more than a story, a book, or many books. It is an endlessly changing scene in a mirror, like Richard Wilbur's nature, "in which we have seen ourselves and spoken," wherein we have or may yet find "all we mean or wish to mean" ("Advice to a Prophet"). In a sense, the game *is* profound all by itself, for in its signs and syntax it speaks to us an ambiguous message of play and strife, both in their ways beautiful, and prompts our speaking, and that speaking in turn changes the game, becomes, in Wallace Stevens's words, "a part of what it is."

NOTES

Introduction

1. The famous case of Eddie Gaedel (1951) offers evidence to support Oscar Wilde's assertion that life imitates art. The parallels between Thurber's dwarf and Eddie Gaedel extend to pinch-hitting with a toy bat, receiving instruction to take a base on balls, and prompting a protest on the part of the opposing manager, a protest that is denied because in each case the dwarf's team has a legal contract making the dwarf a part of the team (Shatzkin 369).

2. For instance, Colin Murray Turbayne claims that metaphor is like the green glasses handed visitors to Oz, who, compelled to look through those lenses, find that the Emerald City is *really* green, and they "believe they contemplate nothing but the un-made-up face of the truth" (27). Also writing in the figural mode, Nelson Goodman says that a metaphor is "an affair between a predicate with a past and an object that yields while protesting" (124).

3. See Marc Manganaro's introduction, "Textual Play, Power, and Cultural Critique: An Orientation to Modernist Anthropology," wherein he traces an evolution in anthropological studies growing from the recognition of traditional anthropology's imposition of control on the anthropological "subject," an evolution from monologue to dialogue, from representation to evocation.

4. See Arthur W. H. Adkins, "Myth, Philosophy, and Religion," for an exploration of the shifting senses of the terms *mythos* and *logos* in Plato and his predecessors. *Logos* ("true account") and *mythos* ("false account") would thus produce, in *mythology,* a term meaning something like, "a true account of lies."

5. Feldman and Richardson provide a useful gathering of eighteenth- and nineteenth-century mythographical texts and pertinent commentary (224–527).

6. At times Barthes seems almost besieged by myth: "The mythic is present wherever *sentences are turned,* where *stories are told* . . . : from interior monologue to the conversation, from the newspaper article to the political speech, from the novel . . . to the advertising image" ("Mythology Today" 68).

7. See the prologue, "Myth and the Body," to Campbell's *Inner Reaches of Outer Space,* which concludes with a speculation about any emerging mythology of the unified earth and a caution about the continuing power of old control systems: "Meanwhile . . . in the old Near East, where in Sargon's time the idea appears to have first been implemented of politically exploitive wars of territorial conquest, contending armies of the only three monotheistic monads of the planet . . . in this delicate moment of imminent global unification . . . are threatening the whole process . . . with the adventure of their scripturally prophesied Armageddon" (22).

8. In his notion of the signified changing into the signifier, Gould takes his cues from Lévi-Strauss, who says, "in the continual reconstruction from the same materials, it is always earlier ends which are called upon to play the part of means: the signified chang-

es into the signifying and vice versa" (*The Savage Mind* 21). In his analysis of archetypes Gould, like Northrop Frye, places the archetype not in the innate structure of the mind but in language, literature, myth. But Gould goes beyond Frye in a linguistic analysis that synthesizes archetypal theory and post-phenomenological criticism by explaining the ubiquitous, recurring, evolving character of archetypes, a character, he says, that is a function of the fact that archetypes offer their structures, figures, and images to the unconscious to use for its own purposes.

9. Although Roland Barthes's analyses of myth evolved over time from a structuralist to a poststructuralist perspective, unlike Gould he wrote in a mode largely isolated from the wider field of myth criticism, focusing particularly on what may be called commercial and political forms.

10. Gould relies on Ricoeur (*The Rule of Metaphor*) to support the case for an alliance of structural and interpretation theory: "There is no strain in linking a theory of reading with a theory of structure. . . . Paul Ricoeur has suggested this function [of supplementary mythic activity in formal analyses]: 'Structural analysis does not exclude, but presupposes, the opposite hypothesis concerning myth, i.e., that it has meaning as a narrative of origins. Structural analysis merely represses this function. But it cannot repress it. The myth would not even function as a logical operator if the propositions that it combines did not point toward boundary situations'" (Gould 191–92). Gennette goes farther, suggesting that structuralism itself is a form of interpretation: "A priori, of course, structuralism as a method is based on the study of structures wherever they occur; but to begin with, structures are not directly encountered objects – far from it; they are systems of latent relations, conceived rather than perceived, which analysis constructs as it uncovers them, and which it runs the risk of inventing while believing that it is discovering them" (11). Although he does not use the term, Gennette's point gives the work of the structuralist critic the quality of "mythicity," as Gould has defined it, a perfectly logical next step and one taken up explicitly by Derrida in "Structure, Sign and Play."

Chapter 1: The Myth of the Gap

1. It is interesting to notice that by 1971 Barthes, whose field was the interpretation of cultural myths, taking his cues from Derrida, already recognized the mythic nature of his and others' endeavors: "A science of the signifier . . . has in fact taken its place in the work of the period; its goal is not so much the analysis of the sign as its dislocation. With regard to myth . . . , the new semiology – or the new mythology – can no longer . . . separate so easily the signifier from the signified, the ideological from the phraseological. Not that this distinction is false or ineffectual, but it has become mythic itself" ("Myth Today" 66).

2. The fourth name is Michel Foucault. When asked whether he saw an intellectual affinity with Barthes, Lacan, and Foucault, Lévi-Strauss replied, "That still both-

ers me, as there are no grounds for that combination. I don't see what the names have in common. Or rather I do see it. It is deceptive" (in Eribon 71–72).

3. Turbayne's subject was the machine metaphor of Newton and Descartes, and he wished to demonstrate that a shaping metaphor like this one actually determines the nature of reality in the minds of observers (scientists and others); he provided the linguistic metaphor to reveal the contrasts in worlds created by the two metaphors or models.

4. Saussure actually insists on a third gap, which lies in his distinction between synchrony and diachrony, a cleavage that results for linguists in the so-called Saussurean paradox.

5. For example, in chapter 12 of the *Biographia Literaria,* Coleridge coined a term for the imagination – "esemplastic power," the coinage *esemplastic* meaning "to mold into one."

6. Ricoeur remarks that whether the "like" is indicated, the principle holds (*Rule of Metaphor* 296–97).

7. The relationship of thought and knowledge to language is still problematic. Some philosophers, as Gerhart and Russell point out, "hold . . . that there is much that we know but cannot express in language, much that we are unable to communicate. We can think about that which we know but cannot express, for if we could not think about it, we could not be said to know it at all." Moreover, they write that "thought and language are not equivalent" (108). My position is that the same claim could be made about any unconscious "knowledge," and my bias is squarely with Lacanian theory, which I explain later, which asserts that language is still the medium and the vehicle of unconscious knowledge and that its modes are radically rhetorical.

8. To take an illustration from English, the analogy is with phonemes and the phones representing them. The phoneme /p/, manifest on the empirical level as either [p] or [pʰ], becomes meaningful only by its contrast, for example, to the phoneme /b/, manifest as [b]. The forms [pʰɪt] "pit" and [bɪt] "bit" contrast with each other and distinguish differences in meaning only within a system that includes at the systematic (phonemic) level a contrast between the never heard phonemes existing in a binary opposition as to the matter of voicing: /p/ is voiceless and /b/ is voiced; at the manifest level [p] and [pʰ] are allophones, alternate forms of the phoneme whose distribution is predictable.

9. M. M. Bakhtin's notion of the authoritative word, which is "religious, political, moral; the word of a father, of adults and of teachers, etc." (342) and which he distinguishes from the dialogic prose of the novel, appears to be something like the language of the engineer – not as written but as perceived; it has "internal persuasiveness" (342). Those who take such texts as authoritative in Bakhtin's sense are those who believe in the *bricoleur*'s "myth of the engineer." The sacred tale, the epic, and the political manifesto may be invested with authority by the text's recipient. To the unquestioning recipient of the authoritative word, it and its text appear remote in time, lofty, sacred, mythic. "Its semantic structure is," Bakhtin says, "static and

dead, for it is fully complete, it has but a single meaning, the letter is fully sufficient to the sense and calcifies it." Furthermore, "it permits no play," and therefore, "one must either totally affirm it, or totally reject it" (343). The authoritative word "by its very nature [is] incapable of being double-voiced" (344). Not always, but at times, Bakhtin speaks as though the authoritative text itself creates its own interpretation and authority, but of course there is no meaning in the unread, unheard text; meaning is always in people, not in texts, and this fact renders Bakhtin's discussion problematic. If, as Lévi-Strauss and Derrida claim, the mythmaker and critic are of necessity *bricoleurs,* their texts always fashioned from the debris of the texts they may seek to revise, reject, or deconstruct, then no text – mythic, political, or moral – can be authoritative, outside the realm of the play of language, in and of itself. It too is bricolage; it too is at the very least double-voiced. Like the deep of Tennyson's "Ulysses," any text, any construct of language, any myth, must of necessity "moan round with many voices." Nothing in my own experience of reading texts – mythic, sacred, scientific, political, or moral – convinces me that there is a fundamental authority inherent in texts themselves. For that reason, it seems to me that there are many positions toward "authoritative" texts between total affirmation and total rejection.

10. In his "Prospectus to *The Excursion*" Wordsworth says of the mind that it is the "haunt and main region of [his] song."

11. Ragland-Sullivan's subtitle, "Prolegomena to a Lancanian Poetics," indicates the preliminary nature of her findings, and Robert Con Davis ("Introduction") reiterates the fact of a still-emerging Lacanian theory of narrative. I refer readers to both of these as cogent discussions of and significant contributions to Lacanian literary theory.

12. What keeps the imaginary and the symbols from merging with Lockean "ideas" is the distinctly Saussurean claim that their meanings emerge in a complex system of binary oppositions.

13. The concept of the real provides a kind of Blakean "limit of opacity" both to the language of the unconscious and to interpretations; unlike Derridean and other forms of poststructuralism, the abyss of the Lacanian mind is not bottomless. The limited number and nature of the symbols restrain the endless proliferation of "readings"; that is, the shared language of the unconscious dictates that there may be both appropriate and inappropriate interpretations of "texts."

14. Metaphor and also metonymy are here seen as semantic condensations, although in Roman Jakobson's analyses metonymy is assigned to the syntactic and metaphor to the semantic (semiotic) components of the grammar. The early Lacan, like Paul Ricoeur, sees these tropes not as existing as polar opposites but as serving similar semantic functions. See Eric Gould (47–55).

15. It is tempting to draw an analogy between Lacan's Law and Desire and Bakhtin's "authoritative word" and "internally persuasive word" (342). If I read Bakhtin correctly, however, his concepts are only in part internal. Moreover, although an agonistic relationship often exists between Bakhtin's two "words," as with Law and De-

sire ("The struggle and dialogic interrelationship of these categories of ideological discourse are what usually determine the history of an individual ideological consciousness" [342]), this struggle appears at least partially – and perhaps mostly – conscious; Lacan's Law and Desire are rhetorical speaking figures, voices of the unconscious.

16. See Ragland-Sullivan for an exposition of the self-revelation implicit in Lancanian interpretation, wherein "literature operates a magnetic pull on the reader because it is an allegory of the psyche's fundamental structure" (381).

17. I use the masculine pronoun here and elsewhere in discussions where subject matter and mythic content demand it. To use "he or she" in this discussion of the phallus-weapon-bat would border on the absurd. Indeed, mythic heroes generally have been male, as has the overwhelming majority of baseball players, baseball writers, and the heroes of baseball. As a result both the personae and symbology of the texts reflect this masculine center. In chapters 3 and 5, where I examine feminine heroes of baseball (or softball) narratives, I explore the curiously altered relationships between protagonist and the field, the game, and the bat when the myth system is made to accommodate the feminine hero.

18. See James Lieberman's "Why Oedipus Loved His Father." The author points out that a loving, nonaggressive relationship exists among Oedipus and his adoptive parents, Polybus and Merope, the "real" parents in the drama, who welcome the infant Oedipus as "a gift."

19. Lacan's account of the vertical dimension of any given word provides a complex psychological counterpart to Bakhtin's account of the word in a "dialogized process," the word "directed toward an object, [which] enters a dialogically agitated and tension-filled environment of alien words," there "to shape its own stylistic profile and tone" (Bakhtin 276–77). In Lacan's case the polysemy is provided diachronically, by the word's history; in Bakhtin's, synchronically, by its environment. Language viewed from a Lacanian perspective can never be monologic.

20. For Gould's full discussion of the sacred, see his chapter 4, "The Mythic and the Numinous."

21. Kenneth Burke demonstrates this point from a more traditionally rhetorical perspective in *The Rhetoric of Religion: Studies in Logology,* in which he analyzes the use of metaphor in religious discourse as a projection of terms from nature, society, and politics into the realms of the sacred and the role in sacred rhetoric of the negative morpheme ("a purely linguistic marvel" [19]). See especially his chapter 1, "On Words and The Word" (7–42).

22. Gould's focus on metaphor and metonymy in his analysis of myth and the sacred is valuable, placing myth criticism in line with structural and poststructural emphases on these two tropes (through Freud, Jakobson, Lévi-Strauss, Barthes, Lacan, Derrida, de Man, Ricoeur, and others), tropes to which Genette refers as "the exemplary figurative pair, the irreplaceable bookends of our own modern rhetoric" (107).

23. In *Tears* Taylor provides a remarkable synthesis of theoretical issues that concern the sacred and exist at the intersection of theology, philosophy, literary criticism, and art. His entire argument bears on the question of the origins, and perpetuation in modern and postmodern art, of the sacred, issues with obvious relevance to this study. Subsequent citations can only suggest that relevance.

24. In *The Masks of God: Primitive Mythology* Joseph Campbell makes an analogy that helps to explain *archetype* in its usual sense. He points out that newborn chicks, some with eggshell still adhering to their down, will flee for cover when the image of a hawk is drawn over their cage; the same image drawn backward resembles the shape of a goose, and the chicks do not respond at all (31). The conclusion is that the chicks are born with the image of the enemy, the hawk in flight, in their brains and react with appropriate behavior when they encounter this archetype for the first time. The Jungian notion of archetype is that similar ideas and possibilities of ideas inhere in the human brain at birth and reveal themselves in the objects of human imagining. In Gould's reordering all that is left of the Jungian archetype is not the image of the enemy, for example, but only the hole, the emptiness of fear, waiting to be filled by language, by particular signs, words like *dragon, serpent, witch,* or *wolf.*

25. The ubiquity of the journey metaphor is explored by George Lakoff and Mark Turner in their recent exposition of poetic metaphor and its meaning-producing potential. See *More than Cool Reason: A Field Guide to Poetic Metaphor,* especially chapter 1, "Life, Death, and Time."

Chapter 3: Paths of Glory

1. I have heard this claim attributed to John Gardner but have been unable to verify its source.

2. The authors cite as support such studies as Charles L. Sanford's *The Quest for Paradise,* wherein Sanford claims that "the Edenic myth . . . has been the most powerful and comprehensive organizing force in American culture" (Jewett and Lawrence 171).

Chapter 4: Mark Harris's Bang the Drum Slowly and the Two Stories

1. Genette asserts that the novelist is not a *bricoleur* but rather an engineer: "The instrumental universe of the *bricoleur,* says Lévi-Strauss, is a 'closed' universe. Its repertoire, however extended, 'remains limited.' This limitation distinguishes the *bricoleur* from the engineer, who (in principle) can at any time obtain the tool specially adapted to a particular technical need. The engineer 'questions the universe,

while the *bricoleur* addresses himself to a collection of oddments left over from human endeavors, that is, only a subset of the culture'" (4-5). Genette wishes to make
the point that the critic *is* a *bricoleur*, a mythmaker, not a writer, creating the critical
text from the oddments of "the work"; the critic "builds ideological castles out of
the debris of what was once a *literary* discourse" (5). But the distinction becomes
impossible to sustain. Harris creates Henry, who may be a "tool" specially adapted
to a particular need, but he creates him as an "Author" from a warehouse of author-
parts, a figure whose ancestors are legion, whose powers are extensive, and whose
method is bricolage. Answering Genette, I claim that the plows of all texts (mythical, literary, and critical) are driven over the bones of the dead.

2. Northrop Frye discusses violence (*forza*) and guile (*froda*) as two essential
forms of sin *and* virtue that, entering literature, "help to create the forms of tragedy
and comedy respectively" (*Secular Scripture* 65-66).

3. Campbell explains that rites of sacrifice "are required to bring the social order to accord and thereby to refresh . . . the force of the play throughout the social
body of the energies of the tide of life" (*The Sacrifice* 37).

Chapter 5: Dimensions of the Field of Play

1. "Plot" is A. Bartlett Giamatti's pun for both story and ground and the relationship between space and story. See his discussion in *Take Time for Paradise* (81-101).

2. At the beginning, Hesiod says, one might have done enough in a day to last
for a year, "with no more working" (43-44). That was the way Zeus planned it, but
things went wrong when Prometheus stole the divine fire for men. In retaliation Zeus
created the first woman, Pandora, who released into the world her "sorrows," among
them death and incessant, exhausting, lifelong labor. Similarly, Adam and Eve enjoyed a leisurely existence in Eden tending the trees that yielded their fruit in all
seasons until, at the prompting of the subtle serpent, the first couple ate the forbidden fruit and were expelled from Eden, compelled to labor and to die.

3. The biblical Eden is only one such image of timeless ease; details of such scenes
vary, but they are alike in insisting on ease and eternity. They may, for example, be not
walled gardens but isolated islands, as are the Sumerian Dilmun, the Babylonian Far
Distant, the Irish Land of Youth, and the Greek Islands of the Blessed or the Garden
of the Hesperides. Although travelers frequently must journey over water to reach a
supernatural realm, sometimes the place is of the world, a walled garden or other structure bounded and set aside from ordinary space, perhaps situated in or coextensive
with heaven or perfected existence, as in the New Jerusalem of Revelation, the Elysian
fields of *The Aeneid,* or Valhalla of Nordic mythology. All these are places for the immortal (dead); that is, they are perfected "homes," points of origin and destination of
the human quest. So enduring is this image that it is already present in the oldest texts
we know. Over five thousand years ago the Sumerian Dilmun was depicted as a land

of youth: "Its old man says not 'I am an old man.'" Without age, there is no death; without death, no sorrow: "Its singer . . . utters no lament" (Kramer 55).

4. One of Giamatti's first works was *The Earthly Paradise*, a scholarly exploration of the image in Renaissance texts; his last, *Take Time for Paradise*, returned him to this same place and preoccupation, where he found that all play, all games, are paths into the lost paradise: "All play aspires to the condition of paradise. . . . Through play . . . we hope to achieve a state that our larger Greco-Roman, Judeo-Christian culture has always known was lost. Where it exists, we do not know, although we have always envisioned it as a garden, sometimes on a mountaintop, often on an island, but always as removed, an enclosed, green place" (42).

5. In "The Creation Myths of Cooperstown" Stephen Jay Gould rejects accounts of an abrupt, inspired beginning for baseball and traces its historical evolution in the nineteenth century.

6. This proposition opposes Rousseau's claim that humans are born free and culturally enslaved with the assertion that it is really nature that enslaves; culture provides a measure of freedom. Joseph Campbell argues that part of nature's enslavement consists of "bioenergies" – the compulsions to feed, to procreate, to plunder, and to have mercy (or to love). Myth, the language of culture, has the task of controlling the bioenergies of this raw human nature (*Inner Reaches* 11–23). Speaking of nature as a "hard taskmaster," Paglia adds her own litany of nature's crimes, saying, "Incarnation, the limitation of mind by matter, is an outrage to the imagination. Equally outrageous is gender, which we have not chosen but which nature has imposed upon us. Our physicality is torment, our body the tree of nature on which Blake sees us crucified." She adds that culture "is our frail barrier against nature" (3).

7. This quotation, attributed to Pete Rose, is contained in William Matthews's poem "Lost Time for Sale" (*The Gettysburg Review* 5, no. 3 [Summer 1992]: 423).

8. Dudley Young argues another point, that war originates in primate populations not naturally, as in some species, but as an expression of curiosity and the impulse to play. That is, first comes play, then war: game becomes war becomes game in the progress of civilization (39–61). The example of the Trukese suggests that modern games may well be a form of what Young calls "rituals for the repair and maintenance of our taboos against inappropriate violence" (59).

9. Joseph Campbell's term *bioenergies* (see note 6 to this chapter) refers to certain behaviors that "are of the essence of life itself, and which, when unbridled, become terrific, horrifying, and destructive." It is, he says, the task of myth to control such "primal energies and urges of the common human species" (*Inner Reaches* 13).

10. Both *garden* and *yard* are words linked etymologically in Indo-European languages to *field* – "Gerd" in Nordic mythology, the frozen field-bride of the god Freyr who melts and becomes fertile in his embrace.

11. As Thompson explains, "Sexual reproduction introduces death, for it produces new individuals that, by virtue of being limited and highly specific beings, must die. The asexual cell divides itself *ad infinitum* and therefore never fully dies; the

parthenogenite reduplicates itself in a daughter that is practically a clone, but the sexual organism reproduces itself and then moves that much closer to death. Reproduction is the climax of life" (53).

12. In *Woman and Nature: The Roaring inside Her* Susan Griffin begins her examination of the profound disfigurement that the metaphoric identification of woman and nature has produced with "a man's view" of woman: "He says that woman speaks with nature. That she hears voices from under the earth. That wind blows in her ears and trees whisper to her. That the dead sing through her mouth and the cries of infants are clear to her. But for him this dialogue is over. He says he is not part of this world, that he was set on this world as a stranger. He sets himself apart from woman and nature" (1). In *The Lay of the Land* Annette Kolodny, with a quite different perspective, speculates that the identification of woman and nature results in projecting onto nature the forms of desire, namely, the nurturing mother and the virginal bride: "The European discovery of an unblemished and fertile continent [America] allowed the projection upon it of a residue of infantile experience in which all needs – physical, erotic, spiritual and emotional – had been met by an entity imaged as quintessentially female" (153–54). Although Kolodny does find that aggression toward the female and ambivalence result from the counterimpulse toward autonomy and independence, she does not find the darker forms of projected fear that are implicit in Griffin's work and evident in baseball's mythology. Evelyn Fox Keller (*Reflections on Gender and Science*) and Ruth Bleier (*Science and Gender: A Critique of Biology and Its Theories on Women*) both examine the ways in which the woman-nature metaphor has negatively influenced the progress of science, Western transactions with nature, and male-female relationships. Keller says that the natural sciences contain "the deeply rooted popular mythology that casts . . . mind as male, and . . . nature as female" (7).

13. That the identification is not archetypal in the Jungian sense suggests that even this most persistent and seemingly changeless of signifiers may yet be modified or abandoned. Annette Kolodny finds fault with this traditional notion of archetype as mental given: "The only fault I find with definitions of this sort is their tendency to imply that these symbol systems, by their very universality, are thereby totally fixed and unavailable to conscious attempts at alteration" (151). She does not, however, propose the sort of linguistic theory adopted in this study, a theory that permits evolution and might permit alteration – not, to be sure, by the consciousness operating to change the unconscious mind but by the slow process, spanning generations, of changing the language from which the unconscious builds its rhetoric.

Chapter 6: Going Back to the Motherland

1. Freud's claim in *Beyond the Pleasure Principle* that "all instincts tend toward a restoration of the earlier state of things," a return to infancy and, even further, to

the womb, presents the ambiguous impulse that moves toward connection and fusion with the mother and toward dependency, powerlessness, and even in the last extremity, annihilation.

2. David Black claims that *Ironweed* reveals a peculiarly Greek view of time, one in which one faces not the future but the past. He says that the Greeks "envisioned the future as being behind us – something unknowable, unseeable – and the past as lying in front of us, before our eyes. The present, to the Greeks, looked into the past. Only the past, not the future, could be known" (177). Thinking of this concept, one sees Michael Phelan walking backward into the train that constitutes his future.

Chapter 7: At Play on the Fields of the Gods

1. A few years ago, in response to a question about the difference between myth and religion, Joseph Campbell remarked, half seriously and half in jest, that the difference was one of point of view; that *religion* is a term we use for our own system of beliefs and *myth* is a word we reserve for the beliefs of others.

2. Paul Giles offers a useful survey of theories from the last two centuries that "attempt to subsume religion and mythology under a rationalist umbrella"; he comments, "It is one of the puzzles for rationalist historians, and one of the frustrations for rationalist philosophers, why 'reason' continues to exert such a slim and tenuous hold upon the general consciousness of mankind, and the perseverance of old religious attitudes is one explanation for this" (9, 13). This explanation is not really an explanation, of course, for it merely raises the further question of why the old attitudes persevere.

3. Looking as far as we can into the past, we find that religion is born as art. The astonishing paintings at Lascaux, dating to Paleolithic times, present a pictorial yet clearly sacred tale (Joseph Campbell, *Way of the Animal Powers* 58–66). The depictions reveal that religion is already centered on the theme of death and the artist-shaman's "craft" to render it harmless. Similarly, our oldest hero tale, *The Epic of Gilgamesh,* which predates Homer by some fifteen hundred years, focuses on death and the attempt to evade it. When we move into history, everywhere myths of origins place death (often of a divine or semidivine being) at the beginning of time, the first death applying once and for all – like the curse of mortality on Adam – and requiring our concerted mythic effort at damage control. In this sense religion and art have traveled together through much of human history, evolving along separate paths only in recent centuries. Yet even today both continue to erect defenses against death.

4. Other constrained or bound figures serve a similar function: Seth in the Egyptian tales of Osiris, Loki in the Norse myths, and even the Greek Prometheus. Prometheus ("forethought") belongs with "the fiend," Satan, Loki, and Seth not only because he is bound like them but because while he is ostensibly a friend of humankind, his efforts on humanity's behalf result not only in the gift of fire (imagination,

creativity, thought and forethought) but also in the sorrows to go along with human consciousness and its foreknowledge of death.

5. Carl Sagan discusses the evolution of the triune brain throughout his *The Dragons of Eden;* see especially pp. 54–57. See also Dudley Young (53–54).

6. Philip Lieberman offers evidence that language and its sentences, the briefest of narratives, in their remotest origins grew out of so-called separation or isolation cries of mammal infants (18–19). Seen in this light, myth – "speech" – is a naturally evolved form of crisis art.

7. In *Totem and Taboo,* a work recently receiving renewed attention, Freud argues that culture arose from an originary "crime" committed by a brother band against a "father," consisting of murder and followed by cannibalism. Dudley Young (102–23) develops a version of this theory in seeking the origins of the sacred.

8. In *The Eating of the Gods* Jan Kott provides an insightful analysis of this motif in Greek tragedy.

9. Campbell, for example, reminds us that Aztec "basketball" was a ritual in which the captain of the *winning* team was beheaded at the conclusion of the game (39).

10. Saint Paul's anguished meditation (Romans 7) reveals the nature of the divided self in almost paradigmatic purity. His "wretched man that I am! Who will deliver me from this body of death?" (Rom. 7:24) is the cry of one who has suffered the Nietzschean spiritual catastrophe.

11. Biblical prophets claim that their words are God's, not only divinely inspired but divinely compelled, as in the cases of Moses and Jeremiah. William James cites a similar experience of George Fox (16–17). Ezekiel's language, too, is God's language, written on a scroll that the prophet is required to eat (2:7–3:4). Jeremiah wishes not to deliver God's message but has no choice, for the word in his heart is "as a burning fire," and he cannot hold it in (20:9).

Chapter 9: Bernard Malamud's The Natural *in the Wasteland*

1. See also Baumbach, Mellard ("Four Version"), Richman (28–49), Helterman (23–36), and Rajagopalachari (37–53), for similar treatments.

2. Kristeva coined the term *intertextuality* in 1967 in her "Bakhtin, le mot, le dialogue et le roman," but interest in the phenomena of intertextuality is as old as literary criticism. In their introduction to *Intertextuality: Theories and Practices,* Michael Worton and Judith Still provide a history of intertextual concerns from Plato forward, a useful survey for anyone interested in the topic (1–44). Harold Bloom's *Anxiety of Influence* (1973) is perhaps the best known among works on intertextuality in a Freudian context, but for me J. Hillis Miller's "The Critic as Host" is one of the most cogent and applicable discussions of the subject. I discuss some of his key figures in the last section of this chapter.

3. Weston says, "Some years ago, when fresh from the study of . . . Frazer's epoch-making work, *The Golden Bough*, I was struck by the resemblance existing between certain features of the Grail story, and characteristic details of the Nature Cults described" (3). Eliot likewise acknowledges Frazer's influence, "To another work of anthropology I am indebted in general, one which has influenced our generation profoundly; I mean *The Golden Bough*" (50).

4. Wasserman claims that "to the twentieth century the Grail story is the archetypal fertility myth" (440).

5. Frazer finds the literary remnant of this tradition in book 6 of Virgil's *Aeneid,* in which Aeneas is required to secure the golden bough as a passport into the underworld.

6. The foregoing material is a highly condensed summary of Frazer's analysis, focusing especially on material pertinent to a reading of *The Natural*.

7. In the Old Testament, for example, Naomi names her sons Mahlon and Chilion, names meaning "sickness" and "wasting." Both sons die young (Ruth 1). Jacob ("he supplants") becomes a supplanter of his older brother Esau, fulfilling the demands of his name.

8. A usual reading of Wonderboy is as "phallic instrument" (see Wasserman 441), but I suggest that although this meaning is present, the bat is also other and more than that; it is the golden bough and external soul.

9. Wasserman sees this confrontation as being like the one between Percival and the Red Knight for the "hero's office" (442).

10. Wasserman finds an identity of the three as "the same fertility hero, displacing each other with each new seasonal resurgence and decline of potency" (443).

11. Wasserman analyzes the women, Iris Lemon and Memo Paris, in Jungian terms, as good and bad mother, one who frees the son and one who prevents his progress.

12. Many critics find that Harriet is the sinister witch, Morgan le Fay, as do Wasserman (442) and Lidston (77), among others.

13. Both Pifer (139–40) and Helterman (23–24) notice this meaning without connecting it to the tarot card.

14. Miller's metaphor of the host cell and the virus brings his theory of intertextuality close to the related notion of archetype as Eric Gould redefines it. The archetype, like Miller's "metaphysics," is passed "from generation to generation in . . . languages and in the privileged texts of those languages."

Chapter 10: Playing God, Playing Man

1. See, for example, discussions by Scholes, Shelton, Gonzalez, Caldwell, and especially, McCaffery.

2. Bishop Ussher calculated in 1654 the exact time and date of the creation as nine o'clock in the morning on Tuesday, October 23, 4004 B.C.

3. Under Milton's influence, however filtered through the culture, many of my students are surprised to find in the first three chapters of Genesis no Satan, no apple, and no sinister, seductive Eve.

4. Coover, acknowledging the influence of Huizinga, has in *The UBA* anticipated recent theories of aesthetics generally and of literature specifically in their emphasis on the creative role of play. Caldwell notices the parallel of two "games" – literature and baseball – and the emphasis on play in recent theories of literature (161–62). Huizinga's formulation is broadly stated, however, and so is Coover's. Play gives rise to *all* aspects of culture, including religion, history, science, and philosophy, as well as art.

5. Coover himself has stressed the element of realism in his fiction: "Maybe I think that all my fiction is realistic and that so far it has simply been misunderstood as otherwise. There are paradoxes, of course. Though the varying perspectives may at times seem to disturb the 'realism' of the book, the overview that embraces them all I think is wholly realistic – and yet this overview includes the book's design, and that design is born of, well, something else. That vibrant space between the poles of a paradox: That's where all the exciting art happens, I think" (in LeClair and McCaffery 67).

6. This account and the following quotations are taken from Gen. 1:1–2:3.

Chapter 11: *Fathers and Sons, Blessings, and Baseball's Myth of Atonement*

1. For an exposition of these matters, see Peter Blos (1–55).

2. The cats in these two episodes are enigmas. One is tempted to see Roy Hobbs's black tomcat drowned in the bathwater as emblematic of the child himself, his father, or both, a sort of embodied masculinity that is slaughtered by the mother and lies dead, "all glossy wet, with its pink tongue caught between its teeth" (Malamud, *The Natural* 201). Gideon Clarke's cat is a beloved animal, a repository of filial love deflected away from herself by the indifferent mother. The effect of her taking the cat when she leaves is to deny Gideon of any sort of maternal love object.

3. Roth has said of *The Great American Novel* that its satire is "directed, however playfully, at aspects of American popular mythology" (in Searles 63–64).

Chapter 12: *"Every Inch a Man"*

1. Cirlot says that the dwarf "is the personification of those forces which remain virtually outside the orbit of consciousness" and a being "with certain childish characteristics befitting its small size" (91). In the Lancanian symbols (those referring to the body, kinship relations, birth, life, and death) the dwarf is clearly an image of the

child's body, and hence of the largely unconscious preoccupations and limitations of the period of childhood and their residue carried into adulthood.

2. Bruno Bettelheim, analyzing the dwarfs in the story of Snow White, points out that "dwarfs are eminently male, but males who are stunted in their development," and that "these 'little men' . . . suggest phallic connotations" indicative of a "preoedipal existence." The author notices the paradox of identifying "a figure that symbolizes a phallic existence as also representing childhood before puberty, a period during which all forms of sexuality are relatively dormant." But, he says, the dwarfs, being free of inner conflicts, "have no desire to move beyond their phallic existence to intimate relations," being satisfied with a changeless, nonevolutionary existence: "This lack of change or of any desire for it is what makes their existence parallel that of the prepubertal child" (210).

Chapter 13: Baseball, Bricolage, and the Beautiful

1. Speaking, for example, of Joseph Smith, Bloom observes that he "did not excel as a writer or as a theologian, let alone as psychologist and philosopher. But he was an authentic religious genius and surpassed all Americans, before or since, in the possession and expression of what could be called the religion-making imagination" (*American Religion* 96–97).

2. So insignificant is LaVerne Rose, Pete Rose's mother, in the story of his life that there are only three brief references to her in Reston's book, and in the Pete Rose–Roger Kahn biography there are nine. One of them recounts an occasion when she called her son for tickets to a Reds game, and he forgot to return her call (Reston 44–45). When Pete Rose hears that his father is dead, his disbelieving response is "You must mean my mother" (44). Reston may have been inspired to include the material on Ty Cobb's relationship with his father and mother by reading the Rose-Kahn account, for all the "facts" are there too, although it is by no means clear that they *mean* the same thing in the two biographies. In the Rose-Kahn account, however, one point is clear: Pete Rose sees a likeness between himself and Ty Cobb in that, as he says, "we both thought the world of our fathers" (27). Both Rose biographies include the story of Mrs. Cobb's shooting of her husband and her affair. In both instances the story seems, if superfluous at a literal level, absolutely necessary at a figurative level, its presence poetic rather than noetic.

3. An interesting comparison might be made between Eliot Asinof's historical treatment of Buck Weaver, one of the Black Sox, in his *Eight Men Out* and Harry Stein's imaginative treatment of the same figure in *Hoopla*.

4. Barthes notices that even the notion of "facts" has been called into question, and he cites Nietzsche as having written that "there are no facts *as such*. We must always begin by introducing a meaning in order for there to be a fact" ("Discourse of History" 138).

5. This theme of the one man who stands alone on the side of the truth of base-ball's record is repeated in Kinsella's *Iowa Baseball Confederacy*. Here the task of Matthew Clarke (and later of his son, Gideon) is likewise to restore the record, to insist that it include an account of a lost league (the Iowa Baseball Confederacy) and of a lost game, all evidence of which, as in Roth's novel, has been erased from human memory.

6. The idea is apparent throughout Gould's writings. For example, in both *The Mismeasure of Man* and "Agassiz in the Galápagos" Gould points out that in the scientific endeavor the scientist's own blindnesses and biases are often projected onto "nature," which then reflects in its "facts" the scientist's own meanings.

7. I have called Gould a "true mythmaker," by which phrase I intend high praise. An avid reader of Gould's books and essays, as I was thinking about bricolage and aesthetics, I found myself recalling the passage in *Time's Arrow, Time's Cycle* where Gould describes James Hampton's *Throne of the Third Heaven of the Nations' Millennium General Assembly*. When I went back to Gould's passage, I understood why it had come to mind in this context, for in its account of Hampton's inspiration and method of sculpture (180–85), Gould's text contains perhaps the best description of the work of the *bricoleur* to be found anywhere. Furthermore, Gould's book itself, he says, "is cobbled together from bits and pieces of time's arrow, quirky and unpredictable moments of my own contingent history" (vii). Gould does not use the word *bricolage* to describe either Hampton's or his own craft, but the concept is surely there.

WORKS CITED

Adkins, Arthur W. H. "Myth, Philosophy, and Religion." In *Myth and Philosophy*, ed. Frank S. Reynolds and David Tracy, 95–130. New York: State University of New York Press, 1990.

Angell, Roger. *The Summer Game*. New York: Penguin, 1990.

Asinof, Eliot. *Eight Men Out: The Black Sox and the 1919 World Series*. Owl Book Edition. New York: Henry Holt, 1987.

Bakhtin, M. M. *The Dialogic Imagination: Four Essays*. Ed. Michael Holquist. Trans. Caryl Emerson and Michael Holquist. Austin: University of Texas Press, 1981.

Barthes, Roland. "The Discourse of History." *The Rustle of Language*, trans. Richard Howard, 127–40. New York: Hill and Wang, 1986.

———. "Mythology Today." *The Rustle of Language*, trans. Richard Howard, 65–68. New York: Hill and Wang, 1986.

———. "Myth Today." In *A Barthes Reader*, ed. and intro. Susan Sontag, 93–148. New York: Hill and Wang, 1982.

Baumbach, Jonathan. "The Economy of Love." In *Modern Critical Views: Bernard Malamud*, ed. Harold Bloom, 21–36. New York: Chelsea House, 1986.

Baym, Nina. "Melodramas of Beset Manhood." In *The New Feminist Criticism: Essays on Women, Literature, and Theory*, ed. Elaine Showalter, 63–80. New York: Pantheon, 1985.

Bettelheim, Bruno. *The Uses of Enchantment: The Meaning and Importance of Fairy Tales*. New York: Knopf, 1976.

Black, David. "The Fusion of Past and Present in William Kennedy's *Ironweed*." *Critique* 27, no. 3 (Spring 1986): 177–84.

Blake, William. "Jerusalem." In *Complete Writings*, ed. Geoffrey Keynes. New York: Oxford University Press, 1966.

Blanchot, Maurice. *The Sirens' Song: Selected Essays*. Ed. and intro. Gabriel Josipovici. Trans. Sacha Rabinovitch. Bloomington: Indiana University Press, 1982.

Bleier, Ruth. *Science and Gender: A Critique of Biology and Its Theories on Women*. New York: Pergamon, 1984.

Bloom, Harold. *The American Religion: The Emergence of the Post-Christian Nation*. New York: Simon and Schuster, 1992.

———, ed. *Modern Critical Views: Bernard Malamud*. New York: Chelsea House, 1986.

Blos, Peter. *Son and Father: Before and beyond the Oedipus Complex*. New York: Free Press, 1985.

Boehme, Jacob. *Works*. Trans. William Law. London: Everyman, 1926.

Boswell, Thomas. *Why Time Begins on Opening Day*. New York: Penguin, 1984.

Brown, Bill. "Waging Baseball, Playing War: Games of American Imperialism." *Cultural Critique* 0882-4371 (Winter 1990-91): 51-78.

Burke, Kenneth. *The Rhetoric of Religion: Studies in Logology*. Berkeley: University of California Press.

Caldwell, Roy C., Jr. "Of Hobby-Horses, Baseball, and Narrative: Coover's *Universal Baseball Association*." *Modern Fiction Studies* 33, no. 1 (Spring 1987): 161-71.

Campbell, Joseph. *The Hero with a Thousand Faces*. 2d ed. Bollinqen Series 17. Princeton: Princeton University Press, 1968.

———. *The Inner Reaches of Outer Space: Metaphor as Myth and as Religion*. New York: Van Der Marck, 1986.

———. *The Masks of God: Creative Mythology*. New York: Viking, 1970.

———. *The Masks of God: Primitive Mythology*. New York: Viking, 1970.

———. *The Way of the Animal Powers*. Vol. 1 of *Historical Atlas of World Mythology*. London: Summerfield, 1983.

———. *The Way of the Seeded Earth*, pt. 1, *The Sacrifice*. Vol. 2 of *Historical Atlas of World Mythology*. New York: Harper & Row, 1988.

Campbell, Joseph, and Richard Roberts. *Tarot Revelations*. 3d ed. San Anselmo, Calif.: Vernal Equinox, 1987.

Cavendish, Richard. *King Arthur & The Grail: The Arthurian Legends and Their Meaning*. London: Weidenfeld and Nicholson, 1978.

———, ed. *Man, Myth & Magic: The Illustrated Encyclopedia of Mythology, Religion and the Unknown*. 11 vols. Freeport, N.Y.: Marshall Cavendish, 1983.

———. *The Tarot*. New York: Harper & Row, 1975.

Chapin, Henry B. *Sports in Literature*. New York: David McKay, 1976.

Charyn, Jerome. *The Seventh Babe*. New York: Arbor House, 1979.

Cirlot, J. E. *A Dictionary of Symbols*. 2d ed. Trans. Jack Sage. New York: Philosophical Library, 1971.

Clark, R. T. Rundle. *Myth and Symbol in Ancient Egypt*. London: Thames and Hudson, 1978.

Clarke, Peter P. "Classical Myth in William Kennedy's *Ironweed*." *Critique* 27, no. 3 (Spring 1986): 167-76.

Cooney, Ellen. *All the Way Home*. New York: Putnam's, 1984.

Cooper, J. C. *An Illustrated Encyclopaedia of Traditional Symbols*. London: Thames and Hudson, 1978.

Coover, Robert. *The Universal Baseball Association, Inc., J. Henry Waugh, Prop.* New York: Random House, 1968.

Crossley-Holland, Kevin, trans. *The Norse Myths*. Intro. Crossley-Holland. New York: Pantheon, 1980.

Culler, Jonathan. *Structuralist Poetics: Structuralism, Linguistics, and the Study of Literature*. Ithaca, N.Y.: Cornell University Press, 1975.

Davis, Robert Con. "Introduction: Lacan and Narrativity." *Lacan and Narration:*

The Psychoanalytic Difference in Narrative Theory, 848–59. Baltimore: John
Hopkins, 1983.

——, ed. *Lacan and Narration: The Psychoanalytic Difference in Narrative
Theory.* Baltimore: John Hopkins, 1983.

De Man, Paul. "The Epistemology of Metaphor." In Sheldon Sacks, *On
Metaphor,* 11–28. Chicago: University of Chicago Press, 1978.

Derrida, Jacques. "Structure, Sign and Play in the Discourse of the Human
Sciences." In *Critical Theory since 1965,* ed. Hazard Adams and Leroy Searle,
83–94. Tallahassee: University Presses of Florida/Florida State University
Press, 1986.

Doctorow, E. L. *Ragtime.* New York: Random House, 1974.

Dolar, Mladen. "'I Shall Be with You on Your Wedding-Night': Lacan and the
Uncanny." *October* 58 (Fall 1991): 5–23.

Doty, William G. *Mythography.* University: University of Alabama Press, 1986.

Duncan, David James. *The Brothers K.* New York: Doubleday, 1992.

Eisinger, Chester E. "Robert (Lowell) Coover." In *Contemporary Novelists,* 3d
ed., ed. James Vinson, 155–56. New York: St. Martin's, 1982.

Eliade, Mircea. *Myth and Reality.* Trans. Willard R. Trask. New York: Harper &
Row, 1968.

Eliot, T. S. *The Complete Poems and Plays, 1909–1950.* New York: Harcourt,
Brace & World, 1952.

Eribon, Didier. *Conversations with Claude Lévi-Strauss.* Trans. Paula Wissing.
Chicago: University of Chicago Press, 1991.

Falck, Colin. *Myth, Truth and Literature: Towards a True Post-Modernism.*
Cambridge: Cambridge University Press, 1989.

Feldman, Burton, and Robert D. Richardson. *The Rise of Modern Mythology,
1680–1860.* Bloomington: Indiana University Press, 1972.

Felman, Shoshana. "Beyond Oedipus: The Specimen Story of Psychoanalysis."
In *Lacan and Narration: The Psychoanalytic Difference in Narrative Theory,*
ed. Robert Con Davis, 1021–53. Baltimore: John Hopkins University Press,
1983.

Frazer, James. *The New Golden Bough.* Abr., rev., and ed. Theodor H. Gaster.
New York: Criterion, 1959.

Freud, Sigmund. *Totem and Taboo.* Trans. James Strachey. New York: Norton, 1950.

Frye, Northrop. *Creation and Recreation.* Toronto: University of Toronto Press,
1980.

——. *The Great Code: The Bible and Literature.* New York: Harcourt Brace
Jovanovich, 1982.

——. *Myth and Metaphor: Selected Essays 1974–1988.* Ed. Robert D. Denham.
Charlottesville: University Press of Virginia, 1990.

——. *The Secular Scripture: A Study of the Structure of Romance.* Cambridge,
Mass.: Harvard University Press, 1976.

Gado, Frank, ed. *First Person: Conversations on Writers & Writing.* Schenectady, N.Y.: Union College Press, 1973.

Genette, Gérard. *Figures of Literary Discourse.* Trans. Alan Sheridan. New York: Columbia University Press, 1982.

Gerhart, Mary, and Allan Russell. *Metaphoric Process: The Creation of Scientific and Religious Understanding.* Fort Worth: Texas Christian University Press, 1984.

Giamatti, A. Bartlett. *Take Time for Paradise: Americans and their Games.* New York: Summit, 1989.

Giles, Paul. *American Catholic Arts and Fictions: Culture, Ideology, Aesthetics.* New York: Cambridge University Press, 1992.

Gonzalez, Ann. "Robert Coover's *The UBA:* Baseball as Metafiction." *The International Fiction Review* 11, no. 2 (1984): 106–9.

Goodman, Nelson. "Languages of Art." In *Philosophical Perspectives on Metaphor,* ed. Mark Johnson, 123–35. Minneapolis: University of Minnesota Press, 1981.

Gordon, Peter H., Sydney Waller, and Paul Weinman, eds. *Diamonds Are Forever: Artists and Writers on Baseball.* San Francisco: Chronicle, 1987.

Gould, Eric. *Mythical Intentions in Modern Literature.* Princeton: Princeton University Press, 1981.

Gould, Stephen Jay. "The Creation Myths of Cooperstown." In *Writing Baseball,* ed. Jerry Klinkowitz, 23–34. Urbana: University of Illinois Press, 1991. Repr., Stephen Jay Gould, *Bully for Brontosaurus: Reflections in Natural History,* 42–58. New York: Norton, 1991.

——. *The Mismeasure of Man.* New York: Norton, 1983.

——. "The Streak of Streaks." *The New York Review,* Aug. 18, 1988, 8–12. Repr. in Stephen Jay Gould, *Bully for Brontosaurus: Reflections in Natural History,* 463–72. New York: Norton, 1991.

——. *Time's Arrow, Time's Cycle: Myth and Metaphor in the Discovery of Geological Time.* Cambridge, Mass.: Harvard University Press, 1987.

Greenberg, Eric Rolfe. *The Celebrant.* New York: Everest House, 1983.

Gregorich, Barbara. *She's on First.* Chicago: Contemporary, 1987.

Griffin, Susan. *Pornography and Silence: Culture's Revenge against Nature.* New York: Harper & Row, 1981.

——. *Woman and Nature: The Roaring inside Her.* New York: Harper & Row, Inc., 1978.

Hall, Donald. *Fathers Playing Catch with Sons.* San Francisco: North Point, 1985.

Hans, James S. *The Play of the World.* Amherst: University of Massachusetts Press, 1981.

Harris, Mark. *Bang the Drum Slowly.* New York: Dell, 1956.

——. *The Southpaw.* Indianapolis: Bobbs-Merrill, 1953.

Hatab, Lawrence J. *Myth and Philosophy: A Contest of Truths.* LaSalle, Ill.: Open Court, 1990.

Hawking, Stephen W. *A Brief History of Time*. Toronto: Bantam, 1988.

Heidegger, Martin. *Poetry, Language, Thought*. Trans. and intro. Albert Hofstadter. New York: Harper & Row, 1971.

Helterman, Jeffrey. *Understanding Bernard Malamud*. Columbia: University of South Carolina Press, 1985.

Hesiod. *The Works and Days*. Trans. Richmond Lattimore. Ann Arbor: University of Michigan Press, 1959.

Hexter, J. H. *Doing History*. Bloomington: Indiana University Press, 1971.

Higgs, Robert J. "The Agonic and the Edenic: Sport Literature and the Theory of Play." In *The Achievement of American Sport Literature: A Critical Appraisal*, ed. Wiley Lee Umphlett, 143–57. Rutherford, N.J.: Fairleigh Dickinson University Press; London: Associated University Presses, 1991.

Homer. *The Odyssey*. Trans. Robert Fitzgerald. Garden City: Anchor, 1963.

Huizinga, J. *Homo Ludens: A Study of the Play Element in Culture*. Boston: Beacon, 1955.

Hulme, T. E. "Romanticism and Classicism." In *Critical Theory since Plato*, ed. Hazard Adams, 767–74. New York: Harcourt Brace Jovanovich, 1971.

James, William. *Writings 1902–1910*. New York: Library of America, 1987.

Jameson, Fredric. *The Prison-House of Language: A Critical Account of Structuralism and Russian Formalism*. Princeton: Princeton University Press, 1972.

Jewett, Robert, and John Shelton Lawrence. *The American Monomyth*. 2d ed. Lanham, Md.: University Press of America, 1988.

Johnson, Don, ed. *Hummers, Knucklers, and Slow Curves: Contemporary Baseball Poems*. Urbana: University of Illinois Press, 1991.

Joyce, James. *A Portrait of the Artist as a Young Man*. New York: Viking, 1964.

Kearney, Richard. "Between Tradition and Utopia: The Hermeneutical Problem of Myth." In *On Paul Ricoeur: Narrative and Interpretation*, ed. and intro. David Wood, 55–73. London and New York: Routledge, 1991.

Keller, Evelyn Fox. *Reflections on Gender and Science*. New Haven, Conn.: Yale University Press, 1985.

Kennedy, William. *Ironweed*. New York: Viking, 1983.

Kinsella, W. P. *The Iowa Baseball Confederacy*. Boston: Houghton-Mifflin, 1986.

———. *Shoeless Joe*. Boston: Houghton-Mifflin, 1982.

———. *The Thrill of the Grass*. New York: Penguin, 1984.

Klinkowitz, Jerry. "Introduction." In *Writing Baseball*, ed. Klinkowitz, 1–20. Urbana: University of Illinois Press, 1991.

———, ed. *Writing Baseball*. Urbana: University of Illinois Press, 1991.

Kolodny, Annette. *The Lay of the Land: Metaphor as Experience and History in American Life and Letters*. Chapel Hill: University of North Carolina Press, 1975.

Kort, Wesley A. *Story, Text and Scripture: Literary Interests in Biblical Narrative*. University Park: Pennsylvania State University Press, 1988.

Kott, Jan. *The Eating of the Gods: An Interpretation of Greek Tragedy.* Trans. Boleslaw Taborski and Edward J. Czerwinski. New York: Vintage, 1974.

Kramer, Samuel Noah. *Sumerian Mythology: A Study of Spiritual and Literary Achievement in the Third Millennium B.C.* Rev. ed. Philadelphia: University of Pennsylvania Press, 1972.

Kristeva, Julia. "Bakhtin, le mot, le dialogue et le roman." *Critique* 23 (1967): 438–65.

Lacan, Jacques. *Écrits: A Selection.* Trans. Alan Sheridan. New York: Norton, 1977.

———. *The Four Fundamental Concepts of Psycho-Analysis.* Ed. Jacques-Alain Miller. Trans. Alan Sheridan. New York: Norton, 1978.

Lagerkvist, Pär. *The Dwarf.* Trans. Alexandra Dick. New York: Hill and Wang, 1945.

Lakoff, George, and Mark Turner. *More than Cool Reason: A Field Guide to Poetic Metaphor.* Chicago: University of Chicago Press, 1989.

Lasher, Lawrence M. *Conversations with Bernard Malamud.* Jackson: University Press of Mississippi, 1991.

LeClair, Tom, and Larry McCaffery. *Anything Can Happen: Interviews with Contemporary American Novelists.* Urbana: University of Illinois Press, 1983.

Lévi-Strauss, Claude. *The Raw and the Cooked.* Trans. John Weightman and Doreen Weightman. New York: Harper and Row, 1969.

———. *The Savage Mind.* Trans. George Weidenfeld and Nicolson, Ltd. Chicago: University of Chicago Press, 1966.

———. "The Structural Study of Myth." In *Myth, A Symposium,* ed. Thomas A. Sebeok, 81–106. Philadelphia: American Folklore Society, 1955.

———. *Tristes Tropiques.* Trans. John Weightman and Doreen Weightman. New York: Atheneum, 1974.

———. "When Myth Becomes History." *Myth and Meaning.* New York: Schocken, 1979.

Lidston, Robert C. "Malamud's *The Natural:* An Arthurian Quest in the Big Leagues." *West Virginia University Philological Papers* 27 (1981): 75–81.

Lieberman, James E. "Why Oedipus Loved His Father." *Harvard Mental Health Letter* 7, no. 12 (1991): 4–6.

Lieberman, Philip. *Uniquely Human: The Evolution of Speech, Thought and Selfless Behavior.* Cambridge, Mass.: Harvard University Press, 1991.

Loomis, Roger Sherman. *The Grail: From Celtic Myth to Christian Symbol.* Princeton: Princeton University Press, 1991.

Malamud, Bernard. *The Natural.* New York: Farrar, Straus & Giroux, 1952.

———. "Reflections of a Writer: Long Work, Short Life." *The New York Times Book Review,* March 20, 1988, 15–18.

Manganaro, Marc. "Introduction." In *Modernist Anthropology: From Fieldwork to Text,* 3–47. Princeton, N.J.: Princeton University Press, 1990.

McCaffery, Larry. *The Metafictional Muse: The Works of Robert Coover, Donald Barthelme, and William H. Gass.* Pittsburgh: University of Pittsburgh Press, 1982.

Mellard, James M. "Four Versions of the Pastoral." In *Modern Critical Views: Bernard Malamud,* ed. Harold Bloom, 101–12. New York: Chelsea House, 1986.

———. *Using Lacan, Reading Fiction.* Urbana: University of Illinois Press, 1991.

Messenger, Christian K. "Expansion Draft." In *The Achievement of American Sport Literature: A Critical Appraisal,* ed. Wiley Lee Umphlett, 62–79. Rutherford, N.J.: Fairleigh Dickinson University Press; London: Associated University Press, 1991.

———. *Sport and the Spirit of Play in Contemporary American Fiction.* New York: Columbia University Press, 1990.

Miller, J. Hillis. "The Critic as Host." *Theory Now and Then,* 143–70. Durham, N.C.: Duke University Press, 1991.

Milton, John. *Paradise Lost* and *Paradise Regained.* Ed. Christopher Ricks. New York: New English Library, 1968.

Neugeboren, Jay. *Sam's Legacy.* New York: Holt, Rinehart and Winston, 1973.

Nietzsche, Friedrich. *The Birth of Tragedy and the Genealogy of Morals.* Trans. Francis Golffing. Garden City, N.Y.: Doubleday, 1956.

Paglia, Camille. *Sexual Personae: Art and Decadence from Nefertiti to Emily Dickinson.* New Haven, Conn.: Yale University Press, 1990.

Pifer, Ellen. "Malamud's Unnatural *The Natural.*" *Studies in American Jewish Literature* 7, no. 2 (1988): 138–52.

Plimpton, George. *The Curious Case of Sidd Finch.* New York: Macmillan, 1987.

Ragland-Sullivan, Ellie. "The Magnetism between Reader and Text: Prolegomena to a Lancanian Poetics." *Poetics* 13 (1984): 381–406.

Rajagopalachari, M. *Theme of Compassion in the Novels of Bernard Malamud.* New Delhi: Prestige, 1988.

Reston, James, Jr. *Collision at Home Plate: The Lives of Pete Rose and Bart Giamatti.* New York: Edward Burlingame, 1991.

Reynolds, Frank S., and David Tracy. *Myth and Philosophy.* New York: State University of New York Press, 1990.

Richman, Sidney. *Bernard Malamud.* New York: Twayne, 1966.

Ricoeur, Paul. "Life in Quest of Narrative." In *On Paul Ricoeur: Narrative and Interpretation,* ed. and intro. David Wood, 20–33. New York: Routledge, 1991.

———. *The Rule of Metaphor: Multi-disciplinary Studies of the Creation of Meaning in Language.* Trans. Robert Czerny with Kathleen McLaughlin and John Costello, S.J. Toronto: Univerity of Toronto Press, 1977.

Rose, H. J. *A Handbook of Classical Mythology.* 6th ed. London: Methuen, 1958.

Rose, Peter I., and Roger Kahn. *Pete Rose: My Story.* New York: Macmillan, 1989.

Roth, Philip. *The Great American Novel.* New York: Holt, Rinehart and Winston, 1973.

Sacks, Sheldon. *On Metaphor.* Chicago: University of Chicago Press, 1978.

Sagan, Carl. *The Dragons of Eden: Speculations on the Evolution of Human Intelligence.* New York: Random House, 1977.

Sayles, John. *Pride of the Bimbos.* New York: Little, Brown, 1975.

Schiller, Friedrich von. *Letters on the Aesthetic Education of Man.* In *Critical Theory since Plato,* ed. Hazard Adams, 418–31. New York: Harcourt Brace Jovanovich, 1971.

Scholes, Robert. "Metafiction." *Iowa Review* 1 (Fall 1970): 100–115.

Searles, George J. *Conversations with Philip Roth.* Jackson: University Press of Mississippi, 1992.

Seidel, Michael. *Streak: Joe Dimaggio and the Summer of '41.* New York: McGraw-Hill, 1988.

Shapiro, Karl. *Selected Poems.* New York: Random House, 1951.

Shatzkin, Mike, ed. *The Ballplayers.* New York: William Morrow, 1990.

Shelton, Frank. "Humor and Balance in Coover's *The Universal Baseball Association, Inc.*" *Critique* 17, no. 1 (1975): 78–90.

Small, David. *Almost Famous.* New York: Norton, 1982.

Sophocles. *King Oedipus: The Theban Plays.* Trans. E. F. Watling. In *The Idea of Tragedy,* ed. Carl Benson and Taylor Littleton. Glenview, Ill.: Scott, Foresman, 1966.

Stein, Harry. *Hoopla.* New York: Knopf, 1983.

Stevens, Wallace. *The Collected Poems.* New York: Vintage, 1982.

Taylor, Mark C. [William R. Kenan Jr.]. *Tears.* Albany: State University of New York Press, 1990.

Thompson, William Irwin. *The Time Falling Bodies Take to Light: Mythology, Sexuality, and the Origins of Culture.* New York: St. Martin's, 1981.

Thurber, James. "You Could Look It Up." *Saturday Evening Post,* April 5, 1941. Rprt. in *Short Story Masterpieces,* ed. Robert Penn Warren and Albert Erskine, 508–24. New York: Dell, 1954.

Todorov, Tzvetan. *Literature and Its Theorists: A Personal View of Twentieth-Century Criticism.* Trans. Catherine Porter. London: Routledge and Kegan Paul, 1988.

Tracy, David. *Blessed Rage for Order: The New Pluralism in Theology.* New York: Seabury, 1975.

Tucker, Tommy Neil. "The Perfect Garden." *Sports Illustrated,* July 6, 1981, 48–62.

Turbayne, Colin Murray. *The Myth of Metaphor.* Rev. ed. Columbia: University of South Carolina Press, 1970.

Virgil. *The Aeneid.* Trans. Allen Mandelbaum. New York: Bantam, 1980.

Vogan, Sara. *In Shelly's Leg.* Saint Paul: Graywolf, 1985.

Walden, Daniel. "Bernard Malamud, An American Jewish Writer and His Universal Heroes." *Studies in American Jewish Litrerature* 7, no. 2 (1988): 153–61.

Wallop, Douglass. *The Year the Yankees Lost the Pennant.* New York: Norton, 1954.

Wasserman, Earl R. "*The Natural:* Malamud's World Ceres." *The Centennial Review* 9 (1965): 438–60.

Weston, Jessie L. *From Ritual to Romance.* Garden City, N.Y.: Doubleday/Anchor, 1957.

White, Hayden. *The Content of the Form: Narrative Discourse and Historical Representation.* Baltimore: John Hopkins University Press, 1987.

———. "The Metaphysics of Narrativity: Time and Symbol in Ricoeur's Philosophy of History." In *On Paul Ricoeur: Narrative and Interpretation,* ed. and intro. David Wood, 140–59. London: Routledge, 1991.

———. *Tropics of Discourse: Essays in Cultural Criticism.* Baltimore: John Hopkins University Press, 1978.

Will, George F. *Men at Work: The Craft of Baseball.* New York: Macmillan, 1990.

Willard, Nancy. *Things Invisible to See.* New York: Knopf, 1985.

Wilson, August. *Fences. Three Plays by August Wilson.* Pittsburgh: University of Pittsburgh Press, 1991.

Wood, David, ed. *On Paul Ricoeur: Narrative and Interpretation.* Intro. Wood. New York: Routledge, 1991.

Woolfe, Virginia. *The Waves.* New York: Harcourt, Brace and World, 1931. Rprt. in *Jacob's Room* and *The Waves.* Harcourt, Brace and World, 1959.

Worton, Michael, and Judith Still, eds. *Intertextuality: Theories and Practices.* Manchester, Britain: Manchester University Press, 1990.

Young, Dudley. *Origins of the Sacred: The Ecstasies of Love and War.* New York: St. Martin's, 1991.

Zavarzadeh, Mas'ud. *The Mythopoeic Reality.* Urbana: University of Illinois Press, 1976.

INDEX

Adkins, Arthur W. H., 313*n4*

All the Way Home (Cooney), 72, 73–74, 117

Almost Famous (Small), 13, 120, 121–22, 247, 249, 250–51, 254, 255, 256–58, 260, 263–64, 265, 294, 306, 310

Angell, Roger, 100, 105, 106

Archetype: as signified become signifier, 8–9, 12, 25, 28, 36, 40, 50, 182, 321*n13;* analogous to Lacanian symbols, 32; and intertextuality, 40; plots as, 40, 49, 64, 245; and the sacred, 47–52; traditional definition of, 48, 182, 318*n24;* as bricolage, 50–51, 181; garden as, 98; feminine nature as, 119; Satan as, 152–67; and metacreation, 223–24; analogous to "metaphysics," 324*n14;* mentioned, 34, 244–45

Art: postmodern, 50; ball field as space of, 77–78, 287. *See also* Crisis art

Arthurian legend: in *The Natural,* 182, 184, 185, 186, 188, 189, 190–92, 203, 205, 212, 217, 324*n4*

Asinof, Eliot, 326*n3*

Augustine, St., 96

Babel, Tower of: as myth of myth, 3–5, 52–53, 303, 311–12; Lacan on, 51–52; and French and American structuralism, 64; in Malamud's *The Natural,* 181; as world of texts, 223; mentioned, 11, 17, 24–25, 35, 43, 44, 208, 218. *See also* Gap, myth of the; Tarot symbolism

Bakhtin, M. M.: on authoritative text and myth of engineer, 314–16*n9;* contrasted with Lacan, 316–17*n15,* 317*n19*

Bang the Drum Slowly (Harris), 12, 19, 80, 81, 103, 161, 294, 295, 298; double plot, 81–92; author-protagonist as *bricoleur,* 82, 91, 92, 294; Henry Wiggen as classic hero, 82, 85, 88, 89, 92; Bruce Pearson as American hero, 82–83; role of language in, 85–86

Barney, William D., 254

Barthes, Roland: on myth and meaning, 1; as mythophobe, 7, 313*n6;* on myth and history, 300–301, 305, 326*n4;* on semiology as mythology, 314*n1;* and structuralism, 314*n2;* mentioned, 314*n9*

Bases, running: and quest, 66–67. *See also* Monomyth

Bat: as phallic instrument, 36, 57–58, 60, 122, 195, 307–8, 324*n8;* as weapon, 36–37, 57, 60, 109–11, 122; energy of, 122; as golden bough, 194–95

Baumbach, Jonathan, 192, 196, 215, 323*n1*

Baym, Nina, 115, 116

Beautiful, the. *See* Myth, and the beautiful

Beginning. *See* Time

Bettelheim, Bruno, 325*n2*

Bible: Genesis, 3–4, 98, 114, 225, 226–27, 228, 232–35, 244, 262–63, 324*n7,* 325*n6;* Revelation, 113, 188, 225; Song of Solomon, 115; Psalms, 117, 180, 235; Corinthians, 160; Acts, 165; John, 167, 244; Matthew, 179; Job, 231; Mark, 244; Romans, 323*n10;* Ezekiel, 323*n11;* Jeremiah, 323*n11;* Ruth, 324*n7. See also* Babel, Tower of; Eden, Garden of

Black, David, 322*n2*

Blake, William, 222–23

Blanchot, Maurice: on the depths of

language, 41–42, 293; on the modern sacred, 43, 47, 188
Blessing. *See* Father
Blier, Ruth, 321*n12*
Bloom, Harold: on religious criticism, 288–89; on the religious and the poetic, 292, 293, 301, 326*n1;* mentioned, 42, 322*n2*
Blos, Peter: on the father's blessing, 246, 325*n1*
Boas, Franz, 5
Boehme, Jacob, 228–29, 230
Boswell, Thomas, 93, 97, 109–10, 122
Bricolage: mythological thought as, 5; and intertextuality, 40, 181, 184, 187, 214, 220; Lévi-Strauss on, 50–52; and the sacred, 50–51; baseball as, 53, 287; baseball history as, 287; and the rhetorical mode, 310; mentioned, 12, 24, 36, 150
Bricoleur: defined, 5; Lévi-Strauss, Derrida as, 23–25, 50, 286, 287, 290–91, 312, 318–19*n1;* as intertextual artist, 40, 310; Tower of Babel as work by master, 52–53
Brothers K, The (Duncan), 13, 247, 255–56, 259–60, 263, 265
Brown, Bill, 110–11
Burke, Kenneth, 317*n21*

Caldwell, Roy C., Jr., 226, 324*n1,* 325*n4*
Campbell, Joseph: on monomyth, 65, 69; on sacrifice, 87, 159–60, 319*n3,* 323*n9;* on the forms of the mother, 131–32, 134, 142, 145; on illumination, 150–51; on archetype, 318*n24;* on enslavement by nature and bioenergies, 320*nn6,9;* mentioned, 7, 13, 48, 186, 313*n7,* 322*n3*
Cavendish, Richard, 185, 186, 204–5, 209, 211

Celebrant, The (Greenberg), 13, 77, 97, 106, 109, 110, 155, 156, 168–80, 294, 303–4, 310
Charyn, Jerome, 2, 14, 120, 261, 267, 268, 273, 305. *See also Seventh Babe, The*
Chomsky, Noam, 17, 20
Cirlot, J. E., 325*n1*
Clark, R. T. Rundle, 161, 162, 163
Cobb, Ty: and Pete Rose, 297, 301, 326n2
Coleridge, Samuel Taylor, 315*n5*
Conrad, Joseph, 169
Conversion. *See* Illumination; Sacred, the
Cooney, Ellen, 72, 73, 117
Coover, Robert, 13, 68, 119, 120, 121, 122, 156, 221–33, 240, 270, 271, 272, 291, 306, 310, 325*nn4,5;* and metacreation, 222–27; and intertextuality, 223–24. *See also Universal Baseball Association, The*
Crisis art, 12, 147–67; baseball, religion, and, 149, 154, 165–67, 168–80
Culler, Johathan, 16, 17

Dacey, Philip, 157, 158
Davis, Robert Con, 316*n11*
Death: as aspect of Satan archetype, 152–63; and baseball, 154–59, 160–63; of gods, 159–60, 161, 178–80, 322*n3;* as sacrifice, 159–63, 179
Derrida, Jacques: on play space as center, 18; on critic as *bricoleur,* 18–19, 23, 314n10; on gap as abyss, 19; on engineer myth of anthropologist, 24–25, 288, 315–16*n9;* mentioned, 28
Doctorow, E. L., 264, 304–5
Dolar, Mladon: on the modern uncanny, 43
Doty, William, 5

Duncan, David James, 13, 247. *See also Brothers K, The*

Dwarf in baseball, 266–85; as archetype, 267, 271–73, 275; as personal primordial, 267–71, 325–26*n1*, 326*n2;* as Oedipal child, 268, 270, 274; as sidekick, 273–76; as hero, 276–85; and manhood, 277–85; mentioned, 2, 13–14, 21–22, 131

Eden, Garden of: as field, 57, 77, 128; as home, 57, 77; as scene of American monomyth, 77, 79, 318*n2;* as gap, 78; baseball's walled garden as, 99–100, 115, 102; and the Fall, 104, 128, 319*n2;* as motherland, 115
Eight Men Out (Asinof), 126*n3*
Eiseley, Loren, 164
Eisinger, Chester E., 226
Eliade, Mircea, 97–98, 99, 112
Eliot, T. S., 181, 184, 187–88, 211, 213, 218, 221, 290, 324*n3*
Emerson, Ralph Waldo, 293
Eribon, Didier, 315*n2*

Falck, Colin, 6, 7–8
Fan: religion and crisis art, 168–80; mentioned, 12
Father: failure of, 2, 262–64; blessing, 13, 246–47, 254–62; father-son atonement, 13, 247, 296; conflict, 55, 59–60, 195–98, 262–63; as double, 56; early death of, 143–44, 247–48, 254–55, 256–57, 260, 262, 264, 296; Orestes and, 245; Oedipal relations with son, 245–46; as object of quest, 253–54; childhood memories of, 254–56; redemption of, 260–61; withheld blessing, 261–62, 297
Feldman, Burton, 313*n5*
Felman, Shoshana, 37, 38, 50
Fences (Wilson), 54–62; Oedipal elements in, 54, 55, 56, 59–61, 68; Eden archetype in, 57, 61; the uncanny in, 62–63, 310; quest for home in, 68, 69; mentioned, 12, 36, 53, 81, 132, 248, 265
Fiedler, Leslie, 182, 212
Field, baseball: in *Fences,* 55; as nature, 77–78; as space of art, 78, 114, 172, 182; as archetypal garden, 102, 128; as time shelter, 103, 128; as battle-field, 108–12; as image of self, 112–14; as primal scene, 114–24; as masculine haven, 120–22; as graveyard, 156–63, 198; as world, 238–43
Fisher King. *See* Arthurian legend
Forster, E. M., 240
Foucault, Michel, 314*n2*
Frazer, Sir James George, 6, 184, 186–87, 192–93, 194–95, 211, 214, 324*nn3,5,6*
Freud, Sigmund, 2, 18, 21, 27, 28, 29, 32, 33, 34, 35, 51, 137–38, 182, 187, 194, 214, 215, 293, 321–22*n1*, 323*n7;* key narratives, 34, 37–39, 49–50, 64, 65
Frye, Northrop: and American structuralism, 3, 6, 8, 48, 64–65, 77, 148, 301; on time, 106; on myth and reality, 222, 224; on archetype, 314*n8;* on forms of tragedy and comedy, 319*n2*

Gaedel, Eddie, 313*n1*
Gap, myth of the: and Genesis, 3–5; as theoretical model, 11–12, 16; as academic myth, 16–17; as void of nonmeaning, 17; as play space, 18; baseball and, 19, 35–42, 45, 47, 107, 287; Derrida on, 19, 24–25; Lévi-Strauss on, 21–24; Genette on, 24, 25; Lacan on, 25–35; and the sacred, 45–47, 215; Tower of Babel as image of, 52–53; space-time continuum of, 93; rhetoric of, 292–93, 310, 311

26*n1;* on rhetorical tropes, 32–34, 39–40, 316–17*n15;* on the dream structured like a sentence, 34; and metaphor of the bat, 36–37; on baseball and the symbology of family, 37; on sex and death, 37, 58; on ellipsis and allegory, 39–40; on the depths of language, 40–41, 118, 317*n19;* on the modern sacred, 43, 47; as *bricoleur,* 50–52; on interpretation and the Tower of Babel, 50–52; and structuralism, 314*n2;* mentioned, 116, 263, 271, 302, 316*n11*

Lagerkvist, Pär, 266

Lakoff, George, 318*n25*

Lasher, Lawrence M., 182, 211

Lawrence, D. H., 212–13

LeClair, Tom, 223, 241, 325*n5*

Lévi-Strauss, Claude: on bricolage, 5, 12, 50; on the *bricoleur,* 5, 50, 286; on mythic thought, 8; on language as myth, 15, 21; on the metaphor of gap, 21; on mythemes, 21–22; as metaphor maker and *bricoleur,* 22–23, 316*n9;* and myth of mythology, 23; on *bricoleur* as distinct from engineer, 24–25, 287–88, 318–19*n1;* on myth and history, 295, 301; on signified and signifier, 313–14*n8;* and structuralism, 314–15*n2;* mentioned, 15, 18, 19, 28, 31, 34, 38, 39, 40, 48, 244, 301

Lidston, Robert C., 212, 219, 324*n12*

Lieberman, James, 317*n18*

Lieberman, Philip, 323*n6*

Malamud, Bernard, 2, 13, 181–85, 187–88, 203, 211–20, 270, 289, 294; "Reflections of a Writer," 181, 213. *See also Natural, The* (novel)

Man, Paul de: on figural language, 7, 39

Manganaro, Marc, 10, 313*n3*

Marvell, Andrew: "The Garden," 114, 119, 221

Matthews, William, 320*n7*

Mazur, Gail, 100, 147

McCaffery, Larry, 226, 324*n1,* 325*n5*

Mellard, James M., 37, 323*n1*

Messenger, Christian K., 14, 66, 67, 68, 71, 93, 106, 289, 290, 291, 292, 295, 303, 304; on counterhistory, 305

Metacreation, 222–27

Metafiction, 222, 226

Metzger, Deena, 71, 120

Miller, J. Hillis, 216–17, 323*n2,* 324*n14*

Milton, John, 226–27, 231–32, 325*n3*

Moffi, Larry, 147

Monomyth, 12; classic, 65; and quest romance, 66–67; of going back, going home, 68, 125–46; American, 76–80; defined, 77; and Eden, 77; of the American hero, 79–80

Motherland, 125–46; as ball field, 128; as church, 129, 131; as graveyard, 129–30; as garden, 130

Mothers: abandoning, 2, 55, 60, 132, 133, 248; terrible, 2, 115, 129–30, 132, 134, 136–38, 144–46, 247, 249–50; Great Mother, 114–15, 118, 128–29, 130; good, 130, 131, 134, 144–46, 253; as nature, 130; forms of, 131–38; violence against, 135, 136, 138–41, 143, 248, 249; separation from, 247–54; image of, 252–53; as spoilers of game, 264; survival of, 265. *See also* Nature; Women

Myth: defined, 3–6, 11; modern, 6–8, 11, 28; literary criticism as, 24, 26; structure of, 25; and the beautiful, 286–312; criticism, 286–312; relation to art, 287–88; and history, 295–310; numbers in baseball, 298; good, 310–12

Mythicity: Eric Gould's analysis of, 8–10; as quality of baseball texts, 9–10; as quality of written and spoken discourse, 10–11, 25, 26

Mythmaking: anthropology as, 23; criticism as, 24; history and, 294–310

Myth of the gap. *See* Gap, myth of the

Mythology: defined, 5–6

Narrative: and time, 94–95; mythic, and time, 95; baseball's plot as, 96–97. *See also* History

Natural, The (film): as classic monomyth, 75–76, 80; as revision of novel, 289–90, 302

Natural, The (novel; Malamud), 2, 13, 75–76, 120, 156, 157, 181–220, 254–55, 258, 260, 263, 264, 270, 271, 272, 289, 294, 297, 302, 324n6, 325n2; mythic intrepretations of, 181, 182, 183, 212; intertextuality in, 211–20; mother-son relations in, 247–48

Nature: ball field as unfallen, 77; and the uncanny, 78; contrasted with culture, 100, 101, 115, 320n6; laws of, suspended in baseball, 100; feminization of, 114–15, 118, 321n12; masked, 115; unmasked, 119; and motherland, 123; devouring, 136–38; Dionysian, 151

Neruda, Paolo, 164

Neugeboren, Jay, 14, 305, 307. *See also* *Sam's Legacy*

Nietzsche, Friedrich, 1, 13, 18, 150–51, 153, 154, 164, 169

Numinous. *See* Uncanny

Odyssey, The (Homer): Lacan on underworld in, 27–28; as key narrative, 37–38, 65; as underlying structure in baseball, 39, 67; Troy Maxson

and, 55; and classic monomyth, 65–70; and American monomyth, 76, 79; mentioned, 12, 36, 41, 85, 88, 89, 104, 142

Oedipus myths: as key narratives, 38, 49, 138, 245; Laius complex, 38; Polybus's heroism, 38; Troy Maxson and, 54, 55, 59–60; Oedipal conflict and home, 68, 143, 144; as themes in Wallop, 70; and American monomyth, 76, 79; satirized, 252–53; mentioned, 2, 12, 14, 21, 33, 37, 38, 183, 216, 218, 245–46, 251–52

Oresteia, The: themes of, in baseball myth, 67, 136, 142, 143, 245, 254; as key narrative, 126, 138

Osiris myth, 161–63, 198

Paglia, Camille: on women and nature, 100, 115–16, 118–19, 120, 123, 130, 320n6; mentioned, 78

Parker, Robert, 103, 120

Percival. *See* Arthurian legend

Pete Rose: My Story (Rose and Kahn): mythic elements in, 296–99, 326n2. *See also* Rose, Peter I.

Pifer, Ellen, 215, 324n13

Play: in the gap, 17–19; place of art in, 18–19; place of baseball in, 19; field of, 93–124, 320n4; and time, 96–107; contrasted with work, 101–3; and space, 107–24; Edenic and agonic, 108–9; in *The Universal Baseball Association,* 228–30, 232–36; and *Deus ludens,* 229, 231, 241–42; and *Homo ludens,* 229, 231, 240, 242; Huizinga on, 229–30; and myth, 230; life as, 238–39, 241; and aesthetics, 240–41. *See also* Gap, myth of the

Plimpton, George, 113

Pride of the Bimbos (Sayles), 2, 14, 267, 268, 269, 273, 276–85, 310

Quest. *See* Monomyth

71–75; and shift to defense, 72; and "leg problems," 72–73; and classic monomyth, 73–75; and failure of quest, 75; excluded from field, 120, 250–51; and batting slumps, 122, 195; as paragons, 141–42; as consorts, 198–203; and goddess archetype, 198–99; attributes of mothers generalized to, 250–51; misogyny, 253, 265

Wood, David: time as central to philosophy, 94

Woolf, Virginia, 295

Wordsworth, William, 316*n10*

Worton, Michael, 323*n2*

Year the Yankees Lost the Pennant, The (Wallop): as classic monomyth, 69–70, 76; and the uncanny, 69–70; Oedipal themes in, 70; time in, 103; Lola as Hecate in, 121; mentioned, 73, 80, 157, 197

Yeats, William Butler, 154

"You Could Look It Up" (Thurber), 2, 268, 269, 270, 272, 313*n1*

Young, Dudley: on the sacred, 125, 155, 320*n8*

Zavarzadeh, Mas'ud, 222

DEEANNE WESTBROOK is a professor of English at Portland State University. Her main teaching assignments are in British romanticism, criticism, myth, the Bible as literature, linguistics, and writing. She has published articles on Coleridge, Wordsworth, Genesis 2–3, and northern European myth. A former sandlot player and Little League mother, she is now a fan in the tragic mode, following the game generally and, in particular, the fortunes of the Portland Rockies and the Chicago Cubs.